THE QUAKER PEACE TESTIMONY
1660 to 1914

William Penn's Treaty with the Indians
The cover-picture is courtesy of Friends House Library, London: being taken from
their circa 1800 repainting of the original oil painting of 1771 by Benjamin West
(1738-1820), which hangs in the Pennsylvania Academy of the Fine Arts,
Philadelphia. Note: Both the 1800 repainting in England, likewise another painting
in Independence Hall, Philadelphia, show the Indians at the left-side of the picture.
The positioning of this cover-reproduction is the same as the Benjamin West
1771 original.

The
Quaker Peace Testimony
1660 to 1914

by

Peter Brock

Professor Emeritus of History
in the
University of Toronto

Sessions Book Trust
York, England
1990

ISBN Card Cover 1 85072 065 7

Hard Back 1 85072 074 6

First Published 1990

Second Impression 1993

North American Distributors:
Syracuse University Press Inc.,
1600 Jamesville Avenue,
Syracuse, 13244-5160,
New York, USA

Printed in 10 on 11 point Plantin Typeface
by William Sessions Limited
The Ebor Press
York, England

Contents

Acknowledgements

BOTH I AND THE PUBLISHERS wish to thank the following institutions for their generous financial assistance in publication: The Joseph Rowntree Charitable Trust, supported by the Sessions Book Trust in the United Kingdom; and in the United States: The Obadiah Brown Benevolent Fund, the Anna H. and Elizabeth M. Chace Fund, the Thomas H. and Mary Williams Shoemaker Fund, the Edna S. Troemner Fund of Philadelphia Yearly Meeting, and the Friends Historical Association.

We would also like to express gratitude to Edwin B. Bronner, Curator of the Quaker Collection at Haverford College, and J. William Frost, Director of Friends Historical Library at Swarthmore College, for their energetic support of the project on the North American continent.

Many other persons have assisted me in my present research on the history of the Quaker peace testimony. I would like in particular to thank the following: Hans Eirik Aarek, Hugh Barbour, Cecil Evans, Kyle Jolliffe, Jack D. Marietta, Rosemarie McMechan, Geoffrey F. Nuttall, Arthur O. Roberts, Thomas P. Socknat, Malcolm Thomas. I am grateful to Shirley A. Fulford for typing almost all my manuscript and to the Department of History, University of Toronto, for its support of my work in various ways as well as to the University's Office of Research Administration for a travel grant in aid of research. Finally, I am especially indebted to the Interlibrary Loan Section of the University of Toronto Library for long-term assistance in obtaining materials unavailable in this city.

Toronto, May 1990   P. de B.B.

KEY TO ABBREVIATIONS IN THE NOTES

BDMPL	*Biographical Dictionary of Modern Peace Leaders*, ed. Harold Josephson, Westport (Connecticut) and London, 1985.
BFHA	*Bulletin of Friends' Historical Association*, (Haverford [Pennsylvania] etc.).
Hirst	Margaret E. Hirst, *The Quakers in War and Peace: An Account of Their Peace Principles and Practice*, London, 1923.
JFHS	*The Journal of the Friends' Historical Society* (London).
PMHB	*The Pennsylvania Magazine of History and Biography* (Philadelphia)
QH	*Quaker History* (Haverford, etc.).
WMQ	*The William and Mary Quarterly* (Williamsburg, Virginia).

Preface

NEARLY SEVENTY YEARS HAVE ELAPSED since the English Quaker scholar, Margaret Hirst, published her comprehensive history of the peace witness of the Society of Friends. The present book represents the first attempt since Hirst's work appeared, to present in a single volume a survey of the Quaker peace testimony before World War I covering not only North America and the British Isles but the European continent and Australasia as well. Much detailed research on the subject has been done since Hirst's time; I have tried to incorporate this in my narrative as well as to explore certain aspects of the topic on my own. In addition, I have attempted to emphasize the important aspects of Quaker pacifist history which Hirst treated lightly or not at all, while sometimes covering in less detail aspects she treated more extensively and where her narrative still stands firm. Hers was indeed a pioneering study to which all later students of the subject are indebted.

Until 1914, Quakerism for most people – at any rate in the English-speaking world – had symbolised the Christian pacifist ethos. Friends have continued their witness for peace down to the present with scarcely abated vigour and not infrequently have won respect for their sincerity in this stand, even from those who disagreed with their position on war and peace. Still, in the era of global warfare when pacifism has drawn the overwhelming majority of its adherents from outside the Society of Friends (or the other historic peace churches), Quaker pacifism no longer plays as central a role as it once did in the general pacifist impulse. The year 1914, therefore, appears to me to be an appropriate date at which to conclude this study.

Detailed references will be found in the notes. The 'Further Reading' list at the end is intended to help those who want to read more deeply in one or another aspect of the topic. I have confined the list to books and pamphlets which should be fairly easily accessible on library shelves or by interlibrary loan.

CHAPTER I

Pre-Quaker Pacifism in England

THE QUAKERS WERE NOT THE first to espouse pacifism in the British Isles.
If we put aside the possibility of early Christian antimilitarists being found
there in Roman times (and their existence then is by no means unlikely), the
followers of the 14th-century heterodox English theologian and philosopher
John Wyclif, who died in 1384, seem to have been the earliest protagonists
of pacifist ideas in this part of Europe. It was only after his death that Wyclif
had been formally condemned as a heretic, though many of his ideas were
officially rejected by the Church during his lifetime. 'It is more conformable
to the law of Christ not to war,' he had written. But he himself never
condemned war as such. Some of his disciples, however, did so.

According to Nicholas of Hereford, who had studied under Wyclif at
Oxford and been deeply influenced by him, 'Jesus Christ, duke of our
battle, taught us [the] law of patience, and not to fight bodily.' And in 1395
the Lollards, as Wyclif's followers become known, presented 'twelve
conclusions' to parliament, the text of which they tacked up on the doors of
Westminster Abbey and St. Paul's Cathedral so as to bring them to the
attention of the general public. The tenth conclusion stated that killing,
whether in battle or under some legal pretence,

> without special revelation is express contrary to the New Testament, the
> which is a law of grace and fully of mercy. This conclusion is openly
> proved by [the] example of Christ's preaching here in earth, the which
> most taught for to love and to have mercy on his enemies and not for to
> slay them . . . We know well that no clerk can find by scripture or by
> reason lawful punishment of death, for one deadly sin and for another.
> But the law of mercy, that is the New Testament, forbad all
> manslaughter: *in evangelio dictum est antiquis, Non occides* . . . by
> meekness and suffering our belief was multiplied, and fighters and
> manslayers Jesus Christ hateth and menaceth. *Qui gladio percutit, gladio
> peribit.*

1

Especially worthy of condemnation was the Church's habit of granting indulgences, at a price, to knights who had killed their fellow Christians in battle – 'that had run to heatheness to get themselves a name in slaying of men.' For the Lollards such a practice was 'an holy robbing of the poor people,' on whom the financial burden would finally rest.[1]

On the other hand, we find two Cambridge theologians, Walter Brut and William Swynderby, in 1393 stating the church's position with respect to the Lollard's pacifist heresy as follows:

> To fight in the defence of justice, against both unbelievers and Christians, is in itself holy and permissible: to hold the opposite is to be in error. Such opinion has it that it is not permitted to Christians to fight against unbelievers, pagans or others, so as to bring about their forcible conversion to the Christian faith: it also claims that no Christian may fight other Christians for the defence of justice.
>
> This opinion is false and erroneous, for the following reasons. First it would not permit any Christian king to defend his kingdom against invaders or false intruders, so that, for example, it would not be right for the King of England to defend his lands against the French or the Scots, nor against anybody else, etc. Secondly, the teachings of the holy Fathers have approved and vindicated just wars as being permissible and righteous when fought by Christians, if their end is the defence of justice or the protection of the Church and the catholic faith. Thus saints approved by the Church have granted indulgences to men going to war for these purposes: God himself has vindicated just wars of this kind, and, indeed, often ordered his chosen people to fight, as is made plain by a reading of almost the whole of the Old Testament. Thus it may be accepted that this is true and catholic doctrine, the contrary of which, propounded by the above-mentioned opinion, is an error.
>
> As for the suggestion that a Christian is forbidden to defend himself and to resist attack by the use of force, that, too, is an error. This opinion holds that Christians cannot freely and forcefully defend themselves against injuries aimed at them, nor against bodily attacks, nor against violence of other kinds. Such an opinion is against the good of the general peace, against all order of government and against all reason. It is an error to uphold it, and the opposite must be maintained, namely that Christians may defend themselves with force, above all against injuries which they suffer unjustly, and may oppose force with force, especially when the hand of correction is not readily available.[2]

Nevertheless nonresistance was certainly not a tenet held by all Lollards. The Lollard lay leader, Sir John Oldcastle, who rebelled against the Crown in 1414, was obviously not a pacifist. When, early in the 15th century, the movement was driven underground and its adherents subjected to all the penalties of heresy, it lost its men of learning and its upper class following and sank into a rural sect surviving into the 16th century and the Reformation era by reason of its obscurity. That pacifist beliefs however survived among the Lollard remnant, at least for a time, is shown for instance by the trial before the bishop's court in 1429 of an illiterate Norwich miller, John Skilly, who confessed to a large number of Wyclifite heresies: after his abjuration he was condemned to seven years' imprisonment on bread and water. Among the heretical beliefs Skilly abjured was 'that it is not lawful for any man to fight or do battle for a realm or a country, or to go to law for any right or wrong.'[3]

The Lollards, we know today, made little impact on the English Reformation. They had become a spent force long before its arrival. The pacifist beliefs that surface from time to time in England from at least the middle decades of the 16th century on drew their inspiration from another source – the contemporary Anabaptist movement in central Europe. To cite one instance of this: England around mid-century became the centre of activity for the small pantheistic sect known as the Family of Love, whose founder Hendrik Niclaes had originated from Westphalia and made his first converts in northern Germany and the Netherlands. A British scholar has summarised the attitude of the sect to war as follows: 'The bearing of weapons is forbidden. But to prevent members from becoming marked men they may carry staves.'[4] The imprint of Anabaptist nonresistance is clear here, even if its influence is indirect.

The Familists, though they survived in England for well over a century, were extremely small in numbers, and their impact was correspondingly limited. The impact of mainstream Anabaptism, however, was much more considerable, and it seems to have had adherents in England from the 1530s, which should cause us no surprise in view of the close commercial contacts at that time between East Anglia and the Netherlands where Anabaptism was already rampant – at first of a not altogether peaceable variety. The English Anabaptists were mostly obscure weavers or petty traders and craftsmen: they left, not surprisingly, few literary traces behind them. A written defence of nonresistance by a semi-literate English carpenter has, however, survived from 1575. There S.B. (we know him only by his initials) declared his belief in unadulterated Anabaptist nonresistance of the Schleitheim variety: 'I thought it not lawful for me to revenge my wrongs done unto me by extremity of law, nor to requite any blows given me with the like, concluding thereby that I need wear no weapon.' True, S.B. went on, rulers were ordained of God and might wield the sword against evildoers but genuine followers of Christ must eschew all acts of revenge and steer clear of civil office or the military profession; they must be ready to suffer 'rebukes and blows' and 'be hated of all people.' For 'Christ is the true expounder of the law, and saith, resist not, and gave us an example to follow his steps.'[5]

Fear of Anabaptist nonresistance as a potentially dangerous, and implicitly subversive element in the country's ecclesiastical life and civil polity is apparent throughout Elizabeth I's reign and into the early Stuart period. We find the legitimacy of Christian participation in 'lawful' warfare being asserted more than once by the state Church of England, the most famous of such declarations of course being the 37th article of the Thirty-nine Articles of 1563. 'It is lawful,' states that article, 'for Christian men, at the commandment of the magistrate, to wear weapons and serve in the wars.' A number of writers expressed alarm not only at the Anabaptists' rejection of war but at their opposition to a specifically Christian magistracy. Even though Anabaptists like S.B. had stressed their loyalty to the Crown, this failed to remove a general suspicion, reinforced by the tendency to equate Anabaptism in general with its Münsterite variant, that the sect was a menace to civil government. John Paget, for instance, in 1618 condemned the Anabaptists because they 'would take the sword from the Christian magistrate, upon the erroneous opinion that the judicials of Moses are at an end.' And the anonymous author of *The Anabaptists' Catechism* of 1645 mocked at the sect's adherents for saying (so he claimed), 'We are free from bloodshed, and will not kill, no not a louse; nor do we hold it fit that any should be punished for his infirmities.'[6] But long before this, perhaps as early as the 1580s, English Anabaptism, from the beginning an amorphous and semi-underground movement, began to lose its separate identity and merge with the growing body of Separatists who, having severed all ties with the established church, eventually gave rise to the Congregationalist and Baptist denominations – England's first free churches.

There were no pacifists among the Congregationalists for a long time to come, but early English Baptism had a pacifist wing. And it is to this we must now turn our attention. We know of a group of English separatists with Anabaptist leanings, who took refuge in the Netherlands in the mid-1590s as the result of the repressive measures then enforced against religious dissidents in their native land. They established an *émigré* congregation, first at Campen and then at Naarden. Among the group's beliefs was nonresistance: 'That magistrates ought not to put malefactors to death . . . they [also] condemn all wars and subjects in armour in the field,' as a pamphlet written against them in 1597 stated. It is not known what became of these people or whether any surviving members had contacts with John Smyth, the founder of the first English Baptist church which he set up in Amsterdam in 1609.[7]

Smyth, along with other like-minded exiles, had left England for the Netherlands shortly before that date. A clergyman of the Church of England and a fellow of a Cambridge college, Smyth came under Mennonite influence soon after his arrival in the Netherlands and, by the time of his death in 1612, he had succeeded in persuading many – though by no means all – of his flock to espouse nonresistance. Those who disagreed separated from him to form a separate congregation under the leadership of Thomas Helwys, who with his followers returned to England in the year of Smyth's death. Smyth's congregation then merged with the Waterlander Mennonites in 1615.

'What simplicity is this to think that it is more lawful to hire men to fight a battle than to fight it themselves,' Helwys had written in *An Advertisement or Admonition* which appeared in 1611.[8] He regarded not merely the form of exemption enjoyed in the United Provinces by Dutch Mennonite conscientious objectors, but the whole nonresistant position as untenable. Smyth, on the other hand, defended nonresistance in a number of statements issued either in his own name or that of his congregation. 'I however recognise Christ as a spiritual ruler,' he wrote (in support of the Mennonite Hans de Ries's *Confession of Faith*), 'and his church as a spiritual kingdom . . . [whose] weapons are spiritual and [whose] laws, punishments, rewards, soldiers, and warfare are all spiritual . . . the primitive church, which was completely perfect, did not acknowledge the magistracy in its midst.'[9] In the Short Confession of Faith Smyth drew up for his congregation around 1610 he stressed that the magistracy was 'a necessary ordinance of God, appointed and established for the preservation of the common estate, and of a good, natural politic life, for the reward of the good, and the punishing of the evil.' Prayers must be offered up for those in office and taxes paid to them 'without murmuring.' But members of 'the church of the new testament,' i.e., those who pursued the nonresistant path, were forbidden to take office of any kind, and would be obliged to resign if they became convinced of the true Christian way while serving in government. 'Yea rather they are called of him . . . to the following of his unarmed or unweaponed life, and of his cross-bearing footsteps.'[10]

Despite the hostility to pacifism of their founder Helwys, it is among members of the antipredestinarian General Baptists rather than among the Calvinistic Particular Baptists, that pacifist views crop up from time to time during the following decades. In 1624 a small group of General Baptists in London, led by one Elias Tookey, even went so far as to ask the Waterlander Mennonite church in Amsterdam – which, as we have just seen, already had an English speaking section – to accept them, too, into membership as a group. Explaining their attitude to the magistracy and to bearing arms

Tookey states: 'We will in no manner accept or undertake them, some of us for conscience and the rest just for peace sake.'[11] The passage indicates that, if complete unanimity on this issue did not prevail, nonresistance must certainly have been a tenet of the majority of the congregation.

Even as late as the 1650s doubts concerning the legitimacy of Christian participation in warfare were voiced among the General Baptists. How widespread such antimilitarist sentiment was we cannot say, but evidently it was sufficiently strong for the question to be discussed at a general meeting in 1657 where it was decided: 'In answer to the queries about fighting we say that in some cases it may be lawful, but . . . we account it exceeding dangerous.'[12] Of course a large number of Baptists joined the parliamentary army and served, many with distinction, throughout the Civil War: pacifists and conscientious objectors remained a very small minority in the denomination.

In 1646 a prominent Puritan divine, Thomas Edwards, had published a virulent attack on all manner of 'heresies' that he entitled *Gangraena*. Among the views he attacked we may note the following: ''Tis unlawful for Christians to fight at all, or to kill any man, yea to kill any of the creatures for our use, as a chicken, or on any other occasion.'[13] Edwards did not specify any particular group which held such views. He was perhaps thinking of the small nonresistant minority within the General Baptist church, for many of his attacks were directed against the Baptists. Or possibly he was merely repeating general hearsay without direct knowledge of the opinions he was assailing or the people who held them.

Early in the next decade at any rate, several small sects emerge which held such views either wholly or in part. There were, for instance, the mystical – and somewhat eccentric – Muggletonians. They opposed the bearing of arms – at least in principle, if not entirely in practice. According to Christopher Hill, John Reeve, the sect's co-founder (with Lodowick Muggleton), who died prematurely in 1658, 'advocated pacifism and abstention from politics, long before the Quakers officially adopted such positions.' He told his followers they were not permitted to 'take the sword of steel, to slay their brothers, because they know that man is the image of God, neither can they go to law with their neighbour.' 'Love,' he said, 'doth not make us to desire after the office of a minister, or to be a Parliament-man.'[14] Even more decisively the advocates of pacifism were the contemporary Tryonites, under the leadership of a prosperous London merchant, Thomas Tryon, who practised vegetarianism as part of a thoroughgoing nonviolent *Weltanschauung*.[15] Even the Ranters produced at least one pacifist, Oxford educated Abiezer Coppe, who wrote in 1649: 'Not by sword, we (holily) scorn to fight for anything; we had as lief be dead drunk every day of the week, and lie with whores in the market place.'[16]

We have now reached the period which saw the emergence of Quakerism. The evidence presented above is fragmentary but I hope it may serve to show that Quaker pacifism did not arise in a vacuum. The pacifist idea was not at that date entirely a novelty in England: it possessed roots there, however fragile. This, I think, is an element that needs to be taken into account in any discussion of the genesis of the Quaker peace testimony.

Before closing this chapter I would like to consider briefly Rufus Jones's thesis that Quakerism marked the culmination of a 'slowly maturing spiritual [reform] movement' stretching back to its continental protagonists of the Reformation era[17]; at any rate in so far as this thesis affects the beginnings of Quaker pacifism. Many of the 'spiritual reformers' considered by Jones held vaguely pacifistic views, even if these were not usually at the centre of their philosophy. One alone, so far as I know, was an uncompromising pacifist. This was Valentin Weigel (1533-88), a German Lutheran pastor whose mystical writings were published only after his death. Weigel greatly influenced the Silesian mystic, Jakob Boehme (whom Jones in turn claimed as a seminal influence on George Fox[18]), and his belief in the inwardness of true religion, and that the word of God was to be discovered not so much in the Scriptures or through the sacraments as within the illuminated human soul, certainly foreshadow later Quaker doctrine. In his treatise *Von dem Leben Christi, das ist, vom wahren Glauben*, which appeared in London in 1648 under the title *Of the Life of Christ: That is, of True Faith*, Weigel wrote:

> The man who has the Christ-Life in him does not quarrel; he does not go to law for temporal goods; he does not kill; he lets his coat and cloak go rather than oppose another . . . If Christ were of the seed of Adam, he would have the nature and inclinations of Adam. He would hang thieves, behead adulterers, rack murderers with the wheel, kill heretics, and put corporeally to death all manner of sinners; but now he is tender, kind, loving. He kills no one. The Lamb kills no wolf . . . Where the Life of Christ is, there is no war made with corporeal weapons . . . The world wars but Christ doth not so. His warfare is spiritual . . . He that maketh war is no Christian but a wolf, and belongs not to the sheepfold nor hath he anything to expect of the Kingdom of God, nor may the wars of the Old Testament, of the time of darkness, serve his turn, for Christians deal not after a Mosaical, earthly fashion, but they walk in the Life of Christ, without all revenge . . . We walk no longer under Moses but under Christ.[19]

All this is finely said. But whether George Fox or any other of the early Quakers read it is doubtful. And even if they did, their peace testimony was woven from so many different strands that Weigel's eloquent advocacy of Christian nonresistance could, I think, have played only a very minor role in its making. It seems that, after all, the spiritual reformers, whose general influence on early Quakerism recent scholarship, in contrast to earlier opinion, has tended to regard as small (though by no means entirely nonexistent), must have contributed comparatively little directly to the emergence of the Quaker peace testimony.[20]

CHAPTER II

Quaker Attitudes to War before the Peace Testimony

QUAKERISM IN ITS EARLIEST PHASE remained essentially a part of Puritanism. As Tolles, one of the most perceptive students of Quaker history, has said: 'We may, if we like, call it the "left wing" of the movement, but we cannot regard it as a separate or alien phenomenon.' Rather, 'it was in a real sense a fulfillment,' 'a natural, almost a predictable outgrowth of Puritanism.' Thus, 'Quakerism was in large measure a native growth in England, rather than primarily the product of mystical influences from the continent of Europe.'[1] Like other Puritans, the early Quakers had sought above all to express the working of the Holy Spirit in their lives. Even if they interpreted this quest differently from their fellow Puritans, they, too, saw the pursuit of righteousness in all its aspects as the surest path to fulfilling the leadings of this Spirit.

We owe such new insights into the origins and the early character of Quaker religion to scholars on both sides of the Atlantic like Geoffrey Nuttall, Frederick Tolles, and Hugh Barbour. Even more important, however, for our purposes here, is the work of a group of British scholars (Alan Cole, Christopher Hill, and Barry Reay are perhaps the most representative names), who from the early 1950s on have been exploring in depth the social and political aspects of early Quakerism. The condition of England around mid-17th-century when Quakerism arose – the year 1652 has been assigned traditionally as its starting point – was one in which 'there was a great overturning, questioning, revaluing, of everything.'[2] The monarchy had been abolished and the king executed after a prolonged civil war between royalists and parliamentarians. Not only novel religious, but also revolutionary political and social ideas came to the surface and found ardent and able exponents to propagate them throughout the country. Levellers had preached radical political democracy and Diggers practised agrarian socialism – until suppressed by the alarmed authorities, whose outloook was circumscribed by the upper middle class *Weltanschauung* of the Commonwealth government's most influential supporters. Yet the

Good Old Cause of radical political reform, though severely restricted, did not disappear altogether. It found fresh channels of expression, including those opened up by new religious sects like the Quakers, which arose during the 1650s on the Puritan left.

'The essence of the Quaker message,' writes Geoffrey Nuttall, 'was that the Spirit of God was in every man.'[3] For many early Quakers this entailed, if not a coherent programme of reform, at any rate a generally egalitarian attitude toward society. They spoke out on behalf of the poorer sections of the population, opposed the payment of tithes, and attacked the church establishment for its privileged position within the community, refused to doff their hats to social superiors or to use the accustomed forms of polite address, and claimed the rights of free born Englishmen when they felt these were being denied them. Some former leaders of the parliamentary left joined Quakers. No wonder, then, that the new sect's opponents called them Levellers and accused them of subversive designs. Indeed, early Quakerism was, in Reay's words, 'far more radical than some historians would still admit.'[4] Drawn at first mainly from small traders and artisans in the towns and from smallholders in the villages (with only a few coming from the highest and lowest strata of society), early Quakers were widely considered to be 'socially disreputable' people who posed a threat to the stability of the state. In short, what they seemed to want to do was 'to turn the world upside down.'[5]

If Quakers during the first decade of the movement were certainly religious and political radicals, were they also pacifists in the sense all agree they became from the Restoration on? Until recently historians of Quakerism, whether Quaker or not, regarded pacifism from the beginning as an important element in the Quaker outlook. It was agreed there were some early Quakers, especially among converted soldiers, who did not reject war at first, though it was believed a growing realisation of what Quakerism meant had soon led them to lay down their arms. If at that time – as well as later – there were Quakers who did not entirely share their sect's view of war, these people, it was felt, formed a small minority, exceptions that prove the rule. Pacifism, then, was an evolving witness borne from the first by the sect's founder, George Fox, whose fidelity to the cause of peace after a short while outweighed any tendency toward a more warlike stance among his followers.

Within recent decades this interpretation has been challenged and a radically different picture presented in the detailed researches of scholars like Cole, Hill, and Reay. For instance, Cole, who pioneered the new viewpoint, speaks of 'the supposed pacifism of the early Friends.'[6] According to Reay, before 1661 'it is impossible to talk, as it is later, of the Quakers as a predominantly pacifist group,' and he also detects 'ambiguity' in Fox's attitude toward war.[7] Reay's mentor, Christopher Hill, while conceding that 'before 1661 there were premature pacifists' among Quakers, agrees with Cole and Reay in his belief that the sect adopted 'the peace principle' only after the Restoration and that even 'Fox had not committed himself to pacifism before the Restoration.'[8]

Consensus, however, exists within these divergent interpretations that in the 1650s there were to be found alongside each other both Quaker soldiers and – almost certainly – at least a few Quaker pacifists. In trying to assess the strength – or weakness – of Quaker pacifism during this period, I would like to look first at the Quaker soldiers and of some expressions of Quaker militancy found in this period, and then to discuss in turn George Fox's attitude to war and violence, the nature and extent of Quaker antimilitarism, and finally the crisis that occurred in 1659 and its immediate aftermath, since the Quaker stance during that critical time seems to mark a watershed in the history of the emergent peace testimony.

The Quaker movement had begun in the rural north of England but it soon spread southward. London and Bristol became important centres of activity, and Quaker missionaries, the 'first publishers of truth' as their coreligionists came to call them, spread the new faith quickly into Wales and Ireland and Scotland, and across the Atlantic to colonial America and the British West Indies as well as across the Channel to continental Europe. Early on, Quaker preachers began to proselytise among the soldiers of Cromwell's army and among the sailors in his fleet. Indeed radical elements of the New Model Army, disappointed in their hopes of political reform and religious renewal, proved 'a major source of Quaker recruitment.' The emergent sect found a sympathetic hearing and valuable support among both army officers and rank and file: not all these men actually became Quakers but they helped the spread of the movement at a critical period in its development.[9] 'The number of Quakers who had been in the Army and Navy, until they were forced out, is legion,' writes Hill.[10] And it was the Cromwellian army in Ireland and Scotland that proved a particularly fertile soil for the growth of the Quaker message during the middle years of the decade.[11]

After a little, however, the army authorities, headed in Ireland by Oliver Cromwell's son, Henry, and in Scotland by General George Monck, began to take alarm at the spread of Quakerism among the soldiers under their command. They proceeded, therefore, to purge their ranks of any, officers or men, who were suspected of sympathy with a group believed by many to entertain subversive designs. Henry Cromwell reported in 1656: 'Our most considerable enemy now in our view are the Quakers. I think their principles and practices are not very consistent with civil government, much less with the discipline of an army.' And General Monck, writing to the Lord Protector around this time, echoed his son's sentiments about the Quakers: 'Truly I think they will prove a very dangerous people, should they increase in your army, and be neither fit to command nor obey, but ready to make a distraction in the army, and a mutiny upon every slight occasion.'[12] Wholesale expulsions of Quakers in the armed forces ensued until soon very few remained at any level.

As we might expect, the cashiered Quakers more than once spoke out against what they considered as arbitrary and unjust action on the part of the army authorities, as base ingratitude from those they had been serving loyally. They protested that they had always been ready to risk their lives for the preservation of liberty. In one such petition they call themselves 'the faithful friends of this Commonwealth, and well-wishers for the peace and good government thereof . . . We as once fellow members, and fellow soldiers with you, in a good cause, and upon good engagements, wish well towards you in the Lord.'[13] Cole has, I think correctly, described the standpoint of the vast majority of the Quakers turned out of the army at this time as 'comprehensible only if we recognise that they were disillusioned not with the cause for which they had fought, nor even with the means by which they had sought to advance it, but with the men who were now betraying it.'[14]

Let us now move on to examine a few samples of Quaker 'militancy' among early Quaker leaders outside the ranks of the army. (George Fox, however, I have kept for separate treatment in more detail below.) Christopher Hill has pointed to a number of statements made by early Quakers, some of them ex-soldiers, in which they clearly supported the armed effort of the English parliamentarians, at any rate until their leaders betrayed the holy cause of freedom.[15] According to George Bishop, for instance, this cause hitherto had been 'the highest on which men were engaged in the field.' 'Did thy sword (till of late) ever return empty from the blood of the slain and the spoil of the mighty?' he demanded angrily of Cromwell in 1656.[16] And Francis Howgill, in 1655, writes in even more bloodthirsty fashion against the unrighteous, a thirst that it seems hard to dissolve entirely into metaphor: 'Spare none, neither old nor young; kill, cut off, destroy, bathe your sword in the blood of Amalek, and all the Egyptians and Philistines, and all the uncircumcised.'[17] To some Quakers of this period, writes Cole, 'even the violence of the Irish campaign . . . appeared . . . as a divine judgement on a rebellious nation.'[18] Edward Burrough who, despite his youth, soon became a leading figure among early Quakers, reflects clearly in his numerous writings this early Quaker militancy. We find him, for instance, in 1655 exhorting the lower ranks of the Cromwellian army in Ireland to repent if they wished to avoid the wrath to come. Let them turn to the Light:

It will teach you in your places to serve the living God, and to do violence
to no man, but to be terrors, and reprovers, and correctors of all
violence, and of such who live in it. And it will teach you not to
strengthen the hands of evildoers, but to lay your swords in justice upon
every one that doeth evil. And it will teach you not to make war, but to
preserve peace in the earth; and this is your place and duty required of
you from the Lord God commander in chief, unto whom you must all
give an account, . . . if you stand in the fear of the Lord your sword will
be a terror and dread to them that fear him not, but live contrary to the
Light in their own consciences, which Light if you love, it is your
command to march by, and your rule to judge by, and weapon to fight
withal, and your chief commission for duty.[19]

In this striking statement we may perhaps detect some glimmerings of
an emergent peace testimony, though Burrough's attitude appears to be
closer to the traditional theory of just war than to later Quaker pacifism. For
him Cromwell's soldiers, armed with righteousness, wield the sword of
justice against evildoers. He seems, moreover, to identify himself with them
unconditionally. He does not stand aside and, as in the case of the
Anabaptist-Mennonite tradition, grant with studied aloofness a conditional
justification to the office of the sword – this he refrains from doing so long at
any rate as 'the sword of the Lord' is 'in the hands of the Saints,' to quote
another contemporary Quaker author.[20]

'And what,' asks Christopher Hill, 'are we to make of Burrough's
Woeful Cry of 1657?' Like the Taborite militants several centuries earlier,
Burrough here presents his vision of the earth after Christ's second coming
and the inauguration of the rule of the saints. 'It shall be said,' he writes,
'"All that would not that Christ should reign, slay them before him."'[21]
But, as we shall see, whereas the Taborites had moved from pacifism to
chiliastic violence, Burrough's militant chiliasm eventually gave way before
his sect's espousal of nonviolence.[22]

It was not Burrough, of course, who led early Quakerism, nor even the
enthusiast James Nayler, dubbed by some of his contempories 'the head
Quaker in England,'[23] but George Fox, whose charismatic personality from
the outset charted the course taken by the new sect, even if during the early
years some others made important contributions almost equal to his.
Speaking in 1660 Fox stated during one of his numerous appearances in
court: 'I never learned the postures of war, . . . I loved all men; I was
enemy to no man.'[24] But how far did the pacifism implied in this statement
reflect a consistent viewpoint held over the previous decade? As we know,
some recent scholars have dated his full acceptance of a pacifist position as
late as 1660.[25] A brief examination of the record should help in the
elucidation of what is admittedly a complex issue.

Very early on in his career as a 'publisher of truth' Fox was twice faced with the question whether or not to serve in the parliamentary army. The first occasion was around April 1651, while he was serving a sentence in the Derby House of Correction for disturbing the peace. Some parliamentary soldiers visiting the prison and seeing this well built and determined young man – Fox was then 27 years old, 'a tender youth' who 'dwelt in the fear of God' – offered to make him their captain if, as he relates in his *Journal*, he would 'take up arms for the Commonwealth against the king. But I told them I lived in the virtue of that life and power that took away the occasion of all wars, and I knew from whence all wars did rise, from the lust according to James's doctrine [James, IV: 1, 2].' So Fox remained in jail where, shortly before the decisive battle of Worcester, which took place on 3 September 1651, a second attempt to make him a soldier was made – this time by the local authorities. 'Justice Bennet sent the constables to press me for a soldier,' writes Fox, 'seeing I would not accept of a command. I told them I was brought off from outward wars.' On their making further efforts to enlist him, 'I told them that I was dead to it. They said I was alive. I told them, "Where envy and hatred are there is confusion."'[26]

This seems to me a pretty clear expression of pacifist conviction: refusal to bear arms stemming from a belief in the virtue of nonviolence and in the origin of wars lying in human lust. It has been argued, however, that 'this must be retrospective mental adjustment,'[27] an unconscious projection backwards of his later pacifism into a period before it had become a fixed article of his faith. Is there, then, further evidence from the earlier period that may decide on the accuracy, or otherwise, with which Fox later described his earlier attitude to war?

In letters he composed during the 1650s the same nonviolent stance his later *Journal* assigns to the period of his sojourn in Derby jail does emerge clearly from time to time. Though in Old Testament days war was legitimate, under Christ's dispensation, he writes in one of these letters, our warfare must be spiritual. 'The Jews did kill with the outward sword the heathen, and one another; but Christ Jesus, the Prince of Life, fulfills the Law, and ends the Jews' types, figures and shadows, ordinances and carnal weapons,' for he 'comes to save men's lives.' Jesus commanded his disciples 'to love enemies, and not to kill them; and love them that hate them, and not kill them.' True, Fox went on, we see Christians since then making war and slaughtering each other; his true followers, however, 'reign (in spirit) over all these fighters with carnal weapons, that are get up, since the days of the apostles.'[28] The only warfare Christians might engage in was the Lamb's War fought with spiritual weapons against the powers of evil[29]: in this world they are obliged to accept persecution and suffering, loving their enemies and forgiving injuries. This, says Fox, 'is the royal command to the royal priesthood.'[30]

However, two elements of ambiguity in Fox's attitude to the sword still remain. In the first place, Fox never attempted to preach – indeed never even mentioned – pacifism to those soldiers in Cromwell's army who were converted to Quakerism nor did he ever try to persuade them to leave the army.[31] Indeed he was as indignant as Burrough and other leading Quakers were when the Quakers were purged from the forces. He even went so far as to claim with satisfaction that one Quaker soldier was equal to at least seven non-Quakers![32] There is nothing in the advice he gave to soldiers in 1657, for instance, that indicates any reservations about bearing arms in a righteous cause: 'See that you know a soldier's place, and see that ye be soldiers qualified, . . . and that ye be content with your wages.'[33]

Secondly, we find Fox during this period urging the Commonwealth to pursue a forward military policy against the Catholic powers on the continent, and in particular against the Pope, and he sometimes chides the government for its failure to take what he considered strong enough measures. In 1654, for instance, he wrote to Cromwell: 'Invite all them that profess against the Pope, in all nations, [to] join with thee against him, . . . and let thy soldiers go forth with a free willing heart, that thou may rock nations as a cradle.'[34] Fox's crusading zeal seems sometimes to have exceeded even that of the Lord Protector and the army authorities. He urged the English armies to subdue not only Spain and the Papacy, but France and Germany and the Turks.[35] Of course some of this was mere rhetoric but in any case it is difficult (though perhaps, we shall see, not impossible) to reconcile such an attitude with a pacifist ethos. The most warlike of Fox's utterances are probably those contained in a pamphlet he addressed early in 1659 *To the Council of Officers of the Army and the Heads of the Nation, and for the Inferior Officers and Soldiers to read.*[36] Here Fox accuses the army of unfaithfulness to their divine mission for not carrying war into the heartland of Spain and into Italy as far as Rome, so as to destroy the Inquisition in those lands, as well as for not bringing the Turks to Christianity and rooting out their idolatrous practices by similar means. 'And if ever you soldiers and true officers come again into the power of God which hath been lost, never set up your standard until you come to Rome, and it be atop of Rome, and there let your standard stand.'

We may, I think, detect greater consistency in Fox's position on war in the 1650s if we recall the position elaborated by the evangelical Anabaptists in the late 1520s and inherited from them by the Mennonites. Here the magistracy, though 'outside the perfection of Christ,' was assigned a positive role in the divine plan for the world: its sword would protect the innocent and punish evildoers. True Christians, while they were bound to practice the precepts of nonresistance, were at the same time under a sacred obligation to obey the powers that be in all things that were not contrary to

God's commands and to suffer unresistingly any penalties the government might impose if its laws were disregarded in favour of a higher law. I think that at this time Fox went far in sharing this view, and that is what, at least partly, explains his 'permissive' views with respect to soldiering and to the violence employed by the state to maintain order.[37]

As early as 1653 we find him writing – 'to the peace-breakers' – as follows concerning the role of the office of the sword. It was the magistracy, he says,

> Which should bear the sword, which should be a terror to evil doers, and that which is a terror to the evil doers keeps peace, and it is for the praise of them that do well, *the righteous whom the law was not made for, but for transgressors* which law was added because of transgression.[38]

The words I have italicised seem to me to be crucial: they might almost have come out of the Schleitheim Confession (though I am sure Fox was unaware of the existence of that document). Is it not the Quakers he is primarily referring to here as 'the righteous whom the law was not made for'? Does not Fox likewise imply that the sword of the magistracy, while divinely ordained to carry out a positive role in society, is nevertheless outside the rule of perfection laid down by Christ for those who wished to follow him exactly?

Fox was even more explicit in another epistle, composed admittedly near the end of the period we are considering, where he elaborated in greater detail sentiments he had been expressing more vaguely earlier. In it he wrote:

> Friends, live in the seed of God, that destroys the devil, who is the author and cause of wars and strife, and bringing of men and people into the earth, where the war, strife and pride is; here the outward sword-men have not learned yet to beat their swords and spears into plough-shares and pruning hooks. Yet ye that are in that seed, see that ye accuse no man falsely, that hath the sword of justice, which is to keep the peace, and is a terror to the evil-doers, and to keep down the transgressors, and for the praise of them that do well; this is owned in its place: But he that killeth with the sword, must perish with the sword. So, there was a time the Jews were to fight with outward weapons with sword and spear; but there is a time, when nations shall not learn war any more, but shall come to that, which shall take away the occasion of wars, which was in the beginning, before the wars were.[39]

We can perhaps now see more clearly how, for his own use, Fox could reject 'carnal weapons,' 'the outward sword,' in favour of 'spiritual weapons' alone, and at the same time vehemently urge the magistrate to employ military force to extirpate evil and establish godliness throughout the world.

Fox's difficulty lay in the fact that he himself as well as most other Quakers of this time were emotionally involved in the Commonwealth regime; their past tied them to the parliamentary cause in countless ways that made it extremely hard to separate decisively from it. Neither the evangelical Anabaptists nor the Mennonites had experienced this dilemma.

In November 1656 a group of Quaker elders had met at Balby in Yorkshire to discuss various problems then facing the movement: according to Braithwaite, the resolutions issuing from this meeting constitute 'the oldest . . . advice on Christian practice issued by any general body of [Quakers].' Concerning government service it was decided, 'That if any be called to serve the Commonwealth in any public service which is for the public wealth and good, that with cheerfulness it be undertaken and in faithfulness discharged unto God, that therein patterns and examples in the thing that is righteous ye may be to those that are without.'[40] Though Fox was not present, he presumably approved what had been decided on at the meeting. The resolution quoted above, while it approves Quakers holding public office, does not make it quite clear whether this approval covers those aspects of government which made use of military force. The fact that the framer of this document was probably William Dewsbury[41], whose early pacifist credentials are generally admitted, would indicate that it did not. On the other hand, at this date there were still many Quakers serving without qualms within the army so that it is not possible to be entirely certain on this point.

Indeed we must admit a certain lack of clarity in Fox's own thinking in this period, resulting from his dilemma described above. It seems likely that at first he had not felt that all other Quakers were obliged to follow his own noncombatant stance. The rulers of the Commonwealth, though beginning to backslide, were still, in Fox's eyes, for the most part godly men who sought to fulfill God's purposes by force of arms if need be. Was it necessarily wrong, therefore, for Quaker soldier converts, whose private search for righteousness had not led them, as Fox's had done, to reject 'the occasion of wars,' to continue to aid the authorities in this endeavour? Were they not following God's will in that path of service, as in turn Fox was by his renunciation of 'carnal' weapons in the fight against the unrighteous? (We shall find, I may remark, a parallel stance in that of the abolitionist William Lloyd Garrison during the American Civil War, which I have discussed elsewhere.[42])

In Fox at this time, as in the case of Quakers – and nonresistant abolitionists like Garrison – during the American Civil War, there existed a tension between peace and justice that had rarely emerged within the Anabaptist-Mennonite tradition. Cromwell – and Lincoln – pursued justice by military means: justice even seemed to demand the two leaders should engage in this pursuit even more vigorously than they were doing. This pulled Fox – as it did the Civil War Quakers – toward enthusiastic support of the government. Their pacifism, on the other hand, separated them from the magistrate's sword. The early Fox, at any rate, did not always distinguish successfully between the demands of the two ideals when they seemed to conflict with each other. The Quaker ethos, moreover, unlike that of the Anabaptist-Mennonite tradition, accepted at least the police functions of civil government. On this issue Fox during the 1650s seems to have experienced, in embryo, some of the dilemmas faced later by Quakers in Pennsylvania when they tried to distinguish between the legitimate police actions of government, in which they might participate, and the war making power of government, which they were bound by their principles to oppose, albeit passively.

If Fox's emergent pacifism was marked by certain waverings and inconsistencies, a more decisive peace witness was made during the Commonwealth period by at least a few Quakers. The evidence is fragmentary, for this was not an issue that Quakers considered to be of paramount concern. Among early Quaker leaders William Dewsbury and the ex-Leveller John Lilburne, both former soldiers, renounced the sword in decisive terms. We know, too, of Peter Hardcastle who resigned from the Commonwealth army explicitly for his opposition to war. In 1657 a similar case occurred of a Commonwealth soldier asking for his discharge from the army because of his conscientious objection to bearing arms: this was Robert Evans, a sympathiser soon to become an active Quaker member. Evans was serving at that time in Ireland under Henry Cromwell.[43] The case of one Richard Smith, a Gloucestershire man, who around 1655 joined the first 'publishers of truth,' also seems to belong in the same category, although the circumstances are not quite as clear as with Evans. Smith, the report ran, 'had been a soldier for many years, but soon after [Quakers] came about,' he abandoned soldiering and became a pillar of the local meeting.[44] 'There were also vague suggestions of pacifist notions among some of the Quaker soldiers in Scotland,'[45] where, it is interesting to note, 'convincement . . . was at first confined mainly to the army . . . of occupation.' There for instance a soldier sympathetic to the Quaker message, Cornet Ward, is reported as saying, if he did become a Quaker, 'he purposed not to make use of any carnal sword, but was resolved for that thing to lay down his tabernacle of clay.' All this so alarmed the authorities in Monck's army that the general was informed that 'these people's principles will not allow them to fight, if we stand in need, though it does to receive pay.'[46]

Further evidence of the adherence before 1660 of a growing, if still small, number of Quakers to pacifism is found in an autobiographical narrative relating how in 1657 one Thomas Lurting turned into a Quaker pacifist while serving as a boatswain's mate in the navy of Admiral Blake during England's naval war against Spain.[47] There seem to have been at this time both 'fighting' Quakers who remained in, and 'peaceable' Quakers who resigned from, the English navy: Lurting had remained a 'fighting' Quaker for some time after his convincement. It was only during an attack on Barcelona that he had developed 'some scruple of conscience on the account of fighting.' He then succeeded in persuading the other sailors who had turned Quaker to become 'peaceable,' too, and leave off fighting. None of them, however, seem to have connected Quakerism with pacifism until Lurting drew this deduction for himself in what appeared to him later as a moment of inspiration during the course of the attack.

We also know of cases toward the end of the 50s of Quaker objectors to militia service. One such was Richard Keene, a colonist in Maryland, who in 1658 refused to train 'as a soldier' and was punished for this offence by a distraint on his property. Besse indeed lists some 30 other Quakers who round about that year received various forms of punishment on account of their objection to bearing arms in the provincial militia.[48] Quakers, at any rate in Maryland, had evidently reached an unambiguously pacifist position by 1658, an earlier date than the arguments of Cole, Hill, and Reay would lead us to suppose was possible. Indeed the Governor and Council of Maryland at this time seem to have become extremely worried by the presence of Quaker pacifists in their midst, for next year they issued an order directed against 'vagabonds and idle persons known by the name of Quakers that have presumed to come into this province.' Not only were such persons opposed to the taking of oaths (already a firm Quaker testimony), but, still worse, they were attempting to dissuade 'the people from complying with the military discipline in this time of danger.' Justices of the peace were, therefore, instructed to apprehend such persons 'forthwith' and have them 'whipped from constable to constable until they be sent out of the province.'[49] It is difficult to say whether Quakers coming to Maryland were really such active antimilitarists as this document portrays them, or whether it does not reflect rather the fear aroused by the unexpected appearance in the province of a few conscientious objectors.

However, further evidence of the existence of Quaker conscientious objectors, in this case even as early as 1657, can be found in the records of another colony, Rhode Island. Some of these men may have been American born and bred, but most had probably come out from England as missionaries of the new sect. In this colony, too, the local authorities soon became anxious at the effect the pacifist propaganda of the Quakers might have on the defensive stance of its inhabitants, and the General Assembly proceeded to pass legislation punishing anyone who refused to undergo military training. I shall return to this subject later in my section on Quaker conscientious objectors in colonial America.

In England before 1660 we hear of Quaker conscientious objectors to militia service only in Colchester – and then only for 1659. But, as Margaret Hirst remarks (with fitting Quaker caution), 'it is almost certain that these were not isolated examples': it was not until after the Restoration that Quakers recorded 'sufferings' of this kind 'with great accuracy.'[50] Scanty as the evidence is, there does seem to be enough to justify the assumption that adhesion to pacifism was growing among Quakers toward the end of the 1650s.

Finally, we must deal with the crisis of 1659, a crisis embracing both the Quaker movement and the radical republicans with whose cause many Quakers were then intimately bound up. When Richard Cromwell, Oliver's son and successor as Protector, fell from power in April of that year and the Rump of the Long Parliament, with a strong radical presence, was restored in May, the way seemed to open up for the inauguration of a rule of the Saints, the elite of the Puritan left. This republican left, under the leadership of Sir Henry Vane, sought at once to enlist the Quakers in support of the new regime. The Quaker response to these overtures appears to have been, on the whole, positive at first. Quakers acted as Commissioners of Militia in Bristol, London, Westminster and elsewhere. Negotiations were set on foot to bring about the reinstatement of those Quakers who had been dismissed from the army. We know of several members who, not waiting for such a wholesale restoration, joined up on their own. Quaker preachers, too, were active in proselytising among the soldiers. A leading Quaker, Anthony Pearson, who had told Cromwell in 1654 'that now . . . should be . . . no more . . . wars and fighting without,' was instrumental in the north of England in raising militia to put down the royalist uprising led by Sir George Booth that took place in August there. While millenarian excitement rose among the sects who awaited the inauguration of the rule of the Saints and the destruction of its enemies, panic increased among those who viewed these expectations with abhorrence.[51]

How far Quakers were united in supporting military measures to bring about the political changes they all hoped for is not entirely clear.[52]

Let us look at some of the expressions of militancy among Quakers in 1659. As Cole remarks, at this time 'several Quakers came closer to direct approval of armed resistance to unjust authority than at any other time in their history.'[53] They also reiterated their belief in the role of military force in bringing about the divine plan. 'The just soldier,' wrote Edward Byllinge in his pamphlet *A Word of Reproof, and Advice to My Late Fellow-*

Souldiers, 'I own in his place.'[54] Isaac Penington, later to become William Penn's stepfather-in-law, who had joined Quakers a year or two earlier, expressed even more cogently his conviction that a reformed army, purged of those elements which had endeavoured to corrupt its noble purposes, might again become an instrument to carry out God's purposes for the nation. He wrote in May 1659:

> There hath been often a naked, honest, simple pure thing stirring in the Army, which the great ones (seeing some present use of) fell in with, and improved for their own ends but destroyed the thing itself; so that it attained not to the bringing forth of that righteous liberty, and common good which it seemed to aim at (and did indeed aim at in those in whom the striving did arise) but was made use of as an advantage to advance them in their particular interest against their enemies, and so set them up.[55]

The militant spirit can be seen most clearly of all in the case of Edward Burrough who addressed two broadsides to the restored Rump during the summer of 1659. He called on that body both to bring Quakers into the work of government, alongside the Presbyterians, Independents, and Baptists, and to readmit the cashiered Quakers to their former places in the army. In the second broadside we find him writing:

> Had the army stood in the power as once it was in, and had not the rulers of this nation lost sincerity, and turned after this world's honour, and become degenerated from their principles, and turned many faithful men out of the army, and their places of trust, which hath sorely weakened you, these things had never come to pass in the nation . . . Had you at your restoring put all these in again into their places, which they were turned out of and are kept out, only for their good conscience sake; and if you had done this then we should have cause to own that you intend to establish righteousness, which if we saw that spirit amongst you that would advance righteousness, and not seek yourselves but the good of the nations; oh then we should rejoice, and our lives would not be dear to lay down. But till then how can we come between you and your enemies to defend you and establish you in power to oppress us and our brethren . . . ?[56]

In 1659 a militant spirit undoubtedly predominated among Quakers. But there were some, we know, who maintained a pacifist position, though not always without a certain vacillation and hesitation. Francis Howgill, for instance, whose sentiments earlier had sometimes been belligerent, now came out strongly against Pearson's activities in recruiting for the militia. He was himself, he said, 'altogether dead to those things,' adding that Quakers in his area were 'quiet and meddle in none of these things.'[57]

William Dewsbury took an even stronger position against any involvement in military affairs – Reay calls it 'an anarchistic stance' – when he wrote: 'There should not be a man in Israel to rule one over another, but . . . the rule and authority of man should be overturned, and Christ alone rule in the hearts and spirits of his people.'[58]

What of George Fox himself during this crisis year? Did he back the endeavours of the militants to rally the Quaker movement behind the revival of radical republicanism and to stand with arms behind the raised standard of the Good Old Cause? Or did he attempt to damp down this enthusiasm and place Quakerism squarely on a nonviolent footing?

At first indeed Fox gave no clear reply to those who looked to him to guide them along the uncertain path that was opening out before the Quaker movement.[59] When he was asked to advise Bristol Quakers who were 'in some little strait about their acting as Commissioners' of Militia, Fox came up with no decisive answer either way. 'There is something in the thing,' he told them, 'and you cannot well leave them seeing you have gone amongst them.'[60] Then from August until near the end of the year he remained in a condition of deep depression – 'a time of darkness' – which evidently stemmed, at least in part, from his inability to resolve in his own mind the dilemma then facing Quakers: whether to help bring in, and maintain, by force of arms a new and more godly political and social order or whether to renounce this opportunity in the name of a nonviolent *Weltanschauung*.[61]

Meanwhile events moved rapidly. In October the restored Rump was replaced in a military coup by a Committee of Safety, which in turn gave way to a second restoration of a now thoroughly discredited Rump Parliament. Englishmen, disillusioned by the attempt to establish utopia, came increasingly to favour a restoration of the monarchy; while, on account of their association in the public mind with radical republicanism and sectarian fanaticism, Quakers became widely suspected of planning violence (suspicions that may have been justified in isolated instances but were surely without foundation in respect of the movement as a whole). They were now subjected to a policy of harassment that in turn brought about a rapid reassessment within their ranks of the policy of political involvement pursued by some of the Quaker leaders. The defeat of the Good Old Cause was imminent, a time of trouble lay ahead. 'Better had it been if all had been kept still and quiet in those times,' wrote a prominent Quaker, Alexander Parker, to Fox in August 1660, 'for because of the forwardness, and want of wisdom in some is one great cause of our present suffering.'[62]

Long before this, however, Fox himself had emerged from his darkness. Before the year 1659 was out we find him telling 'all Friends everywhere' to 'keep out of plots and bustling and the arm of the flesh.' Theirs was the path of peace and not the way of war. 'All that pretend to fight for Christ, are deceived; for his kingdom is not of this world, therefore his servants do not fight. Therefore fighters are not of Christ's kingdom, but without Christ's kingdom.' At last, then, Fox had taken the decisive step and denied the compatibility of military service, even in an army of the Saints, with membership of the Quaker community. 'All such as pretend Christ Jesus, and confess him, and yet run into the use of carnal weapons, wrestling with flesh and blood, throw away the spiritual weapons.' Quakers, to be true Christians, must turn the other cheek. They must learn to love, and cease to kill, their enemies.[63]

The year 1660 brought the Stuart restoration. Within the Quaker family – the Society of Friends (a term we shall frequently use henceforward) – the same year saw the establishment of pacifism as an official tenet of the sect, a collective witness soon to be enforced by a series of sanctions climaxing in the expulsion of the refractory member. Only from this point in time can we speak correctly of a Quaker peace testimony.

CHAPTER III

The Crystallisation of Quaker Pacifism

A NEW PERIOD IN THE history of Quakerism had begun in 1660. The restoration of the monarchy finally put an end to 'the utopian millenarian hopes'[1] that many Quakers had nurtured during the previous decade. The loosely knit Quaker movement now became a Society of Friends bound together not only by a common religious faith but by an efficient organisation and a discipline enforced against those who overstepped the limits of allowable behaviour. Fox's leadership remained unchallenged until his death in 1691: it was he who had been largely instrumental in bringing about those changes, which helped Quakerism to survive the periodic bouts of persecution that continued up to the passing of the Toleration Act in 1689.

Pacifism, now accepted 'as a principle,' became in fact 'an important means of disarming the old order,' political and social as well as ecclesiastical, which had been re-established in 1660.[2] Violence on the part of Friends would have removed the possibility of the slow but steady growth that, despite all the hardships and temporary setbacks, Quakerism was to experience under the later Stuarts. No longer fiery visionaries suspected of perpetrating frequent excesses and of being potential disturbers of the peace, Friends became universally recognised as devout men and women who had renounced 'striving with outward arms'[3] in the fight against moral and material evil in favour of spiritual weapons.

But of course this change was not recognised all at once nor indeed did it come about overnight. In the previous chapter we have seen the peace testimony slowly emerging during Quakerism's turbulent first decade. Throughout 1660, and even beyond, Quaker motives were still under question. In that year, for instance, we find a royalist pamphleteer, Arise Evans, writing: 'The Quakers give out forsooth, that they will not rebel nor fight, when indeed the last year, and all along the war, the army was full of them.'[4] But already the tide had turned. Early in this year Fox had stated his uncompromising opposition to any Friend accepting military rank. 'It was,' he wrote in answer to an enquiry on this point, 'contrary to our principles, for our weapons are spiritual and not carnal.'[5] In June Margaret Fell (who later became George Fox's wife) composed a statement for presentation to the King, which was then signed by Fox and 11 other leading Friends. In it they made clear that Quakers now bore a collective testimony 'against all strife and wars and contests.' 'Our weapons,' they reiterated, 'are not carnal but spiritual.'[6]

The climax in this development came in January 1661 after the millenarian sect of Fifth Monarchy Men had made an unsuccessful attempt to overthrow the government, and several hundred Quakers had been thrown into prison under suspicion of having collaborated with the insurrectionists. An official Declaration 'against all plotters and fighters in the world' was then drawn up by Fox and Richard Hubberthorne 'in behalf of the whole body of the Elect People of God who are called Quakers' and signed by the two authors as well as 10 other leading Friends.[7] This, writes Braithwaite, was 'the only official document of first-rate importance issued by Friends on the subject of war in the Restoration period.'[8] Yet, ironically it dealt primarily not with war or military service but with an issue in domestic politics.[9] Friends felt it was essential, in view of their own past image and present reputation in society, to repudiate categorically any association with those radical elements in the state that still harboured thoughts of replacing the monarchy by a rule of the Saints.[10] Their belief in pacifism only entered in to strengthen the argument they were making for domestic consumption.

In principle as well as in practice, declared Fox and his colleagues, Quakers sought peace and rejected 'war and fighting', which they knew from James 4:1-2 proceeded 'from the lusts of men.' They had renounced the sword forever, for 'the spirit of Christ, by which we are guided, is not changeable, so as once to command us from a thing as evil and again to move unto it; and we do certainly know, and so testify to the world, that the spirit of Christ, which leads us into all Truth, will never move us to fight and war against any man with outward weapons, neither for the Kingdom of Christ, nor for the Kingdoms of this world.' They had ceased to learn the postures of war and broken their swords into ploughshares and their spears into pruning-hooks: they had armed themselves instead with 'the sword of the spirit' knowing that he who takes the sword, for whatever cause, '"shall perish with the sword."'

The Declaration of 1661, despite its rapid composition in order to deal with an immediate need and its failure to bring out adequately many of the positive aspects of Quaker pacifism[11], exercised nevertheless a decisive influence on the Society of Friends. Henceforward pacifism became a hallmark of Quakerism, and for the next two centuries and more the nonpacifist Friend was the exception, whose minority stand might get him into trouble with his Society, especially if he chose actually to bear arms. When, for instance, during Monmouth's rebellion in 1685, some West Country Quakers took up arms on the side of the Duke against the Catholic King James II, they were dealt with rigorously by the Society. 'That any under our profession should any way concern themselves in the late war' was, stated the Society's Quarterly Meeting most closely concerned in the affair, 'contrary to our peaceable principle, and profession, and was and is their grief, and trouble that any such did.'[12]

At first, however, Quaker militancy continued to make its presence felt, especially among those leaders of the Society who had been most closely bound to the Good Old Cause. For some of them the turn toward pacifism proved difficult to accept. In the case of Anthony Pearson, a gentleman by birth who had become a Commissioner for the militia in 1659, this may have been one of the reasons bringing him to break with Friends in the early sixties and rejoin the Church of England. Edward Byllinge, on the other hand, stayed in the Society despite his opposition to pacifism. 'In 1660 and 1661,' writes Hill, 'he refused to give an undertaking not to take up arms or plot against the King.' He headed a faction within the Society that wished to see the Declaration of January 1661 withdrawn, and his threat otherwise to come out openly in opposition led to the withdrawal of references in that document to Quakers being his Majesty's 'loyal subjects.' Moreover, it seems that 'as late as November 1662 some Friends disavowed Margaret Fell's paper of June 1660,' referred to above.[13]

In his book Reay has listed a number of cases dating from the early sixties, where members of the Society still refused, at any rate in theory, to accept their sect's declared noncombatancy.[14] Whether such disagreement took on the dimensions of an internal controversy seems doubtful.[15] We may, however, note the absence from the signatures appended to the Declaration of pacifism of two leading – and strongly antimonarchical – Friends: George Fox the younger[16] and Edward Burrough. The post-Restoration position of the latter, who died in 1662, has been aptly described as 'a minimum pacifist position.'[17] To Burrough the restored monarchy appeared as a punishment from God for the people's sins, which had to be accepted patiently. Let 'the men that now are in power . . . have their day.' Yet, he warned, the people's patience might eventually become exhausted: if the King ruled with excessive 'force and cruelty,' then 'the people . . . will not long bear any degree of the yoke of slavery.' Isaac Penington was another early Quaker leader who, as Hill remarks, 'never abandoned his conviction of the righteousness of the original Cause.'[18] His pacifism around the time of Restoration seems, like Burrough's, to have been somewhat reluctant. He believed indeed that Friends should henceforward stand clear of all political involvement: a foreshadowing of 'a better state' to attain which Christians should ever strive. Yet he took care to make plain:

> I speak not this against any magistrate's or people's defending themselves against foreign invasions, or making use of the sword to suppress the violent and evil-doers within their borders (for this the present estate of things may and doth require, and a great blessing will attend the sword where it is borne uprightly to that end, and its use will be honourable; and while there is need of a sword, the Lord will not suffer that government, or those governors, to want fitting instruments under them for the managing thereof, to wait on him in his fear to have the edge of it rightly directed); but yet there is a better state which the Lord hath already brought some into, and which nations are to expect to travel towards.[19]

Actually, around the very time Penington was praising his Friends for their withdrawal from the magistracy, across the Atlantic in Puritan New England there were still Quakers who did not feel it incumbent on them to refuse military rank. For example, in Kittery, which Quaker missionaries had visited in 1659, we hear of three Quakers among the selectmen in 1662 and 1663, one of whom was a militia commander and the other two also members of that body.[20] A situation of this kind soon ceased to be possible even in such outposts of Quakerism. Yet in North America, we shall see, the office of the sword continued to be a bothersome question for colonial Quakerism until the time of the Revolution.

At this point it may be in order to examine briefly the position George Fox took up with respect to the magistracy during the post-Restoration period. Fox continued to stress that Friends believed that the magistracy was ordained of God. The Law of the state, enforced by the magistrate's sword, curbed the evil doings of 'the unrighteous.' So long as Caesar did not restrict religious truth but kept within his proper secular sphere, he must be honoured and obeyed. 'Caesar's weapons,' he wrote in 1679, 'are for the punishment of the evil-doers and for the praise of them that do well; for which he is to have his tribute, his custom, his due.'[21] Fox never forbade Quaker participation in office (if he had done so, he would have had to repudiate the Quaker experiment in government which his younger colleague, William Penn, launched in 1682). But, a man of action and not a systematic thinker, he never attempted to work out in detail the relationship between Quaker pacifism and political power.

This task was left to the more powerful pen of Robert Barclay, the descendant of Scottish lairds who turned Quaker in 1667 (he died in 1690 a year before Fox). Before joining Friends Barclay had been thoroughly educated in the classics and theology, acquiring in the process extensive erudition that did him good service when he undertook the task of providing a systematic and thorough exposition of the Quaker faith. Barclay's was a logical mind, he knew how to present his arguments cogently and in a sophisticated form that would appeal to his own and many generations to come. If his work generally seems to present-day readers somewhat dry and lacking the fire – as well as the crude force – of Fox's best writing, we should not forget that his *Apology* remained for at least two centuries the classic statement of Quakerism both for Friends themselves and those outside the Society. It had first appeared in Latin in 1676 under the title *Theologiae Verae Christianae Apologia* and then two years later in an English version as *An Apology for the True Christian Divinity.*[22] Here all the tenets of the Quakerism of Barclay's day find extensive – and effective – treatment, the subject of 'revenge and war' being discussed in sections 13-15 of Proposition XV (the main theme of which is, rather strangely, 'salutations and recreations'). In the course of his argument Barclay displays not only his deep Biblical knowledge and classical learning but also his acquaintance with the writings of the Church Fathers and of antimilitarist humanists like Erasmus and Juan Luis Vives.

In his exposition of Quaker pacifism Barclay indulges in some detailed textual criticism and cites key passages in favour of, and refutes other passages that were widely cited against, Friends' position on war. But his emphasis is always on the spirit of Jesus' message rather than on the letter of the text. For him the Sermon on the Mount – 'Matt. V., from verse 38, to the end of the chapter' – is all important. How, he asks, may Christians reconcile Jesus' doctrine of peace, which he taught on the Mount, with the results of war. Through war,

> the world is filled with violence, oppression, murders, ravishing of women and virgins, spoilings, depredations, burnings, devastations, and all manner of lasciviousness and cruelty; so that it is strange that men, made after the image of God, should have so much degenerated, that they rather bear the image and nature of roaring lions, tearing tigers, devouring wolves, and raging boars, than of rational creatures endued with reason.

Christ had replaced the law of Moses with a new dispensation that excluded his followers from warring and fighting, binding them instead to suffer and to repay evil with good. 'Things, which in time past were lawful to the Jews, considering their condition and dispensation,' and 'because of their hardness' of heart, were no longer admissible in a follower of Christ, and among the chief of these things was war.[23]

The teaching given by Jesus in his Sermon on the Mount seemed to Barclay to provide incontrovertible evidence of the unchristian character of war. 'And truly,' he declares, 'the words are so clear in themselves, that, in my judgement, they need no illustration to explain their sense: for it is as easy to reconcile the greatest contradictions, as these laws of our Lord Jesus Christ with the wicked practices of wars: for they are plainly inconsistent.'[24] There were other New Testament texts of course that Barclay was able to bring forward in support of his argument, and he did not fail, either, to refer to the peace witness of the early church before Constantine's reign.[25] He rejected the plea of opponents 'that defence is of natural right, and that religion destroys not nature,' on the grounds that to obey God could never be to destroy nature but rather 'to exalt and perfect it . . . to elevate [humanity] from the natural to the supernatural life.'[26]

All this sounds fairly modern to our ears. Fox and the first generation of Quaker pacifists had rarely, if ever, produced humanitarian arguments in support of their position. They acted in obedience to God's command as recommended by the Inner Light and confirmed in the text of the New Testament. That for them was sufficient. But Barclay, we have seen, while he too based his case for pacifism on the New Testament and made use of textual arguments to buttress it, also appealed against war to human reason and described its horrors in an effort to discredit it. This, I think, is something new in Quaker thinking. Geoffrey Nuttall has rightly pointed to 'the Renaissance strain in Quakerism,'[27] a humanist strand in their thinking on war and society that eventually blossomed out into the humanitarian relief activity that has become so closely associated with the Quaker name in our century. For this development Barclay was largely responsible.

Let me quote from Barclay's *Apology* a brief – and unusually ironic – passage that illustrates clearly his humanitarian approach to the problem of war. It comes at the conclusion of his discussion of that subject:

> If to fight for outward and perishing things, to go a warring one against another, whom we never saw, with whom we never had any contest, nor anything to do; being moreover altogether ignorant of the cause of the war, but only that the magistrates of the nations foment quarrels one against another, the causes whereof are for the most part unknown to the soldiers that fight, as well as upon whose side the right or wrong is and yet to be so furious, and rage one against another, to destroy and spoil all, . . . if to do this, and much more of this kind, be to fulfill the Law of Christ, then are our adversaries indeed true Christians, and we [Quakers] miserable heretics . . .[28]

Here we detect tones that sound through much of 19th and 20th-century pacifist writing and that are largely absent in the exponents of Anabaptist-Mennonite nonresistance or in the very first proponents of Quaker pacifism.

Barclay's exposition of the peace testimony nevertheless contained its
conservative aspects. They arose primarily from what Elton Trueblood has
aptly described as 'the tension between two loyalties' felt by Barclay with
respect to Friends' peace testimony, and in particular to the bearing this
testimony might have on Quakers' attitude to the office of the sword.
Barclay's solution of this tension lay in his 'recognition that what is true for a
separated society is not necessarily true for a government which represents a
great mixture of peoples, problems, and convictions.'[29]

Barclay in fact was prepared, as Fox had done, to grant 'the lawfulness
of fighting to the present magistrates and states of Christians.'[30]
Governments, even Christian governments, might have to employ the
sword both against domestic evildoers and against foreign invaders. In his
Apology he dealt squarely with this problem. A 'truly Christian' magistrate,
he says, ought to follow Jesus' command, 'Love your enemies' – 'and then
he could not command us to kill them,' while, on the other hand, 'if he be
not a true Christian, then ought we to obey our Lord and King, Jesus
Christ, whom he ought also to obey.' But, with regard to the former kind of
magistrate Barclay then exclaims: 'Alas! where shall we find such an
obedience? O deplorable fall!' Nevertheless fallen Christians, Barclay
grants, and not only those who strove to follow the perfection of Christ,
must still be regarded as Christians: their apostasy in this regard had come
about 'perhaps through inadvertency, and by the force of custom and
tradition.' So long as they remained in this condition, warfare in a just cause
retained a conditional validity.

Better for those who had not risen to the standard of the Sermon on the
Mount to fight rather than yield to injustice: this seems to be implicit in the
passage from the *Apology* I quote below, even if everything is not explicitly
stated there.

As to what relates to the present magistrates of the Christian world,
albeit we deny them not altogether the name of Christians, because of
the public profession they make of Christ's name, yet we may boldly
affirm, that they are far from the perfection of the Christian religion;
because in the state in which they are (as in many places before I have
largely observed), they have not come to the pure dispensation of the
gospel. And therefore, while they are in that condition, we shall not say,
that this war, undertaken upon a just occasion, is altogether unlawful to
them. For even as circumcision and the other ceremonies were for a
season permitted to the Jews, not because they were either necessary of
themselves, or lawful at that time, after the resurrection of Christ, but
because that Spirit was not yet raised up in them, whereby they could be
delivered from such rudiments; so the present confessors of the
Christian name, who are yet in the mixture, and not in the patient

suffering spirit, are not yet fitted for this form of Christianity, and therefore cannot be undefending themselves until they attain that perfection. But for such whom Christ has brought hither, it is not lawful to defend themselves by arms, but they ought over all to trust to the Lord.[31]

'Not fighting, but suffering' was how Barclay's younger contemporary, William Penn, defined the essence of the Quaker peace testimony. This was a traditional pacifist approach. But Penn, like Barclay, supplemented his Biblical base with pragmatic considerations for pacifism. Writing in the mid-1690s he states: 'And, Christianity set aside, if the costs and fruits of war be well considered, peace, with all its inconveniences, is generally preferable.' Penn, again like Barclay (and in this case like Fox too), took a positive view of the magistracy. 'Where government doth not interfere with conscience' he regards it as 'an ordinance of God, and where it is justly administered, a great benefit to mankind.'[32]

What both Barclay and Penn omitted to consider was the role pacifism would play if Quakers were once again admitted to the magistracy – that ordinance of God which they believed brought great benefit to mankind but from which they had been excluded by the restoration of the monarchy. In Pennsylvania in particular, as well as to a lesser degree in several more of England's American colonies, a Quaker magistracy soon became not merely a remote possibility but a present reality. This was to raise problems that Barclay had probably never envisaged, and of which Penn himself only gradually became aware.[33] Meanwhile the Declaration of 1661, and perhaps even more Barclay's exposition of pacifism in his *Apology*, had laid a foundation on which Quakers erected a firm structure of war resistance. In addition to a personally nonviolent stance[34], conscientious objection to military and naval service as well as to some, if not quite all, the other demands made by the state for the support of war, now became the established practice of the Society of Friends.

CHAPTER IV

The Pattern of Quaker
Conscientious Objection in England

THE QUAKER CONSCIENTIOUS OBJECTOR in most cases embodied 'the general respectability, piety, self-limitation, and sectarian discipline which marked . . . the men who claimed the rights of conscience'[1] granted in many Protestant lands from the late 16th century on. Eventually he became a symbol of war resistance, and Christian pacifism and the Quaker peace testimony appeared to many to be identical. The Society's conscientious objectors, usually against their own wishes, were often treated with greater consideration than those coming from other backgrounds. Smaller in numbers than the Mennonites for instance, the Quakers came to exert a greater influence than any other pacifist sect on the wider peace movement that emerged in modern times.[2] Yet, we have seen, Quaker pacifism had been born in turmoil, and only after 1660 did it become an established testimony of the Society of Friends. But from that time on Quakers, if they desired to retain membership in the Society, were required to refuse to bear arms, should this obligation be imposed on them by the state. Henceforward, failure 'to find a man for the militia' figured among the chief 'sufferings' of post-Restoration Quakerdom, along with refusal to pay tithes or worship in the established church, rejection of the oath of allegiance, and infringement of various acts passed against dissenters.

The pattern of conscientious objection which was now established covered of course a wider area than merely the refusal to bear arms in the militia, though this was perhaps the most important issue at first. Quakers indeed felt their testimony against war was all of one piece. We find members of London Yearly Meeting expressing this thought in their epistle issued in 1804 during the war against Napoleon: 'Friends,' they then said, 'it is an awful thing to stand forth to the nation as the advocates of inviolable peace; and our testimony loses its efficacy in proportion to the want of consistency in any.'[3] And similar statements might be found earlier on in the Society's history.

We shall, therefore, have also to consider briefly both the Quaker objector to service in the navy and the scruples entertained by Quakers and the dilemmas they underwent in respect of the arming of merchant vessels against privateers and pirates. Auxiliary war services and various other forms of assistance to the waging of war as well as involvement in war industries all provided the Quaker conscience with further problems to grapple with. Conscientious objection to compulsory manifestations of joy for victories and sorrow at defeats played a minor, though symbolically significant role, in the total pattern. Finally, in the interstices of the narrative we shall catch a few glimpses of the Quaker objectors to the peace testimony, i.e., the minority who did not conform to the now generally accepted pattern of behaviour in respect to warlike activities, and see how they fared within their Society. I cannot attempt here to give more than a summary review of the problems which the working out of the practical implication of their pacifist witness involved for English Friends, and I would refer the reader who seeks a more detailed treatment to the relevant sections of Margaret Hirst's classic study of the Quaker peace testimony, *The Quakers in Peace and War* (1923). Indeed throughout this chapter I have drawn on it extensively for illustrative material.[4]

Conscription for the army did not exist in Britain before World War I. But ablebodied males were required to serve in the militia or 'trained bands' for several weeks annually, though this obligation was imposed irregularly. The exact terms of service varied from one period to another; yet the law remained the same in essentials until the abolition of compulsory militia service in 1860. Long before that date, however, compulsion had virtually ceased for what had become an increasingly moribund body. In the 17th century at any rate, we may note, that women were also sometimes required to find a man for the militia if they owned property on which an obligation of this kind was laid (see below).

Friends' position was by this time unambiguous. No Quaker of course could bear arms himself, nor was he permitted by the rules of the Society to pay for a substitute, though this always remained legally a possible way out for those not wishing for whatever reason to serve when the ballot unhappily fell on them. By the rules of his Society the Quaker was not allowed, either, to pay the fine which was the penalty for failing to obey a summons to the militia. As a result militia objectors had their property distrained to the amount (and sometimes more than the amount) of the fine or, if they did not possess sufficient means for this, they were imprisoned for a short period, varying according to time and place.

Distraint and imprisonment seem to have occurred rather erratically throughout the period under discussion. In the 17th century we find that the law was enforced more rigorously in London and the south-eastern counties than elsewhere, because fear of French invasion was felt more acutely there than in other parts of England. 'The minute-books of Kent Quarterly Meetings,' writes Margaret Hirst, 'show only fourteen years in the period 1660 to 1702 in which there is no record of fine or imprisonment for this cause.'[5] Innumerable cases of militia 'sufferings' are recorded for this period in Besse's two volumes, including some where the sufferer is a woman Quaker, who is either imprisoned or has property distrained for unwillingness to send a man to bear arms in the militia.

Usually these entries are terse: they rarely preserve the arguments objectors presumably presented to the authorities in defence of their refusal to train. However, some time ago Henry Cadbury uncovered a document recording the hearing held at the Guildhall of a London Quaker, Philip Ford, who had refused to pay the fine levied on him by the city authorities for refusing to muster in the trained bands. 'Before the first summons came' to bear arms, states Ford at the outset, 'I received a summons from the Prince of Peace to march under his banner, which is love, who came not to destroy men's lives but to save them. And being enlisted under this banner I dare not desert my colours to march under the banner . . . of the kings of the earth.' He was, he said, prepared to pay ordinary taxes to government even when the money was put to military uses, since this was Caesar's and not his concern. He had also paid the tax levied for the upkeep of the city watch (which, we may add, not all Quakers were prepared to do), even though he knew the watchmen carried arms during the performance of their duties. 'I make a distinction,' Ford explained here, 'betwixt the military power and the civil. The military power's command is, Go, fire, kill and destroy. The civil power's command is, Go, keep the peace.' On being asked whether Christians formerly had not assisted their rulers in war, Ford replied: 'Yes, they did . . . when their faith in God began to fail them, and they took to carnal weapons, there the apostasy entered, and the Pope got over most called Christians.' A Christian must obey his master and love, not kill, his enemies. True, tribute should be rendered when Caesar demanded it but, in Ford's view, a fine imposed for refusal to render military service fell into quite a different – and inadmissible – category.[6]

The two Jacobite rebellions, led in 1715 by the Old Pretender James and in 1745 by the Young Pretender Charles, tested the loyalty of English Quakers to their peace testimony. Although they passed that test there were moments of uncertainty in some parts of the country. Quakers, we should remember, were in their subdued way devoted supporters of the Hanoverian establishment, which the wild invading Scots were bent on overturning in favour of a Stuart restoration. In 1715 Quakers remained quiet while at the same time clearly expressing their sympathies for the Hanoverian cause. In Cheshire, for instance, it was reported, their behaviour 'gained them love and respect even from the very soldiers.' On the defeat of the rebels Yearly Meeting handed the king an address congratulating him on the suppression of the 'Black Conspiracy.'

In 1745 some Friends in the North contributed financially to the military effort: this was the area actually invaded by Bonnie Prince Charlie's troops. We read of Quakers of these parts presenting the army of the Duke of Cumberland – 'Butcher Cumberland'! – with various gifts, including 'ten thousand woollen waistcoats to keep them warm.' These presents, though, do not seem to have been made officially on behalf of the Society. There were also a few Friends who in their enthusiasm volunteered to bear arms: such men were at once dealt with and only reinstated as members in good standing after they had acknowledged that they had acted contrary to their Society's principles. More difficult to detect, because done secretly, were transgressions of the peace testimony (for surely they were this?) where Quakers acted as intelligence agents for the royal forces transmitting information that would thwart the enemy's 'base and treacherous designs.' There were certainly not many such cases. But, on the whole, the comment of an eye-witness, 'I have not met with any . . . but what were zealous friends to the Government,' sums up correctly the Quaker position in 1745. Once again, at the conclusion of the rebellion the Quaker Yearly Meeting presented the king with an even more laudatory – even more servile – address than they had compiled in 1715. 'As none among all thy Protestant subjects exceed us in an aversion to the tyranny, idolatry, and superstition of the Church of Rome,' they wrote, 'so, none . . . have greater cause to be thankful to the Almighty for the interposition of his providence in our preservation.' Hirst's comment on these events is apt. 'It is obvious,' she writes, 'that prosperous Friends, in common with other members of the wealthy middle class, had been badly frightened.' For them, too, Cumberland appeared as the saviour of the nation as well as of the Protestant cause.[7]

There were no essential changes during the 18th century in the pattern of Quaker objection to militia service. As earlier, a few Friends agreed to pay for a substitute. But in the overwhelming majority of instances events moved *mutatis mutandis* roughly along the pattern recorded for 1777 in the case of a Reigate (Kent) manservant, Isaac Cox:

> For refusing to serve in the militia when drawn, [he] had taken from him by warrant . . . his chest which had in it most of his wearing apparel and some money. It was . . . some time after broken open, the money taken out and other things retained. And when they had settled the expense of hiring a substitute, they returned the overplus.[8]

Cox's was only one of hundreds of such procedures carried out against Quaker militia objectors in the course of the century: the details changed (the 'overplus,' for instance, was not always returned), but the outline remained constant. There was, however, some variation in the regularity with which imprisonment was imposed on propertyless Quaker delinquents. For instance, the long war with France that began in 1793, and, apart from several short breaks, lasted until 1815, brought a stiffening of sentencing. A number of young Friends from the poorer sections of the Society then saw the inside of prison walls. Sentences, however, were limited to a maximum of three months and conditions inside prison seem to have been remarkably mild. In the case of an impecunious young shop assistant, Richard Elgar, on whom the ballot to serve fell in 1809, local Friends reported: 'During his imprisonment the deputy gaoler and the turnkeys behaved in a quiet and becoming manner towards him, and his fellow-prisoners who were not of our persuasion were as agreeable as could be expected in such a place.'[9] We should remember that by that date their fellow countrymen regarded Quakers as model citizens whose 'tender consciences' – or peculiar foibles – were worth protecting even when they could not be wholly understood.

After the closure of the Napoleonic Wars in 1815 few instances occur of young Quakers being imprisoned in connection with the militia.[10] Militia distraints, however, continued until the abolition of the militia ballot in 1860, though long before that date their number had gradually fallen off until it eventually became a mere trickle. Military conscription was not to come again to Britain until 1916, and then compulsion was to be exercised with respect to the army and not the militia.

From early on conscientious objectors occasionally emerged within the ranks of the professional army. This happened when a serving soldier, brought by some chance into contact with active Friends, embraced Quakerism, including its tenet on peace, and then took steps to join the religious Society of his new found persuasion. (This, we may interpose, is of course a far cry from the early days, when toward the end of the 1650s dismissed Quaker warriors were clamouring for reinstatement in the army they saw as the chosen instrument to fulfill their religious vision.) The record on army objectors is fragmentary. At any rate, we read of a Quaker soldier-convert serving in Ireland who in 1670, having been 'convinced of the unlawfulness of wars and fightings under the gospels,' had laid down his arms, for which offence he was sentenced to ride 'the wooden horse' (a specially irksome punishment). Twenty-three years later we hear of the Meeting for Sufferings (the chief executive body of the Society) concerning itself with the release from jail of a soldier converted while stationed at Canterbury (Kent). The man had refused to bear arms any longer, and this stance of his brought serious ill treatment down on his head. Efforts to secure his release were successfully concluded with the help of local

Friends.[11] More cases of this kind can also be cited from both the 18th and the 19th centuries.

We must now move from land to ocean – or at any rate to the waters adjacent to Britain's shores – to observe the reaction of Friends to that invidious form of conscription for the British navy enforced by means of the press-gang. I suppose one might describe this procedure as a form of selective drafting. During this period, in any one of the dozens of ports and fishing villages dotted along the English coast, an ablebodied young man might be seized by the 'gang' and pressed into service in His Majesty's Navy. If the pressed man had influential family and friends, whom he could contact before being spirited away onto the high seas, he had some chance of release: otherwise his hopes of attaining this were slim. The practice naturally was widely unpopular, especially with the ordinary people of the seacoast on whom the burden fell most heavily.[12]

In the early days especially, but indeed throughout the 18th century, there were many Quakers who gained their living from the sea, who therefore spent most of their lives on ships or in the towns and villages of the coastline. From what I know of Quaker persistence, then and now, I doubt if many of their young men falling into the clutches of the press-gang remained indefinitely a part of the Royal Navy. Friends would not rest until they had gained release for such. Moreover, Quaker pressed men clearly made rather unruly – though of course nonviolent – tars, and thus the Navy was probably glad to get rid of them before too long.[13]

While on board ship the Quaker who had been pressed was likely to suffer severe ill treatment for disobedience to orders, every effort being made to force him into an at least reluctant compliance. A simple Yorkshire fisherman, Richard Seller, who was pressed in the port of Scarborough in 1665, has left a graphic account of his 'sufferings' that was recorded soon after the events he was describing. They form one of the most interesting sections of Besse's massive compilation of Quaker documents.[14] His steadfastness succeeded in winning some of the crew over to his side, though those in command long regarded this steadfastness as stubbornness. After rendering humanitarian aid to members of the crew during an encounter with the Dutch (for it was wartime), Seller's relationship with all on board greatly improved, and he was now allowed to return home as soon as the ship docked in an English port.

It would be tedious for the reader if I were to multiply such narratives. Impressment, though, remained a threat hanging over the heads of young maritime Quakers for a long time to come. In 1678 we find the Meeting for Sufferings concerned with 'the often sufferings of Friends by being impressed into King's ships of war.' Quakers were asked to contribute money to procure their release. 'At times,' adds Hirst, 'in the hunt for seamen the gaols were invaded and Friends lying imprisoned for [refusal to pay tithes] were carried away.'[15] Eventually, it seems, the press-gang, in its voracious pursuit of manpower for the Royal Navy, grew less eager than it had been at first to bring into its net such refractory material as Quakers almost always proved in their hands.

We come now to consider a group of closely related activities, likewise connected with the sea, to which the Quaker conscience objected. But with these activities no outward compulsion was exercised. Here the struggle between the Quaker's Truth and material power took place within the intellect and the heart. Perhaps for this very reason the pressure to yield on a matter of principle was stronger than where the state attempted exterior compulsion to extort conformity. Indeed the measures the state took against conscientious objectors in Britain seem to us surprisingly mild. It was surely not too much of a hardship to have to yield from time to time a part (often a very small part) of one's property in the shape of a distraint. There were worse things in life than having to spend three months in prison, especially when the jailers and one's fellow prisoners were really quite nice. Even physical ill treatment such as was meted out to young Seller, used already to the assaults of wind and wave as well as to the hardships of life on a fishing smack, was probably not much worse than what was given as punishment to non-Quaker sailors who broke the rules. Fishermen in those days were accustomed to harsh conditions – and Seller's sufferings were but temporary. But what of those more subtle temptations that arose when the infraction of Quakers' peace principles meant gaining material profit, bluntly put, meant acquiring more money? As time passed, Quakers, we know, were becoming more bourgeois in outlook, more profit oriented – or at least some of them were who carried weight in the counsels of the Society. Moreover, it was not always easy (though often of course it was) to decide where an action offended against Quaker pacifism and where it did not. There was also the fact that detection, i.e. the possibility of an un-Quakerly action becoming known to one's fellow believers, would not always appear likely. Such moral dilemmas, we shall discover, were not confined to Friends who dwelt by the sea but the dangers of going astray were perhaps more keenly felt by this class of Quaker than by those whose livelihood did not depend on that treacherous element.

For one thing, there was still really no very clear distinction between merchant navy and Royal Navy with its ships of war. Both classes of fleet had to cope with foreign privateers, even in peacetime: in wartime the distinction between the two became even more fragile, and long stretches of war cover the period we have now under discussion. For Friends the most delicate issue of all, however, was that of involvement in armed vessels.

Putting guns on ships was an almost universal practice throughout the merchant navy. There was, in addition, the complex problem of privateering; the privateer being an armed vessel whose owners were private persons authorised by 'letters of marque' from the government to attack merchant ships of foreign countries deemed hostile and confiscate their merchandise for their own profit.

Since Quakers in those days were active both as shipowners and as sailors, the temptation to compromise in this regard was bound up with the problem of occupation. For instance, a Quaker sailor, often a poor man whose daily bread – and that of his wife and children too – depended on his being able to find employment on a merchant vessel, frequently found it difficult to come upon a ship that did not carry guns. His best chance was to be taken on in a Quaker owned vessel. But the well-to-do Quaker shipowner faced his dilemmas here, too. Without arming his vessels – even in peacetime – he would have to face the likelihood of heavy financial loss from the depredations of pirates and hostile privateers – not to speak of the still more difficult conditions prevailing in time of war. It was, moreover, hard for him to resist pressure to place guns on board and make other para-military preparations from crews drawn in many instances from non-Quaker backgrounds.

The official stance of the Society remained inexorably opposed to any compromise on these issues. They became a matter of concern for Friends from the date they adopted their peace testimony until the problem finally ceased to exist in the second quarter of the 19th century. In Yearly Meeting's Epistle of 1693 we find the carrying of guns on Quaker-owned ships is roundly condemned. The passage in question runs as follows:

A complaint being made about some shipmasters (who profess the truth, and are esteemed Quakers) carrying guns in their ships, contrary to their former principles and practice, and endangering their own and others' lives thereby; also giving occasion of more severe hardships and sufferings to be inflicted on such Friends as are pressed into ships of war, who, for conscience sake, cannot fight, nor destroy men's lives, it is therefore recommended to the Monthly and Quarterly Meetings whereunto such shipmasters belong, to deal with [them] in God's wisdom and tender love, to stir them up, and awaken their consciences, that they may seriously consider how they injure their own souls in so doing, and what occasion they give to make the truth and Friends to suffer by their declension, and acting contrary thereunto, through disobedience and disbelief; placing their security in that which is altogether insecure and dangerous; which we are really sorry for, and sincerely desire their recovery and safety from destruction, that their faith and confidence may be in the arm and power of God.[16]

The admonition had alas to be repeated in 1709, and similar appeals continue throughout the 18th, and on into the early years of the 19th century, mixed now with laments about the repeated involvement of some Quakers with privateering.[17]

Such deviations from Quaker rectitude on the part of otherwise probably highly respected – and undoubtedly well-to-do – members were indeed 'lamentable.' It was certainly not an acceptable excuse to plead that the guns were intended merely to 'terrify' an assailant. 'Friends think [this] is chiefly pretence,' stated Yorkshire Quarterly Meeting, under whose supervision the sea captains and shipowners of Whitby and Scarborough came, in 1745.[18] Often offenders confessed themselves at fault, as Joseph Linskill, a prominent shipowner, had done in 1714. The Quarterly Meeting then declared he had 'been so convinced of the evil of that work (of carrying guns in ships) that he has given forth a very sensible testimony in writing against his former practice.'[19] But practices of this kind could not be stopped altogether, for all the 'labouring' and 'dealings' against the delinquents which took place decade after decade. 'Deficiencies' as to proper observance of Friends' peace principles in this area of behaviour continued to be frequent. At one time even the Clerk of Whitby Monthly Meeting held shares in armed vessels, though he was persuaded to dispose of them when the matter became known.[20] Many had finally to be disowned: some of these cases, but obviously only a small selection, are recorded in Margaret Hirst's volume. Often such disownments were only accepted with difficulty in the coastal Meetings, and there were occasions when the bulk of members of a Monthly Meeting like Whitby clearly sympathised with the expelled members. After all, there were probably few whose hands were entirely clear of complicity in this kind of 'misdemeanour.'[21]

Friends did not distinguish, at least as regards their own conduct, between the offensive and defensive use of armaments. But we may perhaps make a distinction between the more gross offenders and those Quaker shipowners – or part-owners – who yielded with reluctance and agreed to place guns on their vessels for defensive purposes. At any rate these armaments were not, we presume, used to attack another ship. But what of those Friends 'concerned in fitting out . . . privateers?' The object for which they had received their letters of marque was clearly aggressive: a share in the 'prize goods' gained through seizure of an 'enemy' merchant vessel.[22] Quakers of this kind were certainly participating in the spoils of war, even if such spoils were sometimes acquired during times of peace, and I think their conduct must be condemned more rigorously than that of the reluctant offenders as being even more inconsistent with the testimony of the Society to which they belonged and of which it seems they were usually active members.

I would like at this point to discuss briefly a curious phenomenon, perhaps legendary but more likely to have existed in reality: 'Quaker guns'! Quaker guns were wooden not iron ones, dummies intended to scare away attackers without the need for actual combat. No blood would be shed; yet all the advantages of military defence would be gained without actually taking life. Cadbury [23] thinks that those shipowners who resorted to this practice were non-Friends: presumably they did so for reasons of economy. But I am not altogether convinced. At any rate, we know of at least one case of a Quaker-owned ship that carried 'Quaker guns.' This was the *Bengal* that sailed from Liverpool in 1814 on her maiden voyage to Calcutta where she arrived next year. Curiously enough, one of the *Bengal*'s part owners was James Cropper, the future father-in-law of our Friend Joseph Sturge. Cropper's other vessels which plied the Atlantic were not, so far as we know, supplied with guns, Quaker or real: he had indeed the reputation of being a sincere upholder of the peace testimony. We must presume it was his non-Quaker partners or the non-Quaker crew whose pressure led to the installation of these dummies.[24] That they were constructed of wood and not iron, may perhaps be regarded as a partial triumph of the peace principle over the God of war! The story at any rate illustrates the peculiarly difficult situation in which the Quaker shipowning community found itself in those days.

There is a mass of materials in the records of the Society dealing with the shipowning bigwigs, though it has never been systematically explored. But information is scanty about the rank-and-file Quaker seaman whose stake in the sea was perhaps even greater than that of his wealthier coreligionist, since for him it was literally a question of his bread and butter. This dearth of sources, however, is understandable, for in general the common sailor figures to a much less degree in history than the naval officer.

Let just one example suffice to illustrate the moral dilemmas that Quaker sailors might have to face. Doubtless other, and better, examples lie buried in the archives. The case I have chosen is an early one, that of Edward Coxere, whose autobiography was first printed only in 1945.[25] Coxere's home town was Dover. It was there, during a shore leave in 1661, that he was converted to Quakerism by two of the First Publishers of Truth, Edward Burrough and Samuel Fisher. After hearing these preachers his conscience at once began to trouble him 'concerning fighting or killing of enemies.' Was his sailoring, to which killing formed a frequent, though not essential accompaniment, in fact an occupation a man who took his Quaker religion seriously might pursue – at any rate after the Quakers' Truth on this point had been set before his eyes? At first Coxere did not know what he should do: elements of doubt concerning pacifism continued for a time to lodge in his mind. But he was already pacifist enough to be repelled by a fellow Quaker convert among the crew, who tried to persuade him that, if their vessel became engaged in combat, even though they were Quakers they might still 'fire at the mast.' 'The Lord,' he writes, 'at that time let me see that piece of deceit : that . . . it was but a cheat [to] deceive them we were with, . . . for I knew that when we came [aboard] we had the men to deal with and not the mast. This would not serve . . .' Therefore, on his next shore leave he plainly told the owner of his ship, who was also his brother-in-law, that he would not fight or take human life any longer.

As a result of his open avowal of pacifism Coxere, despite his 'good acquaintance with many masters of ships,' remained out of employment for some time to come. 'The name of a Quaker and not fighting shut me quite out of esteem with them.' 'I became as one not fit to be suffered in a ship, and how to maintain my family, which increased, I was in a strait.' At that date there were few Friends who were shipowners, but Coxere did in the end succeed in finding a sea captain sympathetic to Quakerism who was ready to have him as the ship's mate.[26]

As Friends entered in larger numbers into the shipowning business, the difficulties Coxere had faced in seeking employment must have lessened. Quaker shipowners indeed usually found difficulty in recruiting sufficient Quaker sailors for their ships : they had to make do with non-Quakers, and this, we have seen, sometimes led to pressures to arm that would not have been felt if the majority of the crew had been Quaker. At any rate, for the later period the records remain largely silent over any dilemmas of conscience suffered by Quaker seamen.

The Quaker seafaring community, together with the Quaker shipowning interest that was intimately linked with it, faced problems in connection with their Society's peace testimony that did not afflict their landed brethren. But the latter's troubles, on the other hand, were not confined to sporadic attempts to make them muster with the militia.[27] Friends from time to time were cautioned against keeping guns in their homes or on their farms. If a crisis situation arose, who knew if temptation to use them for lethal purposes might not prove too strong? Friends were also to resist payment of 'Trophy Money,' i.e., a levy for the buying of various kinds of military accoutrement. If distraint or imprisonment resulted from such refusal, this should be submitted to quietly as in the case of militia service. In the event of a victory, they were not to take part in public rejoicing or participate in victory celebrations, and on the occasion of a defeat they were not to indulge in public fasting or mourning, even if this would probably entail, at least for the Quaker merchant community which now formed a substantial section of the Society, considerable financial loss and sometimes the breaking of shop windows and damage to property from angry mobs as well.[28]

The question of alternative service appears to have arisen only rarely. Dr. Johnson tells us that his Quaker friend, Tom Cumming, had informed him in 1745 that he was not prepared to fight, 'but he would drive an ammunition cart.' But Cumming was scarcely a model Friend; besides, he was never of course actually required to drive an ammunition cart, an activity for which he would certainly have been disciplined by the Society.[29]

In general Quakers were required to refrain from giving any form of assistance, voluntary or otherwise, to the army. In 1810 during the Napoleonic Wars, for instance, Yearly Meeting issued the following warning: 'It is inconsistent with our known testimony against wars for Friends to be in any manner aiding and assisting in the conveyance of soldiers, their baggage, arms, ammunition, and other military stores.'[30]

The story of Quaker involvement with war industry is a complex one. The official position of the Society allowed no doubt that it was a violation of the peace testimony to take part in, and derive profit from, the manufacture of munitions or other instruments of war. Any Friend known to have done so was liable to be disciplined – and then disowned if he persisted in flouting one of the major testimonies of the Society. Yet it was some time before Quakers succeeded in this connection in effectively defining exactly what should be regarded as a contribution to war. Of course it was a question here of marginal activities. Concerning the making of cannon or muskets or military uniforms there scarcely needed to be any discussion.

We learn with some surprise of the Meeting for Sufferings in 1690 taking up the cause of four Quaker carpenters, who had been dismissed from their work in the King's Yard at Chatham, a naval dockyard, 'because they could not bear arms' in the military drill which the authorities had instituted for employees during an invasion scare. The Meeting was concerned in recovering the men's wages which had been withheld at their dismissal. It does not, however, seem to have thought of taking up the question why these members were working at all in an establishment devoted to the construction of men-of-war.

Quaker manufacturers, who emerged in considerable numbers in the 18th century, do not appear to have found it difficult to steer clear of production for war. But this was not always the case, as was shown in the Samuel Galton affair which became a *cause célèbre* within the Society of his time. The firm of Samuel Galton of Birmingham – formally known as Farmer & Galton – had got itself deeply involved in the manufacture of guns. Guns of course were not necessarily used for war, or even personal defence. There was hunting, for instance, or shooting the birds that were eating up the farmer's crops. But from 1746 on Galton's had been accepting large-scale government contracts: whatever the position earlier, there could be little doubt henceforward that military armament was being produced within the portals of Galton's factory.

Strangely enough, it was not until 1792, when Friends were suddenly sensitised to the demands of their pacifism by the imminence of war with France, that objection was raised within the Society to these activities of the firm of Galton. The Samuel Galtons – there was now a father and son in charge of the family business – were highly respected both by their fellow citizens and by their fellow Quakers. They were pillars of their local Meeting, and they had long enjoyed all the authority that men of substance held in the Society of that day. But now some members of Birmingham Monthly Meeting objected to the acceptance of monetary contributions from what they considered a tainted source. 'It seems doubtful', however, writes Hirst, 'whether Friends in general were aware of the Galtons' work for the Government.' Events continued to move slowly. By 1795 the Galtons were being 'dealt with' officially by their Meeting 'for the practice of fabricating and selling instruments of war.'

The elder Galton eventually submitted and gave up his share in the business. But the younger Samuel continued to justify his position; in the course of his defence it transpired that he held strong reservations concerning the peace testimony in general. He was not, he stated, against 'defensive,' but only against 'offensive,' war; and 'the manufacture of arms,' he considered, 'implies no approbation of offensive war . . . for which I profess the most decided abhorrence.' He appealed to the tolerant spirit of the Society, to which he declared himself sincerely devoted. Perhaps the most telling moment in his argument came when he pointed out to his coreligionists : 'My grandfather – afterwards my uncle, then my father and uncle – and lastly my father and myself have been engaged in this manufactory for a period of 70 years, without having received any animadversion on the part of the Society.' But, as we know, times had changed : the era of quietism within the Society of Friends was drawing to a close, while the evangelical spirit was beginning to quicken it and bring about renewal from within. So in the end, but not till August 1796, Samuel Galton the younger received notice of disownment.[31]

We have perhaps strayed rather far from the subject of conscientious objection *sensu stricto*. Still, the two components of conscience and objection have remained central in all these matters, and the connecting link has remained war.[32] The final problem we shall touch on in this section is that of war taxes. (But I must refer the reader to a later chapter for an overview of the subject.)

Were there, we may ask, any tax objectors in Britain in our period ? Quakers, including George Fox, did not usually feel any scruples about paying taxes: in fact rendering Caesar his due was they believed a Christian's obligation. As the Yearly Meeting's epistle of 1693 put it: 'Because we are subjects of Christ's kingdom, which is not of this world, we cannot fight; yet, being subjects of Caesar's kingdom, we pay our taxes, tribute, etc. according to the example of Christ and his holy Apostles, relating to Christ's kingdom and Caesar's; wherein we are careful not to offend.'[33] This indeed had been the position of the Anabaptist-Mennonite nonresistants. With Quakers at this time, as with Mennonites, it was Caesar's responsibility what he did with any tribute he received in this way. Friends in Britain, then, paid all general taxes as a Christian duty as well as those 'in the mixture', i.e., where at least some part was devoted to non-military uses, and even such as were clearly destined to support war. But in the course of the 18th century, not it would seem before,[34] they developed scruples about paying a tax devoted clearly and specifically to a warlike purpose.

An assessment of this kind appeared in the new Militia Act of 1762, which remained in force for 24 years. The act allowed countries not actually raising a militia to impose a rate instead, which presumably went toward covering one or another military need. Friends declared, 'It is our sense and judgement, that we cannot consistent with our well known principles actively pay the rate . . . because such money is required expressly for, and in lieu of such militia.' I do not know whether in actual fact this part of the act was ever put into effect, or if any Quaker was required – and then refused – to pay the rate. Hirst remains silent on this point, merely noting that by a clause of the act the local justices of the peace were authorised to put a distraint on the property of any Quaker householders refusing to contribute.[35] In any case Friends at that time seem to have treated the question as forming part of the wider problem of militia service rather than regarding it as a tax *sensu stricto* and then trying to puzzle out whether or not this constituted a legitimate demand of Caesar's. In their eyes the matter was already settled: as with the acceptance of militia service, the peace testimony would have been set at nought if Friends had paid.

The same attitude comes out in Friends' response to the special war levies imposed at the end of the century during the war against France. In 1796 we find Yearly Meeting censuring 'the active compliance of some members with the rate [imposed in the previous year] for raising men for the Navy'; those who complied should be persuaded of the wrongfulness of their action.[36] And Friends' response to the cavalry rate of 1796 followed the same pattern: an official Quaker admonition to refuse payment, which was sometimes heeded by Friends but sometimes not. There was of course no new principle at work here. But the special war tax, which the government imposed in 1799 to help finance the war against France, caused more intense heartsearching than anything of the kind had done hitherto. While some Friends paid, though with an 'uneasy' conscience, plenty were to be found who refused and had their property distrained to make up the money they should have contributed to the government.[37] These were, I think, indeed true tax objectors, and I will have to allude to them again as well as to the Quaker income tax objector, Nathaniel Morgan of Ross-on-Wye, whose refusal stemmed from that tax's role in financing the long military struggle against Napoleonic France.

In short, the tax objector *sensu stricto* appears to be a rather late comer among English Quakers. But we find him there at any rate by the end of the 18th century. Throughout our period the pattern of conscientious objection had remained fairly stable, with its focus on the militia objector and perhaps the heaviest burden resting on, and the greatest temptation to backslide residing in, the Quaker communities which lived from the sea. By around mid-19th-century a compulsory militia had vanished and the armed merchantman, too, had disappeared for different reasons. Conscientious objection thereafter ceased to play a significant role in the peace testimony of English Friends until World War I brought the reimposition of military conscription in a more onerous form than ever before.

CHAPTER V

Quaker Conscientious Objectors in Colonial America

THE PATTERN FOR QUAKER CONSCIENTIOUS objection remained broadly the same in colonial North America as it was in the home country. Only the atmosphere in which the colonial pattern was set differed as greatly from the English pattern as the physical environment, encompassing the small and scattered groups of Quakers that had found lodgment from New England down as far as North Carolina, differed from that of their English coreligionists.[1]

In the colonies a state of endemic warfare existed all along the frontiers (except along those of Quaker Pennsylvania), and this cold war could on occasion spill over into warfare in earnest even when England herself remained at peace. In wartime the colonists might expect not only invasion by the armadas of enemy European powers but also the depredations of Indian 'savages' (as even Quakers called them). Indian raids, whether carried out in wartime or peacetime, brought a high toll of life on the frontiers as well as extensive material destruction in their wake. Moreover, as the 18th century advanced the western frontiers of colonial North America became the scene of a bitter and long drawn out power struggle between England, with her long string of maritime colonies, and France, which owned the colonies of New France (today's Quebec) and Louisiana: an imperialist battle for ascendancy in that vast area with control of the whole continent as the final goal.

A religious group, however respected otherwise (and Quakers, we may note, were hated rather than respected in places like Puritan Massachusetts), might not be very popular in the community if its members were unwilling to bear their share of the burden of military defence. The vital role the militia often played in colonial defence comes out in the words written by Governor Robert Dinwiddie of Virginia in 1752: 'We have,' he wrote, 'an open and extensive country, without fortifications, so that the protection of our lives and estates depends chiefly . . . on our militia; and it's the maxim of all wise nations, in time of peace, to prepare and provide against the exigencies of war.'[2] And according to an earlier provincial governor, John Seymour of neighbouring Maryland, writing during the War of Spanish Succession, Quakers just 'sit at home without the least concern of the public safety or welfare.'[3] We need not wonder, then, if Quaker conscientious objection failed sometimes to gain the same recognition from the colonial authorities as it had been accorded in England. What is perhaps a matter of – pleasant – surprise is the amount of good will displayed to Quaker objectors in the communities in which they lived: hostility of course occurred, especially in periods of crisis, but such incidents were usually short-lived.

'The theory of conscription that every able bodied citizen must keep himself armed to repel a common foe was,' writes a legal expert, 'part of the colonial heritage brought from England.' Before 1775 provincial governments had passed over 650 draft laws 'of one kind or another': out of this plethora of legislation one point alone remained constant – the obligation of able bodied males from around 18 to 50 to serve in the militia. (Quaker Pennsylvania was the single exception: its assembly did not pass a militia conscription act until 1775.) Penalties were laid down for refusal to muster with arms or for failure to do so without legitimate reason. Delinquency was normally punished by a fine. After mid-18th century four provinces – New York (1755), Massachusetts (1757), Virginia (1766), and North Carolina (1770) – included in their militia laws an exemption for Quakers; in the first three cases they were required either to pay a commutation fee or find a substitute to appear in the conscript's place.[4] As we know from our discussion of Quaker objectors in England, Friends were 'absolutists,' at least officially, and required members to reject any alternatives a government might offer to actually bearing arms and to stand out boldly for unconditional exemption. Therefore, both before and after 1750 Quakers called up for service in the provincial militia suffered distraint of property or imprisonment, if without property, on the English model.[5]

The militia legislation of one province needs special attention, and that is Rhode Island. Because of the important role Quakers came to play in its political life, Rhode Island's militia laws were marked, though not uniformly so, by greater consideration for Quaker scruples than those of any other province in North America (apart from Pennsylvania of course). The first occasion the province had come into contact with Quaker pacifists occurred during the summer of 1657 when a party of Quakers arrived there, much to the disgust of neighbouring Massachusetts which requested their expulsion as an element dangerous to the body politic. The Rhode Island government returned a polite refusal. They abhorred Quaker views, they said, but freedom of religious conscience prevailed under their rule, and moreover they possessed no law to hinder the settlement of such people as the Quakers. On 13 March 1658 the General Assembly went on to inform Massachusetts that, if the Quakers 'which are here, or who shall arise or come among us, do refuse to subject themselves to all duties aforesaid, as training, watching, and such other engagements, as other members of civil societies, for the preservation of the same in justice and peace,' it would have to consult the English government through its agent in London as to 'how to carry ourselves in any further respect towards these people, so that therewithal there may be no damage, or infringement of that chief principle in our charter concerning freedom of conscience.'[6] Rhode Island Quakers, however, had to wait a quarter of a century before legislation was passed granting them exemption from bearing arms in the militia.

The act when it came in August 1673 during the war with the Dutch was remarkable both for the generosity of its provisions for conscience and the liberal sentiments which underpinned its promulgation. It applied to anyone whose conscience forbade him to fight : it did not indeed specifically mention religion in this connection.[7] The Assembly grounded the exemption of the province's pacifists in the need felt to respect conscience of all kind, which since the beginning had lain at the basis of the province's political life. Objection to bearing arms and to killing formed, in its view, a legitimate expression of conscience so that, where sincerely held scruples against performing a certain action existed, compulsion should never be used to try to force compliance. In peacetime the conscientious objector would not be required either to pay commutation money or find a man in his place. Only in time of war, when enemy invasion appeared imminent, might the civil authorities require such objectors '(though exempt from arming and fighting) to conduct or convey out of danger of the enemy, weak and infirm and aged impotent persons, women and children, goods and cattle, by which the common weal may be the better maintained, and works of mercy manifested to distressed, weak persons.' Besides humanitarian service of this kind objectors could be required in time of war 'to watch to inform of danger (but without arms in martial manner and matters), and to perform any other civil service by order of the civil officers for the good of the colony, and inhabitants thereof.'[8]

After three years the exemption was withdrawn,[9] and many years were to elapse before in 1730 an exemption clause was reinstated in the militia act of that year. Meanwhile Quakers seem to have been granted exemption from militia service unofficially; at any rate, writes Worrall, 'despite the law, Friends do not seem to have suffered hardship for the remainder of the century.' In 1700, however, on pressure being exerted by the Society, which felt the unsatisfactory character of their position, the province expressly allowed its militia officers to excuse Quakers and others who objected to bearing arms from service. 'In effect,' comments Worrall, 'the law probably gave the force of legality to accepted practice.' The situation remained unchanged for the next three decades. Then in 1730, in answer to a petition from Friends, a conscience clause was inserted in the new militia law of that year.[10] But now exemption was limited to those whose objections were based on religious grounds (this, however, was in practice likely to encompass virtually everyone who at that time held pacifist views). In 1740 the legislature passed a new militia act, which included exemption for religious objectors provided they were willing, when required, to help remove women and children endangered by hostile attack from places of danger, assist with fighting fires caused by enemy action, and do 'any other duty consistent with their religious principles.'[11] All of this appears to be a re-enactment of the provisions of the act of 1673 that dealt with the duties of conscientious objectors in wartime.

We do not know if the alternative service contemplated in the acts of 1673 and 1740 was ever required of Quakers or other objectors. The first piece of legislation remained in force for only a very brief period, and there is no record, either, of alternative service being required of Rhode Island Quakers in the 35 years intervening between 1740 and 1775. It is possible it was, but my presumption is that the requirement remained a dead letter.[12]

We should note in passing that New York's militia act of 1755 also included a scheme for alternative service for Quaker militia objectors, to be put into operation in time of invasion. Then, according to Worrall, they might be required 'to serve as labourers, building field works.' In fact the scheme was never put into operation. Those sections of the act touching on objectors that were implemented, including the imposition of fines as well as the provision of a certificate of membership for the county clerk and a small registration fee, soon met with opposition from Monthly Meetings in the province, despite an initial period of vacillation. Worrall is surely right when he surmises that New York Friends 'would have probably objected to alternative service provisions that required Quakers to build field fortifications.'[13] But the most Friends in fact had to suffer under this act were some heavy distresses laid on the property of their militia objectors in lieu of the fines these men refused to pay.

I would like now to pass in review several cases of colonial conscientious objection. Some of them, I hope, may illustrate the peculiar circumstances of North American Quakerism, so different on many points from that of the Society in Britain: it would be wearisome for the reader, however, if I were to attempt to do more than give a few examples.

First, however, let me mention one point: if an attempt were made to enforce militia conscription with excessive harshness against the Quakers, this more than likely would have served only to discredit the authorities in the eyes of the community, whose sympathies would have now turned from the latter to the former. We see this in fact happening in the case of a militia act which Governor Cornbury of New Jersey had forced through that province's assembly in 1704. 'Beneath the strict provisions of the act lay the desire of Cornbury and his advisers to injure the [powerful] Quaker interest.' The heavy fines foreseen by the act in case of refusal of service in the militia and its failure to provide for the recovery of any 'overplus,' i.e., money gained by sale of property distressed in excess of the original amount of the fine, eventually proved self-defeating. (In most provinces, we may note, the overplus was automatically returned, though not always so ; in that case it was usually recoverable by law should the objector be willing to file suit, which of course he was not always ready to do.) As a result of the harsh nature of the act, 'so bitter was the feeling in West Jersey [where Quakers were thickly settled[14]] that the provisions of the law could not be carried out.' Local constables in Burlington County, for instance, being required to carry out distraint on the property of Quakers refusing to serve, would not do so, and juries refused to convict such constables when the attorney-general prosecuted them. Property seized from Quaker objectors in lieu of fines remained unsold : their neighbours were unwilling to buy such goods considering that to do so would appear as approval of arbitrary rule. 'The seizures amounted to £1,000 a year, about ten times the real value of the fines.' Due to the widespread unpopularity of Cornbury's act, the assembly in the end balked at renewing it.[15]

Subsequent militia legislation in New Jersey, while retaining the option of imposing a fine on those who refused to muster, left it up to 'the captains of the [militia] companies whether the Quakers should be fined at all.'[16] We shall see below that in New Jersey at least, even in days of crisis, the militia officials were reluctant to enforce the full penalty allowed by law on members of a religious body which enjoyed on the whole the respect of its neighbours and fellow citizens.

We have seen that, already by 1658, Quakers in Maryland were being punished for not bearing arms in the militia, if called upon to do so. At first, some brutal penalties were imposed, like whipping or chaining. But soon here, as in other provinces, a fairly routine procedure was established. From the Quaker side the employment of substitutes[17] or the payment of a fine were strictly forbidden, even if distraint of property or imprisonment remained the only alternatives : these last, suffered unvoluntarily, implied no recognition of the state's right to conscript men for a service the Society of Friends considered to be unchristian.

In contrast to this picture of neighbourly fellow feeling and sympathetic militia officers, the first example I have chosen to illustrate Quaker conscientious objection in colonial America is set in wartime Massachusetts in 1703-4 when Quakers were still highly unpopular among the province's citizenry. Local preachers pointed at the sect as the cause of God's punishing them all by setting the Indians against the white man, and they called for the expulsion of Quakers as the only way to win back the Almighty's favour and putting an end to the atrocities of Indian warfare. At that moment two Quakers from Bristol County, both in their early 20s, John Smith, who has left us an account of his experiences, and Thomas Maccomber, were arrested for refusing the summons to bear arms. Since neither of the young men possessed property to distrain on in lieu of their unpaid fine, they were both sentenced to hard labour in the fort at Boston. The sentence was of indefinite duration, release being contingent on their performing sufficient labour to cover the fine as well as the cost of their incarceration. In fact Maccomber and Smith refused the work that was assigned them in the fort alleging it was of a military character and therefore to do it was contrary to their Quaker principles. Nonetheless they do not appear to have suffered ill treatment as a result of their attitude. Smith indeed speaks of the courtesy shown him while a prisoner in the fort: they believed, he wrote, 'I acted from a religious principle.' By chance the two objectors possessed an eloquent spokesman to present their case to the authorities in the visiting English Quaker, Thomas Story. Story could give a more coherent account of Quaker pacifism than we could expect from two simple country boys (though Smith's narrative, written not long after the events described, shows he at least was by no means inarticulate). Despite Story's pleadings the men remained in the fort for four months more. Then the governor, who during an interview he gave Story had shown himself not unsympathetic, though fearful of the reaction of public opinion were he to release the objectors prematurely, at last gave Maccomber and Smith leave to return to their homes.[18]

My next example is also taken from the period of the War of Spanish Succession, only its setting is Virginia not New England and the year is 1711. The background in each case, however, is not entirely dissimilar. In 1711 Virginia, too, was in the throes of a local Indian war, which had broken out in the early autumn of that year. We find the provincial Governor, Alexander Spotswood, writing on 15 October to the Board of Trade in London as follows:

> On the 22d of last month . . . the Tuscaruro Indians . . . without any previous declaration of war, or show of discontent, and having divided themselves into parties, at sun rise (which was their signal) began a barbarous massacre, on the inhabitants of the frontier plantations, killing without distinction of age or sex about sixty English, and upwards of that number of Swiss and Palatines, besides a great many left

dangerously wounded: . . . since which they have continued their ravages, in burning those plantations, and others deserted by the inhabitants for fear of the like cruelty.[19]

What especially alarmed the Governor in this threatening situation, so he told the Board of Trade, was the province's state of military unpreparedness, 'the incapacity of this country for an offensive or defensive war.' The militia was short of arms as well as ammunition. And, he concluded, if the home government could not speedily remedy these deficiencies, 'I fear I shall not be able to sustain any considerable attack of an enemy,' whether these were forest 'savages' or a European great power.[20]

Spotswood had also informed the provincial Assembly of 'the naked condition of the country.' Though that body's response had been disappointing, the governor reported that it had at least agreed to enact certain emergency defensive measures, including compulsory work for all ablebodied males on building fortifications. This would act as a back up for the activities of the militia. Now, to Spotswood's fury 'a set of Quakers' (Colonel Spotswood seems anyhow to have been no lover of the Quakers), were refusing to comply with the labour order. As he reports to London:

They have not only refused to work themselves, or suffer any of their servants to be employed, in the fortifications, but affirm, that their consciences will not permit them to contribute in any manner of way to the defence of the country . . . I have thought it necessary to put the laws of this country in execution against that set of people, which empower me to employ all persons as I shall see fit for the defence of the country in times of danger, and impose fines and penalties on their disobedience; . . . it is absolutely necessary to discourage such dangerous opinions, as would render the safety of this government precarious, since every one that is lazy or cowardly would make use of the pretence of conscience to excuse himself from working or fighting when there is greatest need of his service and I fear the Quakers would find too many proselytes on such occasions.

Spotswood was particularly infuriated by what he regarded as unreasonable intransigence shown by the Friends of the province, who, in his opinion, were taking an unfair advantage of his difficult position to refuse all co-operation. They had now 'broached doctrines so monstrous as their brethren in England have never owned,' he told the Board of Trade.[21] I think he was probably wrong here;[22] though it is true that English Friends on occasion took an ambiguous stand on the subject of noncombatant duties when accepted in lieu of bearing arms. (So far as I know, no record exists of any comments made by English Friends in the matter.)

The reaction of individual Virginia Quakers to Spotswood's labour decree differed considerably. Some refused to perform such work and were duly fined, with distresses or imprisonment following if the fines were not paid. This was the position officially supported by the Society. Others, however, agreed to work on the fortifications or carry out similar noncombatant duties, or were ready to pay the fines imposed for not doing so. Such backsliders were dealt with in due course by their Meetings. The offer of noncombatant service of this kind was, we may note, exceptional in Quaker history of that period (though we have seen it figure as a possibility in wartime Rhode Island). It was of course not formulated specifically as an alternative to bearing arms in the militia; though implicitly it does seem to have provided such an alternative, its net in fact stretched wider to encompass all the ablebodied male Quakers of the province.[23]

My third example of conscientious objection among colonial Quakerdom is also taken from the South but from a time when Britain was nominally at peace. The scene is set in a small rural community in North Carolina.[24] We learn from the minutes of the Perquimans-Little River Quarterly Meeting for April 1737 that in one of its constituent Monthly Meetings (Little River) the ablebodied male members had suddenly and quite unexpectedly received notice of their incorporation into the militia. There one morning the Quakers had awakened to find 'a note fixed on the Meeting House by Captain David Bayly that he had orders . . . to warn his company [i.e. to be made up from local Quaker draftees!] to meet in the field . . . for training . . . that they might appear and answer to their names.' No time was left for consultation with the Yearly Meeting, whose leading members were situated many days journey from Little River. No one knew exactly what should be done. At first there were some who thought there would be no harm in appearing on the muster field and simply answering when the captain called out their names. But further thought brought the conclusion that this would 'in some measure infringe on our testimony against war.' That 'Friends ought not to appear' was the Meeting's final decision. 'Some Friends in behalf of this Meeting [were] to draw up in writing the reasons and present [them to] the officers and give them what satisfaction they can in the affair.'[25] These explanations appear to have satisfied the latter; at any rate we do not hear of any young Quakers at Little River having to suffer on this occasion on account of their peace convictions.

The episode, with its initial confusion on the part of Little River Friends as to what procedures they should adopt toward the militia captain's demands, illustrates both the physical isolation and the lack of grounding in basic Quaker principles sometimes displayed in those days by rural American Friends. I do not think the more carefully trained – and more delicately nurtured – English Friends of the country Meetings would have displayed such vacillations as to where Quaker duty lay; for one thing, appeal for advice to London could have been carried out more expeditiously than the parallel appeal contemplated, but then abandoned, by these backwoods Quakers of North Carolina. However, in the end Little River reached the same decision in the matter as most other Meetings on both sides of the Atlantic would have reached – which was the correct one of course from the Quaker point of view.

Fourthly, and lastly, I would like to look briefly at an incident involving Quaker conscientious objectors during the French and Indian War (the conflict that was known in Britain as the Seven Years War since it lasted formally from 1756 to 1763). We possess considerably more information about the treatment of conscientious objectors for this period than for the century that preceded that war. I would refer my reader to the relevant sections of Worrall's book on Quakers in the Northeast or of my own work on American pacifism for further accounts of the subject.[26] Here one illustration should suffice, and we take it from New Jersey, the home province of the Quaker 'saint' John Woolman. In the late summer of 1757 we find Woolman noting in his *Journal* that a number of young New Jersey Friends had been caught up in the extensive militia draft that had been imposed so as to raise troops to relieve Fort William Henry in the province of New York from enemy siege. Quakers were being drafted, among other places, from Burlington County, Woolman's own county. Some of the young men, so Woolman wrote, appeared to be unprepared to face the ordeal that lay ahead of them. But most of them were resolved to stand firm. As things turned out, the militia authorities, by no means for the first time, showed a remarkable understanding of Friends' position and did not press the matter beyond a statement of their legal claims to enforce service. Let Woolman's own words tell the story:

> Several young men of our Society were chosen [i.e., drafted by ballot]. On the day appointed to meet the Captain in our town, several of our young men, not less than four or five, came and acquainted him in substance as follows, that for conscience sake they could not fight nor hire any one to go in their stead, and that they should not go out of his way. They were all dismissed at that time, with orders to remain in readiness, and soon after came accounts from the general, that they were not likely to want them this time. It was a day of deep trial to the young men, yet the effect it appeared to have on their minds was such, that I thought I saw the kindness of providence in it.[27]

The cases of colonial Quaker conscientious objection that we have cited above, a mere handful of course from many hundreds more, have all concerned the militia draft. For those Quakers employed on the sea the press-gang does not seem to have been quite as much of a menace as we have seen it was back in England. The coastal areas of the colonies were fortunately free from this iniquitous institution; still, Quaker sailors – along with other sailors – were subject to seizure by ships of the Royal Navy, and it was subsequently no easy thing to gain their release. The practice was still alive during the Seven Years War: we know of local Meetings in New England at that time supplying their Quaker sailors with certificates of membership in the hope, not always realised, of freeing them from impressment if this were attempted or at least proving their *bona fides* as Quakers. The ports of New England, and in particular the Quaker-inhabited island of Nantucket, then a centre of the whaling trade, were the areas most concerned, for there were few Quaker sailors to be found south of New England.

The only account known to me of the experiences of a colonial Quaker pressed to serve in the Royal Navy comes from the pen of the same John Smith, from whom we have quoted in connection with his 'trials' as a militia objector. After release from the Boston fort he had joined the crew of a merchant vessel owned by a New England Quaker and bound for London. In April 1704, on approaching the shores of England, Smith was seized, along with another Quaker sailor named Thomas Anthony, and placed on board a man-of-war. It was wartime of course, and shortly afterward the ship was attacked by a French battleship. 'When they were going to engage,' writes Smith, 'they placed us to a gun, and commanded us to fight, but we told them we could not, for Christ and his apostles spoke to the contrary; but they not regarding what we said, hauled us about the deck to make us work, but we signified we could not on any such account.' The two men continued in their work refusal, fearing at the same time they would be trapped inadvertently into some activity that might be interpreted as giving sanction to fighting. Finally, just over a year since their impressment, and after their ship had more than once been involved in combat, the two Quaker conscripts were deposited on English soil eventually making their way back to their native Massachusetts.[28]

We know that the wealthy Quaker merchants of Philadelphia and Rhode Island, and the Quaker whaling captains on the island of Nantucket, were subject to more or less the same dilemmas and the same temptations as their brethren were in old England. The epistles of New England as well as Philadelphia Yearly Meetings periodically include the same kind of admonitions against arming vessels or taking out letters of marque for privateers or buying 'prize goods' if known to be such, as do those of the parent Society in England: sometimes even the language used by the colonial Yearly Meetings is copied word by word from the epistles issued from London earlier. On both sides of the Atlantic Quakers in equal measure condemned such activities on the part of any of their members as 'a flagrant and lamentable departure from our peaceable principle': offenders were dealt with and disowned if they did not express contrition for their conduct. Profit must not be permitted to override principle; at least that was the official position of all the American Yearly Meetings, even if practice may sometimes have fallen short of the ideal, especially when the delinquent was able to conceal his dubious activities from the watchful eyes of his coreligionists (as was undoubtedly the case, for instance, with some of the Quaker merchant grandees of Philadelphia).

Participation in war industry did not create a problem for North American Quakers at this date for, unlike in Britain, there were then few, if any, Quaker industrialists in the colonies. But the Quaker farming communities of the New World were subject to a special dilemma that English country Quakers did not usually have to face. It was a problem that normally arose only when areas settled by Quakers became, if not the scene of actual battle (though this sometimes happened), at least the terrain over which armies marched in battle array. A situation of this kind had rarely arisen in Britain (it did, though, in 1745)[29] but it was not uncommon in colonial America. Then the marching armies required from the civilian population, if the need arose, certain auxiliary services to assist their passage. Among the most usual services thus demanded was 'the furnishing of wagons, horses and provisions' for the army. Officially Friends regarded this as 'a military service,' which must be refused along with such obviously military activities as bearing arms in the militia – and the consequences of refusal were to be likewise suffered quietly as a religious duty. As Philadelphia Yearly Meeting declared in 1758: 'The care of elders, overseers, and faithful Friends should be extended, in true and Christian tenderness, to such as deviate herein, in order to convince them of their error.'[30] In fact 'deviations' of this kind were not uncommon.

Even less clear was the position with respect to selling merchandise to army or navy. This was certainly done by Friends who remained in good standing with the Society. William Frost cites the case of Whitney Lovell, a Rhode Island Quaker, who remarked when in 1745 a British man-of-war anchored off the coast of that colony: 'Whatever Philadelphia saints may think . . . we are well pleased with the arm of flesh especially if we had more fresh provisions to give them.'[31]

There were still other, mostly minor, problems indirectly connected with the peace testimony that arose from time to time to trouble colonial Quakers. For instance, should Monthly Meetings issue certificates of membership if the militia authorities required these from drafted Friends? In most cases, I think, no objection was made, at any rate if the other conditions accompanying the call-up permitted Friends' collaboration (which of course was by no means always the case). With respect to the watch, the situation was more complicated. English Friends, we know, contributed to the upkeep of the watch, even when it sometimes functioned with weapons, since protecting person and property was one of the functions of civil government, and civil government, Quakers believed, was part of God's plan for the world. But American Friends were frequently required to do more than merely give money for others to do the watching: they found themselves obliged to take their turn, too, in the watch. Worrall cites a case from Rhode Island in 1704 during the War of Spanish Succession. 'Newport,' he writes, 'apparently wanted Friends to take the watch under arms. The Monthly Meeting was firm: Friends could only watch without arms. Two years later the Monthly Meeting apparently successfully petitioned the General Assembly to permit Friends to watch without arms, for the issue does not appear again.' [32] I think the watching in question here was the usual town watch, or possibly an extension of it under wartime conditions to embrace watching for the enemy, too. Some of the Friends involved must have been required to watch as an alternative to serving in the militia (see above); others though – and possibly the greater part – would have been serving in fulfillment of a special civic obligation.

Lastly we should touch briefly on certain aspects of war taxation. This issue loomed up large on the Quaker horizon in 1756 when it was raised directly by John Woolman and several other likeminded reformers within the Pennsylvania-New Jersey Quaker community. I shall leave consideration of this episode as well as an overall view of the problem for later chapters. Here I wish only to remark that, throughout the colonial period, war tax concerns were never altogether absent from Quaker thinking. Colonial Friends, we have seen, followed their English brethren in paying not only ordinary taxes but also 'those in the mixture,' i.e., where some part went for the support of war. There were visitors from England like the weighty Thomas Story, who advised payment of virtually every kind of impost, except a militia fine: Story no doubt spoke here under the influence of his older contemporary, George Fox, whose viewpoint he was expressing. But not all colonial Friends were content with such all encompassing permissiveness. What, for instance, should be done in the case of a rate levied to pay for building fortifications or one whose main purpose was to gather funds to recruit and equip soldiers? During the sessions of New England Yearly Meeting in 1702, which were being held at Newport, the representatives from Rhode Island took the opportunity offered by the presence among them of an experienced English Friend, John Richardson, to ask him how he thought Friends in Britain would expect them to act if one or another of such rates were imposed on them by their government. In England, replied Richardson after considerable thought, 'Friends did not see an effectual door opened to avoid the thing, that tax being mixed with other taxes; although many Friends are not so easy as they could desire.'[33] He went on to point out, very wisely, that what applied in Great Britain might not, however, be the best solution in colonial circumstances: advice that was not always heeded on his side of the Atlantic.

During the French and Indian War Quakers in New England had to grapple with the problem of a poll tax specially levied in connection with the on-going conflict.[34] The new tax replaced direct service in the militia: from this aspect, therefore, it resembled the customary militia fine imposed on – and rejected by – Quaker objectors. Thus refusal of payment might still be regarded as being for a Quaker as much of an obligation as refusal to pay a militia fine had always been. Yet (if I understand its workings correctly) the tax was spread wider than militia fines were, for these concerned directly only the young men on whom the ballot for service had fallen. The new levy, on the other hand, formed part of the general provincial tax. Thus, from another aspect their levy seemed more closely to resemble a tax 'in the mixture,' for whose ready payment a long line of Quaker precedents existed.

Military efficiency seems in this case to have formed the underlying motive behind the substitution of the Quaker poll tax for the military conscription of Friends. An egalitarian impulse may also have been at work here, too, for some of the citizenry appear to have felt that they were forced to carry an unduly heavy military burden because Friends were getting off lightly, and some of them scot free. The poll tax was first introduced as an experiment on Nantucket, where 'the greatest part of the inhabitants [were] Quakers,' in March 1756. The Massachusetts legislators evidently intended also to extend it, in due course, to 'Quakers elsewhere.' The cost of equipping and maintaining a soldier was calculated to be £13/6/8 annually. The Quaker community was ultimately saddled in practice with the responsibility for paying into the provincial treasury the combined sum due from all the Quakers who had been drafted. 'No town,' Worrall writes, 'would have to furnish more troops than its proportion of non-Quakers, making up the difference with the £13/6/8 poll tax for each Friend drafted . . . By this means authorities managed to have their army and avoid jailing Quakers by the score. To be sure there were still problems – some residents resented Friends being excluded, and not everyone understood the act – but there was nothing on the order of what might have occurred had the act not passed.' Though the tax came out of Quakers pockets, they were not entrusted with its collection. Wisely so, for I am not sure if they would have been willing to undertake this task, at any rate for long. As it was, Nantucket Quakers, while they protested against the size of the impost (which was in the end reduced by over a third), never attempted to evade payment.

In December 1757 the Quaker poll tax was indeed extended to mainland Massachusetts. Here, 'though some Friends paid the tax, many others were uncomfortable.' While, at first, protest centred on what was considered the excessively high amount of the poll tax ('sums assessed Quakers exceeded the cost of hiring troops to replace them') rather than on the tax itself, soon the sensitive Quaker conscience made itself felt. But neither Quarterly Meetings nor even the New England Yearly Meeting itself could resolve the question or reach consensus as to how Friends should react. An appeal for advice was, therefore, despatched to London Yearly Meeting which replied in 1760 against payment. The poll tax it considered to be in effect a disguised version, slightly sugared over, of the old fine imposed in lieu of militia service. 'Such payment,' wrote London Friends (perhaps not altogether in harmony with some of their earlier judgements in similar matters), 'is inconsistent with the religious testimony we have to bear in the world . . . Suffer the penalty the law inflicts rather than violate [our] testimony.' As Worrall points out, London's decision really arrived too late to help New England Friends to resolve their dilemma. The war was drawing to an end, and with peace the crisis situation that had led to enactment of the poll tax vanished too. However London's negative judgement 'did serve to set a precedent for many in the War for Independence.' Of that more anon!

Meanwhile, we may note that Massachusetts's example became infectious. In May 1758 the Governor of New Hampshire began a campaign for the passing in his province, too, of 'an act similar to an act passed lately in the government of . . . Massachusetts . . . obliging the people called Quakers, to bear a proportionate part in the present expedition [against the French], either in men or money.' Such legislation was in fact enacted in the following March. A penalty of £10 was to be collected from any Quakers who refused to pay the poll tax. 'Friends protested the act; some even suffered distraint; but New Hampshire was determined to use the tax in support of the war effort if Friends refused to enlist.' While the Monthly Meetings in that province supported the poll-tax resisters as best they could, they could not prevent the authorities from collecting the tax to the full.[35]

In 1762 New England Yearly Meeting agreed to the following – rather convoluted – statement. It obviously incorporates the advice recently received from London concerning the kind of 'military assessments' we have been discussing above, and it also attempts to cover the older type of militia fine that had prevailed earlier. Friends, the document declares, if they were to act consistently with their Society's peace testimony, should refuse to:

actively pay any rate or assessment on any town or class of men which may be imposed, for not raising the quotas or number assigned them to raise for any military purpose; whether it be as fine for neglect, or an equivalent for such quotas or detachment; nor any rates or assessments made for the advancing of the hire or inlisting-money of volunteers, or which may be expressly therein ordered to be given or paid to military men.[36]

Peace came to the American colonies in 1763. The pattern of Quaker conscientious objection now returned into its accustomed channels. A new chapter in its history begins in 1775. This time Quakers in Pennsylvania, no longer Quaker Pennsylvania but a centre of revolutionary action, were ranged alongside their brethren in the other provinces – provinces that were shortly to become states – in an effort to maintain their peace testimony during the struggle between Britain and its erstwhile colonies.

CHAPTER VI

Quaker Conscientious Objectors
in the West Indies

THE QUAKER MESSAGE WAS FIRST brought to the British West Indies during the second half of the 1650s and soon Quaker Meetings were set up there as a result of the conversion of local settlers. Friends never became a numerous community anywhere in the Caribbean area, but Jamaica as well as Nevis and Antigua among the Leeward, and Barbados among the Windward, Islands each contained its Quaker community for a time as did the island of Bermuda lying out in the Atlantic Ocean many hundreds of miles north of the Caribbean Sea. And in the second half of the 1720s Friends appeared, too, on the tiny Virgin island of Tortola. During the 18th century, however, Quakerism began to decline in the West Indies; by the last quarter of that century it had disappeared altogether.[1]

From the beginning the existence of Quakerism in this area remained a precarious one. The islands were ringed by enemies from without, and their white inhabitants lived under the constant threat of Black slave revolts from within. Caribbean Quakers, therefore, led an existence far different from that of their coreligionists across the Atlantic or even of Quakers on the American mainland. France, Spain, and the Netherlands, with whom singly or in combination England was periodically at war throughout the whole period, also owned territory in the Caribbean area: the enemy was, so to speak, on the doorstep. In addition, there was the menace of pirates who roamed the seas, from time to time raiding settlements on land as well as preying on merchant vessels. Quakers during this period had not yet developed their testimony against slaveholding. Though they believed in treating their slaves humanely and giving them some religious instruction, the Quaker conscience was not yet sensitised to the point of liberating the slaves they held. Therefore, it is likely they, too, would have fallen victims if a slave revolt had broken out, along with their less humane compatriots. All in all, it is surprising on the one hand to find Caribbean Quakers adhering so loyally to their Society's peace testimony and, on the other, the island authorities, despite periodic outbreaks of harshness, showing a degree of tolerance of Quaker pacifist opinions that one might not have expected in this war-torn and tormented area. Caribbean Quakers, we may note, seem on the whole to have been well-to-do; many of them were planters, growing chiefly sugar, and some were merchants or shopkeepers who lived in the towns. A few belonged to the lower ranks of society as they still did in Britain or the American colonies. We hear of servants and craftsmen, for instance, being members of Quaker Meetings on the islands.

It is not easy to piece together a coherent account of Quaker pacifist practice in the Caribbean. For one thing, Caribbean Quakerism in general 'is a fragmented and transient phenomenon. The several islands have been rarely under a single political or ecclesiastical jurisdiction. They belong geographically neither to Europe nor to America.' Secondly, sources for the peace testimony, as indeed for any other activity of Caribbean Quakers, are scanty and scattered. Only for little Tortola, where Quakerism bloomed late and only for a very brief while, do we possess substantial Quaker records. Such records are no longer extant for the other – and more important – centres of Caribbean Quakerism, for minute books and similar Meeting documents have disappeared completely, victims of 'climate, disaster and neglect.' While the Quaker scholar, Henry Cadbury, succeeded in unearthing some materials still extant in local public archives, especially in respect of Jamaica, they throw little light on the question of peace. On the other hand, Margaret Hirst, when researching her history of the Quaker peace testimony, discovered relevant manuscript materials in the Public Record Office in London as well as in the collections of London Yearly Meeting. We shall be quoting from some of these documents but, however valuable, they cannot adequately replace the rich documentation we possess for so many important aspects of mainland Anglo-American Quakerism.

Despite these lacunae in the records, Caribbean Quakerism does provide us with a number of significant insights into the workings of the peace testimony in a troubled area. Moreover, as Cadbury has remarked, 'for a time these islands played a real part in what has been called the Transatlantic Quaker Community. Here travelling Friends stopped on their way to and from England en route to the mainland British colonies.'[2] The islands were geographically remote from the centres of Quaker life, they were situated indeed on the very edge of European civilisation. Yet the peace witness of their Quakers, while it bore the imprint of the islanders' peculiar circumstances, still shared the basic assumptions underlying the pacifism of transatlantic Quakerism.

Military service, the requirement to bear arms, formed only one of the causes of those Quaker 'sufferings,' which have been recorded so scrupulously by Joseph Besse with regard to Friends in the West Indies as well as those living elsewhere.[3] For in the West Indies Quakers also clashed repeatedly with the authorities, as they had done in the mother country, with respect both to paying tithes for the upkeep of the established church and to taking an oath for whatever purpose the authorities might require it.[4] Resistance on all these issues combined to make Quakers generally unpopular; at best, they were considered to be difficult characters. They deserved some respect perhaps, but it would be necessary either to punish or placate them as circumstances dictated. In particular, it was their refusal to keep firearms, or muster with the militia, or take part in defensive measures when invasion threatened, that strained their relations with the island authorities as well as with the community among whom they dwelt. As Besse noted of Barbados, 'the laws of the country [required] the personal service of the inhabitants, their servants, and horses, and [inflicted] severe penalties in case of default.'[5] Indeed severity - though not always as extreme as might have been expected – marked the treatment of conscientious objectors in all the islands in contrast to what we have seen their brethren experienced in Britain or the mainland colonies.

The Caribbean authorities genuinely feared the effect Quaker pacifism would have, if it spread, on the state of defensiveness in the islands. Quakers were seen as 'daily seducing others of the King's subjects from their allegiance, by persuading them not to bear arms for the defence of the rights of His Majesty and subjects, contrary to all laws.'[6] Friends tried to explain the religious basis of their objection to bearing arms and stressed they were in other ways loyal and law abiding subjects who paid their taxes without murmuring. In 1661, for instance, Barbados Quakers told the Governor, Council, and Assembly of that island that 'the sufferings that have been inflicted upon us . . . for not bearing of, or sending in to arms, and for not sending help to build and repair forts' stemmed from their desire to witness to the truth. They strove to fulfill the Biblical prophecy, '*Not to learn war any more* and . . . Christ's own words where he saith, *My kingdom is not of this world, therefore my servants do not fight:* And it is likewise according to Christ's precept, *to love enemies.*'[7] But such explanations did not usually remove the fears of the authorities or their annoyance at what they understandably considered the Quakers' intransigence. Moreover, the fact that Quakers on the whole formed a prosperous group, and therefore one whose monetary contribution to defence could make a significant contribution to an island's military budget, made the authorities all the more anxious to get Friends to give at least something for defence. As the Governor of Barbados explained to James II, such was the wealth of the Quaker community there that 'they ought to make one regiment on the island,';[8] i.e., Quaker financial assistance would make it possible to raise and equip a whole regiment of soldiers. The Governor may have exaggerated his Quakers' prosperity, but at any rate the remark illustrates the frustration and anger felt by many of the island rulers at their failure to force the sect to contribute to military needs in proportion to its wealth.

We can watch the growing impatience of administrators and legislators in the series of decrees enacted in Jamaica between 1662 and 1670: the record, here, writes Margaret Hirst, shows 'a gradual tightening of the laws against Friends' with respect to military service. In 1662 they were exempted from personally bearing arms 'provided they shall contribute for the same.' Obviously local Quakers did not comply with this demand, for in 1664 Governor and Council laid down that any Quaker 'not appearing in the field at the several muster days should receive due punishment.' Four years later, in 1668, the island government, expressing its fears of what would happen if the Quaker's recalcitrance in fulfilling their military obligations became widespread, ordered that objectors should be kept in jail 'until they pay the due fine.'

By 1670, however, as Hirst comments, 'Governor and Council had to own themselves beaten.' Trouble had arisen from the refusal of 'Quakers living at Port Royal' to take part in the military guard set to watch for an enemy attack by sea: all ablebodied white males of the town had been required to attend nightly. The Quakers, then, seemed 'to the Council very obstinate in that matter,' and their explanations 'weak and frivolous' and their attitude 'dangerous and destructive to all government: yet, out of pity and compassion to those poor misled people in that particular,' they were to be freed henceforward from bearing arms, provided each objector were ready to pay the officer in command of the town guard sufficient money to hire three men to serve in their place.[9] This of course was not a compromise acceptable to Friends, and Besse continues to list the militia 'sufferings' of Jamaica Friends until near the end of the century when he closes his account.[10] However, in Jamaica as on the other Quaker-inhabited islands, penalties for failure to perform military service grew less severe from the late 1680s on: the disappearance of Quakerism from the area altogether in the next century finally put an end to the problem.

The military obligations of Caribbean Quakers strike us as being more varied and onerous than those laid on Friends in Britain or, except during times of crisis, on American Quakers on the mainland. In the Caribbean not only were ablebodied male Quakers expected to muster with the militia, both regularly[11] and in times of alarm, or to serve in a military guard, but they might be conscripted, too, to help construct or maintain fortifications and bulwarks and to dig trenches for defensive purposes. They would sometimes be required as well to carry arms while travelling so as to be in constant readiness for enemy attack.[12] In addition to such personal obligations, which of course were also incumbent on non-Quakers, owners of land of either sex were required, as happened in Britain too, to provide men for the militia in proportion to the size of their freehold: one foot soldier for every 20 acres, and a cavalryman to be sent if the holding amounted to 100 acres was, for instance, the rule in Barbados.[13] Furthermore, masters and fathers were sometimes held responsible if, respectively, their servants or their sons did not appear for drill, these young men being presumably Quakers also.[14]

Fines, calculated for official purposes in pounds of sugar,[15] inevitably ensued on refusal to perform military duty of whatever kind. Then followed distress of the offender's goods. (This of course we know was standard practice in dealing with any who failed to bear arms on conscientious or other grounds.) Hogs, horses, cattle, articles of clothing, household goods, pots and pans, bags of sugar – and even Black slaves of either sex – were taken by the marshals in lieu of fines and then sold by public auction. We even hear of a Jamaica Quaker, one Thomas Norris, from whom 'a gun which cost 3d' was seized on account of his 'not appearing in arms.'[16] Norris presumably kept the weapon for such non-lethal purposes as hunting game. Friends from time to time complained bitterly of 'rapacious and greedy' marshals, who refused to return the 'overplus' after seizing and selling goods of much greater value than the original fines. Of John Thurborne, 'marshal to Colonel Tidcombe,' for instance, Barbados Friends reported, 'He would scoffingly call the Quakers his milch-cows, often saying, George Gray [17] (one of these people) was one of his best cows, and gave a brave mess of milk every exercising day.'[18]

Caribbean Quaker objectors seem to have suffered imprisonment more frequently than their British or American brethren, and this was not a penalty imposed only on the propertyless. Caribbean Quakers also found themselves in jail for considerably longer periods than Quakers did elsewhere (though the length of the sentence varied according to time and place). In 1668 John Gittings of Barbados, for instance, 'by order of a court of war . . . was committed to prison for a year and one day for not appearing at an alarm': the moment was obviously one of tension and expectation of imminent invasion.[19] Conditions in prison often resembled those back in England so graphically described by George Fox in his *Journal*: of course prison conditions throughout Europe remained extremely harsh until recent times. In Antigua we hear of a Quaker tobacco grower being imprisoned in 1685 for five weeks and five days: in jail he 'underwent great hardships, for he was grievously bitten by vermin, and through much wet and cold was so benumbed, that he was almost like a dead man.'[20] Again, Humphry Highwood from Nevis, while imprisoned in the fort, was 'kept there double ironed' until released by the governor's order.[21]

Cruel punishments were also inflicted on objectors in order to force them to bear arms. In 1687 Peter Dashwood of Jamaica, for instance, suffered serious leg injuries as a result of being 'sentenced to ride the wooden-horse,' a particularly painful form of punishment. Eleven years earlier in Antigua one of the marshals, Major Mallet, made a bad name for himself through his harsh treatment of Quaker militia objectors. 'With a wythe which he had in his hand he gave them many sore and grievous stripes over their faces, backs, and heads, to the shedding of their blood, and bruising the flesh upon their bones.' On another occasion we are told he gave John Haydon 'near fifty stripes with a horsewhip and a blue wythe.' Such treatment, however, met with disapproval from the major's lieutenant who told him, 'They are men who pretend to tenderness of conscience, and I cannot judge of a man's conscience, therefore am not willing to meddle with them.' Even the governor, when he learnt of the major's excesses (so Besse reports), 'seemed to be troubled, that such cruelties should be exercised,' and he therefore 'reproved Mallet for what he had done.'[22]

One specially severe penalty was reserved for members of the servant class who, for whatever reason, refused to attend musters.[23] This consisted in being tied up 'neck and heels' and then left in that condition for at least one hour. The punishment appears to have been a rather painful one (though perhaps no more so than many others then inflicted in the armies and navies of Europe). Richard Pancoman, a Quaker from Nevis, for instance, was in 1677 'for not appearing in arms at an alarm . . . tied neck and heels so close together, that he was almost suffocated. In like manner, and for the same cause, Noah Lewis and several others were tortured, till some of them spat blood, and had their health impaired.'[24] We are told of one of the leading 'persecutors' of Barbados Quakers, Major-General '(so called)' Sir Timothy Thornhill, that, when a Quaker was brought before him 'for not appearing in arms' and pleaded conscience in extenuation of his refusal, he shouted at him angrily, *'God damn your conscience; if I cannot make your conscience bow, I'll make your stubborn dog's back bend*; and so tied him neck and heels with his own hands, with that violence and rage, that almost deprived him of life.'[25] One case is known from Barbados of death resulting from such punishment. This happened with a young Quaker, Richard Andrews, a shopkeeper's servant, after he had been repeatedly 'tied neck and heels . . . so strait, that he could hardly speak.'[26]

In 1660, the year of Quakerism's first establishment in Bermuda, we find the Governor's Council there at its meeting on 6 September dealing with a complaint lodged by the militia captain William Nelmes against Francis Estlake, one of the island's original Quaker converts, for 'refusing to bear arms' when called upon to exercise with the militia. For the present the Council merely 'admonished' Estlake 'to reform upon like occasion hereafter.' But if he continued in his refusal, 'he as likewise any other of the same judgement are to lie bound neck and heels together during such exercise under Captain Nelmes or any other captain of a trained band in these islands. And in case of an invasion of an enemy to be forced to fight in the front thereof.' We discover from Besse that during the following years Estlake and other Quakers persisted in resisting militia service and were punished in the manner the Council had laid down. For 1665 Besse, for instance, records that Captain Dorrell of the island militia, accompanied by eight musketeers, broke into a Quaker Meeting worshipping on a weekday in the house of one of the members 'and rudely took several of the men assembled out of the Meeting and carried away two of them . . . into the field.' One of these was Francis Estlake. Besse continues:

> They charged the said Francis with neglect of duty in not appearing among them in arms, and under that pretence tied him neck and heels together, which punishment the said Captain Dorrell threatened to inflict on him and others of his persuasion as often as they should neglect what he called their duty, for the future. But his wrathful purpose was restrained by the power of God, and he was not permitted to proceed with such extreme cruelty and rigour.[27]

Over the succeeding years, somehow or other, Quakers and island authorities seem to have achieved a rough *modus vivendi*. In 1660 a law was introduced fining 'each person one shilling for each time of his absence from the mustering, or any other military service required.' In 1673 Quakers were exempted from bearing arms if they found a substitute to take their place in the ranks.[28] Of course either alternative was equally unacceptable to Quakers. We presume, therefore, distraints now became the order of the day, with sporadic harsh physical punishments as well as the occasional imprisonment of a propertyless objector. But Besse remains silent. By 1703 there appear to have been only a handful of Quakers remaining on the island.

Friends' readiness to collaborate in defensive measures that did not entail the actual use of lethal weapons probably helped to ameliorate the harshness with which the islands' authorities tended to treat their conscientious objectors in the early period. Some measure of understanding was eventually reached between those who adhered to nonviolence and those who sought to protect the community against its enemies by arms. For instance, in a representation they addressed in 1674 to their Governor Sir Jonathan Atkins, together with his Council and the Assembly, Barbados Quakers stressed that they were not acting out of mere stubbornness and perversity in disobeying the summons of the magistrates to perform military service, but from their desire to keep Jesus' commandments:

We have shown our readiness and diligence in watching, and warding, and patrolling in our own persons and horses, which was for some time accepted, since the late wicked contrivance of the Negroes, which the Lord by his witness in the heart made known for the preservation of the island and inhabitants, and if thou and we be faithful to his holy requiring, he will assuredly yet bring every hidden work of darkness to light, . . . for *Except the Lord keep the city, the watchmen watch in vain . . .*

Four years later we find Barbados Quakers once again addressing the same authorities in an effort to achieve an alleviation of the militia law as this affected Friends. They pointed out that they had always shown willingness to appear for 'any duty as far forth as they can for conscience-sake, either in watching or patrolling,' though 'we brought not swords, pistols or muskets, which we dare not . . .' Moreover, they state, ever since their Society had come into existence, they had 'always [been] willing to pay the King his customs, taxes, and publick levies of money or goods.'[29]

Yet at this very time, when the Quakers of Barbados were emphasising their readiness to go the second mile if the state required it from them and if they felt they could comply in good conscience, Friends on another Caribbean island, Nevis, were raising serious objections to compliance of this kind, which some of them at least felt would only lead to a compromise of their Society's peace testimony. The archives of Nevis Quakers are no longer extant. We know of the misgivings they entertained concerning compromises, such as we have seen were clearly approved by their coreligionists in Barbados, only from an epistle sent by George Fox in November 1675 'to Friends at Nevis and the Caribbean Islands concerning watching.' In their dilemma Nevis Friends had written to Swarthmore Hall to ask Fox's advice: in their letter they evidently tried to explain to him the nature of their scruples 'concerning watching or sending forth watchmen' without arms ('and possibly also not under military command,' adds Hirst). Fox's reply is the only evidence that has come down to us about the incident: unfortunately, as Hirst aptly remarks, 'the letter is confused with many repetitions.' But it does give us an idea of the direction in which the thought of Nevis Friends was turning.

As to Fox, his reaction to their scruples was on the whole negative. 'It is a great mercy of the Lord,' he told them, 'to subject the Governor's mind so much by his power and truth that he will permit you to watch in your own way, without carrying arms, which is a very civil thing, and to be taken notice of.' Friends in Barbados or Jamaica, he pointed out, would have been only too pleased if their governors had permitted them to serve in this way: Fox also reminded Nevis Quakers that in Rhode Island, where Quakers controlled the government, a similar dispensation prevailed in times of danger from without. He asked them, did not Friends in their area keep watch against robbers on their estates, and in the towns were they not ready to call on the watch in case of housebreakers or arsonists and to bring offenders before the magistrate for punishment? 'You are not to be the revenger, but he is the revenger.' 'If any should come to burn your house or rob you, or come to ravish your wives and daughters, or a company should come to fire a city or town, or come to kill people; don't you watch against all such actions? And won't you watch against such evil things in the power of God in your own way?' Moreover, Quaker sea captains 'have their watches all night long, and they watch to preserve the ship, and to prevent any enemy or hurts that might come to the ship by passengers or otherwise.'[30] Therefore, in Fox's opinion the fears of Nevis Friends that watching without arms would undermine the peace testimony were groundless. Instead, he chided them for lack of charity in criticising a practice that was both reasonable and accepted by Friends generally.

Fox's letter lacks a clear comprehension of the situation out of which Nevis Friends had written. He had failed to envisage the atmosphere of constant and warlike alarms that surrounded Caribbean Friends and made such activities as watching – even without arms – so nearly military as to cast a serious doubt in the more sensitive Quakers' consciences whether Friends could carry them out and remain consistent pacifists. True, there were sincere Friends in their midst who took an opposite view, believing unarmed watching and suchlike represented a reasonable compromise that preserved their spiritual integrity while demonstrating their loyalty to the power that be. But Hirst is right when she says, 'It was not the actual advice given by Fox [i.e., to accept unarmed watching], but his commentary upon it, which seemed to open the way to an almost unlimited share by Friends in services auxiliary to war.'

It is not clear indeed whether Friends in Nevis were prepared to follow George Fox's advice in this instance. Shortly afterwards Governor Stapleton (of Montserrat) in a report home wrote of Nevis Quakers:

> They will neither watch nor ward, not so much as against the Carib Indians, whose secret, treacherous, and most barbarous inroads, committing murders, rapes, and all other enormities, discourages the planters in the Leeward Islands more than any one thing, knowing how they have been made use of in the last war by our neighbours.[31]

But we do not know whether this situation arose from continued Quaker reluctance to participate in watching under any circumstances, or whether the authorities had finally decided to reject any compromise and to require Quakers instead to come armed to the watch, for the relevant documentation has disappeared.

Thirty-three years later, in 1708, long after Fox had died, London Friends received from Caribbean Quakers another request for advice on a military question. This time the dilemma had arisen among the now steadily dwindling community of Friends on the island of Antigua. There controversy had broken out among members on the question of alternative service. For the previous three years Antigua had been living under threat of a French invasion, and the island authorities, in order to maximise the defensive potential of its inhabitants, had offered Friends an alternative to bearing arms: they would now be required only to perform certain auxiliary duties of a noncombatant nature in lieu of the military service that was compulsory for the non-Quaker population.

Two groups formed among the Quakers, one consisting of older Friends who supported the acceptance of the government's offer of alternative service and the other of younger members who considered this to be contrary to their Society's peace principles. Each side then wrote to London putting forward its viewpoint: the letter in favour of compromise was signed by the Clerk, Jonas Langford, while that from the young dissidents had six signatures appended to it.[32] The former obviously remembered the persecution Quakers had endured in the past from refusal of military demands and were grateful to the authorities for allowing them now a noncombatant alternative. They also recalled George Fox's advice to Nevis Friends in 1675, considering it as giving approval to their present stand. It seems indeed that Antigua Friends had shared in their Nevis brethren's dilemma at that earlier date, too, for Langford refers to hesitations they had entertained concerning 'planting potatoes for them that watched and builded the forts.' The advice of 'dear George Fox and the Meetings in London,' Langford pointed out, 'was they were innocent things and might be safely done.' Langford's younger opponents, on the other hand, obviously chafed at the use of tradition and authority, albeit Quakerly, to suppress what they believed were the promptings of conscience, and they spoke out against acceptance. Such service, they believed, would in effect be 'all one' with compliance in bearing arms. Even if Friends in the past – or Friends elsewhere – had been ready in good conscience to do these things, that did not seem to them a good reason to continue if their own consciences told them such action was wrong.

In Langford's letter we find a somewhat different account of what was actually being required from the account the younger Antigua Friends gave – or rather, the interpretation of the facts differed in the two letters. According to Langford, what the government was now asking from them was to participate in 'the public service of the island, that is to say, building of watch-houses, clearing common roads, making bridges, digging ponds.' 'Also they [i.e., the military authorities] are willing to accept of us without arms only appearing at their training place, and also that we should [carry] messages from place to place in the case of danger by an enemy.' Once Friends complied with such demands, which Langford obviously considered reasonable in the perilous position the island was then placed in, 'we have been excused from bearing arms.' And that, in his view, should suffice for the Quaker conscience.

Seen from the other side, that of the young dissidents, the picture however appeared in a quite different light. Their version is, I think, worth quoting in full. They wrote:

> Whereas it is often ordered by the Government that fortifications are to be built, for the accomplishment whereof ponds for holding water (for the use of these persons who defend these places and inhabit them) are also to be dug, now the same Friends [i.e., Langford's party] do think that if the Government will excuse them from carrying of great guns to these places, and digging of trenches, building of bulwarks, and such warlike things, and instead employ them in digging these ponds, building of bridges, repairing of highways, building of guard-houses, and such things, they can freely do them, yet we do think that in such a case to dig ponds or the like to be excused from carrying of guns, etc. is not bearing a faithful testimony against such things, but below the nobility of that holy principle whereof we make profession, and (at best) doing a lawful thing upon an unlawful account and bottom.Yet we are very willing to dig ponds, repair highways, and build bridges, or such convenient things when they are done for the general service of the island and other people at work therein equal with us, and not to balance those things which for conscience' sake we cannot do.

Appearing unarmed at militia exercises, was, they believed even less consistent with their peace testimony than compliance with the duties they had just listed in their letter. Certainly Friends might give the magistrate warning of approaching invasion or the sighting of an enemy vessel 'or be serviceable as far as we can at such times' in passing on information concerning an impending naval attack. But where it was a question of 'kill, sink, burn, and destroy the enemy, we are scrupulous and not free in that case.' 'As concerning watching,' their letter concluded on a conciliatory note, 'we are free to do it in our own way,' i.e., without having to carry arms as their fellow citizens were required to do.

It took two years before a reply to the two epistles was received from London. This came in 1709 under the signatures of leading members of the Meeting for Sufferings, including Fox's son-in-law, Thomas Lower, and one of his successors in the leadership, George Whitehead. Hirst calls their letter a 'temporising document . . . instinct with that spirit of timidity and caution, combined with a genuine loyalty to the tolerant English government, which marked Quaker leadership in the first half of the eighteenth century.' Like Fox earlier, London Friends again came out decisively in favour of accommodation with the authorities. They saw nothing unworthy in 'digging ditches and trenches and making walls.' Were not these activities exactly similar in purpose to putting doors with locks and bolts on houses or fences round property to keep out thieves or predatory animals, which Friends had never had anything against? What was wrong, either, in raising an alarm and alerting neighbours 'by messenger or otherwise to prevent their being destroyed, robbed, or burnt?' Would not Friends wish others to do this for themselves? The Meeting for Sufferings cited Fox's advice to Nevis Friends in 1675 to buttress the case for conforming while it virtually ignored the arguments used by the young Antigua dissidents. Obviously, what London Friends feared was that, if Friends in Antigua were to reject the proffered compromise, the magistrates there would regard Quakers as 'a self-willed and stubborn people' and renew their harassment. Therefore, they concluded, Antigua Friends should demonstrate to the utmost their willingness to obey government in every matter 'that is not an evil in its own nature, but service and benefit to our neighbours.'

Unfortunately the story breaks off at this point. The same provoking silence ensues as had occurred in the case of Nevis earlier. No evidence has survived to tell us how the group of younger Friends reacted to the adverse judgement handed down by London. We do not know if they now complied with the authorities' conditions for exemption or pursued a policy of resistance, despite London Friends' opinion. Two of the group, William Hague and Henry Hodge, emigrated a few years later with their families to the North American mainland, though it is by no means clear whether this was for purely economic reasons or because of continued disagreement with the military compromise, which a majority of Antigua Friends had presumably accepted on London's recommendation. Quakerism on Antigua seems to have come to an end altogether around 1730.[33]

Quakerism on the other islands, too, was on the point of extinction. As mentioned earlier, a few Friends persisted on Tortola until the last quarter of the 18th century. Around mid-century we find Tortola Friends awaiting trouble from the authorities because of a recent decree requiring islanders to keep firearms in their homes ready for use in case of an invasion and to contribute money to build forts and watchtowers.[34] But the surviving records give us no information as to whether some compromise was worked out between government and Quakers or whether in Tortola, too, Quakers had to suffer the kind of penalties imposed in an earlier period on the Society's militia objectors in the Caribbean area.

For a brief while Tortola even had a Quaker lieutenant-governor, John Pickering, originally a lapsed Friend who eventually returned to his father's faith.[35] Pickering only came slowly to accept Quaker pacifism. When he finally did so, supported by the persuasions of a leading English itinerant minister, Thomas Chalkley, who had visited Tortola in 1741, his superior, the Governor-General of the Leeward Islands, soon relieved him of his office, probably at his own prompting. In the Caribbean environment Pickering, unlike his contemporary coreligionists in Pennsylvania or Rhode Island, seems to have found it impossible to be both Quaker and magistrate. So long as he 'had not yet got over or seen beyond that of self preservation or defending my country or interest in a just cause' (as he told a London Quaker correspondent),[36] he had felt at liberty, while not hiding his sympathies for Quakerism, to remain in office – even if that entailed the use of the magistrate's sword against foreign invaders as much as against internal disturbers of the peace. Yet once Pickering came to accept the full implications of Quaker pacifism, then the Caribbean fact brought home to this simple and semi-literate planter the impossibility of combining the two roles. Such a realisation, however, came to Pennsylvania Quakers only in 1756 – some historians would even say not really until after 1775.

CHAPTER VII

Early Quaker Plans for World Peace

THE PEACE WITNESS OF THE Quaker conscientious objector necessarily bore a negative character, for the emphasis there was on the refusal of action considered to be contrary to Christian teaching. This negative emphasis long continued to be the hallmark of the Quaker peace testimony as it had been, to an even greater extent perhaps, of Anabaptist-Mennonite nonresistance. But Friends were the first to reach out and explore the positive implications of their pacifism, and to try and discover some way of uniting the efforts of the absolute pacifists and of the internationalists who, without renouncing the use of violence in every instance, still strove to achieve a warless world. Within 60 years of the emergence of Quakerism we find two Friends of note outlining their plans of achieving world peace. (Of course the world, as they saw it, was confined to the states of Europe and their overseas colonies, with Russia and Turkey dimly observed on the peripheries of civilisation.) William Penn published his *Essay towards the Present and Future Peace of Europe, by the Establishment of an European Dyet, Parliament, or Estates* in 1693,[1] while John Bellers brought out his plan, which he entitled *Some Reasons for a European State, proposed to the Powers of Europe*, in 1710.[2] In this section I propose to deal briefly with these two works and with their significance in the development of Quaker pacifism.[3]

Penn's *Essay*, along with his better known devotional work *Some Fruits of Solitude*, originated in a period of forced retirement for the Quaker leader, whose friendship with the Catholic Stuart King James II had brought him during the early years of William and Mary under suspicion of harbouring subversive designs. From early in 1691 until the beginning of 1694 he had lived under the shadow of political disfavour: in October 1692, for instance, he was even deprived of his governorship of Pennsylvania, which was not restored to him until 1694. Penn, however, used this time to good purpose; it 'afforded him,' writes Peter van den Dungen, 'an opportunity for withdrawal, meditation and introspection.' He remained nevertheless a close observer of the international scene and, as he watched

75

the naval and land warfare between England and Louis XIV's France with its mounting material destruction and loss of life, he felt more keenly than he had ever done before the need to provide some machinery to stop the seemingly endless succession of wars that had for centuries devastated Europe.[4] Penn, we know, shared the pacifism of his fellow Quakers to the full. 'I cannot fight against any man,' he had declared publicly, adding 'it is both my practice and all my friends' [i.e., Quakers'] to instil principles of peace and moderation.' But he knew that Quaker peace principles had won so far the allegiance of only a minute fraction of mankind. If, within the foreseeable future, a stop were to be put to war in Europe (not to speak of the wider world), the application of something short of complete pacifism was called for. 'Our present condition in Europe,' he wrote in 1692, 'needs an olive branch, the doctrine of peace, as much as ever.'[5] But the olive branch, to be effective, needed to be dressed out in a way to make it acceptable to those unwilling to swallow the whole doctrine of peace as the Quakers officially presented it. Penn, as we shall see in our discussion of Quaker Pennsylvania, showed himself not unready to adapt his pacifism to the exigencies of the existing situation, provided he at the same time believed (correctly or incorrectly) that its inner core could remain untarnished. His *Essay* is just another example of this attitude on Penn's part.[6]

His peace plan in fact blends realism with idealism, common sense with naivety and, as a German scholar puts it, 'a childlike quality (*eine Kindlichkeit*)' that reflects the man's essential simplicity of character.[7] The plan displays on one hand an appreciation of actual conditions of international politics, we might almost say of *Realpolitik*, while on the other the author's humanitarianism and his abhorrence of the irrationalism of war[8] emerge clearly, alongside the Christian foundations of his case against war.

At the outset Penn stated succinctly the source from which he had derived his impulse to write the tract: it was 'the groaning state of Europe,' 'the bloody tragedies of this war, in Hungary, Germany, Flanders, Ireland and at sea,' that had led him to devise his 'pacific . . . proposal,' a scheme to end wars – at least so far as Europe was concerned. 'For till the millinary doctrine be accomplished, there is nothing appears to me, so beneficial an expedient to the peace and happiness, of this quarter of the world.'[9] Moreover, he saw a precedent for the kind of scheme he was proposing in the recent establishment of the United Province of the Netherlands with a States General to act as a central organ for the separate units making up the whole. This, he thought, provided 'an instance and answer, upon practice, to all the objections that can be advanced against the practicability of my proposal.'[10]

Penn presents the advantages of peace and the disadvantages of war in purely material terms. He is not arguing the case for Christian pacifism here; he knows what needs to be said if his plan is to have any chance of adoption by the hard headed rulers of late 17th century Europe. Therefore, he tells them that

> Peace preserves our possessions: we are in no danger of invasions; our trade is free and safe, and we rise and lie down without anxiety. The rich bring out their hoards, and employ the poor manufactors: buildings and divers projections, for profit and pleasure go on: It excites industry, which brings wealth, as that gives the means of charity and hospitality, not the lowest ornaments of a kingdom or common-wealth. But war . . . stops the civil channels of society. The rich draw in their stock, the poor turn soldiers, or thieves, or starve: No industry, no building, no manufacturing; little hospitality or charity; but what the peace gave, the war devours.[11]

The chief means of establishing peace is to establish justice. And, Penn goes on to argue, 'justice is a fruit of government as government of laws from society and society from consent.'[12] Chaos and confusion, strife and war, result from a society without government. The Fall had led to the corruption of human nature, and now, 'so depraved is human nature, that without compulsion, some way or other, too many would not readily be brought to do what they know is right and fit, or avoid what they are satisfied they should not do.'[13] Even if aggressor states, 'those Leviathans' ambitious to extend their territories at the expense of their neighbours, had, in Penn's view, appeared comparatively rarely in history, still, uncertainty concerning what constituted a legitimate title to territory frequently led to war between the sovereign states of Europe.[14] In effect, Penn tended to uphold the maintenance of the *status quo* in Europe (in this respect differing from his predecessor and model Sully and from his successor and fellow Quaker Bellers[15]).

War, according to Penn, was permissible for two reasons only: to rectify 'wrongs received' and to obtain justice after 'right upon complaint' had been refused.[16] He was of course speaking now not as a Quaker but as one pleading with the princes of Europe to unite in a common effort to outlaw the institution of war. Yet the Quaker peeps out here too, when Penn explains that war, even if from the princes' point of view justified under such circumstances, usually fails nevertheless to achieve the objectives sought: for 'the remedy is almost ever worse than the disease.'[17]

In the key section of his tract Penn succeeds in compressing the essentials of his plan into just over 200 words.[18] Its main goal was the creation of a body representative of the existing European states – 'a general dyet, estates or parliament'[19] – which would meet, if possible annually, to draw up rules of international conduct and to settle disputes between the constituent states. The latter, however, would remain entirely independent, apart, that is, from the obligations they had undertaken in respect of the European Diet. On the other hand,

> if any of the sovereignties that constitute these imperial states [i.e., Estates] shall refuse to submit their claim or pretentions to them, or to abide and perform the judgement thereof, and seek their remedy by arms, or delay their compliance beyond the time prefixt in their resolutions, all the other sovereignties united as one strength, shall compel the submission and performance of the sentence, with damages to the suffering party and charges to the sovereignties that obliged their submission.[20]

Here in embryo we find the concepts of international sanctions, an international police force, and reparations: ideas extremely familiar to us in the 20th century.

Three points should be made at this place with respect to Penn's plan. First we may note its aristocratic flavour.[21] He thinks exclusively in terms of ruling princes and their dynasties and not of their subjects, of the peoples who make up the states; still less of course does he have in view nations or ethnies in the modern sense. In his view, 'wars are the duels of princes,' whose kingdoms play the same role on the international plane as individual citizens do within the state, where, he notes, law has taken the place of duelling as a method of solving disputes.[22] Secondly 'Penn did not believe in the doctrine of equality of nations.'[23] The number of representatives each state would be entitled to send to the European Diet would depend upon an assessment of their material wealth.[24] However, Penn did contemplate the possibility of including powers on the periphery of Europe like Muscovy or Turkey,[25] and there was nothing in his plan to obstruct the extension of representation to countries even more remote from European civilisation than these two were. We find, in the third place, that Penn endowed his European Diet with judicial as well as legislative functions. Hence 'diplomats, rather than judges trained in the law, were to settle controversies,' just as in the English parliament politicians rather than lawyers acted as a final court of appeal. International law would be framed by deputies appointed by the princes and the same body that made this law would adjudicate in disputes arising from its application.[26] Penn has been criticised here for confusing the two functions, but we must remember he lived in an era that had not yet heard Montesquieu's powerful plea for the separation of powers.

Since a state of peace would result, so Penn believed, from the implementation of his plan for a European Diet, a reduction of 'the war establishment' would thereby also become possible. The princes would no longer need extensive armaments in a world from which war would hopefully be banished (yet effeminacy would not ensue, as some feared, for that might be prevented through a strict, even Spartan, discipline in the education of young males). Henceforward no single power, not even that of the Turks, would be strong enough to dominate the rest, whose combined forces could easily crush a threat of this kind. No state would be permitted to 'keep up such an army after such an umpire is on foot, which may hazard the safety of the rest,' for the Diet would nip all aggressive designs in the bud. An all-round reduction of armaments would leave each state in the possession only of 'a small force' capable of defending it against some quite unexpected attack.[27]

Penn depicted the advantages of general European peace mainly in terms of material welfare: the human lives spared from destruction, the wealth saved that would otherwise be squandered in war, the flourishing cities and countrysides that battle would reduce to ruin, international communications and cultural interflow opened out that war would indubitably close, and increased friendship between princes instead of the hatred engendered among rulers in case of renewed conflict.[28] But one consideration Penn puts forward in this connection that reflects his Quaker pacifism, namely that 'the reputation of Christians will, in some degree, be recovered in the sight of infidels.' For Christians had for too long been fighting among themselves under the specious plea of establishing justice, when in fact 'ambition or revenge' were their primary motives.

> Yet their Saviour has told them, *that he came to save and not to destroy the lives of men*: to give and plant peace among men. Of all his titles, this seems the most glorious as well as comfortable for us, that he is the Prince of Peace . . . And it is very remarkable, that in all the New Testament, he is but once called lion, but frequently the Lamb of God; to denote to us his gentle, meek and harmless nature, and that those that desire to be the disciples of his cross and kingdom, for they are inseparable, must be like him . . . War shall yield to peace, and the soldier turn hermit. To be sure Christians should not be apt to strive, nor swift to anger against any body, and less with one another and least of all for the uncertain and fading enjoyments of this lower world.

Once again does Penn, after thus expounding the fundamental principles underlying the Quaker peace testimony and then going on to urge 'the reverend clergy of Europe' – of whatever denomination – to support 'this pacific means I offer, which will end blood, if not strife,' return finally to a rationalist view of the problem of war and peace. The carrying out of his plan, he says, will mean that 'Reason, upon free debate, will be judge and not the sword.' It is not the Sermon on the Mount, then, but the appeal to reason that seems to this Quaker to be the best way of leading the rulers of Europe into the paths of peace.[29]

Penn's peace plan, it is worth stressing, was not a pacifist scheme. Indeed we find him recommending its adoption as a means of intimidating the Turkish Sultan from further attacks on Europe: Penn, we should note, published his work a mere decade after the Turks had only with difficulty been prevented from capturing the imperial capital, Vienna. With the establishment of a European Diet a united Christendom would be strong enough to withstand the crescent. Unity would replace the Europe in disarray which 1683 had presented, when 'some Christian princes' connived at, if they did not actually aid, the Turkish invaders. Penn's plan once adopted, 'the Grand-seignior will find himself obliged to concur for the security of what he holds in Europe: where, with all his strength, he would feel it an over-match for him.'[30] Self-interest might even lead the Sultan eventually to join the comity of European states.

In view of the military aspects and underpinnings of Penn's plan, are those writers[31] correct who have asserted the scheme shows Penn had abandoned his faith in pacifism and hereby 'deserted' the Quaker peace testimony? I think this interpretation, while comprehensible because of the conditional approval of armed force in Penn's tract,[32] does not give a complete picture. It is essential to remember that Penn was not addressing a Quaker audience or presenting the Quaker viewpoint on war and peace to a non-Quaker audience. What he aimed at in his *Essay* was to persuade the rulers of Europe to adopt measures for safeguarding the peace of the war-torn continent without requiring them to abandon their reliance on military defence as a last resort and accept Quaker pacifism (a requirement that would obviously nullify the whole project). He seems to have thought that the implementation of his plan would probably make the future employment of force hypothetical, and that therefore the discrepancy between it and the Quaker position was largely theoretical, for the object of both was to create a peaceable world. But in essence the plan and the peace testimony belonged in Penn's mind to two different dimensions of living. The plan would be carried out in the international arena by the princes of Europe, while the peace testimony would be exemplified in the lives of Friends. True, Penn's view differed radically from that of the Anabaptist-Mennonite tradition of nonresistance and from the standpoint of some early Quakers. But it was not one that was basically incompatible with the evolving peace testimony of Friends. There is no reason to believe, indeed his whole career disproves it, that Penn, unlike his private secretary James Logan, ever dissented from the Quaker position on peace, whatever compromises he was on occasion prepared to undertake to bridge the gap between it and the non-Quaker world. There is no reason to believe, then, that he ever regarded his *Essay* as a desertion of pacifism – momentary or permanent. Only, Penn saw the pursuit of peace as an enterprise that might be carried on at different levels.[33] The Quaker peace testimony indicated what a follower of Christ should do if he wished to follow the teachings of his master. The plan to establish a European Diet, on the other hand, provided a short-cut, as it were, whereby some of the fruits of peace could be enjoyed before the final realisation of the peaceable kingdom.

Penn's *Essay* in fact exerted little, if any, influence either on the European statesmen of his day or on the later movement for international organisation.[34] Even less effective in its impact on the outside world was the tract published 17 years later by Penn's coreligionist, John Bellers, on roughly the same theme as Penn's had dealt with. Despite differences in approach, both authors strove to bring peace to Europe through the establishment of institutions that would resolve conflict between its constituent states. Neither of them were attempting to present the case for Quaker pacifism, their treatises therefore did not appear under the official auspices of the Society of Friends.

Bellers belongs to the type of universal reformer that was to become a familiar figure in the 19th century. His best known proposal, put forward in 1695, centred on the establishment of what he called 'Colleges of Industry' to be run on cooperative principles: the scheme, which aimed at employing the poor in useful labour, was never in fact implemented but later aroused the admiration of socialist thinkers as diverse as Robert Owen, Karl Marx, and Eduard Bernstein. Bellers was also a keen advocate of the abolition of capital punishment. Reformation of offenders and not punishment or retribution should, in Bellers's view, have been the law's aim and society's goal, for crime stemmed from poverty and poverty from a faulty social order. In these ideas Bellers, while his recommendations had little immediate effect, proved himself a forerunner of such well known penal reformers as John Howard or Cesare Beccaria. International peace, therefore, was only one of several reforms which Bellers advocated, all of them products of his Quakerism as well as of the emergent rationalism and humanitarianism of his age.

Born into the Society of Friends, Bellers, whose father was a prosperous London grocer, himself acquired a modest fortune in the City as a result of his commercial activities as a cloth merchant. In later life he settled in Gloucestershire as a country gentleman, having married into the family of a country squire who had converted to Quakerism. The impulse to compose his peace tract was much the same as Penn's had been: in both cases it was a prolonged and bloody conflict between the Great Powers that provided the inspiration. In Bellers's day, as in Penn's, what Europe needed above all was peace, a cessation of 'the deluge of Christian blood and the vast treasure

. . . spent' in endemic warfare. For, Bellers writes, 'war is the greatest misery which attends mortals.'[35]

Bellers in elaborating his proposal on his lengthy title page speaks of his goal as the establishment of a 'European state.' And in his dedication to Queen Anne, with which he commences his tract, he holds up the example of England, Scotland, Ireland, and Wales – 'now happily united in one government, to the saving of much human blood' – as a model for the powers of Europe to unite 'in one peaceable settlement.' But no more than Penn had done, did he in fact envisage the creation of a superstate transcending the existing national sovereignties. On the other hand, in the text he refers to a 'confederacy' or 'alliance,' and this indeed describes more accurately what he intended. It was in fact to be for Europe what in the 20th century the League of Nations was intended to be for the world.

Bellers conceived his plan as an outgrowth of the existing wartime alliance against Louis XIV, of which the English, Dutch, and Austrians formed the major components. At the conclusion of hostilities (which the Quaker hoped would not be long in coming) the allies should draw up 'articles of agreement' to which neutrals and enemies would then be invited to accede. As a bait to gain signatures Bellers offered the increased security and protection against potential aggressors resulting from such an agreement to set up a form of international organisation: the Dutch or English, for instance, would no longer need to fear attack from France, or the Emperor a Turkish invasion, or the Italians partition among their neighbours. Even France, he believed, could be persuaded to join, for then it would 'reap the blessing of a lasting peace' and the irenic dream of Louis XIV's grandfather, Henry IV, would be realised.[36] Bellers also urged the inclusion of the Russians and Turks and hinted even at the extension of the 'peaceable settlement' to lands still more distant so as to make it one that was truly universal. He wrote:

> The Muscovites are Christians, and the Mahometans men, and have the same faculties, and reason as other men, they only want the same opportunities, and applications of their understandings, to be the same men: But to beat their brains out, to put sense into them, is a great mistake, and would leave Europe, too much in a state of war; whereas, the farther this civil union is possible to be extended, the greater will be the peace on earth, and good will among men.[37]

How exactly did Bellers envisage that permanent peace might be established in Europe? His proposal, like Penn's before him, centred on the creation of 'an annual congress, senate, dyet, or parliament,' with representatives from as many states as possible, and the framing of a 'standing European law' (into the details of which Bellers does not, however, enter). Even if at first the number of members fell short of the total number of European states, nevertheless a beginning should be made at once upon the conclusion of peace. Time would indeed be needed to frame the constitution of the confederacy, for the states of Europe possessed many different 'forms of government' and, 'every country being apt to esteem their own form best, it will require time and consideration among the powers concerned to draw up a scheme as will suit the dispositions and circumstances of them all.' At any rate, whatever the final arrangements decided on, the European Diet would certainly be entrusted with the task of settling disputes among members without their having to resort to war in support of their claims. Thus, henceforward 'there may be,' Bellers hoped, 'a full stop to the effusion of Christian blood, which hath often been poured out upon small occasions of offence.'

Penn, we have seen, desired to maintain the *status quo* in his plan. Bellers, on the other hand, wished to make a rather curious alteration in the territorial configuration of existing European states. He proposed 'that Europe should be divided into 100 equal cantons or provinces, or so many, that every sovereign prince and state may send one member to the Senate at least.' The relationship between these cantons and the existing states does not emerge clearly but Bellers appears to have thought of the former merely as subdivisions of the latter and not as autonomous units.

'Each canton,' according to Bellers's plan, 'should be appointed to raise a thousand men, or money, or ships of equal value or charge.' The combined forces of the confederacy, to be recruited in this manner, would serve to deter any state contemplating a military solution of its quarrel, and thereby preserve peace by imposing a settlement on the disputants. Potential disturbers of international peace would then know 'that every man in the Senate, hath 1, 2 or 3 thousand men to back what he concludes there.' In that body great powers would willingly associate with weaker ones because they realised it possessed both sufficient strength 'to preserve the public peace' and sufficient impartiality to reach a just decision in disputes over territory. As Bellers explains:

> That assembly must go by arguments (and not scimitars) grounded upon reason and justice, and the major part of the Senate not being interested in the dispute, will be the more inclined to that side which hath most reason with it. Whilst the greatest monarchs in time of peace own themselves subjects to the sovereignty of reason.

Like Penn, Bellers too saw arms limitation as a prerequisite for permanent peace. But the two Quakers obviously regarded complete disarmament, however desirable in theory, as a Utopian proposal that would have no chance of adoption in the existing international situation.

But unless a sizeable reduction of armaments were implemented, 'the peace,' in Bellers's view, would 'be little better than a truce,' leaving the possibility open for a renewal of hostilities by some dissatisfied power when the opportunity seemed ripe.[38]

When elaborating his proposal Bellers seems to have been aware, if only in the background of his mind, that it fell far short of what might be expected of a Quaker. For reliance on military sanctions, or the threat of such, played, we see, a prominent role in his thinking. At any rate, he took pains to point out that his plan represented a practical means of achieving peace within the framework of *Realpolitik*, which did not preclude a higher way toward, and a more lofty vision of, the peaceable kingdom. 'Therefore [he writes] the best expedient that can be offered, is such a settlement, as will prevent adding more injuries by war, to those irreparable ones already past: After the present are settled in the best manner that time and circumstances will admit of.' But at the end of his outline of the plan, he presents the reader with a more elevated view of peace and one more compatible with the Quaker pacifism in which he had been reared and to which (so far as we know) he gave his life-long allegiance. 'The peace of God be with you [he concludes], and his counsel guide you, and make the earth by your means, like the garden of Eden; that the wolf may dwell with the lamb, and the leopard lie down with the kid, and the lion eat straw like the ox; and that there may be no destroyer there.'[39]

Finally Bellers, having presented his solution for healing the wounds of a continent devastated by war, makes one more proposal that he considers essential if warfare, banished from the international stage, is not to appear again on the domestic scene – and from there perhaps spread back to poison once more relations between the states of Europe. With this in view, he now sought to institutionalise his plea for religious toleration in the form of 'a General Council of all the several Christian persuasions in Europe . . . to meet together with a disposition of loving their neighbours, and doing good to each other, more than to contend about what they differ in.' Bellers's mind obviously harked back here to the not too distant age of religious wars fought out between, as well as within, states. Were they to return, his plan for European peace would be shattered irretrievably. Therefore, as he wrote, we need to tolerate each other's religious faith 'in order to prevent broils and war at home, when foreign wars are ended.'[40] For Bellers, ecumenism was an essential component of any design for international peace.

Bellers's plan lacks the details that are so striking a feature of Penn's proposals. After all, the city merchant did not possess the political experience of the founder of Pennsylvania and close associate of kings and statesmen. However, in a way this seeming defect may in the end even prove an advantage. For Bellers's scheme presents the clearer outline, and this today is what gives value to ideas from an age long past where detailed circumstances are no longer relevant and only general principles remain valid.

Some of the criticisms levelled at Penn's plan apply to a greater or less extent to Bellers's, too. For instance, Bellers, like Penn, is concerned only with the relations between states and between their princely rulers; the subject populations appear in his argument only as the passive victims of war.[41] A Soviet writer, T. A. Pavlova, points, with some justification, to the limitations Bellers's bourgeois background placed on his pacifist vision. He tends to calculate the advantages of peace in the kind of terms that would appeal to the commercial class to which he belonged. 'Bellers's project,' Pavlova writes, 'arose under the influence of the advancing bourgeois development of the countries of Europe, which needed peaceful relations between states – for the growth of manufactures, trade, navigation, etc.'[42] And she also points, not without approval in this case, to his partiality for quantification when assessing the harm done by war and the benefits of peace in material terms.[43] 'It would be much more glorious,' states Bellers, in this connection, 'for a prince to build palaces, hospitals, bridges, and make rivers navigable, and to increase the number of his people, than by pouring out human blood as water, to invade his neighbours.'[44] Here indeed he speaks with the voice of the rationalist humanitarian opponent of war who comes to the fore in peace movements of the 19th and 20th centuries.

It only remains for me to say a few words in conclusion about the consistency, or otherwise, of Bellers's pacifism. How did he square his inclusion of military measures in his peace project with his loyalty to Quaker peace principles, which rejected the use of violence? I think the answer to this question follows closely what we have already said earlier in the case of Penn. Primitive Quakerism strove to exemplify 'pure' Christianity, a universalist creed freed from the trammels of nationalism or ethnicity.[45] It was from beliefs of this kind that the Quaker peace testimony drew its inspiration. At the same time the encompassing world was still held tight within the confines of national passions and state rivalries. In his peace pamphlet Bellers, like Penn before him, was offering an olive branch for use among the people of the world, an instrument that might, even 'before the millenary doctrine be accomplished' (as Penn put it), bring peace to a war-sick world, an institution that would succeed in banishing military conflict by providing means of arbitrating disputes and securing the European states against unprovoked attack. Neither Bellers nor Penn spoke as Quakers here, although their proposals were undergirded by the peace principles of the Society of Friends.

But for Friends, for 'the people of God' (as some early Quakers liked to call themselves), a different rule held. It was the one compactly expressed by Penn when he said, 'not fighting, but suffering' was the essence of their peace testimony. It would, however, clearly be fruitless to recommend suffering as the means to achieve a speedy peace to statesmen and rulers who had not yet renounced violence and who regarded the arbitrament of war as the court of final instance in disputes between states. In both plans there is perhaps an element of compromise and a flexibility that some moralists might regard as a dereliction of principle. But I do not think either Quaker saw the matter in this light, nor seemingly did their coreligionists regard their projects as having cast discredit on the Society's pacifism. Salutary advice like this on international affairs given to the magistrates who occupied the office of the sword was not mistaken for an exposition of Quaker peace principles destined for those who hankered after a higher law of righteousness. The distinction remained clear, at least to the Quakers of Penn's and Bellers's day.

We shall see, however, in the succeeding chapters that in the case of Penn's experiment in Quaker government, which was taking place in colonial Pennsylvania, this distinction becomes blurred. For here the Quaker *is* the magistrate. The question will be, then, how does a Quaker comport himself in the office of the sword?

CHAPTER VIII

The Pacifist Ethic and Quaker Pennsylvania: The First Phase

QUAKERS RULED PENNSYLVANIA FOR NEARLY three quarters of a century, and for almost two decades more some of them at least continued active in the politics of that province. Was the period of Quaker rule indeed, as some have argued, 'a holy experiment' (to use Penn's own words) in which Friends, though fallible human beings and liable to error, yet strove to realise an ideal of brotherhood, where men and women would live together in peace and harmony and endeavour to banish violence and war from their midst? Or was it, as others have maintained, despite the undoubted idealism that impelled its founder and first settlers, really an example of mistaken effort that ended by showing the incompatibility of pacifism and political power? In the first view Quaker rule in Pennsylvania provides a model for a peaceable world of the future, though – largely through the fault of others – it finally came to grief. In the second, its fall was implicit in its beginnings, and the attempt to apply Quaker peace principles in the realm of politics was bound to lead to evasion and compromise and the eventual corruption of the original ideal. Both views have found their supporters among those who have studied Quaker Pennsylvania, the 'idealistic' interpretation predominating among earlier writers,[1] many of them belonging to the Society of Friends, while the 'realist' view has come to the fore since World War II among Quaker as well as among non-Quaker historians.

In this chapter I wish to deal with the period of Quaker rule when its founder William Penn was active as proprietor, though at a distance and through a proxy except for his brief visits to the colony in 1682-84 and 1699-1701. In 1712 Penn was stricken by serious illness that incapacitated him for all further work, and he remained in this condition until his death in 1718. In 1713, with the Treaty of Utrecht Queen Anne's War – the War of the Spanish Succession – came to an end and, with the Hanoverian accession the next year, a new era began in British history. In the small and comparatively remote world of Quaker Pennsylvania, these events, too, meant a transition, though a gradual one, to a fresh epoch in its development. This second phase in the story of Quaker Pennsylvania, which lasted until 1756, will be dealt with, therefore, in the next chapter. I shall of course concentrate throughout on the relationship between Quaker rule and Quaker peace testimony and not attempt a wider picture of the province's growth, which would be a task far transcending the one I hope to accomplish here and certainly one well beyond my competence.

When Penn in 1681 received a royal charter giving him title to the land that became the province of Pennsylvania, several motives induced him to undertake its settlement and subsequent government. He certainly hoped it would prove an economically viable project, and he expected it also to prove a convenient place of refuge for his persecuted coreligionists as well as for others, including men and women in other lands, who had suffered for their religious faith. 'In Penn's own mind, however,' as Melvin Endy has pointed out, 'the primary motivation for the Pennsylvania undertaking was religious.'[2] He wished, as he said, that the new province would act as 'an example and standard . . . to the nations.' In a letter to a Lancashire Quaker in August 1681 telling him of his recent land grant, he underlined this point when he wrote: 'I . . . desire that I may not be unworthy of [God's] love, but do that which may answer his kind providence and serve his truth and people; that an example may be set up to the nations, there may be room there, tho not here, for such a holy experiment.'[3] Thus, Pennsylvania was not to form an ordinary civil polity but an ideal commonwealth,[4] by means of which God's people, Penn's Quaker coreligionists, could exemplify their principles of reconciliation and concord and bring the millennium of love and justice a step nearer and give the peoples of the world an example of how a Christian community should manage its affairs and arrange its relations with its neighbours.

Pennsylvania, then, was to be a commonwealth where brotherhood would prevail not only internally between its citizens but externally in its relations with the outside world. But Penn, who was we know in principle no enemy to the concept of a Christian magistracy,[5] realised the need to set the new province on a firm constitutional basis and to provide guidelines for its proper administration. The magistracy would indeed be drawn from members of the Society of Friends, who formed the majority of the population until around the end of the 17th century. But for Quakers the office of magistrate constituted an entirely uncharted area of activity, whose pitfalls remained for some time largely unperceived even by Penn himself. The Frame of Government, which Penn composed in 1682, was designed as an instrument to help the province's administrators in their task of ruling.

'Government,' wrote the founder there, 'seems to be a part of religion itself, a thing sacred in its institutions and end.' Its aims were not merely negative – the correction of evil doers – but positive, for it should serve as a source of 'kindness, goodness and charity.' Indeed those of its activities that reflected these last qualities seemed to Penn the most important.[6] The inhabitants of Pennsylvania were to enjoy liberty of conscience which, if it was not complete, was at any rate wider than almost anywhere else in the Western world.[7] Among the rights of conscience, as Penn saw them, was of course freedom from service in the militia.[8] Pennsylvania was to possess no military establishment: it would be free of the incubus of army and fortifications.

Penn, though a firm believer in the rights of the free-born Englishman, was nevertheless no egalitarian (as many writers have pointed out). As a Whig, he believed in the rights of property and a social hierarchy as well as a restricted franchise in his new province. Quakers under his constitution enjoyed a politically privileged position that continued to be backed informally by the economically and socially elitist status of many leading Friends. Quaker dominance of the province in fact remained unbroken until 1756. As William Frost writes: 'Law and government and the tone of society would be established by Friends. Others would be welcome, but they would have to be governed by Quaker principles . . . The result was a noncoercive Quaker establishment.'[9]

Pennsylvania, when Penn took control, was lightly inhabited by native peoples. The founder, therefore, was not solely concerned with establishing a settler commonwealth on Quaker principles; he had also to work out a peaceable and Quakerly relationship with the Delaware Indians on whose territories Friends were to establish their holy experiment. Despite certain limitations Penn's attitude to the indigenous population was fundamentally one of respect for them and their culture.[10] He sought from the beginning to exemplify in his relations with the North American Indians the ideas of peace and harmony that underlay his Society's testimony against war. As Penn told 'the Emperor of Canada,' an Indian chieftain with whom he hoped to establish trading relations, in a letter he wrote from London on 21 June 1682: 'The great God that made thee and me and all the world incline our hearts to love peace and justice that we may live friendly together as becomes the workmanship of the great God.' The Indians, he informed the chieftain, had nothing to fear from the Quakers, 'who . . . are a just plain and honest people that neither make war upon others nor fear war from others because they will be just.'[11] In the treaty of friendship Penn concluded with the Delawares of Pennsylvania and New Jersey at Shackamaxon on the Delaware river in November of the same year, the same humanist outlook emerges clearly, especially in the words Penn addressed to the assembled Indians. He tried to convey to them (of course through the medium of an interpreter) the essence of Quaker pacifism. 'It is not our custom,' he said, 'to use hostile weapons against our fellow creatures, for which reason we have come unarmed. Our object is not to do injury, and thus provoke the Great Spirit, but to do good.' Faith and goodwill must become the hallmarks of Quaker-Indian relations. 'No advantage is to be taken on either side but all to be openness, brotherhood, and love.' Christian and Indian should make each other welcome and greet each other as friends. 'I will consider you,' Penn concluded, 'as the same flesh and blood with the Christians, and the same as if one man's body were to be divided into two parts.'[12]

In fact, Quaker Pennsylvania, in striking contrast to Britain's other North American colonies, remained at peace with its Indian neighbours.[13] Only in 1755, after the Quaker policy of friendship initiated by William Penn had finally disintegrated, did war break out on the Indian frontier. The break-down had been presaged by such notorious acts as the Walking Purchase of 1737 when the Indians had been tricked out of considerable tracts of land by the provincial government. But Penn's policy, if shaken, remained intact until shortly before the Quaker withdrawal from politics.

Though Penn envisaged Pennsylvania as a Quaker commonwealth practising in the political arena both Christian pacifism and human brotherhood, he could not be unaware that at the same time the province inevitably remained a part of the British Empire, a link in the chain of imperial defence, and a factor of significance in the power struggle that was rending contemporary Europe and spilling over, too, into the New World. The symbol of this other – and darker – aspect of Quaker Pennsylvania was undoubtedly the Captain-Generalship that was imposed on Penn in the Royal Charter of March 1682. By the terms of the Charter he had been empowered 'to make war . . . as well by sea as by land, yea, even without the limits of the . . . province, . . . and to do all and every other act and thing, which to the charge and office of a Captain-General of an army, belongeth.'[14] It is true that Penn may have accepted this military command in his public capacity as magistrate and not in his private role as a member of the Society of Friends. 'Penn,' writes Wellenreuther, 'made a clear distinction between the religious and the public man.'[15] Still, the tension remained, continuing, as we shall see, after his death to plague the relations between the Quaker provincial administration and the proprietary and home governments.

Penn's secretary, the nonpacifist Quaker James Logan, bore witness later to the trouble the Captain-General's office caused his master, especially during his second visit to Pennsylvania in 1699-1701 when he personally assumed the administration of the province. 'He found himself so embarrassed,' Logan reports, 'between the indispensable duties of government on the one hand, and his profession [i.e., his Quakerism] on the other, that he was determined, if he had stayed, to act by a deputy.'[16] In fact, as William Frost has pointed out, there was a certain ambivalence in Penn's original position with respect to pacifism. He evidently feared it could imperil his tenure as proprietor: his enemies might claim with some plausibility (as indeed they were to do) that it incapacitated him for rulership of the province, which consequently should be taken out of his hands. While Penn had stressed the peaceable nature of his projected commonwealth in his contacts with the Indians and emphasised with his coreligionists the unarmed policy he intended to pursue there, he played these aspects down in his negotiations with the Crown and in his propaganda efforts to attract non-Quakers, including French Calvinists and Scottish Presbyterians, to settle in his province.[17] All this, however easy to justify on a short-term view, stored up future trouble both for Penn himself and for his coreligionists who came to settle in Pennsylvania.

Let us move on now from Pennsylvania's Quaker founder and first proprietor to that province's early Quaker citizens on whose shoulders rested the burden of realising Penn's holy experiment. It has been said of them that, like the Puritans, they 'came to do good in America and ended up doing too well.' Moreover, contrary to the expectations of its founder the history of Quaker Pennsylvania turned out to be 'one of growing political friction and social divisions, rising prosperity, and diminishing plainness and spirituality.'[18] Many writers have pointed to the factionalism that very soon emerged within the Quaker political community. 'Litigious, uncooperative, and almost ungovernable': this judgement of a recent historian is hardly too harsh, at least in so far as the first generation of Quaker settlers is concerned.[19] The fault does not seem to have lain primarily with Penn, who strove to reconcile the contending factions and to damp down the animosity directed against himself and his successive deputies. True, there was a patriarchal streak in his character that served to irritate the feelings of the antiproprietary party which soon emerged, drawing its strength from the sturdy Quaker freemen in the country constituencies; and he once described himself in his role as proprietor as 'lord of the soil erected into a seignory' with 'a royalty and share herein.'[20] Yet in practice he allowed his 'subjects' almost unlimited freedom in arranging their affairs. As he told them in 1691 in a message to the provincial council: 'I can forgive you in what any of you have thought or done at any time against me; can you not for my sake and your own forgive one another?... Strive not, read the fifth of Matthew, the twelfth of Romans ... you will see what becomes Christianity, even in government.'[21]

The trouble with Pennsylvania's Quakers resided chiefly perhaps in 'the anti-authoritarian Quaker ethic,' which they brought over with them from the mother country and then tried to adapt to the new colonial environment. 'The basic problem of authority revolved around the question of whether the representatives of the proprietors or the Assembly should rule.'[22] The one constant factor in Pennsylvania politics down to the Revolution, therefore, was the opposition of the Quaker party of the day to the supporters of the proprietary interest (among whom were also to be found a sprinkling of Friends). In England Quakers, since the Restoration at any rate, had been a persecuted sect excluded, along with other dissenters, from participation in government by means of discriminatory legislation. Although, we have seen, in theory English Friends granted the magistracy a place in God's plan for humanity, in practice they remained suspicious of government as a reflection of the corrupt state of this world.[23] They could not easily abandon this suspicion of government even though in Pennsylvania they had themselves now assumed the mantle of the legislator, if not actually of the ruler. First Penn and then his non-Quaker descendants who retained the proprietorship – as well as their deputies to whom they delegated their powers on the spot – now became the main object of attack for the Quaker party politicians and their supporters in both town and country constituencies.

If Pennsylvania Friends found it hard to apply their antiauthoritarian ethic in the novel conditions of a Quaker-ruled province, they found it even more difficult to reach a *modus vivendi* between their belief in Christian pacifism and their obligations as secular rulers of a culturally pluralistic commonwealth.[24] The main burden of working out a compromise between Quaker peace testimony and Quaker political practice[25] rested on the shoulders of the Quaker members of the legislative Assembly, along with the Society's representatives who gathered annually in the Philadelphia Yearly Meeting. The two groups overlapped of course, for some of the leading Quaker Assemblymen and politically active Friends were also prominent members of the Yearly Meeting or of Meetings subordinate to it.

In fact, until the mid-1750s Pennsylvania usually achieved consensus on the peace issue, though not always without considerable heart-searching and not always without leaving a feeling of uneasiness among the more sensitive Friends at the degree of compromise such consensus demanded. However, it was not until 1755 that this residual uneasiness burst out into a revolt against the interpretation of the peace testimony that had prevailed among Pennsylvania Quakers virtually since the province's foundation.

'The Quaker legislatures from 1693 to 1748,' writes Jack Marietta, 'present a record of apparently confusing, sometimes obscure behavior respecting pacifism and obligations to the state.'[26] In the rest of this and in the succeeding chapter we shall examine this record as well as the repercussions on the life of the Society as a whole. But before doing so I would like to point to certain underlying principles that were held to, with greater or less consistency, by the Quaker legislators in association with their coreligionists. The Society indeed, for the most part, identified itself with the activities and attitudes of those elected representatives who were Friends.

First of all, there was unity among all Quakers, both inside and outside the legislature, that Friends should not perform military service themselves or be required to do so by the provincial Assembly. In fact there was consensus, too, that it would be inconsistent with the principles of the Society if a Quaker controlled Assembly were to impose military service on the nonpacifist section of the population. This in practice precluded the possibility of an officially sponsored provincial militia. (Even the handful of nonpacifist Quakers, the so called 'defence Quakers' like James Logan, for instance, or Isaac Norris, Jr., went along with all this, while privately nurturing their right to dissent over the peace testimony.) But thereafter trouble began. Though Friends grounded both the obligations of a Christian magistrate and the justification of conscientious objection on the Scriptures, yet it might seem, at least in the existing circumstances, as if 'the one required what the other forbade.'[27] Could a compromise be worked out that would reconcile the seemingly opposed duties incumbent on the Quaker as magistrate and on the Quaker as pacifist – and still be acceptable as a genuinely Quaker ethic to the Society as a whole?

'Quaker politicians,' Alan Tully has pointed out, 'were obliged by their own pronouncements on the duties of government to suppress deviant behavior in society and to protect the body politic from outside aggression.'[28] With respect to internal order Quaker Pennsylvania retained the death penalty, though at first for only two offences – treason and murder. This may indeed appear inconsistent with the Quaker respect for human life, but we must take into consideration two things. In the first place the Quaker magistrate in imposing capital punishment in these cases was acting not as a Friend but as a public servant and in the name of the Crown, while secondly the Pennsylvania penal code stood in striking contrast to the widespread use of the death penalty, even for comparatively minor crimes, on the European continent as well as in England and its colonies. We should not forget, either, that it is practically certain Penn's tenure as proprietor would have ceased if he had not been prepared to yield in this matter to the views of the home government, which believed law and order depended on the retention of capital punishment at least for the gravest crimes. But in 1718, as a result of pressure from the mother country, the Assembly passed a new legal code that extended the death penalty to a number of other offences thus bringing the province more into line with the situation in England and, perhaps we should add, more out of line with the Quaker ethic.

Among those who had criticised the Quakers for inconsistency on this issue was the dissident Quaker, George Keith. Keith wrote in 1706: 'Is not a gallows, or gibbet, on which the Quaker-judges in Pennsylvania (some of which were preachers also) caused some to be hanged for suspected murder a carnal weapon as really as a sword, gun or spear?'[29] But, curiously, we do not find explicit protest within the Society against Quaker magistrates wielding the sword of justice in this way; so long as it seemed right for Friends to participate in government, they were evidently willing to approve their coreligionists in office curbing evil doers by means of the executioner's sword. They did not apparently see this as reflecting on the sincerity of their own conscientious objection to war.

The situation with respect to defence against external attack did not of course allow the same leeway in glossing the peace testimony as the law code had done. For one thing, Pennsylvania, although enjoying wide internal autonomy, remained an English colony subordinated politically and economically to the interests of the mother country, whose policies were guided by imperial and military considerations.[30] Nevertheless an acceptable adjustment was worked out before the 17th century had ended between the claims of Quaker pacifism and the demands of government, a compromise that remained substantially intact, though not unchallenged within – as well as outside – the Society, until the middle of the next century. For this resort was had to the gospels. There Jesus had said: 'Render unto Caesar the things which are Caesar's.' It was Caesar's duty, then and now, to protect the state by means of the sword, and thus he could rightfully demand tribute from his subjects to accomplish that essential task. It was the loyal citizen's obligation to supply means, financial or otherwise, for this purpose. Provided Quakers themselves did not expend money on, or allocate supplies directly to, war, they were justified, they argued, both in granting these things as provincial legislators and providing them as private citizens. As one of the leading Quaker politicians, Isaac Norris, Sr., stated concerning the Assembly's grant of 1711: 'We did not see it to be inconsistent with our principles, to give the Queen money, notwithstanding any use she might put it to; *that* not being our part, but hers.'[31]

A crisis of conscience was long postponed by the fact of military operations taking place outside the province; yet ultimately the solution we have outlined proved unacceptable to a growing number of the more sensitive spirits within the Society. The crisis was indeed a long time coming, for Quaker Pennsylvania, we have seen, remained at peace with the

Indians, its western frontier experiencing the menace of French attack only after mid-18th century. Though earlier there had been periodic scares of an attack from the sea by enemy privateers or fleet, or even from pirates, they proved less dangerous in reality than in expectation. Thus the Quaker legislators were spared the difficulties that would have arisen if the province had actually been invaded. The rulers of 'the state without an army' did not yet have to cope directly with a war situation. If that had happened, then indeed they would have been faced (as they ultimately were) with two alternatives: either resigning from office in order to preserve their pacifist conscience and taking the consequences of adopting a stance of 'suffering', or abandoning their Society's peace testimony in carrying out military measures for the defence of the province.[32] To have adopted the first position would have been a very difficult step for at least the Philadelphia grandees of the Society; to have chosen the second would have been even more painful, not only for the 'strict Quakers' but also for all those who, despite their elevated social position, still nurtured a genuine affection for the peace principles their Society had inherited from an earlier period when humble shopkeepers and farmers had led Friends in the Lamb's War against evil.

Meanwhile, the compromise worked out within the Society on the defence issue that had emerged within the first decade of the province's existence held firm, despite periodic rumblings that presaged ultimate revolt among Friends. This compromise centred on a willingness on the part of the Assembly to vote money to the English government for unspecified purposes: at first the formula used designated the funds as 'for the support of government,' later the phrase employed was 'for the King's [or Queen's] use.' On the whole, in defending this procedure, which to some extent cloaked the military ends for which most of such funds were destined, the Quaker legislators muted the pacifist implications in their behaviour, though such motivation remained implicit throughout; sometimes it surfaced in the course of debate. For 'Quakers knew that their peace testimony irritated the Crown,' and they attempted, whenever possible, to minimise any threat it might seem to level at the security of the province, using utilitarian arguments against the proponents of military measures or pleading poverty as a reason for not granting military aid. They also urged on occasion that it was the Crown, and not the province, which was responsible for the wider task of defence, especially in so far as danger threatened from the sea.[33] Penn had told Pennsylvania Friends: 'We must creep where we cannot go, and it is as necessary for us, in the things of life, to be wise as to be innocent.' The Quaker legislators clearly found wisdom came to them more easily than innocence. Yet their position was not an enviable one, since they were subject to pressure on the one side from the

Crown and its representatives and from a growing section of the population unsympathetic to Quaker pacifism to undertake more stringent defence measures, and to pressure on the other side from elements within the Pennsylvania Quaker community, which became periodically uneasy at what they took to be unwarranted application of their Society's peace principles. Such dissent usually remained beneath the surface but never completely disappeared.

Hermann Wellenreuther has written: 'The money grants of the Assemblies of 1693, 1709, and 1711 . . . represent the Quaker politicians' translations of their religious testimonies into political terms.' I cannot quite agree with this interpretation, however plausible.[34] Rather, these money grants seem to me to have been not so much a translation into political terms of an amalgam of Friends' peace testimony and *Obrigkeitsdoktrin* as a compromise between these two testimonies, adopted with a certain uneasiness and even reluctance yet regarded as the best possible solution in the existing political situation.

We should now look a little more closely at some at least of the encounters between Quaker legislators and military demands as these presented themselves during the first three decades of the province's history when Penn was still an active factor in its affairs.

During the first decade the issue remained dormant. At this time Quakers still formed an overwhelming majority of the as yet sparsely populated province, and government – of a primitive and personal kind – was entirely in the hands of Friends who, like the founder, were averse to undertaking military measures and unready to yield to pressure in this direction from the Crown. The situation changed somewhat with Penn's appointment in 1688 of an ex-soldier, Captain John Blackwell, as his deputy. 'Being not a Friend . . . was my motive to have him,' Penn explained; he was, in his opinion, better able to deal decisively with the non-Quaker world than a Quaker deputy would have been. When toward the end of the next year King William's War broke out Blackwell discovered that the Quaker controlled provincial council was unwilling to support, at any rate actively, such war preparations as the home government now requested Blackwell to set up. After some equivocation on the part of several council members, the generally respected Samuel Carpenter rose to his feet and said: 'I am not against those that will put themselves into defence, but it being contrary to the judgement of a great part of the people, and my own too, I cannot advise to the thing . . . But if we must be forced to it, I suppose we shall rather choose to suffer than to do it, as we have done formerly.' Carpenter's view finally carried the day.[35] And Blackwell was left to prepare for war as he thought fit without the council giving its approval.

Penn's loss of the proprietorship in May 1692 as a result of his falling under suspicion of Jacobite sympathies, though only temporary (for he regained possession of his province two years later), brought the first serious confrontation on the issue of defence between the Quaker legislators and the Crown. The Crown was now represented by Governor Benjamin Fletcher of New York, who possessed even less sympathy with Quaker scruples on war than Blackwell had done. In 1693, at a crucial stage in the ongoing international conflict, Fletcher presented the Assembly with a clearcut demand for money to support the war. In the background there was the threat of an amalgamation of the Quaker province with New York, which would have left Friends in a minority in the combined legislature. Though there was resistance at first, the Pennsylvania Assembly finally yielded and assigned the sum of £760 'for the support of government' – but only after Fletcher had promised the money granted should 'not be dipt in blood' but would be employed instead – the distinction may seem over-refined – to cover such expenses as 'officers' salaries and other charges' (with half the sum to go, if possible, to cover the governor's own salary). The money, which was described by the Assemblymen as a 'free gift' and 'a testimony of our affections' toward the King and Queen, was to be raised by a tax on the freemen of the province, among whom of course Quakers formed the majority. As Wellenreuther aptly remarks: 'Two things are obvious: first, that the Quakers did not see a way open to avoid at least a show of good will; second that they knew that the money would be used for military purposes.'[36]

I detect beneath the hesitations and prevarications that preceded the granting of this money a sense of uneasiness among the Quaker Assemblymen, many of whom were prominent in the religious leadership of their Society, at the degree to which their participation in politics necessitated (as they saw it) a conditional support of war. I do not, therefore, agree with Marietta's view that Governor Fletcher, when he assured the Assembly that their money would not be used directly for shedding blood, 'showed uninformed solicitude for pacifism,' i.e., uninformed because the Assemblymen did not in fact entertain pacifist scruples of the kind the Governor suspected them of possessing. On the contrary, it seems to me he showed a nice sense of Quaker sensibilities on the war issue: he, perhaps unconsciously, perceived the underlying uneasiness that in a matter of this kind inevitably afflicted the Quaker conscience – until familiarity blunted its edge and obscured the ethical dilemma that lay underneath it.

In the following May Fletcher, when again approaching the Assembly for money, gave another assurance of his respect for their antiwar scruples – 'your principles that you will not carry arms, nor levy money to make war.'

He promised that their grant would be devoted to Indian welfare and that, moreover, the Assembly would have the right to audit the accounts and thus check how the funds were expended (which in fact gave the Assembly in the future a handle with which to secure a measure of control over money which it had granted for the government's 'use'). On this occasion Fletcher obviously expected that the provision of the wherewithal 'to feed the hungry, and clothe the naked' would serve to win the loyalty of the neighbouring Indians, who might otherwise be inveigled into an alliance with the French. As he said, 'my meaning is, to supply those Indian nations with such necessaries as may influence them to a continuance of their friendship.'[37] The governor's plea, however, was for the time being rejected on the grounds that their recent grant went 'so far as the religious persuasion of the most part of that Assembly could admit.'[38] Although Marietta believes this last statement to be 'untrue,' it seems to me to confirm the existence of pacifist scruples among the Quaker Assemblymen in respect of the money grants being made at that time.

In August 1694, shortly before receiving back his proprietorship of Pennsylvania, Penn gave certain promises to the Committee of Trade and Plantations concerning the defence of that province. If restored to his former office, he told the Committee he would 'take care of the government and provide for the safety and security thereof, all that in him lies.' He was ready to pass on to the Provincial Council and Assembly:

> all such orders and directions as their Majesties shall from time to time think fit to send, for the supplying such quota of men, or the defraying their part of such charges as their Majesties shall think necessary for the safety and preservation of their Majesties' dominions in that part of America.

And, Penn added (though we may wonder if he really believed this), he was sure both Council and Assembly would always obey such orders.[39] Here at last was a clear recognition, at least on Penn's part, of Pennsylvania's role in the network of imperial strategy and an acknowledgement of the obligation that rested on the Quaker magistracy in his province to supply the sinews of war at the behest of the Crown.

Penn undoubtedly feared that without such compliance he would again be deprived of his proprietorship, and all chance of realising the Quaker holy experiment would be finally ended. He therefore did his best in future to persuade the Quaker Assemblymen, led by David Lloyd, that doughty Quaker fighter for the rights of the freeborn Englishman, to respond positively to requests from the Crown to provide money. It was understood, of course, by all sides that the expenditure of such monies was solely the Crown's responsibility. Over the subsequent years the Assembly, after some tussles between legislature and governor, usually, though not invariably, acceded to such demands. Mingled with the latent pacifist scruples felt at least by some Friends were political considerations on the part of the Quaker legislators that had nothing to do with conscience. 'On all occasions,' writes Marietta, the legislature during King William's War 'proffered money only in exchange for power or privilege.'[40] This political manoeuvring certainly weakened the pacifist credentials of the Quaker politicians, if not of the whole Society in Pennsylvania, and provided a precedent that would have unfortunate consequences in the future.

An example of the kind of arguments used by Penn's non-Quaker opponents in his province to undermine the home government's confidence in Quaker government may be seen in a petition sent thence in 1697 to the Lord Commissioners for Trade and Plantations by a group of 'His Majesty's most loyal subjects.' Concerning Pennsylvania Friends the petitioners complain:

> The principles they maintain do militate against the very end and essentials of government, which is the protection of the people in all their just interest, bringing in of those to condign punishment that shall invade them. So they overpowering us with their votes in our public assemblies no bill can pass for the forming of a militia, levying of forces, etc. for the defence of the country or for the collecting or sending of any assistance or quotas for the common defence of frontiers or the raising of moneys to answer any such exigencies of government. And for such their proceedings they allege that it is unlawful that men should be hired to fight, or that the sword should be drawn or made use of in any case whatsoever, by which means the country lies naked and defenceless and exposed to be ruined and made a prey of by any enemy that shall first invade it.[41]

The character of Quaker pacifism as depicted in this petition was, we know, not quite correctly drawn. Still, the document brings out the underlying tension that both the non-Quaker public and the Quakers themselves perceived in the relationship between peace testimony and magistracy.

Only five years intervened between the conclusion of peace in 1697 and the outbreak of Queen Anne's War in 1702. The renewal of international conflict led to a series of requests for military aid from the province, which were put off by the Assembly for one or another reason until in 1709 a more urgent demand emerged in connection with the proposed expedition against French Canada. Penn's deputy as governor was now Charles Gookin, who had replaced the inexperienced and incompetent John Evans. Although Evans had failed to extract money from the Assembly, Gookin, with the threat of direct invasion by sea and the prospect of serious frontier fighting in the north, was able to exploit the heightened war atmosphere in his dealings with the legislature. The Assembly, however, rejected his request for at least £4000 with which to equip 150 men to serve in the expedition as the province's 'quota,' and instead voted a mere £500 'for the Queen's use.' The sum raised in this way was to form an integral part of the Queen's revenue, thus shifting responsibility for its expenditure from the Assembly to the Crown. And, even so, the Assemblymen attached certain political conditions to its 'present' that caused Gookin in the end to refuse acceptance of the money as an inadequate response to the existing emergency.

In the election of the following year the Quaker constitutionalist party led by David Lloyd met with a severe defeat. Conservative Quakers, headed by such bulwarks of Philadelphia Yearly Meeting as Isaac Norris, Sr., and inspired behind the scenes by the indefatigable James Logan, now formed a majority within the Assembly. The Lloydites had in fact gone too far in their attacks on the proprietary interest and thereby alarmed the more moderate – and well-to-do – elements among Pennsylvania Quakers. When Gookin in July 1711 presented the Assembly with a request from the Crown for £2000 to help defray the expenses of another expedition against Canada, he met with success. The formula 'for the Queen's use' was once more employed, and the grant was accompanied with a declaration of Friends' conscientious objection to participation in war along with an expression of their 'loyalty and faithful obedience to . . . Queen Anne.' The money, said the Assemblymen, formed 'a token of our duty' to the Crown. At the same time, there could be no doubt in either the Governor's mind or the minds of Friends that the appropriation would be placed at the army's disposal and used for the purposes of war.[42]

Even though the expenditure of the money was not carried out by Quakers, members of their Society were indeed responsible for collecting it from Quaker and other freemen of the province.[43] Now the latent dissatisfaction that existed among Friends concerning the degree of complicity with war that Quaker rule in Pennsylvania appeared to entail, burst forth. 'Clamours and uneasiness' manifested themselves in many Friends' Meetings. But the leaders of the Society, whose voice counted for most in the counsels of Philadelphia Yearly Meeting, stood inflexibly behind the Assembly's decision: indeed among those who made the grant were weighty ministers of the Yearly Meeting. And their stand gained full support from an influential Friend from England, Thomas Story, who cited George Fox and other such precedents in favour of payment as a fitting tribute to Caesar. 'The application,' said Story, 'is the business of kings and not of subjects.' So those who refused to pay the tax were now dealt with as offenders against the Society's discipline. We learn, for instance, that

Concord Quarterly Meeting, when it heard of cases of tax objection in one of its subordinate Monthly Meetings (the one at Darby), sent word that 'proceedings' against such persons should be instituted.[44] The authorities, largely under Quaker control, also took steps to collect the money even from those Friends, seemingly a minority in the Society, who had scruples about paying. They did not hesitate to distrain the property of such objectors in order to obtain the sum they owed as tax, and several Friends found themselves in jail for refusing to pay. On the other side, one of Lloyd's supporters, William Rakestraw, published a pamphlet in support of the dissidents, which he entitled *Tribute to Caesar, How paid by the Best Christians, And to What Purpose.* In its pages he attacked Story with considerable vigour and even rancour, and was shortly afterwards expelled from the Society for his refusal to withdraw his accusations.[45]

Henceforward, for over four decades the Quaker controlled Assembly was to employ the formula 'for the King's use' when appropriating money that all knew would be used for military purpose. Quaker consciences – or rather, the consciences of most Pennsylvania Quakers – were set at rest by the knowledge that it was the Crown, and not Friends, that would apply the money in this way. The responsibility for bloodshed rested, therefore, not on those who had renounced war but on those whose consciences were at ease with the idea of military defence. As Wellenreuther has written of the wider implications of this attitude:

> This ruling . . . signifies nothing else than that the Quaker politicians gave up on religious grounds a part of their obligations as magistrates, namely the defence of the citizenry against enemy attack. In their capacity as subjects they handed over the task of defending the colony to another branch of the magistracy, hoping thereby to be able to preserve their peace testimony intact.[46]

In fact, however, this solution, though it endured for several decades, did not in the end prove tenable. It broke down, as we shall see, when war threatened the province directly, and the business of defence could not be shuffled off by the legislature onto others' shoulders.

Meanwhile, from 1713 to 1739 a period of peace ensued. During this time important changes took place in the political and social structure of Pennsylvania. Demographically the balance tilted decidedly against the Quakers who sank to a minority *vis-à-vis* a rising non-Quaker population often hostile to the ideals, including pacifism, for which Friends stood. All this affected the relationship between the Quaker witness for peace and the Quaker role in the magistracy, so that the delicate balance that had been established between the two during Penn's lifetime, though not yet upset, became shaken. This new epoch in the history of the peace testimony in Quaker Pennsylvania needs, however, a chapter to itself.

CHAPTER IX

The Pacifist Ethic and Quaker Pennsylvania: The Second Phase

THE 26 YEARS OF PEACE THAT elapsed between the end of Queen Anne's War in 1713 and the outbreak of the War of Jenkins' Ear in 1739 were free from any confrontation between Quakers and Crown on the defence issue. The Philadelphia Yearly Meeting continued to stress its opposition to war and the need for Friends to observe strictly their Society's peace principles. As Philadelphia Friends stated in the discipline they drew up in July 1722, while Quakers might expect 'the benefit of those good laws which are deemed our birthright as *English* subjects,' they should not seek 'the protection by gun and sword which others make the terms of their allegiance.' At the same time they reiterated their belief that 'magistracy is an ordinance of God' (within the limits of the province this was of course a Quaker staffed magistracy), and they made a distinction between 'the material or carnal sword, invented by men to execute their wrath and revenge upon their fellow-creatures' and 'the sword of justice "ordained of God for punishment of evil doers, and praise of them that do well".'[1] The distinction might be valid. What the ensuing years were increasingly to put in doubt was whether Quakers could continue to wield the magistrate's sword and still remain loyal to their pacifist principles.

Two factors independent of Quaker control accentuated the dilemma already implicit in the concept of a Quaker magistracy: first, mounting prosperity within the Society and then the demographic expansion of the province's non-Quaker population. Each played its role in bringing about the crisis of conscience that emerged within Pennsylvania Quakerism in the mid-1750s.

Of course, not all members of Philadelphia Yearly Meeting became rich: humble artisans and plain farmers continued to predominate numerically. But the Quaker merchant elite of Philadelphia, which has been studied so perceptively by the late Frederick Tolles, certainly prospered – and grew worldly. And the counting houses of the provincial capital tended to set the tone, morally as well as materially, for most of the Meeting Houses of Pennsylvania Quakerism. The economic achievement of Quaker rule should not be underestimated. 'Within six decades the inhabitants of Pennsylvania had created out of an uncultivated wilderness one of the richest English colonies of North America.'[2] But, as always, such gains came at a price – at least they exacted a price from Pennsylvania Quakers that lessened both their spiritual vigour and the effectiveness of their religious message. Quaker merchants usually differed little now from non-Quakers in their economic and social ethos, and lived without too much unease in an increasingly competitive world. As the Quaker reform movement gathered momentum from the mid-1740s on, wealth came increasingly under attack from the reformers, who sought to restore the Society's pristine simplicity as a means to reinvigorate its declining witness in areas such as the peace testimony. I shall have more to say about this in the next chapter.

The second external element of change that affected the position of the Society within the province and thereby also the development of its peace testimony was the large-scale and continuous influx of non-Quakers into Pennsylvania. 'There is,' writes Wellenreuther, 'general agreement among historians that the Quakers constituted a minority of one third to one fifth in the colony in the fourth decade [of the 18th century] and that the political success of the Quaker Assemblymen at the polls was mainly due to a superb political machine.'[3] This shift in population resulted from trends that the Quakers were powerless to stop, even if they had wished to do so. Both financial and demographic considerations – the small Society of Friends could not provide sufficient immigrants to people the wilderness – and religious reasons – Penn had striven to make Pennsylvania a haven of refuge for all, regardless of creed – had led to the pursuit of an open-door policy that eventually resulted in the swamping of the original Quaker element. Some of the newcomers, like the Mennonites or Dunkers or Schwenk-felders from central Europe, shared much of the Quaker ethos, including a belief in nonviolence, and voted for Quaker candidates at the polls. But there were others like the Anglicans and Scotch-Irish Presbyterians, the latter settled thickly along the western frontiers, who for the most part remained unrelentingly hostile to Quaker ideals, and to their pacifism in particular, and regarded themselves as an element suffering political discrimination from the province's Quaker minority.

By means of electoral geometry and a limited franchise, the Quaker Party, which came into existence in course of the 1730s, succeeded at every election, down at least to 1756, in gaining an overwhelming majority of the seats in the Assembly: a powerful group that pursued its goals with tenacity and even a degree of aggressiveness not always consistent with Quaker values. To quote Wellenreuther again: 'The unity of the Society of Friends and the close rapport of Quaker politicians particularly with their German electorate made the colony practically a one-party state.'[4] 'Whiggish and antiproprietary in nature,'[5] the Quaker Party depended for its success largely on the cohesion displayed by members of the Society in giving it support. There were a few Quakers whose allegiance went to the Proprietary Party, just as there were some Anglicans and Scotch-Irish Presbyterians who voted for the Quaker Party.[6] But the Quaker Party formed, as it were, a projection of the Society of Friends into politics, an embodiment of at least some of their ideals in a shape that could function on the political level.

Quaker Meeting Houses throughout the province served at election times as organisational centres for party activities. Above all, the Party leadership was drawn from Quakers active in the concerns of the Society, men who held at one time or another some of the most responsible offices within the Philadelphia Yearly Meeting. This political oligarchy of course drew its personnel from the Quaker elite of Philadelphia rather than from the country Meetings, though this was not always the case. In particular, certain Quaker families from the elite repeatedly occupied provincial office or sat in the Assembly: Pembertons and Norrises, for instance, occur in this connection from one generation to another. In fact, 'the same persons who managed the Assembly business ran the church business as well.' 'Considering the close tie between Quaker church and Quaker Assembly-men it is not surprising that down to 1754 political decisions were as often taken in the vestibules of Quaker Meeting Houses as in the chambers of the House of Assembly.' For instance, for some years the Clerk of Philadelphia Yearly Meeting, John Kinsey, was also speaker of the Assembly (until he became chief justice of the provincial supreme court). Prominent Quaker politicians like the Israel Pembertons, father and son, or George Ashbridge, were both prominent in provincial politics and also weighty Friends, whose coreligionists entrusted them at one or another level with responsible positions within the Society. The list could be prolonged.[7]

Pennsylvania Quakers, despite their genuine, if narrow, attachment to their Society's peace testimony, were extremely reluctant to dispossess themselves of power even when possession of power ever more clearly conflicted with the Quaker perception of truth and Friends' vision of peace. The basic reasons for this are well put in the following passage by Alan Tully. He speaks of

the Quakers' fierce possessiveness about Pennsylvania. Pennsylvania was *the* Quaker province. It was William Penn's land, with the fine constitution and libertarian heritage he had conferred on them in trust.

With the defection of the Penn children from the Quaker fold, the guardians of this land felt themselves to be the true Quakers – the sons of those who had walked with Penn and shared his dreams in their new land. In the minds of most Quakers, their identity depended on continued political control of Pennsylvania.[8]

This feeling was so powerfully ingrained in Pennsylvania Friends that it took not one, but two crises – in 1756 and again in 1775 – before they finally renounced the vision that had inspired Penn and their forefathers of a Quaker commonwealth set apart from the harsh realities of interstate conflict and yet sharing in the political culture of the mother country and owing allegiance to the English Crown.

Meanwhile, we must return to the situation in which the renewal of war in October 1739 placed Quaker Pennsylvania.[9] The governor at that date was George Thomas, a crusty old soldier, who was to prove somewhat tactless in his dealings with the Quaker legislators, themselves not always models of restraint and understanding.[10] The governor's first act after his proclamation of war was to issue letters of marque authorising the warlike activities of privateers against Spain. The Philadelphia Yearly Meeting reacted immediately to the new situation by issuing a circular letter for transmission to all subordinate Meetings, in which Friends were urged to witness faithfully to their 'peaceable principles' and avoid participation in all 'warlike preparations offensive or defensive.'

The main authors of this letter were three leading Quaker politicians: John Kinsey, elected shortly afterwards Speaker of the Assembly; Samuel Preston, who was Provincial Treasurer and who also sat at one time or another in the Pennsylvania Assembly and Council, and Michael Lightfoot, also active in politics who became Preston's successor in the Treasurer's office.[11] All three were active members of the Yearly Meeting, thus illustrating the close connection between Meeting House and political life. Nevertheless a distinction should clearly be made between men like these and the small group of nonpacifist Quakers, like James Logan, or the wealthy Philadelphia merchant Robert Strettell, or the prominent Judge, Samuel Chew, who all believed in the legitimacy of defensive war.[12] In 1741 we even find Logan urging his coreligionists to withdraw from politics on the grounds that the peace testimony was incompatible with participation in civil government for, in his view, no meaningful difference existed between police action and war in defence of the state. This attitude reflected a view of things very far from that of Quakers like John Kinsey (they were of course also divided in their political allegiance since Logan favoured the Proprietary party). There was, however, consensus in the Society on the importance of its peace testimony: Friends' cherished principle of 'love and unity' needed unanimity on this issue, or at any rate required that dissent such as Logan manifested should be kept within the confines of the Society and not voiced outside its ranks or expressed in any overt act that ran counter to Quaker peace principles.

Governor Thomas now endeavoured to persuade the Assembly to sanction the establishment of a provincial militia and the building of fortifications, especially on the seaward side. He also wanted it to finance the raising of troops and provide money for various military operations. A prolonged debate ensued between governor and assembly which body, seemingly with considerable support from the electorate, remained adamant in refusing to authorise directly either the setting up of a militia or other defence measures. When in the summer of 1740 it finally agreed to pay 'tribute to Caesar' in the form of a grant of £3,000 'for the king's use,' the legislators attached to it a condition which proved unacceptable to the governor; namely, that the indentured servants whom the governor had meanwhile recruited for war service – arbitrarily in the Assembly's opinion – should be restored at once to their former masters. The lengthy controversy that ensued soon got bogged down in a curious amalgam, on the Assemblymen's side, of pacifist and constitutionalist arguments, and ended only two years later. Then, in August 1742 an accommodation was finally reached, and the Assembly's appropriation – '£4,000 to the king's use' – was accepted by the governor, though rather ungraciously.[13] He may have been put out by 'the complete identification of Quakerism with popular rights and legislative privilege' over against the claims of the proprietors and their deputy governor, an identification that remained intact throughout the whole crisis of 1740-42.[14] He could not have been pleased, either, that the Assembly ruled to place its grant at the disposal of the authorities in London rather than in the hands of the governor on the spot.[15]

In July 1745, at the time of the Cape Breton expedition, the Assembly presented Governor Thomas with a grant of £4,000 'for the king's use.' In a message to the governor the legislators explained their attitude as follows: 'Altho' the peaceable principles [held] by divers members of the present Assembly do not permit them to join in raising of men or providing arms and ammunition, yet we have ever held it our duty to render tribute to Caesar.'[16] Again, in the following year when making a similar grant, this time of £5,000, the Assemblymen expressed their reluctance on grounds of conscience to allocate money directly for military ends. As they said: 'Many of us labour under great difficulties when called upon to be concerned in warlike enterprises, such as appear to us inconsistent with the peaceable principles we profess. The only expedient hitherto found to remove these difficulties, hath been, to demonstrate our loyalty and hearty affection to the Crown, by giving a sum of money to the king's use.'[17] On this occasion, however, they did not appoint Friends to spend the money but left it all at the governor's disposition.[18]

The years 1747 and 1748 were marked by fears of invasion on the part of the French and Spanish fleets as well as by enemy privateers. A new crisis, therefore, arose in the relations of Assembly and Executive (whose interim head from the end of May 1747 was Anthony Palmer); it centred primarily on the defence issue over which the two sides remained divided. At the same time Pennsylvania Friends themselves displayed an open division of opinion on the matter – for the first time in the Hanoverian era. Its cause lay deep, in the slow growth of a movement of renewal within Philadelphia Yearly Meeting that, gathering strength, finally led in the middle of the next decade to the withdrawal, on grounds of conscience, of a small body of Friends from the legislature.

During the summer of 1747 and throughout the following winter, pressure mounted among the non-Quaker community for establishing at least a voluntary militia as well as for initiating other measures for the defence of the province. Public leaders like Benjamin Franklin, and clergy like the prominent Presbyterian minister Gilbert Tennent, spoke and wrote on behalf of these measures. There were also some Quakers who sympathised with such efforts, although the overwhelming feeling within the Society, including probably that of a majority of the Quaker Assemblymen, continued to be against giving them official approval. Several spokesmen for the Quaker point of view rallied to defend Friends' peace principles, the most influential of whom was the wealthy patrician John Smith. His pamphlet entitled *The Doctrine of Christianity, as held by the People called Quakers, vindicated: In Answer to Gilbert Tennent's Sermon on the Lawfulness of War* appeared in print on 30 January 1748. In its pages Smith defended his coreligionists' stance on war, while at the same time approving their participation in the magistracy. (He himself was a justice of the peace and had participated in that capacity in judicial proceedings leading to the execution of offenders.) Around this time, too, Philadelphia Monthly Meeting, despite opposition from a few patrician members, took steps to purge its ranks of those involved in arming merchant vessels or in outfitting privateers.[19]

With the spring of 1748 came a heightening of the defence crisis, since many Philadelphia citizens now believed a seaward attack on the city was imminent. In May the Assembly transmitted a message to Palmer and his Council promising, though still not without a certain reluctance, a limited support for such measures as he deemed necessary to enable the province to resist an enemy attack. The legislators asked for mutual tolerance of their divergent views on this issue, while they assured Palmer that they were indeed grateful for the protection the ships of the English navy had given to the trade of the province. Their gratitude, they claimed, did not manifest any disloyalty to the peace principles held by the majority of the Assembly, since that body represented not Quakerism but all the inhabitants of the province irrespective of religious affiliation. Though it was true they felt no confidence in 'such a mode of defence,' they realised others among their fellow citizens felt differently. 'It is difficult for us to express our sentiments; the most of us as well as many others within the province, you know have professed ourselves principled against the bearing of arms; and yet as we enjoy the liberties of our own consciences, we think it becomes us to leave others in the free exercise of theirs.'[20]

So far all defence measures taken – a voluntary militia and batteries along the river – had been privately financed. As Palmer had complained to the commander-in-chief of the British forces at Cape Breton in March, 'we have the misfortune to have an Assembly consisting chiefly of Quakers.' But the mood began to change, so that early in June the Assembly now declared its readiness to support the executive in efforts to protect the civil population and the trade of the province. It was their duty, stated the legislators, to contribute toward this end 'proportionately to our circumstances.' For the first time they showed willingness to give money, hitherto designated for the king's use, directly into the hands of the provincial executive rather than proceeding indirectly through a representative of the Crown.[21]

Meanwhile, at the end of May John Smith, whom we have seen appearing early in the year as an eloquent spokesman for Quaker pacifism and conscientious objection, now reappeared in what at first sight might seem a surprising – indeed a contradictory – role. For, in association with another leading Friend, James Pemberton, he had initiated a subscription to raise funds for defence purposes. Smith designed to hand the money over to the Council to be used as that body thought fit during the existing emergency.

The entry that Smith made on 31 May, the date on which he opened – and closed – his subscription list, is, I think, interesting enough to quote at least in part, for it reveals an aspect of Quaker pacifism that greatly differed from its later visage. Smith then wrote:

> I considered what Friends could do in the present circumstances of things – 5 or 6 privateers at the capes – the Assembly had made no provision for any exigencies of government – and the Council either could or would not borrow money upon the credit of the Assembly's repaying it. I thought if a scheme could be drawn up and reciting what [John] Kinsey the Speaker had said in Council viz. that he believed if they were put to any expense in discharge of what they conceived to be their duty, that an adequate provision would be made by the Assembly, in support of government – and binding the subscribers to fulfil the intent and

meaning of that declaration, it would help to still the clamours and noises of the people and be a means of healing the disturbances at present among us.

But Smith, after consulting a number of Friends who all counselled him against continuing, decided before the day was out to stop the enterprise. It was, he realised 'imprudent, let the intention be ever so good . . . What might be lawful was not expedient.'[22]

We know that Smith, in his pro-pacifist pamphlet had refused to condemn the English government for reliance on arms for the country's defence (for it did not share the peace principles of the Society of Friends), and he was ready as well to concede that government still retained a Christian character and that England might hope God would grant it success in battle. He also defended the compatibility of Quakerism and magistracy. At this juncture he was obviously afraid that the Quaker controlled Assembly's reluctance in a crisis situation to grant the government money would, albeit indirectly, bring the Society into disrepute and alienate the authorities from the idea of Quaker rule. A recent writer has suggested Smith had now changed his position with respect to pacifism and speaks of his 'erratic wanderings' from one stance to another.[23] While his action in May 1748 may have been imprudent, as he soon came himself to believe, because it would have been widely misunderstood outside Quaker circles as a compromise of their peace principles and within the Society would have caused dissension and unease and have destroyed the consensus that Friends had so long and so carefully nurtured on this and other issues, it was not, in my view, inconsistent with the Quaker peace testimony, at any rate as Smith and many of his contemporaries conceived it.

In reality, however, consensus on the peace testimony had already broken down. This became evident when at the beginning of June a country Quaker minister named John Churchman asked permission to address the Assembly, which that overwhelmingly Quaker body granted only with some reluctance. Churchman, a prominent representative of the rising movement of revival within Pennsylvania Quakerism and soon to become a close associate of John Woolman in its work, had, while on a visit to Philadelphia, become increasingly disturbed at the readiness of Quakers there to contribute financially to war. He realised they acted thus out of a feeling of loyalty to the Crown. But for him the peace testimony implied a very different course of action. Put your trust in God, he told the Quaker Assemblymen, and not in 'carnal weapons and fortifications.' Otherwise He will not let you prosper. And, Churchman went on, 'may it with gratitude be ever remembered how remarkably we have been preserved in peace and tranquillity for more than fifty years! no invasion by foreign enemies, and the treaties of peace with the natives . . . preserved inviolate to this day.' It was wrong, he thought, for Friends to water down their witness for peace on the excuse that the province now had a non-Quaker majority that did not share its pacifism. For the latter, he believed, since they realised the peaceable character of the polity in which they had come to settle, would surely show understanding of the Quaker position on war.[24]

The Assembly listened respectfully to the prophetic voice of their rural Friend – and then pursued their accustomed course with regard to the 'reasonable' demands of the state in such a situation. They told the Council, 'as we remember no instances past, so we believe not any such will hereafter happen wherein a suitable provision will not be made in the support of government.'[25] Shortly afterwards, in October 1748, peace was signed at Aix-la-Chapelle and the cloud of war temporarily lifted from both the old and the new worlds.

The spiritual revival within Pennsylvania Quakerism gathered further momentum in the years of peace that followed.[26] Its strength lay in the country Meetings but it drew valuable support from urban Friends as well (witness the saintly Philadelphia Quaker Anthony Benezet). Spiritual renewal brought with it a demand for moral and social transformation that embraced greater simplicity of lifestyle and emphasised the dangers of wealth, even when used circumspectly, and called as well for a reinvigoration of Quaker peace principles. This last demand soon clashed with long accepted views: views, moreover, held by weighty Friends enjoying positions of trust within the Society and often high political office as well. What the reformers stood for was a return to their Society's 'original emphasis on person-to-person relationships rather than political structures.' What they tried to bring home to their coreligionists, a message that was accepted only slowly, was 'that, instead of transforming the world, they had been transformed by a too close accommodation to it.'[27] This accommodation to the world seemed to the reformers to be especially true in regard to the peace testimony. They saw the Quaker witness in this area as one tarnished by evasion and by compromise. The realm of politics and the dominion of truth had proved incompatible entities. Quakers, they felt, must make a choice: withdraw from politics or abandon their heritage as it had been handed down since the Restoration. The reformers believed Friends had no other options.

In recent years historians have usually been extremely critical of the Pennsylvania experiment in Quaker magistracy. This is no longer viewed as a model of applied pacifism, an inspiration and an example for the contemporary peace movement. The critics seem to me to have penetrated deeper than the earlier writers did: Quaker Pennsylvania certainly failed to exemplify Quaker pacifism in action. Yet perhaps something more can be said in favour of the dominant attitude within Pennsylvania Quakerism during this period than is now usually done. The Quaker leaders who succeeded Penn inherited, we must admit, an impossible task, a task that had indeed begun to prove impossible even during the lifetime of Pennsylvania's founder. If the province had been an independent state, the overwhelming majority of whose inhabitants remained Quakers or sympathisers with Quaker peace principles, a pacifist magistracy might perhaps have had some chance of success (though this of course remains a matter of speculation).[28] But with the province subject to the English Crown and forming part of Britain's strategic defence system, and with its Quaker population fairly soon reduced to a minority, the idea of a Quaker pacifist magistracy was inevitably doomed to failure, a failure whose full force was postponed for many decades by 'the tactics of political temporisation.'[29] But not only temporising and the politics of expediency caused this delay. There existed a more positive factor at work here. We have noted the prolonged existence among Pennsylvania Friends of a strong feeling that Quaker rule in that province was something precious, not only for Friends but for the world as a whole, a long lingering belief that the end of the Holy Experiment, however much its holiness had been exposed to the erosion of time, would mean a diminution of God's goodness among men. As James Pemberton wrote to his brother John on 18 November 1752: 'We in this province have been favoured above all the families of the earth.'[30]

However, as far back as 1710 a more realistic view had been expressed by one of the then leaders of the provincial Society, Isaac Norris, Sr.. Norris told Penn that a Quaker-governed Pennsylvania 'must either be independent and [we Quakers] entirely by ourselves' or, if its inhabitants were diluted by those of another faith, the non-Quakers must be immigrants who shared the same views as Friends.[31] The reformers of mid-century drew much the same moral as Norris, the Quaker conservative, had done, but from a situation that from the Quaker standpoint had now deteriorated still further. This moral was, that only political withdrawal could salvage their sinking peace testimony.

CHAPTER X

John Woolman and the Renewal of Pacifism among Pennsylvania Quakers

I

QUAKER PENNSYLVANIA FINALLY CAME face to face with war in the early autumn of 1755. A new situation then emerged with the first Indian attacks on the frontier settlements, and behind the now hostile Indians hovered the danger of French invasion. Thus began the struggle known in the New World as the French and Indian War, the American counterpart of Europe's Seven Years' War that broke out in the following year. For the province's Quakers a second novelty lay in the presence among them of a strong reform movement bent on restoring what they considered the purity of the Quaker ethos. The good name of their Society, the reformers felt, had been tarnished by practices that went ill with the claims Friends made to be following more exactly than other denominations the pristine teaching of Christianity. In no sphere did the reformers think Pennsylvania Quakerism had betrayed its mission more plainly than in that of the peace testimony. One of their first objectives now was to induce the Society to institute a stricter observance of Quaker pacifism and to avoid all action, however sanctified by precedent, that might imply a Quakerly involvement in war. Among leading reformers the name of John Woolman stands out not only because of the saintliness of his character, the simplicity of his lifestyle, and the devotion he gave to the cause of Quaker revival but also because of the impact his writings, and in particular his *Journal*,[1] made on succeeding generations, including non-Quakers as well as Quakers.

A prophetic radical,[2] Woolman succeeded, along with other leading figures in the reform movement like Anthony Benezet, John Churchman, John Pemberton, Daniel Stanton, and the visiting Quaker minister from England, Samuel Fothergill, in arousing the consciences of a creative minority within their Society, even if they were unable to carry the whole membership with them in their effort to detach Quakerism from what they considered to be a harmful involvement in the world of politics and business. Their cause, however, was ultimately to triumph many years later.

Woolman was born in 1720 at Northampton, a rural community near Burlington in New Jersey. He gained a basic education in a Quaker country school, and then lived out his adult life at Mount Holly in the same province, that is, when he was not either on Meeting business in neighbouring Philadelphia or travelling in the Quaker ministry. He died at York in 1772 on a pastoral visit to England. For Woolman, Christianity meant 'universal love' extending to the whole creation, animal as well as human. Our lives, he pleaded, should exemplify the divine love that embraced every living being. More sensitive than most of his fellows to all forms of suffering, and a believer in the equality of humankind, he tirelessly campaigned for a number of humanitarian causes. Peace and antislavery formed his chief endeavours but he also worked for improved relations with the indigenous Indians and for better conditions for indentured labourers. He pleaded with his coreligionists to adopt a simpler and more frugal lifestyle and denounced, in so far as this was compatible with the mildness of his character, the greed accompanying the accumulation of wealth as well as the cultivation of luxury. It was in this human greed he saw the basic cause of war and human strife.

Moreover, Woolman did not remain merely a theoretical critic of the social and moral order; he practised what he preached. The Sermon on the Mount, which he regarded as the quintessence of the Christian spirit, provided the touchstone for all his actions. By its standards violence as well as the quest for riches stood condemned, and one man could not hold another as his slave. In 1743, the year when Woolman was approved as a Quaker minister though only 23 years old, he had refused in his capacity as a conveyancer to write a bill of sale for a black slave. In a moment of vision he saw the evil of slavery even if most of his fellow Quakers, not to speak of his non-Quaker fellow citizens, still perceived nothing reprehensible in that institution. Then, when he found he was growing too prosperous as a retail trader in dry goods (he seems indeed to have possessed considerable business ability), he gave up his shop and maintained himself and family by tailoring and by work on his small family farm. Later he stopped wearing dyed clothing and hats; looking on these as unnecessary luxuries he braved the ridicule that this step entailed, for many of his neighbours regarded the unusual garb he now adopted as eccentric even in a Friend.

Among the reformers it was perhaps Anthony Benezet who came closest to Woolman in character, outlook, and aims. Unlike the birthright Friend Woolman, Benezet was a Quaker by convincement, having arrived in

Philadelphia in 1731 as a lad of 18, a refugee from France along with his Huguenot family. After joining Friends he devoted the rest of his life to promoting a number of philanthropic causes that included antislavery, peace, and the care of the sick: he was active in Philadelphia Monthly Meeting as well as in his Yearly Meeting where he gave strong support to the reformers, and he was tireless in agitating by word of mouth as well as in print for the causes he had at heart. Although a staunch upholder of his Society's peace testimony, he did not approve of the current practice of disowning members who bore arms: he was in favour of tolerance here as in many other areas of behaviour, provided views were honestly held. Friends, he thought, would be 'wiser . . . in allowing some of their members to dissent in the article of defensive war . . . without casting them from their religious care and example.' His fellow reformers, however, for the most part looked askance at such broadmindedness, and a century or more passed before the Society of Friends adopted his position.

Like Woolman, Benezet believed that war, including the conflict being waged in 1755, resulted from human acquisitiveness, from 'the deceitfulness of wealth and honour' that had blinded Pennsylvania's leaders, including many Friends. He held, too, that Quakers were mistaken in thinking it possible 'in times of war . . . to maintain the government and be honest and true to that noble, evangellike testimony which God has given us to bear.'[3] They would have to learn once again how to endure suffering as their forefathers had done. In the crisis that approached, however, he noted that 'many of our Friends begin to rouse from that lethargy in which they have been too long plunged, through a love of this world and [an] endeavour to reconcile those two contraries, the world and heaven.'[4]

Alongside the reformers, led by such men as Woolman and Benezet, the Quakers of Philadelphia Yearly Meeting included two other groups, which recent historians like Sydney V. James and Richard Bauman have described respectively as 'politiques' and 'politicians.' All three groups of course were to some extent overlapping: an individual Quaker's sympathies might switch from one group to another. Whereas the 'politicians' had for the most part abandoned pacifism as a personal creed and retained only a formal link with their ancestral faith, the 'politiques' usually took an active part at various levels in the life of the Society, while at the same time seeking 'to uphold and defend the Society by worldly political means, and with close reference to the partisan arena and to government.'[5] On the war issue the 'politiques,' while nurturing a personal belief in the peace testimony, tended to support the traditional stance of Pennsylvania Quakerdom, which allowed Quakers to vote money, and pay taxes, for military purposes provided this was veiled by the euphemism, 'For the king's use.' If Isaac Norris, Jr., Speaker of the Assembly from 1751 to 1764, was a typical

Quaker 'politician,' the Pemberton brothers, Israel and James, may be taken as representative of the 'politique' position.[6] Events were to show that in fact the 'politiques' were closer to the reformers than to the 'politicians,' for they eventually proved willing to abandon office and withdraw from politics for a time, which the 'politicians,' though desirous of maintaining their affiliation to the Society of Friends, were not ready to do.[7]

Controversy on the defence issue broke out inside Pennsylvania Quakerdom in the spring of 1755. In fact, a crisis over this had long been brewing as the reform movement gathered strength and, though a minority within the Society, began to gain new supporters through the preaching and teaching of its travelling ministers, who were by now active throughout the whole area covered by Philadelphia Yearly Meeting. 'Our Christian testimony,' stated Catherine Payton (a visiting minister from England working closely with the Quaker reformers) in February 1755, 'is against defensive as well as offensive war.' And she noted with apprehension that some Pennsylvania Friends involved in government were not ready to uphold this position.[8] The fact that the Assembly, engaged in a struggle with the proprietors of the province and fearing the latter would take advantage of financial compliance on its part, now claimed the right to supervise appropriation of any monies voted 'for the king's use,' served to increase the alarm felt by the reform Quakers that the Society's peace principles were seriously in danger. Quaker Assemblymen sat on the committee that body had appointed to oversee the manner in which such money was used: thereby they became directly responsible for the purchase of war supplies. In fact, as Marietta remarks, 'the Assemblymen were not rendering to Caesar; they were Caesar.'[9] By claiming the right of appropriation they would have to take an active role in the waging of war: they could no longer shield themselves from this by the ambiguous phraseology that had been employed in the matter hitherto.

A vague unease started to permeate Pennsylvania Quakerdom as the message of the reformers began to percolate through the membership. Dissatisfaction increased with the long accepted view that allowed a limited – though cloaked – Quaker support of the state's warlike activities. A more vigorous and militantly pacifist stance appeared to a growing number of the more sensitive Friends to be the appropriate response to the approach of war on the province's frontiers. Yet undoubtedly the majority of Quakers still clung to the traditional position on this issue; they were reluctant to break with a compromise formula that seemed to preserve the purity of their peace principles, while at the same time allowing them to participate in government and thereby safeguard the heritage of political freedom and religious toleration their province enjoyed under Quaker rule.

The ferment at this time within the Pennsylvania Quaker mind comes out clearly in a letter Philadelphia Quarterly Meeting addressed to the Meeting for Sufferings in London on 15 May 1755. The relevant passages run as follows:

As it is well known that many have voluntarily declined acting in the executive powers of government and some in the legislative as they found themselves incapable of preserving the peace and tranquillity of their own minds and steadily maintaining our Christian testimony in all its branches; and were there a sufficient number of men of understanding, probity and moderate principles proposed for our representatives in whose resolution we could confide to preserve our liberties inviolate, we should be well satisfied to have the members of our Society released from the disagreeable contests and controversies to which we are now subjected. But while arbitrary and oppressive measures are publicly avoided by those who desire to rule over us and our country so heartily calls upon us to maintain the trust committed to us, we cannot . . . judge we should be faithful to them, to ourselves or to our posterity to desert our stations and relinquish the share we have in the legislation . . . Such is the confidence reposed in us that, after the utmost efforts had been used and the pulpit and press exercised against us, our former representatives were at our last election chosen throughout the province by the greatest majority ever known . . . And it is remarkable . . . a set of men conscientiously principled against warlike measures have been chosen by those, of whom the majority were not in that particular of the same principle.[10]

Philadelphia Friends, we see here, were aware of the ambiguous position of Quakers in government – an awareness of course that was in large part the creation of the propaganda of the reform movement bent on sensitising their coreligionists to the requirements of the Quaker ethos in the peace question as in other areas of ethical conduct. Yet at the same time, the writers of the letter drew back from advising a total withdrawal from government, a demand that would soon become a central plank in the reform programme.

In July of the same year General Braddock met with a disastrous defeat at the hands of the French near Fort Duquesne. The Quakers' old friends, the Delaware and Shawnee Indians, now turned against the English and toward an alliance with France. 'With news of the French victory came knowledge that Pennsylvanians were in a war that they would have to fight.'[11] While the Assembly planned to give financial support to Britain's war effort and organise a compulsory militia (with a saving conscience clause of course for Quakers and other religious pacifists),[12] the reform movement among Friends stepped up its activities. As the new governor, Robert Hunter Morris, reported on 28 August: 'All the Quaker preachers and others of great weight were employed to show in their public sermons, and by going from house, the sin of taking up arms, and to persuade the people to be easy and adhere to their principles and privileges.'[13]

The crisis within Pennsylvania Quakerdom reached a climax toward the end of 1755. Commenting on the current situation in the province James Pemberton told the English Friend, Dr. John Fothergill: 'A few months have produced a greater and more fatal change both with respect to the state of affairs in general and among us as a Society than seventy preceding years.'[14] In November the Assembly passed a supplies bill appropriating £60,000 'for the king's use,' the money to be raised by taxation on the inhabitants of the province and its expenditure to be supervised by selected members of the House. Of course everyone knew the funds would be devoted to the prosecution of war. Therefore, while the measure was being debated a deputation of 20 Friends, including the leading reformers and some of the 'politiques' who now began to veer toward the former's stand, presented an address to the Assembly in which they protested in no uncertain terms against both the raising of money for war and its administration by committees on which members of their Society would sit.

While stressing their readiness to pay taxes for peaceable purposes – for example, 'to cultivate our friendship with our Indian neighbours and to support such of our fellow subjects who are or may be in distress,' they declared emphatically they were unwilling to do so when they deemed the purposes to which their taxes would be put were inconsistent with the peace testimony of Friends. In that case, they warned, 'we apprehend many among us will be under the necessity of suffering rather than consenting thereto by the payment of a tax for such purposes.' The imposition of a war tax of this kind they branded as a violation of liberty of conscience, 'for the sake of which our forefathers left their native country and settled this, then a wilderness.' After expressing their sympathy with the Assemblymen's difficulties 'in discharging the trust committed to you . . . in these perilous times,' the authors of the Address concluded with an appeal to the consciences of the still predominantly Quaker legislature and the hope 'you may be enabled to secure peace and tranquillity to yourselves and those you represent by pursuing measures consistent with our peaceable principles' and to trust in God, 'whose providence has heretofore been as walls and bulwarks round about us,' to protect the province in its hour of danger.[15]

The house received the Address with cold politeness: indeed the legislators in their reply made it plain they regarded it as an uncalled-for intervention in affairs of state. They pointed out, moreover, that appropriation of money for the Crown's use was a long established practice which their Society had not censured hitherto. In fact only seven Quaker Assemblymen voted against the supplies bill at its final reading – despite the pleas of the petitioners to have it thrown out. After the supplies bill became law, and with the prospect looming immediately ahead of a tax being collected from the province's inhabitants to provide the military supplies granted therein, Woolman and 20 of his colleagues, including leading reformers like Anthony Benezet, John Churchman, Samuel Fothergill, John Pemberton, Daniel Stanton, and Mordecai Yarnall, issued *An Epistle of Tender Love and Caution to Friends in Pennsylvania*, which was dated 12 December 1755. Since its promulgation marks the initiation of the first major tax refusal movement in the history of the Society of Friends, we shall quote the most significant passages from it in full. The authors of the *Epistle*, among whom Woolman seems to have been the moving spirit, having stated their belief that the gospels taught love of enemies and therefore renunciation of war, went on:

> And being painfully apprehensive that the large sum granted by the late Act of Assembly for the King's use is principally intended for purposes inconsistent with our peaceable testimony, we therefore think that as we cannot be concerned in wars and fightings, so neither ought we to contribute thereto by paying the tax directly by the said Act, though suffering be the consequence of our refusal, which we hope to be enabled to bear with patience.

> And [we take this position] even though some part of the money to be raised by the said Act is said to be for such benevolent purposes as supporting our friendship with our Indian neighbours and relieving the distresses of our fellow subjects who have suffered in the present calamities . . . And we could most cheerfully contribute to those purposes if they were not so mixed that we cannot in the manner proposed show our hearty concurrence therewith without at the same time assenting to, or allowing ourselves in, practices which we apprehend contrary to the testimony which the Lord hath given us to bear for his name and Truth's sake . . . [We trust though] our fidelity to the present government and our willingly paying taxes for purposes which do not interfere with our consciences may justly exempt us from the imputation of disloyalty.[16]

Thus, we see Woolman and his friends objecting here not merely to a tax imposed for a specifically warlike purpose, but to taxation 'in the mixture' when the greater part of it would certainly be assigned to war (as was now felt to be the case). This constituted an innovation; at any rate it reversed the accepted practice of Pennsylvania Quakers and contradicted the position of Quakers in England, who had regularly paid taxes to their government, even though they realised some – not easily calculable – part of what they contributed would be assigned to the use of the military.

I do not think it is clear if Woolman's group envisaged nonpayment of 'mixed' taxes as a general rule and regarded nonpayment as the only acceptable Quaker response even when only a small part was used for war. It is indeed more likely they felt that in the existing political circumstances in Pennsylvania, when the Quaker peace testimony was in their opinion in danger of being obliterated through considerations of expediency and *Realpolitik*, a radical protest was called for that would shake the Society – 'a backsliding people' (in Samuel Fothergill's words) – out of its present torpor and indifference and make it aware of the demands placed on Friends by the peace principles they professed, at least in theory if increasingly less so in practice. Their *Epistle* surely implies doubt whether any substantial part of the present grant would in fact be put to 'benevolent purposes'; indeed its authors appear sceptical if any money at all would be spared for peaceable uses. The reformers, we see, had a very practical aim in view: to arouse Pennsylvania Quakerdom to a serious threat to their peace testimony. They were, then, essentially pragmatists bent on averting the decline of their Society, and not political theorists seeking to formulate a logical basis for tax disobedience.

The proposal to break the law, albeit on grounds of conscience, created much heart searching among Pennsylvania Quakers. For although Friends had traditionally prided themselves on being conscientious lawbreakers and on the sufferings this had entailed, the laws they had broken hitherto were made by those outside their Society and never before by Quaker legislators. No wonder then that views were divided as to the right response to the call of the reformers. Discussion at Philadelphia Yearly Meeting, when it convened in September 1755, had foreshadowed the rift in opinion that displayed itself clearly only after the contents of the *Epistle of Tender Love and Caution* became known to members in December, and the committees appointed by Yearly Meeting to deal *inter alia* with this problem had failed to come to a unanimous decision, with some members urging the payment of the proposed tax and others supporting Woolman and his colleagues in their consistent opposition.

As Woolman wrote in his *Journal*:

Friends thus met were not all of one mind in relation to the tax, which to such who scrupled it made the way more difficult. To refuse an active payment at such a time might be construed an act of disloyalty and appeared likely to displease the rulers, not only here but in England. Still there was a scruple so fastened upon the minds of many Friends that nothing moved it.[17]

The majority of Pennsylvania Friends still clung to the view, hallowed by the authority of George Fox and early Friends, that a Christian, in paying taxes whenever government required them of him, was merely rendering Caesar his due. Such Friends would probably have preferred to be free of this burden not merely for material reasons but also on grounds of conscience, for the situation was undoubtedly troublesome, especially since so many of the revered leaders of the Society advocated refusing payment. Yet the view expressed by William Forster soon after attending Yearly Meeting probably sums up fairly accurately the position of the tax assenters. Forster wrote to John Smith, whose pacifist credentials we have seen were impeccable if of a conservative hue:

> When the Roman Emperor's collectors queried of Peter: Doth your master pay tribute, Peter answered yes . . . and as we understand, the Roman Emperor was at that time in a war, it seems to me difficult, to distinguish between paying the Emperor's tax at that time, and the King's now . . . Render therefore to Caesar the things that are Caesar's and to God the things that are God's.[18]

The Society in Pennsylvania was now split between tax assenters and tax objectors, each claiming to represent the true Quaker position. Before we go on to describe the tax boycott movement, however, something should be said about the role played by English Friends during the crisis which Pennsylvania Quakerism was now undergoing. The London Meeting for Sufferings was especially concerned to mediate the crisis: its motives in this instance, as Marietta points out, 'mixed altruism with personal economic security.'[19] Among the prominent members of that Meeting there figured wealthy merchants like John and Capel Hanbury and bankers like David Barclay, who were nervous of the effect the Pennsylvania crisis might have on the state of public opinion at home. On the one hand, refusal to pay taxes reflected adversely on the integrity of British Friends who had always paid theirs dutifully and without murmuring.[20] It also threatened the material interests of entrepreneurs like the Hanbury brothers, who were deeply involved at this time in the Ohio Company and the defence of Pennsylvania's frontiers against the French. Many English Friends, too, genuinely considered the Pennsylvania reform movement mistaken in advocating such a radical step as tax refusal, which they felt could only prove harmful to the Society on both sides of the Atlantic. On the other hand, Friends in Britain did feel a temporary withdrawal from politics on the part of Pennsylvania Quakers would help to ward off attacks from the proprietary party and its allies grounded on the argument that Quaker pacifism incapacitated any member of the Society from a post in government. When the crisis had passed Quakers would be able to return to power, with renewed strength to uphold the liberty and toleration they had defended successfully in the past. Without a strategic retreat of this kind London Friends foresaw the imposition by parliament of a compulsory oath on all candidates elected to the Pennsylvania Assembly: at any rate such a measure was the declared objective of the Quaker Party's political foes, for these realised an enactment of this kind would effectively exclude all Quakers – even 'defence' Quakers – from the legislature.

As John Fothergill reported to Israel Pemberton on 16 March 1756: 'Though I and many others know that the Assembly is in no way connected with the Society, nor is the Society answerable for their behaviour, yet the multitude here knows no better and therefore throws all the blame, whether just or unjust, that proceeds from any part of the administration in your province entirely upon us as a Society.' And again on 3 April: 'Many here scruple not to assert that Friends will never relinquish their seats in Assembly on any account; others think they will do it cheerfully whenever their country is of opinion that others can serve them better, or that the constitution of their country will be in danger from their persisting to keep them; of this last number I am one, and believe I shall not be disappointed.'[21]

Thus, advice from London Friends, whose authority in that period stood high with colonial Quakerism, pointed in two seemingly contradictory directions. London opposed the reform movement, which had placed political withdrawal in the forefront of its programme, in its refusal to pay the current tax passed by the Quaker dominated legislature, while at the same time calling for the resignation of all Quaker members of that body. Yet the contradiction was only a seeming one, for in each case London's objective was the same – to defend the Society's established position in Pennsylvania from the assaults of the proprietary party and its Anglican and Presbyterian allies. London Friends believed Woolman's group was endangering this position by the extremity of its pacifism while at the same time they considered that Quakers in a wartime Assembly would only stoke the fires of the Society's enemies, since these were convinced that a body dominated by persons calling themselves Quakers was incapable of successfully prosecuting a war (a thesis that unfortunately may not have been entirely correct).

The tax boycott certainly frightened London Friends – or at any rate the well-to-do and conservatively inclined Quakers who presided over the Meeting for Sufferings there. They failed to see – perhaps they did not want to see – any difference between British Friends' position in paying taxes 'in the mixture' to a government in which they had no part, on the one hand, and the position of the Pennsylvania reformers (whose objections were to a military impost voted by an ostensibly Quaker house with the civilian admixture scarcely visible), on the other. And the Londoners evidently felt threatened at home: war tax objectors might appear on the English scene and then the respectability of their Society as well as its good standing with ruling circles might come into question. So London Meeting for Sufferings despatched two emissaries, John Hunt and Christopher Wilson, who were furnished with evidence proving, at any rate to London's satisfaction, the obligation that rested on Friends to pay their taxes, even when the money was used 'for carrying on a war.'[22] The emissaries were also entrusted with the task of inducing as many Quakers as possible to give up their seats in the Assembly, in which area we shall see they had some success. But they made little headway with members of the reform movement, for whom tax refusal soon became a symbol of their drive toward a renewed peace testimony; and the suffering such refusal entailed became for the latter a sign of purification and rejection of material prosperity.

The Pennsylvania reformers, on the other hand, did succeed in winning some support among Friends in the home country, especially in the rural Meetings. In the metropolis where Quaker opinion went strongly against the idea of tax refusal, John Fothergill and, after his return to England in 1756, his brother Samuel, tried to convince Friends of the difference between the situations of English and Pennsylvania Quakers – but without much success.[23] Samuel Fothergill in particular came under attack, for he was considered – rightly – to have been one of the prime movers in the American movement of renewal and in the tax boycott that emerged from it. London Yearly Meeting, despite the efforts of the Fothergill brothers, backed the stand of its Meeting for Sufferings and proclaimed, somewhat pompously, the need of Friends 'for conscience sake' to 'be punctual in the payment of every tribute which we can justly do, without acting in opposition to that sacred illumination bestowed upon us by the Father of light.'[24]

II

Let us now return to trace the steps taken by the tax objectors to implement their protest against what they considered an infringement of conscience. The tax was collected by officials many of whom were Friends, and the full rigour of the law was directed against any who resisted payment. Quaker constables seized the goods of Quaker objectors in distraint, and Quaker justices of the peace confirmed such action – 'in the plain language' used by Friends at that time.[25] Thus the internal unity which the Society had so carefully and so long preserved was now shattered: the sight of Friends confiscating the property of other Friends, who were acting according to the dictates of their conscience, and even threatening them with imprisonment for so doing, distressed all who had the good of the Society at heart and feared that schism might result from this clash of views.

The Society's opponents on the other hand, rejoiced at the dissension created within it by these diverging interpretations of what its peace testimony entailed. After the tax boycott had been in existence for nearly a year, James Pemberton writing from Philadelphia, commented sadly to his English colleague, Samuel Fothergill: 'Our situation is indeed such as affords cause of melancholy reflection that the first commencement of persecution in this province should arise from our brethren in profession, and that such darkness should prevail as that they should be instruments of oppressing tender conscience which hath been the case. The tax in this county being pretty generally collected and many in this city particularly suffered by distraint of their goods and some being near cast in jail.'[26] But Pemberton admitted that tax objecting Friends remained a small minority in comparison with those in the Society who complied with the law and who even censured those who refused to pay. He nevertheless felt the protest was worthwhile.[27]

The radicals indeed soon realised their stance was unlikely to find immediate acceptance among the membership. For, as Woolman said, 'scrupling to pay a tax on account of the application hath seldom been heard of heretofore, even amongst men of integrity who have steadily borne their testimony against outward wars in their time.' But, he argued, unless they took such action, it would be impossible to bring home to their Quaker brethren in office the need to preserve the Society's peace principles in government as much as in private life.[28] In a discussion of tax refusal that Woolman engaged in with a Quaker justice of the peace, he presented his case as follows:

Men put in public stations are intended for good purposes, some to make good laws, others to take care that those laws are not broken. Now if those men thus set apart do not answer the design of their institution, our freely contributing to support them in that capacity when we certainly know that they are wrong is to strengthen them in a wrong way and tends to make them forget that it is so. But when from a clear understanding of the case we are really uneasy with the application of money, and in the spirit of meekness suffer distress to be made on our goods rather than to pay actively, this joined with an upright uniform life may tend to put men athinking about their own public conduct.[29]

Readiness, then, to suffer material hardship of this kind seemed to Woolman the only way still open for supporters of the revival movement to demonstrate their opposition to war and any form of Quaker complicity in waging it.

Philadelphia Yearly Meeting at its fall sessions in 1756 and 1757 attempted to stay neutral on the tax question and thus avoid the much feared split that threatened the Society on this issue. In the latter year, after 'deep exercise' of mind and many hours of consultation, the committee appointed by the Yearly Meeting to consider the question (at which Hunt and Wilson were present) recommended that, 'as we find there are diversity of sentiments, . . . it is not proper to enter into a public discussion of the matter' at the full sessions of the Meeting. 'Friends everywhere' should, however, 'endeavour to have their minds covered with fervent charity towards one another.'[30]

Meanwhile, a second issue, connected with the tax question and almost as controversial, had arisen to further endanger the unity of Pennsylvania Quakerdom. This was the proposal to withdraw, for the time being at least, from provincial politics. As we know, the policy drew support both from the Pennsylvania reform movement and from the London Meeting for Sufferings, though for rather different reasons. Thus, the weight of opinion in Philadelphia Yearly Meeting soon came down heavily on the side of withdrawal, especially as many prominent members of that body (though not those Friends belonging to the movement of renewal) viewed withdrawal merely as a temporary wartime expedient to save the Society from permanent exclusion from the legislature.

During the spring of 1756 feeling against Quakers had risen among the non-Quaker population, who began to hold them responsible for the scalpings and burnings on the frontier perpetrated by the formerly friendly Indians, now allies of France. Up from the country to attend the spring session of his Yearly Meeting, John Churchman records with horror the war frenzy that he found was being aroused in the city. 'Two or three of the dead bodies,' he reports, 'were brought to Philadelphia in a waggon, with an intent as was supposed to animate the people to unite in preparations of war to take vengeance on the Indians, and destroy them: They were carried along several of the streets, many people following, cursing the Indians, also the Quakers because they would not join in war for the destruction of the Indians.'[31] In this situation the association which the popular mind made between Quakerism as a whole and the Pennsylvania government, however incorrect formally, created an unfortunate impression that many Friends felt could only be removed effectively by a thoroughgoing withdrawal from politics.[32] They already had good reasons to urge this policy, and increasing pressure therefore was exerted on Quaker Assemblymen to give up their seats.

On 4 June 1756 six Assemblymen, headed by James Pemberton, resigned from the House giving as their reason both personal conviction as to the incompatibility of their present position with the pacifist principles they held as Quakers and the belief of many of their constituents that their duty as representatives of the people entailed support of warlike measures.

We may well describe the men who now resigned as Quaker 'politiques': they had not hitherto scrupled to vote money for war or demonstrate in other ways their conviction that their Society's peace principles should not prevent them from rendering Caesar his due. In 1755, for instance, James Pemberton had actually 'supervised the buying of grain destined for use by the British troops,'[33] while three among those now resigning had voted for the supplies bill appropriating £60,000 for the Crown's use shortly before giving up their seats. Still, the six reflected the growing influence of the Quaker revival in sensitising Friends to the requirements of their peace testimony,[34] and their action marked a further stage in the rapprochement between reformers and 'politiques.'

After elections were held in October, four more Quakers were persuaded to give up their seats. In this instance at any rate, not so much emerging pacifist scruples as 'orders from London and the two emissaries of London Yearly Meeting' were the decisive factors in bringing about their resignations.[35] However, though Quakers now for the first time became a minority in the Assembly, 12 Friends still remained in the House and refused to yield to the entreaties of their coreligionists on both sides of the Atlantic to give up politics for the time being.

Already in August Speaker Norris had joyfully declared: 'We now no longer lie under the characteristic of an Assembly against all defence and have in truth an inclination to defend the King's colony to the utmost of our abilities.[36] The Quaker Party continued to exist – a party, in Alan Tully's words, that was now 'willing to build forts on the frontiers, raise, equip, and maintain provincial troops, and lay the taxes that these wartime expenditures necessitated.' Whatever the suspicious Scotch-Irish frontiersmen might think of this 'conversion,' and although Quakers as a whole continued to support the party at the polls and even as prominent a 'politique' as James Pemberton returned to the House in 1765, the Quaker element, now a decided minority, ceased to form the core of the party and yielded first place to secular politicians like Benjamin Franklin. Moreover, as R. A. Ryerson has pointed out, henceforward 'the Quaker lawmaker played a diminished leadership role within his own sect; . . . he became . . . a backbencher – or a nonattender – at Friends' major business meetings.' The Quaker Party, until its final demise on the outbreak of the Revolution, did not entirely lose its Quaker colouring: 'politically . . . it was still Quaker in a profound sense.'[37] But the link between Party and Society that existed for decades had been broken by the events of 1756.

As a surrogate for politics we now find Quaker 'politiques' joining hands with Quaker reformers in working for the Indians. Such activity harmonised with the Quaker witness for peace: Friends could carry on privately the cultivation of good relations with the Indians that had now been abandoned by the administration in exchange for hostilities. As Dr. John Fothergill put it, 'Friends . . . are the fittest to transmit business with them. They have sense enough to see that those people who will not take up arms to defend their own, will never by force of arms invade the Indians' property.'[38] The project also attempted, though as it proved not altogether successfully, the kind of philanthropy for which Quakers later became deservedly well known. The Friendly Association for Regaining and Preserving Peace with the Indians by Pacific Measures, which was set up in Philadelphia in the summer of 1756 under the unofficial sponsorship of the Yearly Meeting, continued for nearly eight years until its work, as we shall see, was brought to an end by the Paxton Riots of 1764. Even before that, its promoters had become involved in political controversy and the usefulness of the Association was thus brought into jeopardy. Pacifism and politics, here as elsewhere, proved uneasy bedfellows.[39]

At the Yearly Meeting, held at the end of September 1758, Woolman and his colleagues succeeded in inducing their fellow Quakers to censure Friends who continued to hold offices where they might be required in the course of their official duties to compel members of the Society to carry out 'any act which they may conscientiously scruple to perform.' True, those who refused to resign from such offices would not be excluded from the Society altogether, but they were henceforward regarded as officially ineligible for participation in its business meetings.[40]

The reformers also succeeded in getting Yearly Meeting to condemn Friends who furnished the army with horses and waggons for transporting military supplies: the Assembly had passed in the previous year a law requiring this under penalty of a fine for refusal. It was rural Friends of course who were affected by this law; for Quaker (and other) farmers, supplying waggons with teams to draw them proved quite a lucrative business since the military paid handsomely for such services. The matter was an urgent one, because a number of Friends had fallen in with such demands arising out of General Forbes's expedition against Fort Duquesne in the spring, and further requests of this kind appeared imminent. 'At the same time,' writes Marietta, those Friends involved 'were uneasy about the morality of supplying an army and being paid for it. Because there was no dearth of Quaker magistrates ready to reassure the vacillating owners that supplying wagons and teams violated no Quaker precept, most of them complied.'[41] In these circumstances it was no easy task to put a stop to this practice, even though it had been censured by Yearly Meeting.

In the course of the next six years proceedings were instituted against 32 members for contravening the Society's discipline in this matter, but many delinquents seem to have escaped scot free. In Chester County the Quarterly Meeting complained there were so many offenders that it could not properly deal with them all. Throughout Pennsylvania Quakerdom cases were usually settled privately without open proceedings being instituted in the Meeting, an acknowledgement of regret on the part of the offender being gladly accepted as sufficient penance.[42] Nevertheless, a year later, in 1759, Philadelphia Yearly Meeting was forced to admit that, while 'love and unity in a good degree prevail, though not so generally extensive as desired, the interruption of unity among Friends in Pennsylvania [continues] by reason of the conduct of many in being still concerned in furnishing waggons etc. to carry military stores.'[43] Even though Woolman and his fellow reformers now enjoyed widespread support at Yearly Meeting level, laxer views with respect to the peace testimony obviously continued among many members of the local Meetings. There a majority often demonstrated their sympathies with those Friends who resisted a stricter observance of that testimony than had been customary hitherto, and only yielded with reluctance to pressure from above.

With such lukewarmness toward Quaker pacifism displayed by so many rank-and-file Friends, it is no wonder that, despite the efforts of the revival movement to put new vigour and fresh meaning into the Society's peace testimony, there should still be uncertainty about it, as well as a lack of enthusiasm among some of the younger generation, who saw their elders' evasions and equivocations on this issue. Thus, early in February 1764 there took place what has been well called 'the first massive public deviation from the "peaceable principle"' among American Friends.[44] This occurred during the disturbance known as the Paxton Riots, which began in a small township of that name near Pennsylvania's western frontier. The movement represented an upsurge of anti-Quaker sentiment among the Scotch-Irish-Presbyterian elements there that held the Society responsible for the recent loss of life and property at the hands of hostile Indians; the Friendly Association and especially Israel Pemberton, the leading figure in that body, became a particular target for the animosity of the frontiersmen.[45] Their discontent was then fanned by the Quaker's political and religious opponents in Philadelphia, who accused the Assembly – and by implication Pennsylvania Quakerdom as a whole – of failing to protect the province's frontiers, while at the same time taking care of their own material interests. The cry of Quaker 'hypocrisy' was now heard, not indeed for the first time.[46]

When the 'Paxton Boys' approached Philadelphia, having massacred a number of defenceless Indians before leaving home and now vowing vengeance on the Quakers and death to any Indians whom they might seek to protect,[47] its citizens – and especially its Quakers – became seriously alarmed. Some 200 young Friends, disregarding the official pacifist stance that their Society had always maintained, took up arms, and were joined by a handful of older members.[48] 'Look, look! A Quaker carrying a musket on his shoulder!' cried the street urchins in surprise as they watched one of the fighting Quakers on his way to join an armed company of his coreligionists. In addition, Friends at Germantown allowed armed volunteers to take shelter in their Meeting House during a heavy downpour of rain.[49] This incident, which perhaps was not in itself particularly significant, led an anti-Quaker poetaster to compose the following lines:

> Cock up your hats! Look fierce and trim!
> Nor wear the horizontal brim;
> The house of prayer he made a den
> Not of vile thieves, but armed men;
> Tho' 'tis indeed a profanation
> Which we must expiate with lustration;
> But such the present time requires,
> And such are all the Friends' desires;
> Fill bumpers, then, of rum or arrack!
> We'll drink success to the new barrack![50]

In fact, the expected assault on the city never took place and the Paxton Boys, after presenting a list of their grievances to the provincial administration, went back home without firing a shot. Friends were left both with the task of answering a spate of anti-Quaker pamphlets, which sought to utilise recent events to cast doubt on the sincerity of Friends' peace principles,[51] and with that of dealing with members who had taken up arms. The latter duty was the more serious one, and it occupied several years before it was completed.

The defection of so many Friends of the younger generation administered a salutary shock to the leaders of the Society. True, this defection may have been due mainly to what James Pemberton described as 'the instability of youth,' but it revealed the failure of the older generation to pass on intact its belief in the power of nonviolence and it highlighted the breakdown of the Society's discipline in a moment of crisis. The Quaker witness for peace had been publicly flouted, and its peaceable image had been visibly tarnished in a way that the backsliding of Quaker Assemblymen within the walls of the House had not done. For in that period a Quaker in arms seemed an especially ominous development, at least for those Friends who prized their Society's peace testimony. True, many Philadelphia Friends probably sympathised with the aims of their delinquent young brethren: these had after all taken up arms because they thought this was the only way open to them to defend innocent lives threatened by the advance of the Paxton Boys. But for most Quakers there could be no doubt that steps had to be taken to clear the good name of the

Society that was already coming under attack as a result of the actions of these fighting Friends.

Therefore, in March 1764 Philadelphia Monthly Meeting appointed a Committee of 11 members, including such stalwart reformers as John Pemberton, Daniel Stanton, and Anthony Benezet (who, we have seen, favoured tolerance in regard to divergent views on the peace testimony). For the next few months this Committee laboured hard with the deviants in an effort to convince them of their error in resorting to arms and to persuade them to make acknowledgement of wrongdoing in thus having contravened the discipline of their religious Society. When Yearly Meeting convened in September, the Committee, however, could report only a modest success. Of those who had agreed to discuss their conduct with the Committee (and not all were ready to do this), 'some,' writes Sloan, 'were wavering, but many felt they had acted out of honest convictions at that time, which [for them] was justification enough, while others still maintained that their conduct was unqualifiedly correct. The Committee also mentioned that many of those visited [did] not seem to have a clear idea of the Quaker position on "wars and fighting".'

The Yearly Meeting attempted to dodge the issue, arguing that the problem of officeholding must be satisfactorily solved before the issue presented by the Paxton disturbance could be taken up effectively, for the prospect of Quakers in office promoting war gave a fatal example to the rest of the Society. Philadelphia Monthly Meeting nevertheless continued in its efforts to bring at least some of the delinquents to express contrition for their deviation from the Quaker norm. It was not until October 1767 that Yearly Meeting finally decided that the matter should be closed: Friends, it stated, 'have proceeded as far therein as they found themselves capable under their present circumstances.' In the end no one was disowned, even though some of the deviants refused to toe the line while, on the other hand, some of the pacifist rigorists, especially those from the country Meetings, could scarcely contain their dissatisfaction with so tame a conclusion to the affair.[52]

If dealings with the armsbearing Quakers of 1764 thus ended inconclusively, Yearly Meeting's attempts, backed enthusiastically by Woolman and his fellow reformers, at achieving a total withdrawal of Friends from politics, finished likewise in stalemate. Quakers continued to sit in the Assembly. As late as October 1773 they constituted as much as 43% of that body. Nine months later, on the eve of the Revolution, an outside observer surveying the Assemblymen as they carried on their proceedings, remarked sarcastically: 'Our honourable House made a scurvy appearance . . . it was enough to make one sweat to see a parcel of countrymen sitting with their hats on, in great coarse cloth coats, leather breeches, and woollen stockings in the month of July.'[53]

Pennsylvania Friends as a whole could not perhaps help adopting a somewhat ambivalent attitude with regard to political withdrawal. As Philadelphia Meeting for Sufferings (set up in 1755 on the English model) had reported in March 1761: 'The offers made by the governors of places in the magistracy and the inclination of the people in the choice of their representatives in the legislature have tended to increase the number of the members of our Society in the offices of government.'[54] We know even James Pemberton in 1765 could not resist standing for re-election in order to 'keep out an envious Presbyterian.' Indeed, a strong Quaker presence in the Assembly – or at any rate a majority there which sympathised with the political ideals of Pennsylvania Quakerdom – provided the best guarantee for preserving such ideals intact (they appeared to be menaced by the proprietary party and various anti-Quaker elements in the province).[55] On the other hand, the reformers' view that Quaker politicians supporting military measures, as was now unavoidable at least in wartime, seriously compromised the Society's integrity as a pacifist body had gained cogency as the war proceeded.[56]

In a letter James Pemberton wrote in November 1763 to a friend in London, he referred to 'the uneasiness . . . arising from the scruple some Friends have, of paying the provincial tax, while others hold offices in the government in the execution of which they subject their brethren to sufferings on that act.'[57] By that date the position with regard to the tax objectors was already beginning to ease. But the reformers kept up the pressure for withdrawal even after hostilities were finished: the *débâcle* over the Paxton Riots only added fuel to their arguments. Yet even then Yearly Meeting failed to issue an unambiguous condemnation of Quaker participation in government. Persuasion in favour of withdrawal might be exerted, but there were to be no disownments – or even any individual dealings of the kind that were applied in the case of those Quakers who had actually taken up arms during the Paxton disturbances.[58]

The movement for revival succeeded in reinvigorating the peace witness of Pennsylvania Quakerdom, though it was not able to achieve all it wished to accomplish in this direction. A total severance between Quakerism and government came only as a result of the Society's experiences during the Revolution. Then Woolman gained as it were a posthumous triumph: the character of the American Society of Friends was transformed and remodelled according to the image the Pennsylvania reformers had held up to their coreligionists as an ideal. In respect of the peace testimony the reformers had urged a new view of its obligations based on their understanding of the New Testament, and in particular of the Sermon on the Mount and of what it implied for the Quaker ethos. In that sense they were innovators.[59] At any rate, they denied the validity both of the prevailing opinion in the prestigious Meeting for Sufferings in London that went back to Fox's time and of the prevailing practice of Pennsylvania Friends for over half a century. But for Woolman and his associates prestige and precedent counted for nothing if they believed these ran counter to the voice of conscience and the spirit of the gospels.

CHAPTER XI

The Quaker as Magistrate in Colonial Rhode Island

THE QUAKER CONTROLLED GOVERNMENT ruled Pennsylvania from the foundation of that province in 1682 down to the crisis year of 1756. A Quaker magistracy may also be found functioning in several other provinces of colonial America, though for briefer periods and never in complete control. There was a Quaker presence, we have seen, in New Jersey at the very beginning. Moreover, in North Carolina, for instance, a Quaker squire from England named John Archdale had held the governorship between 1694 and 1696, and around this time too Friends occupied 'half of all the seats in the Assembly.'[1] Quakers remained active in the politics of that province well into the next century. Despite initial persecution Quakers had also participated in early Maryland politics on a local level, accepting office as justices of the peace and sheriffs. They sat in that province's Assembly, though they formed a minority there. In the mid-1680s, however, they withdrew altogether from political life, due to their increasing reluctance to take the oath of office. But before that time Quaker politicians had taken part in the work of such bodies as the 'Committee of Security and Defence'; possibly, though, their presence there was in part due to a desire to protect their coreligionists from the full rigour of militia conscription,[2] which in Maryland had previously been enforced against Quaker objectors with considerable harshness.

Apart from Pennsylvania, the province where the Quaker input into politics was greatest was Rhode Island. There 'Quaker governors held office for thirty-six terms,'[3] and Friends sat in considerable numbers both in the Governor's Council and in the provincial Assembly, occupying, as well, a whole array of subordinate government offices from that of Deputy-Governor and Provincial Treasurer at the top down to the village constable's.[4] As in Pennsylvania, the Quaker magistrates of Rhode Island had to face the problem of war and the impact of their Society's peace testimony on their position in government. But the reaction of Quaker politicians in the two provinces differed, and these differences, we shall see, stemmed from the differing structure of Quaker politics in each area.

The first Quaker converts in Rhode Island had included some of the religious exiles who left the intolerant atmosphere of Puritan Massachusetts determined to set up a polity of their own, in which diverse religious views would enjoy freedom of expression, where conscience would not be pressed into the mould of religious conformity, and where those who wished to do so would be able to follow the promptings of the inner spirit. Such men and women formed a suitable seed-bed for Quakerism; some had already rejected war on principle and refused the taking of oaths in true Quaker style. While not all of them joined the new movement, many of them did so: by the end of the 1650s we find future Quaker political leaders in Rhode Island, like Henry Bull, William Coddington, Caleb Carr, Walter Clarke, Joshua Coggeshall, and John and Nicholas Easton, already members of the Society.[5] They and their like, substantial citizens living for the most part in Newport where in the course of time they built fine mansions for themselves and practised a life-style similar to that of the Quaker grandees of Philadelphia, formed an elite within the Society. As such, they sometimes clashed with the country Friends, mostly farmers and craftsmen of 'the middling sort,'[6] who were centred in the rural districts on the mainland.

Rhode Island had gained its charter from Charles II in 1663, and already we find Quakers like Nicholas Easton and Caleb Carr holding prominent positions in government. Two wars against the Dutch ensued in 1664-7 and in 1672-4: New Amsterdam, the centre of Dutch power in the New World, being situated not far from Rhode Island meant close involvement in warlike action for the latter. This warlike situation was compounded by the fact that England's enemies possessed allies among the Indian tribes of New England, who provided an additional threat to the colony's security. Easton occupied the office of Deputy-Governor for the latter part of the First Dutch War and he was Governor throughout the second war against the Dutch. Clearly he felt his Quakerism should not impede his participation in defensive measures undertaken during wartime. In May 1667, for instance, we find Easton as Deputy-Governor, along with three other Friends, accepting appointment to a committee for raising money for the defence of Newport and for 'mounting the great gun . . . in order to prevent such mischiefs and miseries as may happen for the want of the same.'[7]

A similar situation occurred during the war of 1672-4: Easton was now Governor and William Coddington Deputy-Governor, with Walter Clarke, a leading light among Newport Friends, and other Quakers occupying prominent posts in the wartime provincial administration. The nomination of commanding officers and militia captains rested with the Governor and his assistants, who were made up for the most part of active Quakers. The Assembly in its emergency legislation of 1673 (for a combined Dutch and Indian attack were considered to be imminent) also required the provincial administration to give its military commander 'special and particular directions as the danger shall then occasion, for the safety of the whole.'[8] Payment of troops mobilised in Rhode Island to carry on the war lay in the hands of another Friend, Peter Easton, who was Provincial Treasurer: he was responsible for the distribution of pensions to wounded soldiers as well as to families of those killed in battle. As Arthur Worrall aptly remarks: 'Perhaps to ease the conscience of Quaker members of government . . . the Assembly [in 1673] also passed the most favourable law for pacifists in seventeenth-century New England':[9] a law that we have already discussed in an earlier chapter.

Two years later the long expected Indian attack was launched by the chieftain known to history as 'King Philip.' Before hostilities broke out, the Quaker politicians had attempted to negotiate with King Philip, to whom they proposed an arbitration of the issues dividing the two sides. John Easton, the colony's Deputy-Governor, who headed the deputation sent to the Indian headquarters, explained to King Philip 'that our desire was that the quarrel might be rightly decided in the best way, not as dogs decide their quarrels.' 'Fighting was the worst way,' the Indians agreed, 'but they inquired how right might take place without fighting. *We said by arbitration.* They said by arbitration the English agreed against them, and so by arbitration they had much wrong.' In the end the Indians' sense of wrong done them by the white man prevailed over the genuine concern of the Quaker politicians to avoid war through a negotiated settlement. A week later King Philip attacked.[10] The outbreak of war, however, did not lead to the resignation of the Quaker politicians from government: they evidently thought their duty lay in another direction from that taken later by the Pennsylvania Quaker Assemblymen who resigned their seats in 1756.

At this point we may note that most of the Quaker politicians of Rhode Island stood at the centre of their local Society's life. Their role was not marginal, as was the case with some of the Quaker politicians who continued in the Pennsylvania Assembly after 1756 sitting loose to the peace testimony and in effect often little more than nominal Friends. But we know that Governor Coddington, for instance, lived on intimate terms with George Fox when the latter came to New England, and Fox does not appear to have disapproved of his political activities. Moreover, Newport Friends availed themselves of the Governor's large mansion to hold their Meetings regularly in its salon. While Fox was visiting, it was there that New England Friends held their Yearly Meeting.[11] According to Rufus Jones, John Easton, Caleb Carr, and Walter Clarke, all leading members in one capacity or another of the wartime administration in the colony, 'were among the foremost spiritual leaders of the Quaker Society during the period of their political activity. Easton and Clarke were ministers of the gospel and frequently went forth on public religious service.'[12] In early April 1676 Walter Clarke, shortly before being elected Governor, wrote to the citizens of Providence:

> Only this for your present encouragement: we well approve your advice and willingness to maintain a garrison, and have agreed to bear the charge of ten men upon the Colony's account, till the succeeding authority take further order, and that you may take four of our men to strengthen you, or if it be wholly by yourselves, we, as above said, will bear the charge of ten of them, and after the election, if those concerned see cause, and the colony be of ability to do it, I shall not obstruct, if it be continued all the year. Be pleased to dispatch our ketch. I have no more to you but my kind love and desire of your peace and safety as my own.[13]

Heavy Quaker involvement in government continued in Rhode Island into the second decade of the 18th century; and during much of this time the colony stood on a war footing. England's major enemy, however, was no longer Holland now but the France of Louis XIV. I would refer the reader to Rufus Jones's account for further details concerning the succession of Quaker governors and other high ranking administrators of Quaker persuasion whom their fellow citizens regularly elected to office. Despite allegations that Quaker rulers were incapable of carrying on an effective defence policy, the inhabitants of Rhode Island, a growing majority of whom were non-Quakers, do not seem to have suspected them of pacifist softness. Indeed we find John Easton, son of Nicholas, one of the founding fathers of Quakerism in the colony, during his governorship from 1692 to 1695 in the forefront of the struggle to keep control of the militia in the province's hands against the encroachments of Crown officials. Quakers, like Walter Clarke for instance, staunchly upheld the rights of their province against the claims of the mother country, as in the struggle to maintain the privileges granted in its charter: undoubtedly this was a factor in winning widespread popularity for the Quaker politicians throughout Rhode Island.

Clarke's death in 1714 brought to an end the first period of Quaker participation in Rhode Island government. 'Clarke,' writes Jones, 'had been four times elected governor, and twenty-three times deputy-governor, dying in the office to which he had been fifteen times *successively* elected.'[14] During the half century and more when these Quakers, many of them active and highly respected members of their Meetings, conformed in their political roles to the exigencies of military policy, voices of dissent within Rhode Island Quakerism, though muted, had not been entirely silenced.

The English Quaker minister, William Edmundson, who paid a visit to Newport in 1676 at the end of King Philip's War, has recorded in his *Journal* the uneasiness of Friends in the area generated by the atmosphere of hatred and fear surrounding them, with 'the people who were not Friends . . . outrageous to fight.'[15] But before 1700, opposition among Quakers to the military aspects of political life in which their coreligionists participated, still remained weak.

Moreover, when in 1702 the War of the Spanish Succession broke out, and Friends feared the imposition of 'a lay or tax' by the provincial government to finance the construction of fortifications and other warlike enterprises, the Quaker community was in a quandary. Some Friends thought it would be right to pay and others that it would not be, for the object of such a tax they fully realised 'was for carrying on a vigorous war against France.' Another visiting minister from England – John Richardson – was in the colony at this time attending the sessions of New England Yearly Meeting in Newport. Richardson, being appealed to for his opinion, felt the behaviour English Friends followed in such matters should not serve as a precedent for colonial Quakers, whose situation differed greatly from that of the mother country where Friends remained unrepresented in government. In Rhode Island, on the other hand, Richardson thought the powerful Quaker interest might even succeed in averting the imposition of a war tax. (In fact, we may note, the deputy-governor at this time was our old friend, Walter Clarke, while his nephew, Samuel Cranston, held the governorship and, though not himself a Quaker, was extremely sympathetic to the Society of Friends.) Whereas, according to Richardson English Friends paid such taxes, though often with an uneasy conscience, 'there is a great disparity between our circumstances and yours here.' Therefore, he told the Meeting, 'mind your own way in the truth, and look not out' for a solution to a problem that only those on the spot could find.[16]

Dissatisfaction, however, with the close association of some leading Friends with government's military functions continued to simmer. We do not know how strong such feelings were; they seem to have been stronger among the country Quakers on the mainland than among affluent Friends of Newport, though it might be hard to demonstrate this assertion with reliable statistics. In 1709 discontent of this kind broke out openly in the provincial Assembly when three Quaker members – William Anthony, Jacob Mott, Jr., and Ebenezer Slocum – denounced Quaker involvement in warmaking activities since, as they stated, this was clearly 'contrary to our principles.'[17]

A new period of Quaker participation in Rhode Island politics, though no longer on the scale of the previous century, began in the mid-1730s and lasted down to the Revolution. It is associated with the name of the Wanton family, Quaker shipbuilders whose rise to wealth and political prominence begins early in the 18th century. The Wantons soon came to be numbered among the Newport grandees, whose Quakerism did not prevent them from adopting the life-style of their prosperous non-Quaker neighbours. John Wanton, elected governor in 1733 in succession to his brother William, who had early left Friends to join the Church of England,[18] was throughout his public career an active and dedicated member of his Meeting. 'He early developed a powerful gift in ministry, and devoted much of his time to religious service, preaching both in the home Meeting at Newport and travelling far and wide to deliver his messages when he felt called to go forth.'[19] A confrontation nonetheless eventually developed between him and his coreligionists over his complicity as a politician in the warmaking aspects of government, including the issuing of military commissions and the enlistment of troops, both of which activities became an important part of his duties after England became involved in war in 1739 and the long period of peace under Walpole's guidance at last came to an end.

Next year Wanton had come under attack in his Meeting for his warlike activities as governor. However, he stubbornly defended his conduct arguing that his official position required him to take steps to defend the lives and liberties of the people who had elected him. 'I have endeavoured,' he told the Committee appointed by his Meeting to interview him in the matter, 'on all previous occasions, as on this, to do my whole duty to God and to my fellow-men, without doing violence to the law of my conscience, but in all concerns listening to the still small voice of divine emanation and being obedient to it.' In other words, his Quaker conscience dictated behaviour opposed by the consciences of his fellow Friends, and he claimed the right to follow the course of action he himself believed to be correct. Eventually, with the approval of New England Yearly Meeting, the Governor was excluded from sitting on Meeting Committees, though he was never actually disowned. He died in 1742.

Why at this particular moment Rhode Island Friends as a whole became unusually sensitive regarding the implications for their Society's peace testimony of Quaker participation in government is not altogether clear, for, as Worrall points out, neither before nor after did Monthly Meetings in the colony think of censuring 'political leaders who had modified their pacifism.' Perhaps it was because during the long years of peace they had grown unaccustomed to their Quaker politicians entering so closely into the military aspects of government: these last protruded less obviously into public view in peacetime than they did now that war had come again to the colony. But Worrall suggests another reason – 'that someone within the Monthly Meeting was evening an old score' – since Wanton had aroused ill feeling among some wealthy Quakers by his support of a land bank.

Nevertheless, the proceedings against so weighty a Quaker as John Wanton show a strong sentiment persisted within Rhode Island Quakerdom against the complicity of prominent members in war. A sizeable number of Friends must have resented this as a serious compromise of their peace principles, even if their discontent seldom found a voice; otherwise the 'dealings' against Wanton could scarcely have got under way since personal grudges against the Governor, if indeed they were present in the affair, would surely have been insufficient to generate such powerful feelings against a man of Wanton's reputation and influence.[20]

However, pacifist sentiment of this kind does not seem to have found its head again before the outbreak of the Revolution. John's nephew, Gideon Wanton, for instance, who held the governorship for two terms between 1745 and 1748, acted while in office in precisely the same fashion as his uncle, issuing military commissions and providing money for the forces. He was responsible, too, for despatching troops for service in the expedition against Cape Breton Island in 1745. And yet he remained unchallenged in his role as an active member of Quaker Meetings for business and worship.[21] Or take the case of Richard Partridge. Partridge was an American-born convert to Quakerism, who lived most of his adult life in England where he became a Quaker minister and a member of the Meeting for Sufferings. His connection with Rhode Island stemmed from his appointment in 1715 as the colony's London agent, a post he held until 1759. 'He was always called upon in times of war to arrange the quotas and contributions which Rhode Island was to furnish.' After the expedition against Cape Breton Island had been successfully carried out, it was Partridge who was entrusted with the delicate task of extracting financial compensation from the British Treasury to reimburse the province for its expenses in that connection. 'He finally succeeded in getting an appropriation of £6322 : 12 : 10, which was precisely the amount which the colony claimed.'[22] And, again, what about Thomas Richardson, who acted as clerk of New England Yearly Meeting 'for over three decades before 1760'? He combined this office, among the most influential within the Society of Friends, with that of Treasurer of the Rhode Island colony during the Seven Years War. In the latter capacity, Worrall remarks, 'nothing seems to have hindered his handling of funds specifically designated for military use or from continuing as Yearly Meeting clerk until 1760, five years after Friends had begun to reform the Society.'[23]

Lastly we may look briefly at the prerevolutionary career of Stephen Hopkins of Providence and its implications for the pacifism of Rhode Island Quakers. Hopkins, whose mother was a Friend, joined Quakers only in 1755 when he was already 48 years old. In that same year, having had a long career in provincial politics, he was elected governor and between then and

1768 served altogether nine terms in that office, over half of this period being occupied by war. In the 1750s Hopkins was active in the colonial Congress movement, and during the years leading up to the Revolution he played a prominent part in the efforts of the colonial 'patriots.' We need not be surprised that, like his Wanton predecessors in the governor's palace, he made no attempt to adjust his political practice to the requirements of his Society's peace principles. Though in 1773 Hopkins was disowned, this was for unwillingness to free a woman slave and not in connection with any failure to observe the peace testimony.[24]

Yet, despite Friends' continued tolerance of 'belligerence' on the part of such prominent members of the Rhode Island Society as Stephen Hopkins or Thomas Richardson, the contemporary pacifist renewal generated inside Philadelphia Yearly Meeting by John Woolman and his fellow reformers does seem to have made some impact in the sister colony. Fairly soon, echoes of the reformers' position may be discovered there, too. In 1757, for instance, we find five Quaker members of the Rhode Island Assembly publicly acknowledging they had been wrong in voting for the imposition of a levy for war: this, they declared, was inconsistent with their Society's principles.[25] Nevertheless, despite such demonstrations of a growing sensitivity on the part of Rhode Island Quakers to the demands of their Society's peace testimony, it was only after the outbreak of the Revolution that they arrived at a full realisation of what that testimony implied in the way of a collective witness. Only then did the overwhelming majority of them view the appearance of Friends in public offices carrying serious military obligations as clearly inconsistent with Quaker principles.

The relationship existing in this period among Rhode Island Quakers between their peace testimony and the participation in politics of leading members of their Society possesses special features not present either in contemporary Britain or in colonial Pennsylvania or in the remaining American colonies. We may well ask how it came about that Rhode Island Friends (like Quakers elsewhere) 'dealt with' and, if such dealings proved fruitless, finally disowned the humble Quaker apprentice or simple farm lad who consented to bear arms either voluntarily or when called up for compulsory service in the militia, and yet, when it was a question of some Newport grandee or politician-*cum*-Quaker minister, who agreed in his official capacity to recruit troops, raise war taxes, and commission highranking military officers, then, with the single – and somewhat equivocal – exception of Governor John Wanton in 1740, Friends took no disciplinary action whatsoever and continued, it would seem happily, to entrust the religious concerns of their Society to these men, whose political activities were clearly at variance with the pacifist ethos professed by Quakers since at least 1660.

In England Friends, since the latter part of the Commonwealth era, had withdrawn from all direct participation in political life: the Stuart Restoration made such nonparticipation obligatory for them, and it was not until the second quarter of the 19th century that British Friends returned to the political arena. In colonial America such nonparticipation prevailed for the most part, too. Under these circumstances, the kind of tension that we have seen existing in Rhode Island Quakerism between peace principles and political participation could scarcely arise. In Pennsylvania, where we know Quakers ruled the province from 1682 to 1756, the tension we have just spoken of, while it was indeed present, took a rather different form. In that province there was no militia and no military conscription, and therefore there were no conscientious objectors and (except at moments of crisis as during the Paxton Riots of 1764) no Quaker volunteers for military service. We have seen, moreover, that Quaker Pennsylvania dealt with the question of military appropriations by a series of subterfuges that sometimes amounted to guile. Evasion of the issue in this way was not possible in Rhode Island. For in Rhode Island Quakers never formed more than a significant minority of the colony's inhabitants, and no political geometry existed in their favour there. Yet they constituted a sufficiently powerful section of the population for them to gain a decided influence on provincial politics.

To George Fox and most early Quakers the magistracy had appeared to be an institution created to fulfill God's will on earth. Its aims were divinely set and designed to safeguard human welfare, even if its methods in pursuing such benevolent goals were not always those of 'the people of God called Quakers.' Quakers, therefore, never – or almost never – ruled out entirely the possibility of a Quaker role in politics. But in a polity where Quakers formed a minority (and this was the case everywhere except for Pennsylvania in its earliest phase), could a Quaker, if he entered government, refrain from the use of force either for maintaining internal order or for repelling external aggression? The answer, at any rate during the period with which we are dealing, could only be no. In the circumstances surrounding government in colonial Rhode Island it is difficult to envisage how a Quaker administrator could have pursued a pacifist policy that was clearly in contradiction to the views of the majority of the electorate. Here pacifism and political office appear to be irreconcilable. That this was not clear to Rhode Island Quakers may appear strange. The key to this puzzle lies in what Sydney James has called 'the easygoing assumption . . . that a Quaker could hold office with a serene conscience as long as he had nothing to do with oaths or compelling men to serve in war': an assumption that prevailed until the Revolutionary years.[26]

With respect to military compulsion, we have seen that since 1673, despite changes in the law, Quakers and other pacifists in the province had enjoyed practical exemption both from the militia and from fines imposed in lieu of such service. Though we do not know much about the background leading to such a generous measure of exemption for conscientious objectors, it must have been due, at least in part, to the Quaker presence in government. Thus, it looked as if the purity of Quaker peace principles would be preserved, and at the same time, hopefully, the leaven of Quakerism could begin to permeate provincial politics through the mediacy of those Friends – many of them leaders of their religious Society – who had accepted the tasks, including the military burdens, of the magistrate's office. But such hopes proved ungrounded. There is little evidence that in the long run the Quaker politicians of Rhode Island made any significantly Quaker impact on the politics of their province. There is every reason, on the other hand, to think that these conscientious Quaker magistrates, carrying out faithfully all the military tasks their office imposed on them, served after all only to discredit the peace testimony which their coreligionists nurtured so carefully in the separate enclosure of their Society's life.

CHAPTER XII

Quaker Conscientious Objectors
and the American Revolution

THE AMERICAN REVOLUTION MARKED the end of an epoch for Friends on this continent. The new era in their history began with a decisive break with Quaker involvement in government: thereafter, Friends lived more withdrawn from the society that surrounded them than they had done hitherto. This was especially true in Pennsylvania and Rhode Island. Quaker pacifism, as it had been reshaped by the reform movement of mid-century, gathered renewed strength from the trials Friends underwent during the war years. During the Revolutionary War indeed all members of the Society who remained loyal to its peace principles became in a way conscientious objectors, and not only male Quakers of military age. For the Society then objected collectively not only to fighting, whatever the cause, but to any change of government achieved by violence rather than by consent, and it resisted being forced to abandon its cherished allegiance to the British monarchy that such a change involved. With the outbreak of hostilities, therefore, not only the Society's peace testimony but the Quaker's *Obrigkeitsdoktrin* was at stake.

During the decade of revolutionary gestation that preceded 1775 Friends were active in opposing what they, along with many others in the colonies, considered to be arbitrary acts of the British Crown. This was true, for instance, of the well-to-do Quaker merchants of Philadelphia; they had been especially hard hit financially by the Stamp Act of 1765. Some 40% of the signatories to the nonimportation agreement that was organised in Philadelphia to protest against this measure came from the Quaker community.[1] The same elements within the Society two years later opposed with equal vigour the Townshend Acts that also attempted to raise money in the colonies for revenue purposes, despite the fact that the colonists had no part in framing such legislation. The colonial movement of resistance was at this time still largely nonviolent, though most participants viewed

142

nonviolence as a pragmatic technique for redressing grievances deemed the most effective one in the existing circumstances: only for Quakers were there religious or ethical underpinnings.[2]

As violence increased on the patriot side and the threat of separation grew, so Quaker suspicion mounted and Friends, especially those concerned for the Society's reputation as a pacifist body, became more and more reluctant to see their coreligionists participate in the resistance movement, even if the country's ties of loyalty to Britain remained as yet unbroken. 'The employment of economic sanctions [to obtain redress of colonial grievances] had at first seemed to be a plausible device . . . [But] many Pennsylvania Friends, and to a certain degree other colonial Quakers, were becoming convinced that the constitutional connection with Britain must be maintained as a bulwark against the overturn of the political and governmental status quo.'[3] As early as 1770 Philadelphia Yearly Meeting had warned its members against participation in those activities aimed at 'asserting or maintaining their civil rights and liberties, which are frequently productive of consequences inconsistent with . . . our peaceable testimony.' They should avoid associating too closely with any 'who are not convinced of our religious principles.' Next year the Meeting for Sufferings declared one of its chief tasks now to be 'to guard our brethren against any attempts to contend for civil liberty, or privileges, in a manner unbecoming our peaceable profession.' The message was clear: Quaker reformers had united with former Quaker 'politiques' to proclaim the need for the Society to stand clear of all action that might lead to armed resistance to England. While the reformers took this stand chiefly for fear the peace testimony might be endangered, the politiques' main concern lay in averting the overthrow of the existing political order in Pennsylvania which they supposed – correctly – a victory of the radicals would bring about.[4] But with each group motives were mixed: pacifism and political allegiance to the monarchy mingled inextricably in most Friends' minds so that ultimately they became in effect what we may call 'passive loyalists.'[5]

In December 1773 open violence erupted in the famous Boston Tea Party. The dispute between mother country and colonies increased in rancour, and Quaker leaders became increasingly concerned about members who co-operated closely with the political radicals and their various committees and associations.[6] When early in September 1774 the First Continental Congress met in Philadelphia, it was dominated by patriots who clearly would not baulk at violence if they considered this necessary to achieve their goals. There were some Friends – and near Friends – among the Congress's members, and soon these found themselves disowned by the Society unless they had already severed their link with it voluntarily. In the following January Philadelphia Yearly Meeting, expressing the standpoint of other Yearly Meetings on the continent, made its position clear with respect to the impending conflict. 'To fear God, honour the king, and do good to all, is our indispensable duty,' it announced at the same time as it called on Friends 'to discountenance and avoid every measure tending to excite disaffection to the king, as supreme magistrate, or to the legal authority of the government.' Any attempt to overthrow these institutions constituted a 'usurpation of power': Quakers, therefore, might have no part in such an undertaking. A year later, in their 'Ancient Testimony and Principles of the People called Quakers', issued on 20 January 1776, Pennsylvania Quakers declared even more emphatically their loyalty to the monarch and their 'abhorrence' of actions designed to sever the colonies' connection with Great Britain.[7] With the adoption of the Declaration of Independence on 4 July 1776 the breach between American Quakers and American patriots became complete.

Meanwhile, English Friends had watched with growing alarm the alienation of their coreligionists across the Atlantic from the supporters of the Continental Congress. They felt this to be an impediment to their own efforts to mediate the dispute, for it reflected on the neutrality they themselves attempted to preserve in the quarrel. They were striving above all to get the British government to pursue a more liberal policy in the face of colonial demands, and they felt the attitude of American Friends made their task more difficult. As Dr. John Fothergill, more of a radical perhaps than most members of London Yearly Meeting, told his Philadelphia friend, James Pemberton, in a letter dated 17 March 1775: 'Mind your own business and neither court unworthily the favour of your superiors on this side nor oppose with vehemence the party which steps forward in the protection of your liberties which are all at stake.' It was the latter side, he emphasised, which expressed 'the general voice of America': submission to this party, therefore, as 'the prevailing power must be your duty.'[8] Such warnings, however, failed to dissuade the leaders of Pennsylvania Yearly Meeting, followed – sometimes a little reluctantly – by the other American Yearly Meetings, from pursuing a collision course with the new régime.

There were naturally some Friends who took a less hostile view of the cause of independence. One of them was Moses Brown, the wealthy Rhode Island merchant who played a leading role in New England Quakerdom.[9] Even within Philadelphia Yearly Meeting, where eventually opposition to the colonial cause proved most adamant, there were a few prominent members who adopted a different line: Fothergill's friend, James Pemberton, for instance, or John Reynell who still spoke of the home government's 'oppressive measures' and 'unrighteous laws,' or David Cooper, perhaps the most positive in his assessment of the American cause. A short time after the Declaration of Independence, Cooper in his diary had expressed his belief 'that Providence was bringing about some [great] event . . . and that . . . he would establish the freedom of America, and that she would never be again in subordination to England.'[10] Nevertheless, the prevailing sentiment not only among Pennsylvania Quakers but throughout the whole Society on this continent supported the stand taken by Philadelphia Yearly Meeting, which finally in September 1776 came out unambiguously against Quaker participation in any public office – administrative, executive, or legislative – that was even remotely connected with war making.[11] This stand had the support of surviving members of the revival movement leadership, men like Anthony Benezet and John Pemberton, as well as of many former Quaker 'politiques.' For it was not merely an expression of political opposition to a change in government, it clearly stemmed from the basic Quaker revulsion from violence.

Was the average American Friend a loyalist – 'a Tory' – or, we may ask, would it be more correct to describe such a person as a neutral? There has been considerable debate on this question.[12] I think in one sense most Quakers were indeed loyalists. Certainly loyalism is a characteristic of the numerous wartime documents put out by the official organs of American Quakerism. We have seen this already in several key statements of the Philadelphia Yearly Meeting. Or take 'The Address of the People called Quakers on Rhode Island in Monthly Meeting assembled,' which they drew up on 2 January 1777 for presentation to the British general, Henry Clinton, who was in command of the forces then occupying the island. In it Quakers describe themselves as 'We the King's peaceable and loyal subjects . . . such who have not deviated from their allegiance to the King.'[13] There could be no ambiguity here on which side Quaker sympathies lay. At the same time it is true that, even though Quakers viewed the Revolutionary cause as a rebellion against legitimate authority, they strove as religious pacifists to remain neutral with regard to the fighting. They tried to remain, as it were, 'above the battle,' and they consistently rejected any attempt from the British side to enlist them actively or passively in the struggle against the Revolutionary cause.[14] They would really have liked just to have been left alone, as the German peace sects in America wished too. But this was not possible. Instead, the Revolutionary period proved a time of troubles for the Society of Friends when their peace principles were indeed severely tested. As New England Quakers put it, 'We have enlisted ourselves as soldiers under the Prince of Peace, must wear his uniform and march according to his step.'[15]

Collectively, then, the American Society of Friends maintained its peace witness intact throughout the Revolution.[16] We must now turn to consider briefly Friends' response to the various pressures put on them by one or other side to contribute to the war effort, either directly by some form of military duty or indirectly by collaboration in measures designed ultimately to promote victory by arms.

The most direct of such pressures was of course the compulsion exercised on able-bodied male Quakers to bear arms in the militia or other military forces. While conscription was not imposed on Friends in the areas under British control, the Continental Congress had in July 1775 recognised in principle the exemption from military duties of authentic religious pacifists. This recognition, however, was not unconditional. Conscientious objectors were urged 'to contribute liberally in this time of universal calamity to the relief of their distressed brethren [i.e., fellow citizens] in the several colonies, and do all other services to their oppressed country, which they can consistently with their religious principles.' The state militia laws proved less generous and, as had been the practice before the Revolution, usually required objectors to pay a fine since they were unwilling to purchase a substitute – which Friends' religious principles we know precluded them from doing. Thus a clash with the law inevitably ensued.

Draft resistance during the Revolution sometimes brought harsher penalties for the Quakers than it had usually done during peace time. 'A number of Friends were imprisoned or made the butts of jeering mobs for refusing to perform military service.'[17] Several cases of severe ill-treatment are also recorded: one young Quaker in Virginia, for instance, received 'forty stripes . . . very heavily laid on, by three different persons, with a whip having nine cords,' for refusing to stand guard after his call-up. John Pemberton, who relates the story, adds, 'the faithfulness of this Friend, and the severe suffering he underwent, spread the testimony of truth': a captain after witnessing the scene, had even handed in his commission in disgust.[18] Recent converts to Quakerism as well as those who attended a Quaker Meeting but had not yet joined the Society experienced greater difficulty in convincing the authorities of the sincerity of their objection to fighting than did birthright Friends or those of longer standing, to whom alone the official exemption applied.[19] The former category, when called up for service, more likely than not had to spend a short term in jail. A certificate of membership, therefore, proved to be an extremely important document for the potential Quaker objector, and most Friends' Meetings were now prepared to supply these.

For *bona fide* Quaker conscripts, then, the worst they usually had to suffer was distraint on their property to cover the fine that the law imposed for failure to find a substitute. Of course, if they were very poor they might still find themselves in prison, usually for a matter of weeks only. The authorities sometimes presented Friends with unforeseen dilemmas, as they did in Rhode Island in 1778 when they started to hire recruits directly instead of calling up Quakers for service. They then charged the cost of maintaining those so hired to the Quakers in the area who were liable for the draft. The New England Meeting for Sufferings advised members not to co-operate – and suffer the consequences in loss of property by distraint. Otherwise they would 'wound the cause of Truth, depart from their testimony, and bring a burden upon the faithful.'[20]

In addition to military service there were a number of other paramilitary duties for which compulsion was exercised from time to time. Take the town watch, for instance, which we know had caused Friends trouble in the past. As early as 1775 the matter aroused anxiety in the Quaker communities of Lynn and Salem in Massachusetts. They wondered, now that hostilities had broken out, whether they would be acting in accordance with their Society's peace principles if they still continued to perform this function that had appeared in peace time to be entirely harmless. They therefore applied for advice to the Meeting for Sufferings, and this body recommended abstention, the duty having become they said 'mixed with, if not wholly for military purposes, and we conceive will have a tendency to leaven you into the prevailing spirit thereof.' The town authorities appear to have accepted the Quakers' explanations and henceforward they were not called up for duty. The problem reappeared at least once during the course of the war, this time under British rule. In the spring of 1782 the British commandant in New York, having previously exempted Quakers from military duties on condition they would 'exert themselves in any cases of emergency,' now came forward with a demand they take over complete responsibility for the city watch. This they refused to do on the grounds that the requirement was presented 'in lieu of military service' and was therefore in conflict with their witness for peace.[21] Once again the authorities accepted Friends' arguments and did not attempt to coerce them into compliance.

Work on constructing fortifications, earthworks, and trenches, occasionally required from able-bodied males even in peace time, became a more frequent obligation in war. We hear of two young Friends from Philadelphia being jailed in December 1776 for 'refusing to . . . work at the entrenchments near the city' (they were also unwilling of course to bear arms). We also learn of Quakers in other places, who consented to perform work of this kind. They were invariably dealt with by their Meetings, and were finally disowned if they failed to 'make satisfaction' by acknowledging their offence against the Society's discipline, as we read happened, for instance, in the case of Joseph Brownell of Portsmouth (Rhode Island), who assisted 'in building a fortification.'[22]

For country Quakers (as for the other rural peace sects of North America) demands from the military for horses and waggons to convey military supplies or for teamsters to drive them caused considerable concern, especially as such requisitions were often paid for handsomely and this naturally added to the temptation to conform. Equally troublesome, and equally tempting, were the demands of the armies that crossed and recrossed the land for forage and for provisions or for such articles as blankets, especially necessary in wintertime. Friends were strictly forbidden to accept payment for any requisitions made on them of this kind or to act personally in any capacity that might aid the armies of either side. Disownment inevitably resulted if such admonitions were not heeded, for, as the Western Quarterly Meeting of North Carolina put it, such 'requisitions or demands' were made by men engaged in 'the shedding of blood.'[23]

Moving on into the area of business and commerce we find Friends' consciences exercised there, too. In Bucks County, Pennsylvania, for instance, 'Quakers carried their principles to the extent of refusing to sell or grind grain for George Washington.'[24] With regard to prize goods, any Quaker trading in these might expect to come 'under dealing' by his local Meeting, with expulsion from the Society as the ultimate sanction if he persisted in such practices. 'Rejection of trade in prize goods and contraband paralleled rejection of the slave trade, as all were fruits of war.'[25] Friends, since the expansion of the Quaker movement throughout the continent, had become increasingly sensitive to such issues: gone were the days, at least in North America, when even a weighty member of their community might trade in smuggled articles and participate clandestinely in privateering – and get away with it. Temptation to become involved in activities 'tending to promote war' (to use the phrase then current among Quakers) was strongest perhaps among their seafaring communities: participation of Quaker crews in manning armed ships, for instance, came under the ban. We find a case in point at Portsmouth Preparative Meeting on Rhode Island. Its minute of 29 October 1776 ran as follows: 'Benjamin Stanton hath been on a cruise in a private vessel of war, which being directly contrary to the peaceable principle we profess, we do disown him.'[26] Even at the risk of becoming unemployed, Quaker sailors might serve only on ships that did not carry guns: the rule was enforced with equal strictness in wartime as in the days of peace.

Whether or not to pay war taxes presented Friends of the Revolutionary era with one of their most delicate problems. It was often difficult for them to know where to draw the line between the valid demands of government for tribute and the opposing rights of religious conscience. The issue was complicated by the fact that for most Quakers the King of England remained their lawful sovereign while the Revolutionary authorities appeared to be usurpers. A lively controversy on the tax question ensued within the Quaker community that was terminated only by the conclusion of hostilities and the Quakers' recognition, at first rather grudging, of the government of the New Republic as the legitimate ruler of Britain's former colonies. I shall be discussing this subject in greater detail in chapter XV below, and I would refer the reader to it for further information.

If differences of opinion over the tax question existed even among the stricter Friends, there was virtual unanimity in regarding it as improper for a Quaker to become a collector of taxes, at least in wartime. For one thing, Friends were now required to abstain from all political offices that were in any way implicated in the waging of war. A tax collector could scarcely avoid involvement of this kind. Moreover, with many conscientious Friends now refusing to pay taxes they considered to be in conflict with their peace principles, for which action they had the support of their Yearly Meeting if not the agreement of all their fellow members, a tax collector in the course of his official duties would inevitably have to collaborate in enforcing the law against his conscientious coreligionists. 'I dare not do it, let my suffering in consequence thereof be never so great,' wrote Eli Yarnall from Chester Country (Pennsylvania) in 1779 after being selected for this office. The fine incurred for refusal to serve and the consequent seizure of a horse for refusal to pay the fine seemed to this young Quaker farmer a light penalty for remaining faithful to the peace testimony of his forefathers.[27]

Whether or not to handle the Continental paper currency issued by the Revolutionary authorities proved an even more controversial issue than the tax question. Opinion among Friends remained divided. The money was issued by the Congress and state governments, whose legitimacy we know most Friends questioned, for the express purpose of assisting the prosecution of the war: there could be no doubt about this – or of the currency's rather shaky financial basis. Many Friends, therefore, were prepared to face immediate material loss by refusing to handle the currency as well as unpopularity – and even ill treatment – from American patriots. That earnest-minded Southern Friend, Warner Mifflin, for instance, would not touch it. Another such objector was Job Scott, a Quaker minister from Rhode Island who strictly hewed to the reform programme. Scott wrote in his *Journal*: 'Fears and reasonings of one kind or other prevailed on me to take it for a season; and then it became harder to refuse than it would probably have been at first.'[28] He finally resolved to have nothing to do with the money and face the consequences. On the other hand, Moses Brown, his fellow Rhode Islander – and an equally convinced Quaker – took a different view. More sympathetic perhaps than Scott to the American cause, Brown believed there was no essential distinction between handling paper currency and using specie, which everyone agreed was necessary to carry on everyday life. In fact, most Yearly Meetings, while they expressed sympathy for the stand of the paper currency objectors, urged Friends to display tolerance equally toward those who accepted and those who rejected it.[29]

If Friends were divided on the paper currency issue, they united in repudiating the 'Test,' i.e., the loyalty oath – or affirmation (which those with scruples about oath-taking might substitute). This comprised a renunciation of allegiance to the monarch and a declaration of loyalty to the Revolutionary régime. Refusal entailed heavy fines, confiscation of property or imprisonment, as well as the loss of many civil rights. Quakers objected to the Test on both political and pacifist grounds. In the first place, they felt they could not collaborate in any way in a violent change of government such as was then taking place in North America: such action they held to be entirely contrary to their *Obrigkeitsdoktrin*. Secondly they regarded taking the Test as incompatible also with their peace testimony. For this they said demanded they 'keep clear from any party engaged in disputes that are to be determined by military forces.'[30]

The pacifist element in Friends' objection to the Test, which surely was the fundamental one, comes out clearly in a passage from the address North Carolina Yearly Meeting presented in October 1777 to the state Assembly. That body had recently passed a law requiring the Test from those suspected of being disaffected toward the Revolutionary cause. In explanation of why its members could not make an affirmation of this kind, the Yearly Meeting stated:

> As we have always declared that we believe it to be unlawful for us, to be active in war, and fighting with carnal weapons, and as we conceive that the proposed affirmation approves of the present measures, which are carried on and supported by military force, we cannot engage or join with either party therein; being bound by our principles to believe that the setting up and pulling down kings and governments is God's peculiar prerogative, . . . and that it is not our work or business to have any hand or contrivance therein, nor to be busybodies in matters above our stations . . . We hope that you will consider our principles a much stronger security to any state than any Test that can be required.[31]

The confrontation over the Test that took place between Quakers and the new régime ceased only with the conclusion of hostilities and the Society's becoming gradually reconciled to the change of government that had occurred. But while the war was on, Quakers had suffered severely by fines and distraints, imprisonments and confiscations, and even banishment[32] on account of their resistance to the Test.

Readiness to suffer loss of liberty or material possessions, whether on account of refusal to take the Test or for some other cause, had marked the conduct of most Friends during the Revolutionary War: an attitude summed up after it was over by Warner Mifflin when he told his wife, 'if every farthing we were possessed of, was seized for the purpose of supporting war, and I was informed it should all go, except I gave voluntarily one shilling, . . . I was satisfied I should not so redeem it.'[33] There was of course backsliding as well as evasion of moral duty on the part of some Friends, who acted in this way usually with an uneasy conscience. True, no Quakers lost their lives in the war because of their pacifist stand. (For the two Pennsylvania Quakers executed as British spies in November 1778, whatever the degree of their actual guilt, had clearly been acting in a way that was inconsistent with the peace testimony.) But a perusal of the relevant pages of Mekeel's monograph on their conduct in the American Revolution reveals the extent of Quaker losses in property and of their other 'sufferings' in consequence of their anti-war stand.

Earlier, in September 1777 the Revolutionary authorities had arrested 17 prominent members of Philadelphia Yearly Meeting, along with three Anglicans, on a charge of treasonable relations with the British and had then deported them to Virginia. The moment was a critical one for the American cause, with Philadelphia threatened by British troops. Moreover, Quakers in Pennsylvania were suspect at that time, and especially the wealthy city merchants among their number who, for all their pacifism, scarcely concealed their sympathies with Britain. Thomas Paine, for instance, though he claimed to respect Friends' religious principles, spoke of this group as 'fallen, cringing priest-and-Pemberton ridden people,' and many of his fellow revolutionaries shared his opinion.

On the eve of their arrest, several of the deportees had protested to the Supreme Executive Council of Pennsylvania that there was indeed no 'reason to deprive us, who are peaceable men and have never borne arms, of our liberty by military force.' The charge of Quaker complicity with the enemy proved in fact to be unwarranted: it was based partly on hearsay and partly on forged documents. While some of those arrested, like Samuel Rowland Fisher for instance, were what we may perhaps call Tory pacifists (though by no means Tory militants), the group included Quaker ministers like John Pemberton or the English-born John Hunt who had been associated with the Woolmanite reform movement, as well as Edward Penington, who, though he took up arms during the Paxton disturbances of 1764, had thereafter returned to his ancestral Quaker pacifism. Eventually the American authorities realised these men were not hypocrites hiding connivance with the enemy under the cloak of religion, and released them from captivity. But this only happened after they had been in detention for seven months.[34]

If the politics of some Friends brought them into disrepute with the Revolutionary authorities, Quaker relief work during the war years[35] brought them recognition even from some who were otherwise hostile to the Society. This was an area where the Society in more recent times has gained widespread respect and admiration for its humanitarian endeavours. The most extensive work of this kind was carried out in the Boston area, first during the British blockade of that city in the second half of 1774 and then during its siege by American forces under Washington's command after the outbreak of hostilities the next year. And it was the Meeting for Sufferings of Philadelphia Yearly Meeting that had financed and operated the work of relieving those hit by war in and around Boston. At first assistance was confined to the small Quaker community; soon however Friends extended aid to all who needed help – 'without distinction of sects or parties' – and their programme of relief eventually embraced the numerous refugees scattered around the neighbourhood. The Quakers took care to explain to the contending generals that such activities expressed in positive form their religious witness against fighting and war: it thus gave them an opportunity to bring the nature of their peace testimony to the attention, among others, of military men. In a letter composed at the outset of 1776 Moses Brown, who played an active role in the distribution of supplies, wrote as follows of the impact he hoped Friends' relief would make generally on the non-Quaker community: 'The name Quaker, though little known in these parts, will be remembered and perhaps some may no more think it [a] reproach.'[36]

Friends also assisted victims of war, though on a considerably smaller scale, on the island of Nantucket as well as in Virginia and Pennsylvania. Whereas here the aid went mainly to their coreligionists, in North Carolina we find members of the New Garden Monthly Meeting looking after the wounded as well as burying the dead who had fallen nearby at the Battle of Guilford Courthouse early in 1781. Here Quakers tended impartially to the needs of the distressed on both sides. The Revolutionary General Nathaniel Greene, who had himself been a member of the Society of Friends until his disownment for bearing arms, commended them for their action. 'I know,' he wrote, 'of no order of men more remarkable for the exercise of humanity and benevolence; and perhaps no instance ever had a higher claim upon you than the unfortunate wounded in your neighbourhood.'[37] Thus Quakers showed they were also willing to extend their care to the fighting man, provided they could do it to the 'foe' as well as to soldiers on their own side.

This chapter has been concerned mainly with those Friends who accepted their Society's peace testimony and conscientiously objected to war. Something, however, must now be said about members who disagreed with Quaker pacifism and were prepared to bear arms in the struggle against British rule. (There were of course also a few Friends who fought on the British side.) Most Quakers who joined the Revolutionary army or served in a state militia were young, often in their early twenties. Many of them seem to have been influenced by radical and Revolutionary propaganda or by friends or relatives who had felt its impact. In other words, they had been led to become 'patriots' and now thought the colonial cause worth fighting for. They came to see America's future in an independent republic and no longer as a sharer in the British Empire's destiny.[38] Some of them, too, had already distanced themselves from the ideals nurtured by their ancestors, even before their decision to respond to the call to arms finally severed their link with the Society of Friends.[39]

Disownment inevitably resulted from persistance in their stand. Indeed expulsion from the Society was, we have seen, the fate of all who had collaborated in any way with the war effort and who would not desist when called to account by their Meeting.[40] A few 'fighting Quakers' returned to the Society after having made the required acknowledgement of error; this happened usually after the conflict was over. But most left the Society for good. A minority joined the splinter group known as the Free Quakers, which actively supported the American war effort.[41] The Free Quakers claimed to stand for freedom of conscience: they had separated, they said, from the main body of Friends in order to free themselves 'from every species of ecclesiastical tyranny.'[42] The leading figure among them was a Philadelphia Quaker minister, Samuel Wetherill, Jr.; in fact, apart from a few adherents in New England, the group was confined mainly to Pennsylvania. 'They served actively in the armies of the American side, they appeared in the Committee of Public Safety, they were seated in the Legislature, they were concerned in the printing of the Continental money, and aided by their money and their goods the cause of the American colonies, and . . . the first flag made for the American armies was made by one of them.'[43] Yet they failed to make any headway against the main body of the Society,[44] and with numbers slowly dwindling, the Free Quakers finally ceased to hold Meetings for Worship in the 1830s.

The Quaker pacifists, who controlled the Society of Friends, would have been wiser perhaps to do as Anthony Benezet had wished, and to have exercised tolerance toward its nonpacifist members. But such an attitude ran counter to the narrowly circumscribed morality of the day that underlay the idea of a strictly enforced Quaker discipline. Thus, along with many who had become lukewarm or indifferent, the Society lost some valuable members from this cause. If, for instance, the young Edward Penington of 1764 had been disowned, there would have been no mature Edward Penington the Virginia exile. The stiffening of the discipline in the decade before the Revolution that climaxed in the rigidity of the Revolutionary years certainly brought certain advantages: the Society of Friends emerged at the end of the war a more cohesive body than it had been when hostilities broke out. It is arguable that its peace witness might have been swamped if it had not adopted stern measures to prevent such an outcome. On the other hand, the events of this period seem to show that the overwhelming majority of Friends, whether they inclined politically to the one or the other side, stood wholeheartedly behind the peace testimony and were prepared to make considerable sacrifices to maintain it intact. A few fighting Quakers alongside their solidly pacifist brethren could scarcely have constituted a serious threat to the integrity of their Society's collective witness for peace.

Apart from the small minority of Friends whose participation in the conflict led to their ejection from the Society, Quakers had made it plain that they did not wish to have anything to do with the war. As the fighting drew to a close and it became increasingly clear that the British would have to recognise American independence, they refused to take part in any victory celebrations. When the first of these occurred after the British defeat at Yorktown in 1781 and houses were illuminated and shops closed as a sign of public rejoicing, Friends adamantly refused to do likewise. An outburst of anger on the part of outraged patriots followed, with attacks in many places on Quaker property in its wake. In an address they then sent to the Pennsylvania Assembly the Meeting for Sufferings of Philadelphia Yearly Meeting, whose members were among those chiefly affected, had explained that their conduct on this occasion flowed from their religious convictions and not from 'party views.' The object had been 'to labour for the spreading and propagation of the gospel of peace among our fellow citizens, countrymen, and mankind in general.'[45] These words indeed apply as well to the whole pattern of behaviour American Friends had attempted to follow throughout the course of the long and painful struggle that finally ended in the establishment of an American republic.

After Washington's election as first president of the United States Warner Mifflin sought an interview with his country's new ruler. In the course of their conversation the president asked the Quaker: 'Mr. Mifflin, will you please to inform me on what principles you were opposed to the revolution?' Mifflin replied: 'Yes, friend Washington; – upon the same principle that I should be opposed to a change in this government. All that ever was gained by revolutions, are not adequate compensation to the poor mangled soldier, for the loss of life or limb.' After a few moments of reflection Washington commented: 'Mr. Mifflin, I honour your sentiments; – there is more in *that*, than mankind have generally considered.'[46]

This interchange of views between the general and the pacifist augured well, I think, for the future relations of the Society of Friends with the new American state, despite the breach that had occurred between them during the revolutionary years.

CHAPTER XIII

Quaker Pacifism in the United States
between the Revolution and the Civil War

THE IMMEDIATE POSTWAR YEARS CONSTITUTED for Quakers a period of slow adjustment to the new political circumstances under which they would now have to spend their lives. Those Friends unable to accept the transition from monarchy to republic emigrated to Canada where they formed the first Quaker communities in that country. All these emigrants were loyalists, some of whom had abandoned pacifism to fight for the British (and been disowned for their stand), while others retained their conscientious objection to war but wished, because of their faithfulness to the Crown, to continue to nurture their peace witness under British rule. We shall return to these people when we come to discuss Quaker pacifism in Canada.

The vast majority of Friends remained in the new republic and sucessfully came to terms with the new situation within a comparatively short time. Despite the Test Law being repealed in 1787 and the way thus opening up for a re-entry of Friends into the political arena, Quakers henceforward played only a very limited political role. They voted of course at elections and a few of them sat in the state legislatures. But there was no return to the pre-revolutionary situation as it had existed in Pennsylvania or Rhode Island. The Yearly Meetings advised members against active participation in politics: the Society as a whole now lived withdrawn from political life and frowned on those who took on political office. Instead, Friends concentrated on such activities as antislavery and work for Indians.[1] They continued, too, their witness for peace: their pacifism, we have seen, had survived the trials of the Revolution, even if in the postwar years it lacked the vigour the Woolman generation of reformers had infused into it earlier.

Several special issues connected with the peace testimony remained over from the Revolutionary period. One of these was the question of confiscated estates, which had already arisen during the course of the war. The Quaker

155

authorities forbade members to purchase lands that had been forfeited by 'Tories': disownment followed for those who failed to obey these instructions, even when obedience entailed a considerable financial loss. Postwar taxes that went to cover the government's wartime indebtedness constituted another problem for the Society. Some Friends paid but others, like the ever scrupulous Warner Mifflin, refused to do so and subsequently suffered the customary distraint of their property. In 1786, the Philadelphia Yearly Meeting, on the insistence of certain concerned members and against the opposition of other members, had pronounced such losses as genuine 'sufferings' on behalf of Friends' testimony for peace.[2] In addition, war veterans if they subsequently became Friends, were expected to give up any pension they might be entitled to receive from the government: such money was tainted in the eyes of the Society.[3]

Conscientious objection to military service remained of course central to the Quaker peace witness, as it had done before and during the Revolution. In 1789 James Madison, the future U.S. President, had made an unsuccessful attempt to include an exemption clause for religious objectors in the Bill of Rights. 'No person religiously scrupulous of bearing arms,' it stated, 'shall be compelled to render military service in person.' But the proposal, though supported by some members of Congress, soon ran into strong opposition and was eventually deleted. When the exemption issue cropped up again in the following year while Congress was discussing the question of militia organisation, we find James Jackson from Georgia, for instance, arguing that the exemption of conscientious objectors would lead to a mass conversion to Quakerism! Probably the Quakers' opposition to the Revolution had alienated a number of Congressmen while in addition the representatives of the Southern states resented Friends' advocacy of antislavery. But the chief reason for the persistent rejection by Congress of 'federal conscientious-objector exemptions' went deeper: it in fact stemmed from 'the desire of the individual states to retain their own separate militias' without interference from the federal government. Thus, despite the petitions Quakers presented at this time to Congress asking for unconditional exemption of their members from service in the militia, their efforts were doomed to frustration. 'In the rejection of national provisions for conscientious objectors was reflected the failure of a uniform American militia.'[4]

Thus the pattern of Quaker conscientious objection continued to be governed by state militia legislation. Usually the law, as earlier, exempted Quakers from bearing arms provided they paid a small commutation fee. And as before, Quaker objectors, rather than pay, allowed their property to be distrained, or suffered brief imprisonment if they did not possess sufficient worldly possessions to cover the distraint.[5] If they yielded and paid, their Meetings dealt with them as offenders against the discipline of their Society. By the 1850s, however, the state militia system had passed into desuetude, and the question of militia service no longer exercised the minds of Friends in the way it had done hitherto.[6]

In the antebellum period a more vital aspect of Friends' peace witness emerged among the Quaker communities in the mid-West. There Quaker farmers, who had immigrated into these territories either, like other settlers, in order to gain more and better land for cultivation or because they wished to escape from the increasingly uncongenial atmosphere of the slave states of the South, faced dangers they had rarely, if ever, met with in the more tranquil East. Often the organs of orderly government functioned ineffectively, or not at all. There was sometimes trouble from hostile Indians, who feared – with justification – the effect the westward advance of the white man would have on their independence and lifestyle. Conditions were often disordered, especially in the 1850s when in addition to the other dangers attack by pro-slavery gangs, like the Kickapee Rangers, menaced in particular the antislavery elements among the frontier population. Therefore, settlers normally carried firearms to protect wife, children, and homestead from attack by native Indians or white marauders. Frontier lawlessness presented a challenge to the peaceable Quakers that they had seldom had to face before – even during their 17th-century beginnings on this continent.

Any Friend who carried weapons specifically for self-defence would, if detected by his coreligionists, have been disowned unless he acknowledged his error and agreed to abandon reliance on arms. But, in moments of crisis, the temptation to seize a hunting rifle or a kitchen knife and use it against a potential attacker, must surely have been great. We know, however, from autobiographical accounts left by such wilderness Friends[7] that some of them at any rate put their nonviolent principles into practice and refused to resort to armed defence even in the most trying circumstances.

Endemic warfare marked the life of the American frontier throughout the period under consideration. But between 1783 and 1861 the United States became involved in only two regular wars – and in each case hostilities were brief and located outside the country's boundaries. In fact neither the War of 1812 nor the Mexican War, which erupted in 1846, seriously affected the tenor of everyday life in America. In both conflicts Friends were careful to point out that their objection to war was based on religious principle and not on political grounds, and they took pains to avoid association with the political opposition to the current war that emerged in 1812 as well as in 1846.

In October 1814, for instance, Philadelphia Yearly Meeting issued a statement explaining to 'our Fellow Citizens of the United States' that 'subjects of a political nature make no part of our religious assemblies.' During that conflict the endeavours of Friends had mainly been directed to defending the sincerity of Quaker conscientious objectors, though in 1814 one Quaker (Lucretia Mott's father-in-law, James Mott, Sr.) did publish a tract expounding his Society's pacifism which he entitled *The Lawfulness of War for Christians, examined.*[8] The situation was a little different when the Mexican War broke out in 1846. 'The Friends were doubly offended by the war: their traditional pacifism affronted by armed hostilities, and their antislavery convictions assaulted by the aggressive war's apparent relationship with the extension of slavery.'[9] Moreover, there was now a flourishing Quaker press, the *Friend* since 1827 representing the Orthodox branch of the Society and the *Friends' Weekly Intelligencer* since 1844 the Hicksites, with the *Friends' Review* making its début in 1847 as the organ of the evangelical wing of the Orthodox. In the pages of all three journals antiwar articles appeared regularly throughout the period of hostilities that put the Quaker case against war and slavery and even went so far as to report generally on antiwar activity. Antiwar pamphlets were distributed, provided they expressed the Quaker point of view, and peace petitions presented to Congress and state legislatures. In addition, the Yearly Meetings of the two branches of the Society that had emerged as a result of the schism of 1827 issued a number of addresses expounding the peace testimony for the general public and exhorting their own members to remain loyal to it. Thus we find in fact a rather more political tone in 1846 than had occurred in Friends' utterances in 1812 but they still stressed that their opposition to war was based on religious principle and not motivated in any way by party considerations.

Despite signs such as we have just alluded to of a broadening of the Quaker witness for peace, Friends on the whole continued to regard the peace testimony in a traditional way. They were often narrowly conservative here as in other aspects of their religious life. Moreover, now as earlier, there were some Friends who gave only an external allegiance to their Society's pacifist tradition failing to live out its spirit in their everyday lives. Herman Melville in chapter 16 of his famous novel *Moby Dick* (1851) has given a portrait of this kind of Quaker which, though fictional, undoubtedly reflects a degree of truth. Here Melville depicts Captain Bildad, the pious but money-loving Quaker sea captain and whaling-ship owner from Nantucket, as something of a hypocrite. He was, as Melville puts it, lacking in 'common consistency.' 'Though refusing, from conscientious scruples, to bear arms against land invaders, yet himself had illimitably invaded the Atlantic and Pacific; and though a sworn enemy to human bloodshed, yet had he in his straight-bodied coat, spilled tuns upon tuns of leviathan gore.' Melville goes on to comment sarcastically that the captain most likely reconciled this vast expenditure of animal blood by 'the sage and sensible conclusion that a man's religion is one thing, and this practical world quite another.'

Yet Bildad, not unreasonably, might have pleaded here the difference between animal and human bloodshed as well as the long line of Nantucket Quaker whalers stretching back over a century before his time. But what can we make of the Quaker pacifists who disowned one of their members and excoriated another for condemning the sanguinary wars conducted by the Jews in Old Testament times? Around the turn of the 18th century Hannah Barnard, a young Quaker from New York, had expressed such views while on a pastoral visit to the British Isles. 'As to war,' she had stated to the shocked surprise of most English and Irish Friends, 'in no age of the world [had] the great and merciful Creator ever comissioned any nation or person to destroy another.' She could not understand how a beneficent deity could ever have sanctioned war and human slaughter under the old dispensation any more than under the new, which Jesus Christ inaugurated later. This, in her view, would have been to impeach 'the divine attributes' of love and goodwill toward all mankind in which – at least so she thought – all Quakers believed. Old Testament wars, like modern ones, had originated, she asserted, wholly from humankind's lust and passions; they surely did not flow from the will of God. First London Yearly Meeting branded her opinions as 'erroneous' and then, on returning to the United States, this intrepid young woman in 1802 received sentence of disownment from her home Meeting.

It was almost half a century before another American Friend voiced publicly sentiments similar to Hannah's. However, in 1846, John Jackson, a minister in the Hicksite Yearly Meeting of Philadelphia, had brought out a booklet in which he denied categorically that divine sanction had been given to any of the wars recorded in the Old Testament. How, he enquired, could the policy of extermination carried out there by the Jews against the Canaanites and other tribes be reconciled with the Christian spirit which Quakers endeavoured to follow in their own lives?[10] Jackson was not disowned, for his Hicksites, though few of them shared his views in the matter, were now more liberally disposed than Hannah Barnard's coreligionists had been at the beginning of the century. But they made it plain that they disapproved strongly of Jackson's standpoint.

One of those belonging to the small minority that sided with him was the redoubtable Philadelphia philanthropist, Lucretia Mott (a Nantucketer by birth but of course a more consistent Friend than Melville's Bildad). She reports that Jackson's supporters were 'charged with unsound doctrine' by their fellow Quakers, many of whom refused to read Jackson's tract for fear of moral contamination.[11] Lucretia Mott was to get into even more serious trouble through her association with the New England nonresistants, radical pacifists and extreme abolitionists whose Society came into existence in 1838 under the leadership of William Lloyd Garrison. I would like now to turn to discuss the curiously unsympathetic attitude of Friends both to the New England Non-Resistance Society and to the other nondenominational peace societies that had grown up in the United States (and elsewhere) from around 1815 onwards.[12]

By temperament as well as in outlook Friends of that time might be expected to feel a sense of kinship and common purpose with at least the more moderate and conservative peace organisations that had preceded the foundation of the radical nonresistant body. The Massachusetts Peace Society and its successor, the American Peace Society, published in their periodicals and pamphlets a number of enthusiastic – and often uncritical – accounts of the peace witness the Quakers had maintained over nearly two centuries. They held up the Quaker experiment in governing Pennsylvania as an example of pacifism in action, and they frequently cited the work of the English Quaker peace publicist, Jonathan Dymond (see below), in their arguments against war. But these societies did not confine their membership to absolute pacifists, and that, curiously enough, proved a major stumbling block in the way of official Quaker collaboration with them. Peace advocates like William Ladd, the first secretary of the American Peace Society, were disappointed at Quaker aloofness, considering how much Friends had in common with the emergent peace movement, and they did not fail to point out the contrast with English Quakers who formed the backbone of the London Peace Society, founded largely by Quakers in 1816. True, there were some American Friends who participated actively in the work of the peace movement. The venerable Moses Brown, for instance, a leading figure in New England Quakerism, had helped with his time and money to establish a peace society in his native Rhode Island. And in the small Pennsylvania Peace Society Quakers naturally predominated, but its influence was limited to Philadelphia and the immediate neighbourhood. The work of promoting the idea of peace at large, uphill and extremely slow labour in those days, rested almost entirely on the shoulders of non-Friends: it is Congregationalists and Baptists, Presbyterians and Unitarians, whose names we find on the roster of the first nondenominational peace societies.

For the overwhelming majority of American Quakers, still shut up in their sectarian enclosure, the activities of such societies appeared worldly, 'creaturely.' Apart from expressing condescending approval from time to time and drawing on the literature of the peace movement in their own publications, Friends adopted a cautious stance. They did not of course condemn the movement but they did much less than might have been expected from them to further its activities in the face of widespread hostility or indifference. A representative example of Quaker thinking on the subject can be seen in an article published in the Orthodox *Friend* in the mid-thirties. There the author wrote: 'These societies, in their collective capacity, do not fully come up to the Christian standard according to our estimate of . . . the New Testament doctrine bearing upon this subject; and it therefore may not be expedient that our members should be found in their ranks . . . it is safer, at least in the present state of the world, that we keep much to ourselves, and not act as a body in reference to this important testimony, lest by joining with others we should unawares be led into a compromise or evasion of any of its requisitions.'[13]

If such was the attitude of official Quakerdom to the non-Quaker peace moderates, we need not wonder at the downright hostility most Friends displayed toward the peace radicals who formed the New England Non-Resistance Society. The nonresistants, who were all ardent abolitionists of the Garrisonian variety, opposed not only war but civil government. In fact, these people were really Christian anarchists, and their doctrine was closely akin to Tolstoy's idea of nonviolence, a correspondence indeed that the Russian was freely to acknowledge. But Quakers, we know, had never renounced the political realm and, despite their retreat from politics at the time of the Revolution, withdrawal was never complete. A few Friends continued to sit in the Pennsylvania legislature and act as magistrates (though they were now more careful to see they did nothing that was clearly incompatible with their peace testimony). Above all, while a few Quakers refrained on principle, most voted at elections both at the federal and the provincial levels. 'The peaceable exercise of the right of suffrage, Friends have always left to the private judgement of the members,' declared the Meeting for Sufferings of the Orthodox Yearly Meeting of Philadelphia in an epistle it issued in 1834.[14] Quakers frequently expressed approval of the positive aspects of government: their opposition was mainly directed against its warmaking powers. Few of them shared the total rejection of government and the whole political process that the nonresistants were now calling for. As the Hicksite leader, Benjamin Ferris, himself a conscientious objector in the War of 1812, put it: 'The Society [of Friends] never set up the doctrines of nonresistance . . . The wise men who formed the Discipline have never made any rules that would unfit or disqualify us for human society.'

The appearance of the nonresistants and the vigour with which they propagated their views both inside and beyond New England aroused alarm in conservative Quaker circles. 'The ultra Hicksites generally favour them,' reported John G. Whittier in 1840.[15] This perhaps explains the rancour with which one conservatively minded Hicksite minister in particular, George F. White of New York, proceeded to attack the nonresistants and any Friends who showed sympathy with them. 'Hireling lecturers,' 'hireling bookagents,' 'emisissaries of Satan,' were just some of the names he applied to the Garrisonian propagandists who were active in spreading the new gospel. Among those who became the special targets of his wrath was Lucretia Mott; she was indeed a formidable antagonist, a woman who enjoyed widespread respect within the Society and outside its ranks. She never joined the Non-Resistance Society but she attended its annual conventions when her busy schedule allowed this. A militant herself – in a quietly Quaker way – she admired the nonresistants for the energy and fervour with which they spread their message of nonviolence, and she was not afraid of gaining a reputation for stirring up trouble; she knew such a charge had been levelled against early Friends, too. 'The elders and others,' she wrote of White and the Hicksites of New York, 'have been quite desirous to make me an offender for joining with those not in membership with us.'[16] In Philadelphia, however, her own Meeting supported her and she escaped disownment, a fate which overtook some others among the Garrisonians' Quaker collaborators.[17]

Garrisonian nonresistants were undoubtedly extreme in their views. Indeed they prided themselves on their extremism, believing this would help shake contemporary society out of its apathy and force it to take seriously the threat posed by the associated evils of war, slavery, and societal violence. While most of them, practically speaking, were respectable members of their communities, a few were fanatics or cranks – and this helped to discredit the Non-Resistance Society with the public at large. Their anarchism, summed up in the slogan 'no human government,' breathed an 'ultraism' that understandably was unacceptable to most Friends who were, in addition, put off by the harsh tones in which the Garrisonians attacked their opponents and by their lumping together so many reform causes in one bundle that had to be accepted – or rejected – as a whole.

A more reasoned, less vitriolic, repudiation of Garrisonianism than White's came from the Quaker poet, John Greenleaf Whittier. In 1840 Whittier wrote: 'I do not yet see how the non-resistance doctrine as laid down at the Convention in Boston [in September 1838] *can* be reconciled with *Quakerism* – or can be carried out *in practice* without a violation of, or open opposition to, our Discipline.' 'The new doctrines of non-resistance . . . with the kindred peculiarities which cluster around them . . . seem to be just such doctrines as George Fox contended against when establishing his "Discipline".' While Whittier showed understanding of the position of those Quaker dissidents who had been disowned for joining the Garrisonians, he felt the nonresistant doctrine, if ever put into practice, would lead to disorder, for it showed an unwillingness to submit to a proper ordering of things.[18]

The nonresistants at the beginning had expected support from the Quakers, and they emphasised the similarities between their own standpoint and that of Friends. But, as Quaker hostility opened up, they grew angry and started to attack them in print, accusing them of hypocrisy as well as stolid conservatism. Quakers, they declared, were being false to their own principles of peace in supporting, and sometimes participating in, 'present-day governments' based on the 'life-taking principle.'[19] A typical nonresistant response came from Henry C. Wright, a close friend of William Lloyd Garrison. Wright commented in reference to the government question which, rather than war, constituted the bone of contention between Quakers and nonresistants:

> Friends say we carry things too far, because we will not imprison evil doers . . . Now we cannot imprison evil doers, by existing governmental means, without endangering or threatening their lives. Let us suppose a case. A man is to be arrested and imprisoned; what could a Quaker policeman do in such a case? The Friend seizes him; the criminal is armed and resists. What shall the policeman do? . . . The friends of the criminal come to his rescue, with arms in their hands, and set government at defiance in the person of the policeman. The Friend, when it comes to the point, finds that he is out of his sphere. He, an unarmed man, who believes it to be a sin to make war upon individuals or nations, has undertaken to administer a government, which assumes the right to enforce all its decrees at the point of the bayonet.

Wright concluded by arguing it was Quakers' unconscious realisation police duties under existing governments were incompatible with their pacifism that had kept them from entering this branch of public service.[20]

Friends shared with nonresistants their desire to have slavery abolished, though they differed as to the precise means of accomplishing this objective. In the 1850s both found their hatred of war and violence and their love of freedom and humanity set on a collision course. After the Civil War broke out in 1861 most nonresistants – and some Quakers – abandoned their pacifism in order to fight a war they regarded as one waged for the freedom of the slave.

Among Quakers there were none who experienced this dilemma more acutely than did Lucretia Mott and John G. Whittier. Both were torn between two cherished yet now diverging ideals: peace and freedom. They both remained pacifists, even after the resort to arms, but both experienced the mental agony which this struggle between two ideals brought with it. In Whittier's view (which Lucretia Mott and many other Friends shared with him), 'Liberty and slavery cannot dwell in harmony together.' And without liberty lasting peace was impossible.[21] Though the abolition of slavery might – indeed should – be accomplished by peaceful methods, such Friends felt a sense of kinship with those who wished to realise their common goal by violent means. This feeling came out clearly in 1859 at the time of John Brown's raid on Harper's Ferry. On that occasion Whittier, in order to clear up any misunderstanding arising from his poem 'Brown of Ossawatomie,' had written to Garrison as follows: 'No one who knows me, or who has read my writings, can be doubtful for a moment as to my position; utter abhorrence of war and of slavery as in itself a state of war, where the violence is all on one side.' He still believed in the power of nonviolence to get rid of slavery and would not urge the slaves to use violence to gain their freedom, for 'I dare not encourage others who have not my scruples to do what I regard as morally wrong.' In conclusion, he told Garrison: 'My conscience bears me witness that I have . . . honestly striven to be faithful alike to Freedom and Peace.'[22] Yet he could not restrain his feelings of admiration for Brown and what he had done for the cause of liberty, even if the Quaker poet still held that 'the Christian's sacrifice' by means of nonviolence was a morally better method to achieve this goal.

Lucretia Mott expressed much the same viewpoint as Whittier when she spoke, not long after Brown's execution, at the annual meeting of the Pennsylvania Anti-Slavery Society in October 1860. She told the Assembly on that occasion:

It is not John Brown the soldier we praise; it is John Brown the moral hero . . . the . . . patient martyr . . . Robert Purvis [a well known Black abolitionist] has said that I was 'the most belligerent Non-Resistant he ever saw.' I accept the character he gives me; and I glory in it. I have no idea because I am a Non-Resistant, of submitting tamely to injustice inflicted either on me or on the slave. I will oppose it with all the moral powers with which I am endowed. I am no advocate of passivity. Quakerism as I understand it, does not mean quietism. The early Friends were agitators; disturbers of the peace, and were more obnoxious in their day to charges which are now so freely made than we are.[23]

Here, then, on this antislavery platform in Philadelphia, we hear once again the prophetic voice that had sounded earlier in the declarations of Woolman and his associates during the Quaker reform movement of the mid-1750s. True, Friends' testimony for peace in the period now under consideration had often lacked the vital spark. It was on the whole traditional, conservative, hostile to new ideas and to new strategies for peace. There was little creativity in Quaker thinking on war and violence, in contrast to the fermentation that was then occurring, for instance, in the organised American peace movement of the 1830s. Yet the presence within Quakerdom of persons like Lucretia Mott or Whittier (we could mention other names too) signified that Quaker pacifism was not dead: it smouldered under the ashes. The test for Friends would come in 1861 when in April of that year the firing at Fort Sumter ushered in America's Civil War.

CHAPTER XIV

Quaker Conscientious Objectors in the American Civil War

THE CIVIL WAR PROVED PERHAPS the most difficult war of any for the preservation of American Friends' peace testimony – at least this was so for Friends in the North. The abolition of slavery and the maintenance of the Union were goals which Friends shared with the administration. Indeed they possessed better antislavery credentials than did Lincoln's government, which only made abolition a war aim fairly late in the conflict. Quakers, after all, had been pioneers in the antislavery movement; its consummation with the freeing of all slaves in the American Republic remained one of their most cherished aims. But of course they always sought this through nonviolent means; Black liberation, they held, must come without the shedding of blood. Their young people were brought up in the spirit of Quaker pacifism, and this implied not only witness for peace but belief in human brotherhood, the solidarity of humankind irrespective of race or colour. Friends did not always live up to their ideals but, on the other hand, those ideals remained to inspire their best actions and their choicest souls.

How, then, would male Quakers of military age respond to the call that came in 1861 to defend the Union against internal disruption and – hopefully – to achieve emancipation at last, by force of arms? How were the older men of their community and their women to react to this situation? Was it possible for Quakers to stand by their historic peace testimony and at the same time remain loyal to the idea of national unity and to their belief in human freedom? Or was it necessary to make a choice, at least temporarily, and reject one Quaker testimony for another? The dilemma was a difficult one for many Friends, who agonised long and hard over the issues involved. Some chose one alternative, some the other, while still more tried uneasily to preserve their Society's witness for peace intact without at the same time ignoring the call to promote human freedom and brotherhood.

The Quaker dilemma comes out clearly in a letter contributed to the Hicksites' journal after Lincoln's proclamation of emancipation on 1 January 1863 had deepened the rift in the Quaker mind still further. 'There is danger,' says the writer, 'under present circumstances, of allowing our testimony against war to be modified or lessened, from the fact that this war will certainly be the means of putting down slavery. This war having been begun by slaveholders more firmly to secure themselves in their authority over slaves, we cannot be sorry to see that authority overthrown; yet it is done by a means that we, as Christians, cannot recommend or uphold.'[1] From the beginning, in all their public utterances Friends, irrespective of the branch of the Society to which they belonged, had stressed their abhorrence of the Southern 'rebellion': their prayers and sympathies were with the Unionist cause, even if their peace principles precluded them from approving the means by which that cause was being upheld.[2] They shared the anxieties of the nation at war and rejoiced at the final outcome bringing the release of their Black brethren from bondage, while at the same time they mourned 'the destruction of human life and the sad consequences ever attendant upon a state of war.'[3] For President Lincoln, in particular, they expressed the warmest sentiments of gratitude for his understanding and sympathy of their 'conscientious scruples in relation to war.'[4] And they carefully pointed out the distinction between their own pacifist witness founded on religious belief and the politically motivated antimilitarism of the so called 'peace democrats' or 'copperheads' (as they were derisively dubbed by their opponents), whose opposition to the current struggle stemmed from their hostility to the war aims of the Union administration and frequently from some degree of sympathy with those of the Confederate States, too.

Above all, Friends shared with their fellow Americans a sense of deep grief at the mutual slaughter. 'Why should the young and beautiful be swept away?' exclaimed Lucretia Mott on news of the death of a cousin in battle. And she expressed the divided heart of many Quakers at this time when she went on to write: 'If, by this means, these cruelties [inflicted on the slaves for centuries past] can be arrested and an end drawn . . . to man's claim of property in his fellow man, we need not . . . "be troubled" – knowing that "these things must needs be" . . . My faith however in the superior force of the "mighty weapons" that "are not carnal" is unshaken.'[5]

For many Friends like Lucretia Mott – the poet Whittier, for example – the war against the South was essentially a war to end the monstrous evil, the sin, of slavery. Secession to them was the occasion and not the basic cause of the conflict. Therefore, once war had become an established fact, those who did not believe in nonviolence were in duty bound to pursue hostilities to a successful conclusion. A negotiated peace in the circumstances would constitute a betrayal of the ideals the North had set before itself. 'Regarding the present calamity,' wrote Lucretia Mott early on in the conflict, 'terrible as war must ever be, let us hope it will not be stayed by any compromise' that would leave slavery in existence in the South, for slavery was itself a still more ruthless form of war.[6] I do not think it is correct, as one writer has done,[7] to call the attitude of a Whittier or a Mott 'vocational pacifism' or to speak here of 'a double ethic' with respect to war.[8] For these Quakers, like the rest of their coreligionists who held to their Society's peace testimony, believed this testimony represented an ethic open to all mankind: they never regarded it as exclusively the ethic of a spiritual elite. They hoped the rest of mankind would eventually adopt their peace principles. In the meantime, those who had not yet done so, including some in the Quaker community itself, must follow their consciences and strive for justice by the best means they believed were available to them.

Whittier, I think, put the point admirably in a letter he sent to the Newburyport *Herald* on 15 May 1861. He wrote there:

> No one who knows me can doubt my deep sympathy with the united North, and with those who, with a different idea of duty from my own, are making generous sacrifices of person and property; but as a settled believer in the principles of the Society of Friends, I can do nothing at a time like this beyond mitigating to the extent of my power, the calamities and suffering attendant upon war, and accepting cheerfully my allotted share of the privation and trial growing out of it.[9]

What the peace principles of the Society of Friends were we know from earlier pages. These principles were fairly well known at the time of the Civil War throughout American society both in Unionist and Confederate territory. In the South of course, because of Quakerism's association with antislavery, Friends were considerably less popular than they were in the Northern states. In view of the somewhat moribund state of Friends' pacifist witness at the outset of hostilities and the split loyalties of many Quakers torn between the ideals of peace and freedom, we need not be surprised if the war years produced few, if any, original contributions to the theory of Quaker pacifism, although discussion of practical wartime issues took place in the columns of the Quaker papers. There, too, we find various problems of Quaker wartime behaviour being threshed out in editorials, articles, and letters from readers. Among such problems those of the conscientious objector naturally occupied most space. And to these we must now turn our attention.

Conscription legislation ran roughly parallel in the Union and the Confederate States. At first the armies on each side were composed of volunteers and recruits drawn from the state militias. Soon, however, the belligerent governments discovered they could not depend on voluntary enlistment together with reinforcements from the militias, if they were to wage war successfully. In April 1862 the Confederate Congress passed a conscription act allowing the able bodied exemption only on condition of furnishing a substitute. After prolonged lobbying by the peace churches of the South a supplementary act was passed in October permitting their conscientious objectors to opt out of military service by paying a fine of $500. The exemption was eventually withdrawn; however, 'this last development came so late in the war that little if any repercussion was heard.'

Meanwhile, Lincoln's administration had proceeded to extend the scope of the federal draft until, in March 1863, it introduced universal military service allowing, however, a way out to any conscripts not wishing to serve – either by the familiar method of furnishing a substitute or by paying up to $300 'for the procuration of such substitute.' 'Thereupon,' stated the act, 'such person so furnishing the substitute, or paying the money, shall be discharged from further liability under that draft.' As earlier in the South, Quaker leaders in the North now busied themselves with obtaining specific recognition of the right of conscientious objection for those who objected to fighting on religious grounds. After nearly a year of such lobbying, Congress in February 1864 was persuaded to pass an amendment to the previous law: 'the first federal provision of noncombatant service for religious objectors.' This provision ran as follows:

> That members of religious denominations, who shall by oath or affirmation declare that they are conscientiously opposed to the bearing of arms, and who are prohibited from doing so by the rules and articles of faith and practice of said religious denominations, shall, when drafted into the military service, be considered noncombatants, and shall be assigned by the Secretary of War to duty in the hospitals, or to the care of freedmen, or shall pay the sum of three hundred dollars . . . to be applied to the benefit of the sick and wounded soldiers.[10]

The terms were certainly generous, and we know they satisfied the requirements of the Mennonite and Dunker conscience. But for Quakers they stopped short of what their leaders, in line with the traditional standpoint of Friends, had asked the administration to grant. Though most Quaker conscientious objectors complied, there were some we shall see who did not, and thereby caused the army authorities some trouble before a satisfactory solution was found by Lincoln's remarkably tolerant administration.[11]

Concerning the hiring of a substitute to take the objector's place in the ranks unanimity prevailed among Friends. 'The answer is clear . . . it must be wrong,' wrote the editor of the Orthodox *Friend*:[12] he was expressing here the opinion of all branches of the Society. Yet some conscripts we know did take this way out. Often they were dealt with by their Meetings and disowned if they did not express regret for conduct that had long been defined as thoroughly un-Quakerly. But we do know of cases during the Civil War when proceedings were not instituted against such offenders, one illustration out of many that the Society's discipline was relaxing, especially among the more liberal Hicksite Meetings in the cities. Failure to enforce the discipline in such cases may also have been due to a consciousness among older Friends of the difficulties and dilemmas faced by younger members and a desire to demonstrate in practical fashion sympathy and understanding for their plight.[13] We know also of several cases where the substitute was hired by a relative anxious to free their family member from the draft: a generosity that was not always appreciated by the recipient of such kindness.

The question of paying commutation money aroused more discussion within the Society. The consensus, as in the past, was against paying – but we do know that many young Friends did pay and in this way escaped service. In fact, in the South almost all Quaker conscripts, who were actually members of the Society and thus qualified for this type of exemption, complied and their Meetings in practice turned a blind eye to their infraction of the Society's discipline – or at any rate merely treated them 'in a tender manner' without going so far as to disown anyone for it. Here, what to do was thus left for the individual Quaker conscript to decide according to his conscience.[14] In the difficult circumstances in which Friends were placed in the Confederate States, an uncompromisingly absolutist stand in the matter obviously appeared unrealistic to most members, including both those of military age and those not liable to the draft themselves.

Friends in the North found it easier to accept the payment of commutation money after the act of February 1864 consigned the sum paid to a humanitarian purpose and not, as earlier, to purchasing a substitute. While the latter procedure was totally unacceptable to most Quakers, the former provision, too, proved difficult for many to swallow, since the money was destined to relieve sick and wounded soldiers and thus to help the military, albeit indirectly. But on the whole Friends went along with commutation after February 1864 – not, it is true, with the near unanimity with which Southern Friends had accepted it but on a wider scale than the usual official Quaker disapproval of this practice might indicate.

Take the case of Indiana, for instance, for which area we possess a detailed study by Jacquelyn Nelson of the behaviour of Civil War Quakerism.[15] Here, 'the majority of conscripted Quakers paid the commutation fee of $300. Church records show that eighty seven Indiana Friends from twelve Monthly Meetings chose this option . . . At the suggestion of the Yearly Meetings in Indiana, the Quakers donated money to reimburse those who paid the commutation fee.' Local Meetings requested members to contribute an appropriate proportion of the funds required for this purpose, and the money was then divided equally among the draftees needing reimbursement.[16] An investigation of other Yearly Meetings on a similar scale as Nelson's for Indiana would probably result in roughly the same picture with respect to this problem. We may note, finally, that just as conscripts' relatives had occasionally hired substitutes on their behalf 'secretly' and without their cognisance, this also happened with paying commutation money.[17] But these cases were of course exceptional; we may presume that normally the Quaker conscript, even if his father had supplied him with the cash, knew exactly what he was doing when he paid over his $300.

Though Friends generally seem to have relaxed their traditional opposition to paying military fines, Congress, we have seen, in February 1864 had provided those objecting to this procedure (as well of course as to procuring a substitute) with two further alternatives: work in a military hospital and care of freedmen. With regard to the first option we hear of Quaker conscripts either volunteering for such duties or accepting them after being inducted into the army.[18] But many Quaker conscripts still felt that working in a military hospital, at least, would seriously undermine their testimony against war. We read, for instance, in the report of a Quaker Committee set up by Pennsylvania Friends 'to advise and assist such of our members as might be drafted for service in the army of the United States,' how a Quaker draftee from that State reacted to this problem:

> One young man, when before the Provost Marshal, in his anxiety to escape being sent to the field, inadvertently expressed his willingness to serve in the Army Hospitals. He was soon sent to Camp, where he was expected to drill, and to do other acts which were trying to his feelings; and the more so, because he felt that he had compromised the testimony of Truth by choosing hospital duty . . . When assigned to a hospital, he found the associations and examples extremely repugnant to his moral and religious feelings, and in several letters, deplored the mistake he had made, and the sad situation into which he had introduced himself . . . He was [finally] . . . discharged, and restored to his . . . family, deeply impressed with his error, and more than ever attached to the principles of Friends.[19]

In fact opinion within the Society, among the Orthodox and Conservatives as well as among the Hicksites, was divided in the matter.[20] Some Friends felt it would be wrong in the circumstances for their members to refuse to succour the helpless and needy just because these were in uniform, or because such humanitarian work was carried out under the auspices of the military or a belligerent administration, or because it was undertaken as an alternative to bearing arms. The important thing was that the task was in itself such as a peaceable Christian might perform with a clear conscience: it should not be regarded as 'a penalty or as a purchase' of the right to follow conscience. Let us not manufacture 'crosses' for ourselves unnecessarily, one Friend observed. We should be grateful to Congress and Lincoln's administration for providing our objectors with an alternative form of serving their country which they could conscientiously fulfill. Other Friends, however, stressed the traditional opposition of Quakers to being forced to pay money or perform work in exchange for permission to do what conscience and religion told them was right. Army hospitals, Friends of this way of thinking stressed, formed an essential part of the military establishment: their aim was to help fight the war to a successful conclusion. To work there as doctor, nurse or orderly, or in any other capacity however innocent in itself, was to aid and abet the prosecution of hostilities and to become an integral 'part of the machinery for carrying on war and maiming and destroying our fellow creatures.' For army hospitals aimed solely at getting soldiers back again into the firing line, to make them once more capable of killing, of pursuing 'their murderous employ.' Even work with the freedmen, in which many Quakers were participating on a voluntary basis, seemed objectionable to some Friends if accepted in lieu of military service (though more approved of this alternative than of work in army hospitals). For, purportedly those engaged in such work as alternative service would be subject to military discipline and control, and remain in reality part of the army machine.

Edwin M. Stanton, who held the position of Secretary of War in Lincoln's cabinet, found it difficult to comprehend such arguments as these, despite his understanding in general of the position of the religious objector to war.[21] He felt that since the alternative proposed constituted 'a work of mercy, and in accordance with the commands of Christ,' Friends would be wrong if they rejected 'so liberal an offer' as he had made them – merely in pursuit of what he called an 'abstraction.'[22]

Before moving on to describe what happened to the Quaker absolutists and other Friends – and friends of the Friends – who eventually found themselves in the grasp of the army, I would like to deal briefly with the Quaker 'draft-dodger,' who sought to escape conscription by hiding or deserting or even by crossing the enemy lines. This was mainly a Southern phenomenon, since the draft there bore much more heavily on the conscientious objector than it did in the territory under Unionist rule. In the South it was of course a phenomenon by no means confined to the Quakers but embraced Mennonites and Dunkers as well as many others who, while they did not object to war in the abstract, were reluctant to fight in a cause which, for one or another reason, they did not regard as their own. 'There is abundant evidence,' writes Richard Zuber in his study of Quaker conscientious objectors in the Confederacy, 'both that the Quakers themselves frequently deserted and that they offered strong encouragement to non-Quakers who abandoned the army.' When called up, many young Friends simply failed to respond, hiding in the woods and forests or in caves or in the farmsteads of relatives or friends. And Quaker farmers not only helped to hide their own sons or the sons of their Quaker neighbours but also 'soldiers from both the Union and Confederate armies,' regarding this as a Christian duty. As a result, they naturally came under suspicion from pro-war neighbours as well as the Confederate authorities. They also found that some of the deserters they aided from outside the Quaker community proved to be less pacific than they had expected. As a disillusioned Quaker, who had experienced this, remarked in a letter to a friend, 'We don't believe in war, nor do we believe in a deserter, particularly those that rob, steal, and murder.'

Often an important consideration with those Quakers who either hid or escaped over into Unionist territory lay in their unwillingness to buy their way out of the army by paying a commutation fee. Many Southern Friends had Quaker relatives in the mid-West, who willingly took these refugees into their homes: there had been a considerable Quaker migration in the antebellum period from North Carolina and Virginia north-westwards to the fertile prairie lands then opening up to cultivation. Occasionally one of the escaping conscripts got caught by the Confederate authorities like the unfortunate Elias Parks, aged 18, who in 1862 was imprisoned in the notorious Castle Thunder 'because,' wrote Delphinia Mendenhall, a North Carolina Friend, 'he is a Christian, and therefore he cannot fight . . . After he was drafted . . . he tried to reach the free States but was arrested in Western Virginia. It is said [he receives] . . . nothing but bread and water.' Much more tragic was the fate of another conscript John Burgess, who along with several other young Quakers, was uncovered early in 1865 by a gang of Confederate vigilantes in a forest hide-out. Burgess was selected for execution and thereupon hanged. According to Sowle, 'Burgess appears to be the only conscientious objector who died as a direct result of his peaceable principles.'[23]

In the Confederate area very few Quaker conscientious objectors took the absolutist stand. According to Zuber,[24] in North Carolina only seven Quakers who were *bona fide* members of their Society, remained steadfast throughout the war and neither hid nor fled nor paid commutation money. Even if this figure is unduly low, we may agree the main burden of resisting conscription and the hardships this entailed rested almost entirely on two categories whose Quaker credentials were not recognised by the Confederate authorities: first, those accepted into membership of the Society after the passing of the draft law of 11 October 1862, whom later historians have sometimes labelled, I think a little unfairly, as 'War Quakers,' and secondly, attenders at Quaker Meetings who, while they had not applied for membership, were yet close to the Society in belief and religious practice, sharing *inter alia* its peace testimony. The behaviour of the Confederate authorities – to their credit – was not always consistent with the letter of the law, for they quite often allowed persons in these two categories to qualify for exemption under the commutation clause in the conscription legislation. Such men of course were not necessarily absolutists, for whom commutation was unacceptable; indeed probably they were rarely so, for we have no reason to believe such opinions were more prevalent in their ranks than among Friends of pre-October 1862 standing.[25] But many of them were refused exemption and, their claim to qualify as a Quaker rejected, they were inducted into the Confederate army like the handful of absolutists who were officially recognised members of the Society.

Once inside the army these men were sometimes subjected to harsh and prolonged punishment for refusal to obey orders, the military authorities hoping to break their will to resist and make pliant soldiers out of them, in which endeavour they succeeded only rarely. In all cases where the objector persisted in resisting, the authorities eventually gave up and released him, except for a few recent draftees still remaining in the ranks at the conclusion of the war. The treatment meted out to refractory objectors included the officially approved practice of 'bucking down'[26] that was applied also to other recalcitrant soldiers in an effort to subdue their spirit, as well as beating and kicking, hanging up by the thumbs, deprivation of sleep, restriction of diet – and threats of execution by hanging or shooting. Responsibility for ill-treatment, especially its illegal forms, usually rested with excessively zealous junior officers. The higher command often showed considerable understanding when the situation was brought to its attention. As Wright remarks, 'Taking all things into consideration, it is apparent that the cases of extreme severity in the South were the exception rather than the rule.'[27] Moreover, the plight of these objectors, and the steadfastness with which they faced it, frequently aroused sympathy among their fellow soldiers that took various forms, including in at least one instance petitioning President Jefferson Davis on their behalf. In May 1863, for instance, 10 soldiers sent the following letter to Davis:

> Your petitioners respectfully request of you to exempt . . . Himelius M. Hockett and Jesse D. Hockett, Simeon Barker, and Isaiah Cox. They are all in feeble health, not able to stand a camp life. They all have

helpless families to support, no person to work on their farms but themselves . . . Your petitioners pray that you will duly consider this petition and, if judged expedient, will exempt the four persons above stated as we believe they can render this Government more service at home on their farms. Your petitioners on duty bound ever pray [10 names follow].[28]

Concerning the new and near Quakers who sought the same status as Friends of firmer standing, there was naturally fear in the community at large as well as in the government that granting them exemption would encourage shirkers to join the Society of Friends or claim informal affiliation with it. Quakers, too, were apprehensive lest advantage be taken of their privileged position *vis-à-vis* the draft. As one of them wrote in July 1863 when the net of conscription was being drawn more tightly over the Confederate States, 'There seems to be quite a looking and leaning to our Society in this part of the land, quite a number of men and women have requested to become members.' However those accepted into membership 'are mostly such as have in some measure been connected with [our] Society, and thus seem to have been awakened to a sense of duty by the calamities of the present war.'[29] Among these new members there were a few who had previously been disowned for minor infractions of the Society's discipline: presumably they now felt their return to the Quaker fold would facilitate their procuring exemption from military service. We do not necessarily have to doubt the sincerity of their conscientious objections: marrying out of the Society, for instance, that brought speedy disownment in that period did not automatically mean rejection of its peace principles. And, as for the second category being considered here, we may well feel in general like rating the credibility of those who shared Quaker views on war yet refrained, for one reason or another, from actually joining the Society, higher than that of any of the 'War Quakers.' But all this of course was not immediately obvious to outsiders, who continued to suspect the credentials of all these new and near Friends. It was puzzling in particular to the army authorities.

The Quakers, on the other hand, felt an obligation to defend the interests of all who on Quaker grounds sincerely objected to bearing arms, whether or not they satisfied the legal requirements for exemption. 'Out of this situation,' writes Zuber of the South, 'developed one of the most revealing aspects of the contest between conscientious objectors and the Confederacy.'[30] Southern Quakers indeed were unwilling to stand by and watch without a struggle a member whom they had disowned (or who for some reason had chosen to leave the Society) fall into the hands of the military, provided, that is, he still claimed to be a pacifist.[31] They also tried to help 'near Quakers' as well as members of other denominations who shared Quaker views on war (they sometimes overlapped). Among such persons there were certainly a few Baptists as well as Wesleyan Methodists, members of a small antislavery breakaway group from the mainstream Methodist Episcopal Church which had been founded in 1842. Due to close contacts between the Wesleyan Methodists of North Carolina and the Quakers of that State, which were established already in the antebellum period, Quaker peace – and abolitionist – principles infiltrated the Methodist ranks. After war broke out, we find, for instance, Micajah McPherson, a leading layman in that church, openly espousing the Quaker position on war – and narrowly escaping lynching when a proslavery mob left him for dead after stringing him up on a tree near his farm.[32]

Southern Quakers and their associates faced a fiercer ordeal than did their counterparts in the North. Perhaps their hearts were less divided, for few of them felt the same empathy for their wartime government as Northern Quakers did for theirs. Still, they had to put up with more widespread unpopularity in their local communities as well as more extensive ill-treatment in the case of their objectors inducted into the army. The Unionist administration, we have seen, sought to meet the Quakers more than half-way in their unwillingness to take part in the war. It failed, however, to recognise a right to unconditional exemption which some Friends stood out for (after all this was what their ancestors as well as their own convictions held was right). And, as in Confederate territory, the problem of the new and the near Quaker also cropped up in the North to complicate the problems of the Union army and administration. Here too, for instance, 'persons in whom thoughts of religion had lain dormant for years, began to renew or trace back their Quaker connections.'[33] Put more positively, this meant the crisis of war awoke some hitherto lukewarm consciences to the implications of their ancestral faith with respect to fighting. Such men, often young and inexperienced, were not, I think, necessarily insincere in their now adopting – or readopting – the Quaker position on war. Even less is scepticism justified regarding those admitted to membership after war had broken out; it seems that now Quaker Meetings exerted perhaps even more care than usual in screening new applicants, and therefore shirkers can seldom have got through their screening.

Let us look for a while at the treatment of those Quakers who, despite all the good will and the genuine attempt at understanding displayed by the civil authorities, found themselves at last in the hands of the Union army. Wright in his study, to which I am once again greatly indebted, devotes much space to these people. We possess, moreover, in the posthumously published *Civil War Diary* of Cyrus Pringle, a newly joined member of the Society from Charlotte (Vermont), an autobiographical account of the army experiences of a Quaker conscript.[34] True, his treatment appears to have been harsher than most Quaker conscripts had to undergo under similar circumstances; yet his narrative from the outset on has a genuine ring about it.[35]

Pringle, along with two other Quakers from his neighbourhood, was drafted on 13 July 1863: the men did not qualify for exemption since they had joined Friends only after the commencement of the war. Impressed by 'the abstract beauty of Quakerism,' Pringle and his companions decided to manifest their faithfulness to its peace testimony by rejecting exemption, should it be offered them eventually in exchange for a commutation fee, and by resisting military orders. Eventually they were transported first to the military camp located on Long Island in Boston Harbor and later to Virginia near the battle front. Throughout these Quakers' sojourn in the army the officers made a series of efforts to break them down, the ordinary soldiers, on the other hand, once again proving generally sympathetic. Pringle and his associates were now subjected to various penalties, including the customary 'bucking down.' But perhaps even more trying to them than the physical hardships was their need to decide where to draw the line between commands they felt in duty bound to disobey and those they considered they might submit to in good conscience.

Members of the Quaker community with whom they remained in touch had advised them to accept the offer made by the army authorities, and several times repeated, to allow them to work in a military hospital. 'In our discussion of the subject among ourselves, we were very much perplexed,' Pringle records. They feared a refusal would be misunderstood even among Friends and that they would 'be exposed to the charge of over-zeal and fanaticism even among our brethren.' Pringle then goes on:

> . . . Regarding the work to be done in hospital as one of mercy and benevolence, we asked if we had any right to refuse its performance; and questioned whether we could do more good by endeavoring to bear to the end a clear testimony against war, than by laboring by word and deed among the needy in the hospitals and camps. We saw around us a rich field for usefulness in which there were scarce any laborers, and toward whose work our hands had often started involuntarily and unbidden. At last we consented to a trial, . . . reserving the privilege of returning to our former position.

> At first a great load seemed rolled away from us . . . But soon there prevailed a feeling of condemnation, as though we had sold our Master. And that first day was one of the bitterest I ever experienced. It was a time of stern conflict.

After a few days they finally decided, after more heartsearching, against work of this kind as something that would compromise their witness for peace. Later, however, they agreed to work in a civilian hospital in Washington, D.C., after receiving an assurance that their employment there 'would release none for active service in the field.'[36]

We should note, however, that not all Quakers drafted into the army took the strict line pursued by Pringle and his companions. Henry D. Swift, for instance, a young Friend from South Dedham (Massachusetts), who was drafted around the same time as Pringle was, consented temporarily to help in the camp hospital on Long Island but, according to the account of his experiences he 'refused all remuneration for his services.' Later, after 'bucking down' had failed to break his spirit, he received sentence of death from a military court. Before this could be carried out, however, Quaker intervention with President Lincoln and Secretary Stanton led to Swift's being amnestied, his parole arriving 'shortly before the time he had been informed his execution was to take place.'[37]

In fact no Quaker (or other) objector in the North suffered death for his refusal to fight, though court martials sentenced several of them to be shot and many more threats of death were issued, almost invariably without the desired effect. Lincoln and his administration, apart from their sincere desire to avoid penalising men for genuinely held religious convictions, very wisely did not wish to create martyrs. Such men, they thought, could serve the Unionist cause far better at home than in the ranks of the army, where their presence constituted an unnecessary burden for the hard worked military administration and might even cause disaffection among the common soldiery. From 1863 onwards a parole system came informally into force to deal with cases like Pringle's or Swift's. Though these men received no written certificate of exemption, they were furloughed indefinitely – and remained free of conscription for the war's duration.[38]

There were, we see, Quaker objectors who found themselves involuntarily in the Union army. But there were also Quakers in the Northern forces who had volunteered for service or willingly responded to their call-up when conscripted. The fighting Quaker of course was not a new phenomenon: his existence had led to schism at the time of the Revolution. But whereas earlier, Friends who bore arms could usually expect eventual disownment if they did not condemn their actions, in the Civil War at least some Northern Quaker Meetings relaxed the stringency of their discipline and allowed those who had fought for the Union – and implicitly for the freedom of the slave – to retain membership in their Society. Among Southern Friends, however, where to fight was to fight for a proslavery government, no such leniency existed. A leading Quaker in North Carolina, Delphinia Mendenhall, was expressing the opinion of her coreligionists there when she wrote: 'It is sorrowful . . . that some have taken up arms but in our Saviour's own family there was not only a Peter, but a Judas.'[39]

In the North no Quaker, however firmly pacifist, would have dreamt of calling a young Friend, who had joined up in the crusade against disunion and the slave power, a Judas. He might be mistaken in the means he had adopted to oppose these evils but, however, deplorable his conduct might seem to some, most Friends were prepared to recognise the dilemma their young men of military age faced when pacifism and antislavery, two of the most cherished Quaker principles, appeared to be in head-on confrontation with each other. Some Meetings felt, therefore, that their members who had joined up were following the Inner Light as it appeared to them, and it would be quite wrong to penalise conscience by expelling such persons from their midst. It seems that urban Hicksite Meetings were least prone to disown their soldier members. But opposition to disownment on this score existed, too, among the Orthodox and even among the Conservatives who drew their strength very largely from rural Meetings. (On the other hand, all three branches of Quakerism contained Meetings which carried out the discipline by unfailingly disowning their unrepentent fighting Friends.)

We find the more liberal viewpoint expressed after the war was over by the editor of the New York *Friend*, the organ of the Hicksite Yearly Meeting in that State. It was quite wrong, he said, to require 'a Friend to be dis-owned for acting up to his highest conviction of duty. Warfare is horrible in the flesh – but it is heaven-born innocence by the side of a war upon conscience.'[40] We do not know, even approximately, the number of Friends who joined up – certainly a minority of those liable to serve – or the number of Quakers of military age who became conscientious objectors, either. Nor do we know exactly how many Quaker soldiers were dealt with by their Meetings, though we may presume the majority met with this fate, and how many escaped such proceedings. With the systematic record keeping of the Society of Friends such quantification might be possible but it has not yet been done.[41]

Motives for Quaker enlistment included patriotism as well as antislavery and abolitionist sentiments. They also undoubtedly included youthful love of adventure and a desire to do as one's peers were doing.[42]

We see the patriotic *motif*, for instance, in a letter a young Richmond, Indiana, Quaker sent to his girlfriend shortly before enlisting. 'We all know,' he wrote, 'the Bible says *thou shalt not kill*: but what are we to do with those persons that rebel against the law of our country, are we to just lie down and let them have the reins of this republican government. No! Never! So long as *God gives us* the power to quell them by any means.'[43] The abolitionist impulse, on the other hand, was clearly uppermost in men like Lucretia Mott's son-in-law Edmund M. Davis, who enrolled in the Union army during the first summer of the war. Like his mother-in-law, Davis during the antebellum era had warmly supported the New England Non-Resistance Society and helped to propagate its ideas at the risk of offending more conservatively minded Friends. As Lucretia Mott wrote to his sister (letter of 18 August 1861): 'Who would have thought, when Edmund was exerting himself – spreading Adin Ballou's works [on nonresistance] – to make converts to peace principles, that he would be among the active officers in this war? He flatters himself that the abolition of slavery – end, justifies the means.'[44]

The dilemma experienced most acutely by Friends of military age was reflected, too, in the minds of older men as well as of the women of the Society, who were not subject to conscription. Whittier, for instance, in an open letter he addressed 'To Members of the Society of Friends' soon after the outbreak of hostilities, outlined perceptively what he thought Quaker civilians should do in a situation where their peace testimony and their antislavery witness appeared to conflict. He wrote there on 18 June 1861:

> Steadily and faithfully maintaining our testimony against war, we owe it to the cause of truth, to show that exalted heroism and generous self-sacrifice are not incompatible with our pacific principles. Our mission is, at this time, to mitigate the sufferings of our countrymen, to visit and aid the sick and the wounded, to relieve the necessities of the widow and the orphan, and to practice economy for the sake of charity. Let the Quaker bonnet be seen by the side of the black bonnet of the Catholic Sisters of Charity in the hospital ward . . . Our Society is rich, and of those to whom much is given much will be required in this hour of proving and trial.[45]

And, in line with such sentiments as these, many Quaker women worked hard to provide comforts for the troops, especially for the sick and the wounded. They did this of course without distinction of the side on which the soldiers had been fighting. We find them contributing such items as bandages and sheets or warm clothing which they had either collected or made themselves. Quakers, both men and women, distributed Bibles and religious tracts in army camps and among Confederate prisoners of war. Others concentrated on work with the freedmen, an activity they often found more congenial than work with the troops and one which they continued for some years after the war was over. Some Friends collaborated with the privately run United States Sanitary Commission or one of its state affiliates; however, this organisation, though its objective was humanitarian aid, worked of course very closely with the military.[46]

As we have seen was the case with Quaker conscientious objectors in the army, it was not always easy, either, for the civilian Quaker pacifists to draw the line between genuinely humanitarian activities, whose recipients happened to be soldiers, and activities which, though seemingly humanitarian, in fact contributed primarily to the prosecution of the war. Some more sensitive souls indeed wondered if work for soldiers, especially those on one's own side, was at all compatible with Quakers' rejection of war. Most Friends, however, considered that, like the good Samaritan, they should help to ease suffering wherever it existed. 'War work' could be peace work if carried out in this spirit.[47]

But there were certain ostensibly civilian activities that the vast majority of Friends considered would, if undertaken, compromise their Society's witness and prove inconsistent with a genuine testimony against war. While only a handful of Quakers refused to pay ordinary taxes because these went in part to finance the current war,[48] many Friends, at any rate among those who held strictly to their pacifist principles, regarded the payment of Bounty Money and taxes imposed for the specific purpose of raising troops as incompatible with their Society's peace testimony. There were, however, some members who paid bounties and similar imposts – either unthinkingly or because they saw nothing wrong in a Quaker doing so. A Committee of Philadelphia (Orthodox) Yearly Meeting explained the situation as follows:

> Another source of trial and discouragement to us has been that some members have subscribed to funds raised for the payment of bounties to soldiers, and others have paid taxes levied and applied expressly for the same object; both which are clearly violations of our Christian testimony and discipline, and have tended to discourage and weaken the hands of faithful Friends, as well as to lessen the weight and influence of the Society when appealing to government for the relief of our drafted members. If those who thus aid in hiring men to fight were transported to the field of battle . . . surely they could not but lament that they had incurred the responsibility of helping forward the dreadful business, with its awful consequences. Distance from the scene of action does not lessen their accountability.[49]

The trouble, however, was that for at least a minority of Friends, especially those with sons serving in the Union army, anxiety to give support and comfort to the fighting men outweighed too nice a consideration of how far a noncombatant Quaker might go in this direction. What Nelson writes of Indiana Friends probably holds for Quakers in most other states: 'During the war . . . only a few Meetings took disciplinary action against Friends who gave material aid to the federal and state governments for war-related purposes.'[50]

Whatever the fears of some Northern Quakers that their coreligionists had on occasion gone too far in their support of the Unionist cause, Friends on the whole gained increased respect from their fellow citizens on account of their humanitarian work for the victims of war, both in and out of uniform. Often such exertions formed part of Quakers' general concern for all who suffered or were in need and they harmonised with their ideal of service. As the chaplain of the 14th Wisconsin Volunteers remarked after observing at first hand this kind of Quaker 'war work': 'I saw the difference . . . between talking Christianity and acting it.'[51] In the North at any rate a realisation that the Quakers, if most of them remained noncombatants, were nevertheless anxious to serve their country in so far as such service was compatible with their principled objection to war, helped to smooth their relations with the civilian authorities from the President and his administration in Washington down to local officials at the county level. It also, we have seen, eased their contacts with the military when these became necessary in order to rescue Quaker conscientious objectors from the clutches of the army. Even in the South where Friends' long standing opposition to slavery made them suspect generally, we often find understanding of the Quaker viewpoint at any rate among senior civilian officials, if not always on the lower levels of the Confederate bureaucracy.

If we compare the Quaker response to the Civil War with the stance the Society occupied at the time of the American Revolution, we are struck by the contrasting attitudes it adopted toward government during the two periods. To the Revolutionary authorities Quakers for the most part remained passively hostile, at best neutral. With Lincoln's administration, on the other hand, they enjoyed friendly relations, each side respecting the other's viewpoint even if it did not share it and feeling a number of aims and ideals were held in common. The same could not be said, of course, of Southern Quakers' relationship with the Confederate government but even here the mutual suspicion of the Revolutionary era was absent. A second difference between the two periods lies in the prevailing attitude within the Society of Friends toward those members who bore arms. In the Revolution such persons were almost invariably disowned: most Friends at that time felt they had rejected their Society's heritage by their conduct. True, Friends during and after the Civil War continued to disown fighting Quakers and those who flagrantly violated the peace testimony. But now there were many instances when disciplinary action was not taken for such offences, and when disownment under existing circumstances was considered a violation of those rights of conscience which Quakerism had always sought to defend.

The Civil War saw no mass defection from the Quaker peace testimony such as would occur among certain sections especially of evangelical

Quakerism over the next century. Most Friends, whether liable to the draft or not, made clear their continued allegiance to pacifism. But they were conscious, more than ever before probably, that their witness against war was shared by very few of their fellow Americans and was able to exert little, if any, influence on the conduct of affairs. This witness was, perhaps, during those dark years of civil war 'comparable to a little taper casting a glimmering light through the surrounding gloom.'[52] The gloom lifted after the coming of peace but Friends continued to need the light generated by their testimony against war to illumine the darkening shadows now cast by renewed preparation for battle.

CHAPTER XV

Quakers and War Taxes: An Overview

THE QUESTION OF WAR TAXES EMERGES periodically in the history of the Quaker peace testimony, and we have already referred to it more than once in the previous pages. At the risk of having to repeat some of this material I feel it may still be helpful to give a consecutive account of the reactions of Friends on both sides of the Atlantic to this problem.

Almost all early Quakers had believed it was right to pay taxes to the state – render tribute to Caesar – regardless of the use to which such monies would be put. While they consistently refused to pay tithes to the established church, they considered taxation for secular purposes fell into a different category; in their view acquiescence in this had been expressly commanded by Jesus when he said, 'Pay Caesar what is due to Caesar, and pay God what is due to God' (Luke 20:25). When a poll tax was imposed in 1667 to finance the war against Holland and again in 1678 for the war against France, George Fox as well as Margaret Fell (who became his wife) and her daughter Sarah Fell paid without murmur. Moreover, Fox, in 'a paper concerning tribute . . . sent to some Friends' in connection with one or other of these poll acts, himself endorsed payment as a matter of conscience in the following unambiguous terms:

> To the earthly we give the earthly: that is, to Caesar we give unto him his things, and to God we give unto Him His things . . . So in this thing, so doing, we can plead with Caesar and plead with them that hath our custom and hath our tribute if they seek to hinder us from our godly and peaceable life . . . Which, if Friends should not do and had not done – give Caesar his due, and custom and tribute to them that look for it, which are for the punishment of evil-doers – then might they say and plead against us, How can we defend you against foreign invaders and protect everyone in their estates and keep down thieves and murderers.[1]

This statement reflects the conditional justification of force if exercised by the state to protect the good and the defenceless and to suppress wrongdoers that Fox, we know, shared with the Anabaptist-Mennonite tradition of nonresistance.

Fox's position on war taxation, however, did not go entirely unchallenged in his day. We hear, for instance, of the dissident Friend, John Pennyman, arguing with Fox on the matter in 1670, the year of his expulsion from the Society. Pennyman thought it inconsistent of Fox to support disownment of members who were willing to pay the fine imposed for not bearing arms, and yet at the same time himself pay the tax levied for 'carrying on the war against the Dutch.' 'This practice,' Pennyman told the Quaker leader, in his opinion 'was not agreeable with Truth, for that it seemed to be more justifiable to pay towards the trained bands, to prevent the invasion of the Dutch (which was then feared, they being then at Chatham) than those taxes you allowed of, inasmuch as defensive wars are more allowable than offensive.' To Pennyman evidently, financing the defence of English soil appeared more justifiable than contributing money for a naval war against the Dutch. In reply, Fox had simply told Pennyman (according to the latter's account), 'That the Son paid taxes' and Quakers should therefore follow his example.[2]

In 1693 London Yearly Meeting officially confirmed Fox's standpoint as that of the whole Society. While as disciples of Christ, said its minute, Friends were forbidden to fight, by the same authority they were obliged to pay any taxes and tribute money Caesar might demand from them. For, if they did not do so, the ruler might justifiably take offence and act harshly toward them. There was no talk here of Friends having an obligation – still less a right – to refrain from contributing if they judged the use to be made of their money was wrong.[3]

The attitude on war taxes of William Penn, whose authority in the Society weighed second only to Fox's, reflected that of the older leader. This comes out clearly in a letter Penn wrote from Bristol on 5 September 1695 to some politically influential Friends in his colony of Pennsylvania in an effort to persuade the Assembly to grant money for the Crown's military needs – 'for a common defence' of their province and New York against impending French and Indian attack. Penn, who we must remember in his capacity as proprietor held the honorary rank of 'Captain-General,' had only recently recovered possession of Pennsylvania and was understandably fearful of jeopardising the continuance of Quaker control there. He, therefore, chided his coreligionists for their reluctance to make the financial contribution the Crown was requesting from them. He writes:

> Now our case is this. Here [i.e., in England] we pay to carry on a vigorous war against France. And Friends here admire [i.e., wonder] at the difficulty of the people there to pay, saying it seems to contradict us here; especially since it may be given under the style of peace and

safety or to defray the exigencies of the Government, and deposit it in such hands as may keep Friends clear from breach of their testimony and the country from such complaints as may overset the Government again or contradict Friends here that pay much more barefacedly. Others there will give besides Friends and others pay as well as Friends, so [it] is a mixt thing, and for mixt services. I intreat you to weigh this matter and apply some speedy remedy to this affair as you in wisdom should think meet.[4]

In fact Penn's view of the matter as expressed here became the standard practice of Pennsylvania Friends until the mid-1750s. Throughout this period, as shown in an earlier chapter, the Quaker Assemblymen regularly acceded to the Crown's requests for money to carry on England's wars or to finance preparations for military defence, their tribute to Caesar being given the name of money for the King (or Queen's) use.

Yet it is clear, I think, not all Friends, at any rate in North America, felt easy with this situation. There were members of the Society who regarded the payment of money they knew would be assigned to military purposes as incompatible with their peace testimony. We see from Penn's letter cited above that, at least at that time, some of the Pennsylvania Assemblymen entertained such reservations. While visiting Rhode Island in 1702, the English Quaker minister, John Richardson, noted similar qualms among Friends there as to the correctness of paying 'a lay or tax . . . for building some fortifications, and to provide men and arms for the security of the island.' (He also noted a similar uneasiness in the matter among English Friends, though they had, he said, failed to discover a viable alternative to paying, since taxes there were 'mixed.')[5] But no action appears to have been taken by Rhode Island Friends, for they continued to pay their taxes even when these were obviously destined for military use.[6]

A more serious 'revolt' against the accepted view with regard to war taxation came in Pennsylvania in 1711 after the victory at the polls in the previous year of the more conservative Quaker faction and their subsequent grant of £2000 'for the Queen's use' – in fact to help equip an expedition against the French. Most Friends paid the tax levied to raise this money but some objected and had their goods distrained (by Quaker constables!), while several objectors – presumably persons possessing insufficient property to distrain – spent a brief period in jail (one Friend was even disowned for tax refusal). Among those Quakers vigorously defending the Assembly's position in voting the grant was British-born Thomas Story, who had emigrated to Pennsylvania and was at that time a member of the provincial council – as well as an influential figure in Philadelphia Yearly Meeting. Story now cited the precedent of the Anglo-Dutch wars of the previous century when Dutch Friends, on the one hand, and English

Friends led by George Fox, on the other, had dutifully paid the taxes which their respective governments raised to finance their war efforts, responsibility for the blood then shed resting, in Story's (and Fox's) view, with the two warring states and not with the Quaker communities in each country.[7]

Story's arguments met with a vigorous rebuttal in an anonymous pamphlet entitled *Tribute to Caesar, How paid by the Best Christians, and to What Purpose*. Its author, who wrote under the name of 'Philalethes,' was one William Rakestraw, a member of Philadelphia Monthly Meeting, who was disowned by that body in 1713 for his public and vocal opposition to the official stand the Pennsylvania Society had taken in the matter.[8] His pamphlet, writes Marietta, constitutes 'the first airing of a caveat that divided [American] Quakers throughout the colonial period and the . . . Revolution.' Rakestraw, who seems to have been of a rather cantankerous disposition, worked closely with the antiproprietary party led by that militant constitutionalist – and Quaker – David Lloyd. In fact, though we have no reason to doubt his attachment to Quaker peace principles, the former had long been feuding on largely personal issues with Penn and his secretary James Logan.[9] As Marietta rightly points out, Rakestraw, like many contemporary polemicists, lacked charity so that his rancour against his opponents and general bad temper spoilt his claim to be an advocate of peace. In his arguments he foreshadows those used by Woolman and other Quaker reformers later but, practically speaking, he appears as a party apologist, a demagogue who acted – so far as we can see – largely from personal, rather than strictly ideological, motives.

Less controversial support for Quaker war tax objection might have been derived, indirectly, from the work of a contemporary of Rakestraw's, the German-born Francis Daniel Pastorius, who had emigrated to Pennsylvania in 1683 and then helped in the foundation of Germantown situated a little to the north of that city. A Pietist by conviction and a man of wide learning, and possessing a thorough knowledge of Greek and Latin as well as of the Bible and of the law, Pastorius had become a Quaker after his settlement in the New World. We find his name among the signatories of the pioneer antislavery protest drawn up in 1688 by the German-speaking members of Germantown Monthly Meeting. At some unspecified date prior to his death in 1719, Pastorius composed a short essay on taxation, which he entitled 'The Matter of Taxes and Contributions briefly examined by Plain Scripture Testimonies and Sound Reason.' This clearly written and well argued piece remained in manuscript until it was discovered and published by Henry J. Cadbury in 1934.[10] Cadbury could find no indication of the date of its composition but Pastorius must of course have written it before 1720. It does not, however, deal specifically with the question of war taxation. This indeed is rather strange considering the fact that war taxes, in a veiled form, were being imposed by the Quaker controlled Pennsylvania legislature during the last decade of the 17th, and the first two decades of the 18th century.

Probably Pastorius shared the prevalent view among Friends on both sides of the Atlantic approving payment to the state of all forms of taxation and not that of Rakestraw and the small group of Quaker war tax objectors active between 1711 and 1713. At any rate, in his essay Pastorius states, 'All loyal subjects are oblig'd . . . to pay unto [those in authority] taxes, customs and the like, so that . . . they may be able continually to attend upon their respective places of eminence, care and trust.' Christ Jesus, he says, had expressly commanded the payment of tribute to Caesar both in his teaching and 'by his own practice.' Nevertheless, Woolman's war tax resistance movement of mid-century, if its members had known of Pastorius' essay (which of course they did not), might have drawn from his work some effective arguments to buttress their case. For Pastorius demonstrates clearly his belief that, despite the gospel injunctions, Christians must refuse Caesar his tribute if to contribute goes against conscience. He writes:

> But, whether all . . . impositions may with good conscience be paid or not? is a question, which deserves seriously and solidly to be considered by those who desire to be true to God, their magistrates and themselves too . . . Some taxations are made in general terms, for the use of the respective higher powers, and for the maintenance of the present government we live under; and these, I think, none dare refuse to pay, though even unto Nero himself. For subjects, not being above their sovereigns, can't set themselves upon the tribunal-seat, to call them to account, or to inquire how their tribute-money is spent . . . [But] if money be levied for a certain use, which directly tends to the dishonour of God, or is expressly forbidden by him, we can't pay anything to it without the violation of our conscience . . . In short, whatever we make conscience to act or do ourselves we dare in no wise contribute the least farthing thereunto, to have it acted or done by others, unless we be willing to partake of their sins, and the just punishment thereof. *Quod quis per alium facit, per se fecisse putatur*[11] . . . What should we do then in this case? Answ.: It's our duty to hearken more unto God, than unto men, Acts 4:19.[12] and to be obedient passively, and not oppose the collectors, when they are taking away our goods, nor resist 'em when seizing on our persons.

The only illustration Pastorius gives of the kind of impost he thinks should be resisted in this way is that of 'a tax or tribute . . . demanded for the building of a mass house [i.e., Roman Catholic church], or other idolatrous temple.' But the scenario he envisages here exactly fits the response made by Woolman and his colleagues to the war tax imposed by the Pennsylvania Assembly in 1755.

I have dealt in an earlier chapter of this book in some detail with the Woolman-inspired tax refusal movement and its background, and I do not wish to repeat what I said there (where I think such treatment is most appropriate, for otherwise the mid-century crisis of Quaker pacifism in Pennsylvania is not intelligible). Woolman in this case was prepared to face not only the personal consequences of conscientiously breaking the law but also the pain this would cause the majority of his fellow Quakers, who did not share his view. The tax objectors who had followed Woolman's lead, of course, often felt isolated within the Society, like the North Carolina Quaker who in 1757 told Woolman that hitherto he had been the only member of his Yearly Meeting to refuse payment of taxes that went toward the support of war.[13]

The Woolmanite protest was directed against all forms of taxation, however camouflaged by innocuous sounding phrases, that were raised largely – or entirely – to cover the expenses of war. The Woolmanites, it would seem, did not oppose taxes, the greater part of which went to support the legitimate nonmilitary aspects of government, for of course they shared the belief common to all Friends that government was a necessary instrument of God's plan for mankind. But I do not think they ever attempted to say exactly where the line, admittedly a fine one, should be drawn between general taxation which Friends should contribute – without murmuring – and those taxes in which the military component was so large that, in their view, it would be wrong for a conscientious Quaker pacifist to pay.

The idea implanted by Woolman and his colleagues grew slowly. But by the American Revolution the notion of war-tax resistance had already spread from Pennsylvania into the other sections of the colonial Society of Friends. Opinion, however, remained divided on the issue; there was lively, and sometimes acrimonious, debate between supporters and opponents of payment; but the ranks of the war-tax resisters had widened and their stand had ceased to be regarded by the majority of Friends as a threat to the Quaker establishment. The Revolutionary War situation, however, was complicated by the fact that some Friends objected to paying wartime taxes not so much because a large proportion of the money they contributed would be allocated to prosecuting the current war but because they did not recognise the change from the royal to the republican régime. Here the basis for objecting had shifted from the purely Christian pacifist grounds urged by the Woolmanites earlier, but it is not always easy to distinguish between these two variants of war-tax objection, for often they were inextricably interwoven within the thinking of the same person.

Anyhow, as early as 1776 we find Philadelphia Yearly Meeting approving a statement 'that a tax levied for the purchasing of drums, colours, and other warlike purposes, cannot be paid consistent with our Christian testimony.'[14] Two years later, when the subject of war taxes was raised at the same Yearly Meeting, a minute was passed, which dealt more broadly with the subject. 'We find,' it declared, 'in several different quarters a religious scruple hath appeared and increases among Friends, against the payment of taxes, imposed for the purpose of carrying on the present war; they being deeply concerned and engaged faithfully to maintain our Christian testimony against joining with or supporting the spirit of wars and fightings, which hath remarkably tended to unite us in a deep sympathy with the seed of life in their hearts.' The minute went on to urge Friends to watch carefully for the still voice of conscience within and be extremely careful 'to avoid complying with the injunctions and requisitions made for the purpose of carrying on war, which may produce uneasiness to themselves and tend to increase the sufferings of their brethren.'[15] Such a resolution would have been impossible at the time when Woolman launched his campaign of tax refusal in 1755, for then, we know, Friends in office collaborated without qualms of conscience in distraining the property of Quaker tax objectors and in addition putting a few of them in jail. Nevertheless, even now, as Marietta correctly remarks, 'the refusal to pay taxes for war remained a voluntary and personal decision, which the Yearly Meeting commended but did not require.'[16] The commendation, however, marked a victory for the war-tax objectors, even though their position did not become a requirement of membership and was probably not shared by the majority of Friends, despite their increased openness to it.

Thus, when hostilities commenced opinion in the Society had become split. It embraced many who took the traditional view and argued that all taxes should be paid irrespective of the use the authorities would make of them or of any change of government that might take place. Such persons could of course cite a host of precedents from the practice of Friends on this continent as well as the even more telling example of the Society in Britain. There Quakers demurred to paying tithes but so far never to other forms of taxation. As one American Friend declared in 1775: 'If we receive advantage from civil government, we ought to bear our part of the charge of maintaining it, or else we have no recourse to it in any case whatsoever.' How the state employed the money it received from its citizens remained its business alone. Even Moses Brown, a leading Rhode Island Quaker, who advocated refusal of taxes destined exclusively for war purposes, considered that Friends should not 'raise their testimony so high as to refuse paying taxes mixt with civil government,' however large the proportion allocated to war might be.[17] We even find some isolated Friends, like the group at

Gilmanton in New Hampshire, apparently unaware, at any rate early on in the war, that war-tax refusal was an acceptable Quaker position at all. For in 1776 they told the Provincial Congress: 'We agree and consent to the Declaration of Independence of the British Crown and are willing to pay our proportion to the support of the United Colonies but as to defend with arms, it is against our religious principles and pray we may be excused.'[18]

But as the war progressed, the tax problem emerged more prominently as a concern of the Society. For one thing, most Friends, even if they inclined toward the American side, refused to subscribe to, still less join, any military association set up to prosecute more effectively the revolutionary cause. They, therefore, became subject in most areas under the control of the revolutionary authorities to double, sometimes even treble, the amount paid by 'associators.' Increased taxes were also laid on those, including Quakers and members of other peace churches, who would not make a declaration of allegiance to the new régime.[19] Discrimination of this kind brought home the tax issue to many Friends who had not perhaps given it much thought before. It was now linked not only with their Society's peace testimony but with its *Obrigkeitsdoktrin*: the combination led them to reconsider their whole attitude.

Some Yearly Meetings advised their members to refuse to pay levies associated with the war or collaborate in any way with their collection, at any rate so long as the existing state of political uncertainty lasted.[20] Particularly objectionable was the policy, pursued for instance in North Carolina, where the revolutionary administration increased the amount of taxation imposed on members of peace sects – in exchange, as it were, for their exemption from military service. Not all Friends there conformed when their Yearly Meeting told them to practice tax resistance, nor did all sections of the Society recommend this in similar circumstances, although everywhere it had become at least a permissible form of Quaker behaviour.[21]

In some areas where tax resistance was widespread on the part of Friends, these suffered severe losses by distraint of property (that is, in addition to distraints imposed in connection with other forms of opposition to the war).[22] We even hear of one case from Rhode Island where, during the summer of 1781, a Quaker was put in prison for nonpayment of tax but soon released, after his Friends had intervened on his behalf with the Governor and Council.[23]

In addition to the practical dilemmas and decisions Friends faced in responding to demands from the State for war taxes, lively debate also took place among members of the Society over the issue. The first to appear in print was Timothy Davis, a prominent New England Friend, who

published in 1776 a short *Letter . . . on the Subject of Paying Taxes*. In its
pages he vigorously defended payment of all tax demands made by the
revolutionary authorities. He did not seek to undermine the Society's
pacifism, as the Free Quakers of Philadelphia would do;[24] instead, he
argued (correctly) that unconditional payment of taxes, including those
destined for war, had for long been accepted by most Quaker pacifists,
including George Fox and Thomas Story. Since he had failed to obtain
official permission for publication from his Yearly Meeting, he was
therefore disowned two years later when some 40 other Friends followed
him out of the Society. Davis then found a champion for his views in Joseph
Taber, whose *Address to the People called Quakers* was published in Boston in
1784.

The most eloquent statement of the case against paying war taxes came
from the pen of Samuel Allinson, a weighty New Jersey Friend, trained in
the law and sometime Surveyor General of his native province. He
composed his 'Reasons against War, and Paying Taxes for Its Support'[25]
during the summer of 1780. Since Friends felt it wrong on religious grounds
to fight, they should therefore abstain, Allinson argued, from giving money
for others to do what they themselves believed was unchristian. Moreover,
they ought in no way to assist in overthrowing an existing government and
replacing it by another. For Friends to contribute financially to the
Continental Congress or any other revolutionary authority was therefore
doubly wrong. 'We pay our proportion to the support of the poor, the
maintenance of roads and the support of civil order in government (if the
demand is unmixed with war or tithes). These include every benefit we ask
or receive. We desire not war or any of its consequences, nor do we
apprehend any benefit arising from it.' The main thrust of Allinson's
argument was against taxes imposed specifically for carrying on war. The
more radical viewpoint that also rejected all mixed taxes which included
both a warlike and a peaceful component – a position Allinson was
sympathetic to – found a cogent exponent in the Rhode Island minister
Job Scott. Like Allinson's work Scott's 'Truly Conscientious Scruple,'
which he composed around 1780, also remained in manuscript.[26] Although
Allinson's tract circulated widely among Friends, the Quaker authorities
seem to have been reluctant to allow anything at all controversial to appear
in print, for they feared the effect this might have on a membership divided
in its views on the subject. Neither work, therefore, was printed, their
authors submitting loyally to the censorship the Society then exercised over
the publications of its members.

The Revolution thus marked an important stage in the evolution of
Quaker thinking on war taxes. For the first time the American Society had
officially supported refusal of war taxes when clearly designated as such:

this registered a decisive break with the stand taken earlier by such Quaker leaders as Fox, Penn, and Story. Disownment, at least theoretically, might now result if a Friend flouted the discipline on this point. How to react when the tax was 'mixed' remained of course a matter for individual decision but here, too, tax objection had gained greater recognition, at any rate if such objection was manifested in time of war.

Turning back to Great Britain we may observe a similar trend, though not so marked as in North America, taking place toward the end of the century after the outbreak of the long war first with Revolutionary, and then with Napoleonic France. For the first time for several centuries England faced invasion from the continent: military matters, therefore, loomed large in the minds of the whole populace, including the peaceable Quakers. In 1799 the government levied a special 'Aid and Contribution for the Prosecution of the War.' Some Friends paid this as they had paid all previous taxation, others felt 'uneasy' but nevertheless paid, while still others (we do not know exactly how many) refused to pay and distraint was then made upon their property. In addition, two acts, even more closely associated with the actual performance of military service, were passed during this period – a Navy Act in 1795 and a Cavalry Act in 1796: the one imposing a rate for providing sailors for the Royal Navy and the other a rate for cavalrymen and horses for the army. London Yearly Meeting appears to have regarded these imposts in much the same light as they viewed fines for refusing to find a substitute for service in the militia. And, as we know, finding a man for military service was, in the opinion of Friends, tantamount to fighting oneself. In 1796 the Yearly Meeting censured members who contributed to the Navy rate. Although disownment of those who paid does not appear to have been contemplated, local Meetings were told to take the delinquents 'under their care.'[27] We do not hear any longer of the obligation incumbent on Friends of paying every tribute Caesar might demand, and Fox and Story were no longer cited in defence of this view. (Perhaps indeed their injunctions in the matter were now forgotten, while those of John Woolman were probably remembered on both sides of the Atlantic.)

The most striking instance of war-tax resistance among British Friends comes from an obscure Herefordshire merchant, Nathaniel Morgan from Ross-on-Wye. He and his father, whom Nathaniel had converted to his point of view, refused to pay the new income tax from 1799 on because they believed this was used to finance the ongoing war. They had informed the Commissioners of the Income Tax that they were willing to 'suffer loss of goods, fine, or imprisonment' for their stand and also that their objection was not to the tax as such – 'it being the most just mode of raising money' adopted hitherto – but to the uses to which it was then being put. Their property of course suffered distraint to cover the fines imposed regularly for nonpayment, but in exchange, they got, as Nathaniel put it, 'peace of mind, which was worth all.' Few, if any, Friends followed their example, and the Morgans failed to persuade London Yearly Meeting to adopt their position, despite many attempts to do so. For the Morgans, in wartime income-tax resistance seemed an essential part of their witness as pacifists. But for the overwhelming majority of Friends, paying taxes 'in the mixture' (and as such they regarded income tax) continued to be acceptable behaviour, and they did not regard this as incompatible with their Society's peace testimony. After attending Yearly Meeting in 1813, Nathaniel wrote in his diary: 'I fear my fellow [Quakers] are led by paltry interest and fear of offending the high people of this day.'[28] The judgement was not altogether fair, but it expressed the frustration felt by this ardent advocate of peace when his coreligionists failed to adopt what he considered the only course open to Friends, if they wished their conduct to be consistent with the principles of peace they professed before the outside world.

So far as I know, after the Morgans the war tax question ceased to be a concern of British Friends. Almost a century of peace now ensued for England after 1815; conflicts like the Crimean War or the Boer War were all fought far from home. There was thus no longer the same urgency among Friends concerning such problems as there had been during the long struggle against France. Nevertheless the tax question continued from time to time if not exactly to agitate, at least mildly to interest, American Quakers: this was especially the case during the Civil War.

In the aftermath of the Revolution Friends in the New Republic had warmly debated the question whether they might consistently pay the taxation now imposed to sink the Revolutionary war debt. Once again there was divergence of views. It was the old story: some Friends paid while others refused and suffered distraint. We find Baltimore Meeting for Sufferings, for instance, taking a stern view of its members who conformed to the new state's demand for money. 'Notwithstanding the effusion of human blood has been stayed,' it declared in February 1784, 'Friends cannot be clear in paying taxes imposed for sinking the debt incurred by the late war.' Since this admonition was not always heeded, the Meeting four years later called for the disownment of the delinquents. Inside Pennsylvania Yearly Meeting support for tax payment of this kind seems to have been stronger, or at any rate more vocal. In one Quarterly Meeting we learn there was 'some tight rubbing work' needed in order to enforce the official Quaker view that such taxes should not be paid. 'We had it up and down about taxpaying,' wrote one of the members a little later. Other Yearly Meetings, while sometimes urging mutual toleration of divergent views, followed a similar line in requiring members not to pay such taxes as were clearly incompatible with the Society's peace testimony.[29] But by the end of the 1780s, and as Quakers came to terms with the new political situation created by the successful revolution, the question ceased to be a live issue. The old resolutions against 'paying taxes for the express purpose of war,' passed by the various Yearly Meetings, usually remained in force, and they were sometimes adopted in part or *in toto* by the new Yearly Meetings that were established with the advance of Quakerism into the newly opened up territories in the West.[30] But such resolutions do not appear any longer to have aroused much concern among Friends.

In the 1790s, and again during the War of 1812, we find a few Quakers objecting to payment of import duties, which they believed were in fact concealed war taxes.[31] Joshua Evans, for instance, a Quaker minister from New Jersey, avoided the use of imported articles of this kind. 'I could see no material difference,' he wrote, 'between paying the expenses relating to war, in taxes, or in duties.' The apothecary Isaac Martin during the War of 1812 took the same stand as Evans had done earlier. He refused to stock his shop with items on which import duty had been laid, even though this meant turning many customers away and consequent financial loss. For men such as Evans and Martin discomfort and material disadvantage were compensated for by the feeling that they were acting in accordance with their Society's testimony against war.

The same exact observance of Quaker peace principles comes out in the behaviour during the Civil War of Joshua Maule, an obscure mid-Western Friend. Maule was reared in Ohio among the Conservative (or Wilburite) branch of the Society. Already middle-aged when war broke out Maule, a man of strong, if somewhat rigid, views, felt that the Wilburite Friends, for all their strictness in other ways, had 'flinched and failed' to bear a consistent witness for peace. For he would have liked them to have followed 18th-century Quaker reformers like Woolman, Churchman, or Scott in refusing to pay all taxes that went toward support of war. He was himself prepared to do this: he regarded payment of these levies as complicity in bloodshed. The situation, however, was not quite so simple as in Woolman's day, for now most taxes were mixed ones. Maule's solution was to deduct 8½% from his total tax bill, 'which was,' as he explained to the county treasurer when handing in his money, 'the part expressly named in the tax list as for the war.' After some hesitation at first on the part of the local tax authorities, who showed respect for Maule's conscientious scruples, distraint came to be made regularly on his property so as to recover the amount he had refused to pay. Even if he had failed to keep his 'tribute' from being forcibly assigned to the prosecution of war, still, Maule's conscience was now at rest: 'what appeared at first like a mountain of difficulty,' he wrote, 'has passed comfortably away.'[32]

A few other Friends followed Maule's example in not paying wartime taxes 'in the mixture,' but on the whole Quakers – whether in the North or in the South – failed to see inconsistency here between their pacifism and their payment. They felt little sympathy with the sort of tax radicalism Maule was espousing. And their position was upheld by the various Yearly Meetings irrespective of the branch of the Society to which these belonged. Most Yearly Meetings, however, did advise members to refrain from paying when the tax was clearly – and exclusively – designed to carry on the war, though no disciplinary action of the kind often taken against young Quakers who joined the army seems to have been contemplated against Friends who conformed in this case to the state's demands. Decision was left to the individual conscience.[33] However, many Friends in the North did suffer distraint for nonpayment of such levies as the bounty money for raising recruits for the Union army.

With the conclusion of the Civil War discussion of war taxes virtually ceased for over half a century. It had stopped, we have seen, being a live issue among British Friends long before 1865. In the postbellum United States, writes Edwin Bronner, 'references to responsibility in this regard disappeared from many books of *Faith and Practice*, although the Wilburite or Conservative Yearly Meetings continued to include such admonitions.'[34] The problem revived again within the Society of Friends only in the aftermath of the two World Wars.

In sum, we may say there existed three alternative Quaker responses to war taxation in the period before 1914. In the first place, there was the view predominating among early Friends that did not distinguish between different kinds of secular taxes. Though ecclesiastical imposts were a different matter, the conscientious Christian was otherwise obliged to pay every form of tribute exacted from him by Caesar. If the ruler put such tax money to war purposes, this was his business and not that of his subjects. Secondly came the attitude associated with John Woolman's initiative in the 1750s that considered payment of any tax that was entirely – or very largely – destined for military use to be incompatible with Friends' objection to fighting. This position was adopted in North America, at any rate by most sections of the Society, as a result of the turmoil and stresses of the Revolution. Finally came the most radical attitude of all: the rejection of the war component contained in taxes 'in the mixture.' This view, which emerged fairly late and seems to have surfaced only in time of war, never attracted the support of more than a handful of persons in any given period. It was, however, the position which corresponds most closely to that of tax objectors at the present day when taxation is usually raised for combined support of both the civil and the military enterprises of the state.

The Shaker Peace Testimony: A Variant of Quaker Pacifism

THE SHAKERS – OR, TO GIVE THEM their official title, the United Society of Believers in Christ's Second Appearing – originated in England as an offshoot of the Quakers. But the new sect, while preserving traces of its Quaker roots, soon developed along different lines: celibacy and communitarianism (with men and women living separately in the same community) became its distinctive characteristics as did also an ecstatic form of communal worship that contrasted sharply with the sober and quiet Quaker Meeting. However, when Ann Lee, the founder of Shakerism (who was to become widely known as 'Mother Ann') arrived in New York from England in 1774 along with eight companions, the shape the new religious movement would take was as yet uncertain. Ann Lee, while still living in her native Manchester and working there as a factory hand, had come into contact with two religious enthusiasts, James and Jane Wardley, former Quakers who were ardently awaiting the second coming of Christ on earth – this time as a woman. They eventually chose Ann Lee for this role. Although illiterate, Mother Ann proved indeed a charismatic personality, a capable leader whom adversity failed to quell and whose faith in her mission served to surmount the hostility which the sect's peculiarities at first evoked in the outside world.

Mother Ann and her small band of followers had settled near Albany in upstate New York, then largely a wilderness. Growth came slowly but eventually a number of other religious seekers joined them and the sect began to expand: the new members consisted mostly of farming folk and rural craftsmen with a handful of converts coming from the educated classes. One such was Joseph Meacham, a former Baptist who succeeded to the Shaker leadership after Mother Ann's death in 1784. It was in fact Meacham, and not Mother Ann, who established the communitarian way of life and gave the Shakers a firm, though loosely congregational, organisation. The sect spread first into Massachusetts, Connecticut, and New Hampshire, and later into Maine, Ohio, Indiana, and Kentucky.

Mother Ann had learnt about pacifism from the Wardleys: she succeeded in making it a fixed tenet of the Shakers. During the Revolutionary War she and her followers had come under suspicion both as pro-British and as antimilitarists who preached against war. Several times they faced mob attack and met it nonviolently, refusing to ask for police protection. They did not hide their unwillingness to bear arms and spoke out openly against war, which more than once caused their arrest and imprisonment by the Revolutionary authorities. From the beginning they had made clear their principled opposition to fighting. As early as 1778 we hear of Shakers of military age being required to serve in the New York militia and being excused from appearing on muster days on payment of a fine (a way out open we know to the unconscientious as well as the conscientious). Meacham seems to have been the first to formulate a brief statement of Shaker pacifism: it was aimed primarily at enlightening the authorities concerning the sect's stand. He wrote:

> We cannot consistent with our faith and conscience, bear the arms of war, for the purpose of shedding the blood of any, or to do anything to justify or encourage it in others. But if they require, by fines or taxes of us, on that account, according to their laws, we may, for peace sake, answer their demands in that respect, and be innocent so far as we know at present . . . We believe we are free by the gospel, and that the time is near when others will be so far enlightened that they will be willing to exempt us.[1]

In line with the last sentence of this declaration, Shakers, once the war was over, launched a campaign to obtain official exemption from militia service, a campaign that was to be continued off and on for many decades to come. In November 1788, at a time when the militia question, including exemption for religious objectors, was being discussed in Congress and in the State legislatures, one Daniel Goodrich and a number of other brethren from the Hancock community in Massachusetts petitioned their State legislature 'praying to be exempt from military duty to which they were conscientiously opposed.' In fact Massachusetts in 1809 did grant exemption to Shakers (along with Quakers), provided they produced 'annually . . . a certificate to the commanding officer of the company within whose bounds such Quaker or Shaker resides; such certificates [to be] signed by two or more elders . . . and countersigned by the clerk of the Society with which such Quaker or Shaker meets for religious worship.'[2] Shakers, however, were less successful in persuading other states to grant such generous terms to their objectors.

The sect at first had seen no harm in paying commutation money, where this was still required, in lieu of militia service. A change in attitude, however, occurred during the War of 1812; by the conclusion of hostilities Shakers had come to adopt the same absolutist position as Quakers held in the matter. Henceforward they refused to pay fines in lieu of service and asked, therefore, for unconditional exemption from the authorities. The reasons for this change are not quite clear. Perhaps closer acquaintance with Quaker doctrine influenced the Shaker leaders, who felt they should not take a less uncompromising stand than Friends had done; probably too, the increased separation from the world brought about by their communitarian lifestyle inclined Shakers to a more rigid stand on the question of military service.

During the War of 1812 militia conscripts in the Eastern communities had continued to pay their fines, except in Massachusetts and New Hampshire where they were unconditionally exempt. They therefore encountered little or no trouble over their objection to bearing arms. In the new communities in the West, however, things were different. Shakerism had grown rapidly there as a result of the proselytising activities of a number of capable missionaries: their campaigns were conducted on territories recently affected by the Kentucky revival. Shakerism in these areas was new and exposed to the same kind of popular hostility as Mother Ann had met with on her arrival on this continent. The Shakers' kindly treatment of the Shawnee Indians, who inhabited the area in which they had come to live, added to the ill feeling with which the local white settlers regarded the communitarians. Softness toward the Indians on the Shakers' part, coupled with their unwillingness to fight, led therefore to calls to expel them from these territories. In fact, the Busro community in Indiana was virtually – though only temporarily – abandoned in the autumn of 1812. 'At this juncture many of the brothers were drafted; their failure to serve resulted in heavy fines.' Eventually, after the successful intervention of a friendly colonel who had known the Shakers in Kentucky, Governor William Henry Harrison took a more lenient view. 'The Brethren were allowed to do hospital work rather than serve.'

A year later, in the autumn of 1813, it was the turn of the community of Union Village (Ohio) to encounter difficulties in respect of the draft. Then, seven brethren were called up into the army where attempts were made to force them to bear arms. The leaders of the community reminded the draftees, as they departed from the community, that they should 'consider themselves as a kingdom of priests or tribe of Levites,' separated from the world by their religious profession and – so at least they hoped – 'lawfully exempted from the contaminated services of a military life.' The men were instructed as follows:

Preach the word – be constant in season, out of season – be an example to all men. Go forth as lambs in the midst of wolves – be wise as serpents – harmless as doves – do violence to no man – render not evil for evil but overcome evil with good. Do good to them that hate you, pray for them that despitefully use you.

Once enrolled, the draftees endeavoured to keep their peace witness intact. 'Not only did they refuse to perform military duties, but they even refused to care for the sick and wounded' (a contrast to the attitude of the Busro brethren the previous year). The army seems to have been puzzled to know what to do with its Shaker conscripts, obviously sincere men who were not likely material from which to shape willing soldiers. So, after six weeks the Shakers were released and their back pay used to hire substitutes to take their place in the ranks. Though this resolution of the problem may have offended their pacifist conscience, the men were probably glad nevertheless to be sent home.

'At South Union, Kentucky,' writes Upton, 'the story was much the same. Early in 1813 many brothers were drafted. The fine for not reporting for service was one hundred dollars.'[3] Even though heavy, the fines seem to have been paid, for the Shaker conscience was not yet sensitised to the point that such payment appeared as a dereliction of their peace witness.

The coming of peace in 1815 brought a new vigour to the Shaker peace witness. In the first place, leaders of the sect sought to explain its faith in pacifism to the general public of the areas in which Shaker communities were located. Secondly they attempted to obtain official exemption for their members of military age not only from bearing arms in the militia but from paying a fine in lieu thereof, for Shakers now, as Quakers had always done, believed the State possessed no right to require an equivalent for service the objector considered to be wrong. One of the most eloquent statements of Shaker pacifism appeared in February 1815. This 20-page *Declaration*[4] was drawn up for presentation to the New York legislature and reprinted in the following May in Hartford, with only minor changes, this time with a view to influencing the Connecticut lawmakers, who had also drafted brethren in the recent war. The authors based their case against war on the New Testament ('under the Mosaic dispensation' fighting being, in their view, 'figurative of the spiritual warfare of God's people against the corrupt and contentious passions of human nature'). By refusing to bear arms they were helping to usher in the era of peace whose advent was foretold in prophesy. Theirs was in fact a special mission.

We believe, beyond all controversy, that God has called us to this very work; and that it is required of us to set the example of peace, and to maintain it at all hazards. And, tho' the work, in its present stage, may appear very small and inconsiderable, perhaps even contemptible in the eyes of mankind; yet it ought to be remembered that every important dispensation of the work of God, always had a small beginning, and increased through the labours and example of its subjects.[5]

The declaration stressed the benefits society received from the Shaker communities. These maintained their own poor, contributed to the relief of other paupers as well as of the needy in times of natural calamity, and expended money and labour on the upkeep of roads and bridges in their areas. 'We believe these things are not generally known and considered.' Within the confines of their own communities they kept good order without the use of force. True, 'those who will not be governed by the law of Christ, must submit to the laws of man. But there is no need of the compulsion of human laws to govern those who are governed by the laws of Christ.' Shakers refrained from taking part in politics, whether national or international, for they lived separated from the world that surrounded them and only asked a single benefit from government: 'protection against the abuses of those lawless members of society who violate its internal regulations. For this we pay liberally; and what more can justly be required of us?' Shakers, while prepared as this last passage shows to accept police protection (presumably under the supposition this employed only nonlethal force), rejected categorically any responsibility for 'protection and defence against foreign invasion.' Viewing all humanity as their friends and nourishing sentiments of 'universal benevolence and goodwill to all the human family,' they could not therefore, 'by a partial connection with one [national] community, assist in the destruction of another.'[6]

So much for the foundations of their peace testimony. Moving on to its practical implications for Shakers of military age we find the *Declaration* first attacking conscription *per se*, even for those who were not pacifists.[7] As for their own communities:

We have heretofore paid muster fines in time of peace, for peace' sake, being unwilling to make difficulty; altho' we have always remonstrated against it. But the war has materially altered our situation in this respect. We cannot now do anything of this nature, without directly supporting the cause of war and bloodshed; consequently we cannot proceed any further in this manner: for it is as decidedly against our consciences to procure a substitute, or pay an equivalent, as to render our personal services; since they equally promote the same cause.

The recent period of war, then, had served to stiffen their resistance to the demands of the military. They were now, we see, unwilling under any circumstances to accept any alternative to behaviour they believed was the correct one for the Christian.[8]

For more than a decade Shakers, in those states which had failed to provide the unconditional exemption they sought, continued to publish and present to the respective legislatures a series of petitions, addresses and observations on the subject.[9] In New York, where the Shakers concentrated the main impetus of their successive campaigns, they even succeeded in enlisting the support of non-Shakers. Over 100 of these signed the Shaker *Memorial* of February 1816 asking for unconditional exemption of their militia draftees. Whether because of this outside backing or for some other reason, in the following March the State legislature in 'An Act for the Relief of the People of the United Society called Shakers' agreed to give them what they wanted. In peacetime, though not during a war, members of their communities were now 'exempted from all manner of military services within this State and from any commutation in lieu thereof.' But this respite proved of brief duration: unconditional exemption was withdrawn two years later and an annual commutation fee of four dollars was imposed on Shaker conscientious objectors, with distraint or imprisonment for failure to pay such a fine. 'It is obvious,' writes Upton, 'that the law of 1818 dealt a harsh blow' to the Shakers. Despite some amelioration of the law in 1820, 'the problem of militia fines continued to plague the Shakers' in New York State. Cases of imprisonment of Shaker objectors became fairly frequent, for Shaker property was communal and the individual member was technically without worldly possession (which did not, however, prevent the State on occasion from seizing joint property to make up an individual member's fine).

Out of this situation two new developments emerged. In the first place, with the consent of their fellow communitarians most of the brethren of military age now transferred their residence from New York State to Massachusetts where, we know, the Shakers enjoyed full freedom from militia obligations. 'The moves . . . were seen as the only way of escaping the reach of harsh militia laws.' Secondly, the Shaker leaders, at least temporarily, shifted their main efforts to the federal level and tried, though without success, to get Congress to come to their aid. Shakers had long maintained that to compel a man to act against his religion, as was happening now with their objectors, was contrary to the Constitution of the United States, since this had secured both religious liberty and freedom of conscience for its citizens. Moreover, in 1826 a committee of the New York legislature, while rejecting the Shakers' current *Memorial* on the problem, had advised them, perhaps in an effort to divert pressure from themselves (and surely incorrectly?), that only 'Congress has the power to exempt the memorialists from militia service totally and absolutely.'[10]

After 1830 Shaker petitioning of the New York legislature on behalf of their militia objectors appears to have ceased: the militia system in any case was growing moribund. However, 'even as late as 1832 Shakers were suffering imprisonment for nonpayment of fines.' And there may have been later instances the record of which has been lost. In 1846 a law was passed abolishing imprisonment for nonpayment of militia fines altogether: however, New York Shakers had probably been free of fear on this score long before that year.

In Kentucky where the State had ceased to fine Shaker objectors after 1815, the outbreak of the Mexican War in 1846 raised the question of military conscription again, since the unconditional exemption they had enjoyed in peace time might, it seemed, no longer be valid during war. On enquiry from rank-and-file members whether paying a fine in lieu of service was still an admissible alternative for the brethren, the Shaker leadership in that state answered in the negative. 'As far as going into the army,' they added, 'and mingling with the vilest of the vile, without doing military duty, to save a little consecrated money, [this] would not be wise according to our best judgement; for we consider our souls and bodies, our time and talents as fully consecrated to God as any property in our possession.' It is not known, however, if in fact any of these Shakers were called up for militia duties and, if so, whether or not they opted out of service by means of the fine.[11]

Despite the prosperity of their community farms and the high standards of craftsmanship they uniformly maintained in their industrial products, the Shakers' organisation had begun to decline by mid-century. They were ceasing to gain young recruits from outside, at any rate on the scale this had happened in earlier decades. Since they observed rigidly the rule of celibacy so that there was no internal demographic growth, the average age of members slowly rose. And this brought with it a gradual diminution of vigour that affected the Shaker peace witness as it did other aspects of their intellectual and spiritual life.

When the Civil War broke out in 1861, the communities were suffering from an 'acute manpower shortage. Written down in black and white, the figures were appalling.'[12] In Kentucky the situation seems to have been a little better than in New England, New York or the mid-West: here Shakers were known widely, too, as agricultural pioneers and specialists in the production of medicinal herbs. There also appear to have been more young people. In the North a few Shakers of military age found themselves under army arrest after Federal conscription was introduced in 1862; for no special exemption was provided for them in the legislation, and they continued to reject the alternative that was still open to all conscripts of either hiring a substitute or paying a commutation fine.[13] Frederick W. Evans, the extremely capable and intelligent Shaker leader at this time, more than once interviewed President Lincoln and Stanton, his Secretary of

War, and explained to them his coreligionists' position with respect to war. As a result, even though successive federal conscription acts failed to mention the Shakers, the administration in fact issued a blanket exemption furloughing Shaker draftees for an indefinite period. After that they experienced no further trouble from the Union army authorities.

In Kentucky, which at the beginning of the war formed part of the Confederate States, the Shakers of the Pleasant Hill and South Union communities were not forced into the Southern armies, their pacifist principles being respected despite the known Shaker opposition to slavery. They had indeed made clear their unwillingness to fight against the Confederate government, and this was accepted. At Pleasant Hill,[14] however, the community suffered by the constant marchings to and fro of the Union and Confederate forces, beginning from the Spring of 1862 on. When in September of that year the community was occupied by Confederate troops some of its young people got carried away by martial enthusiasm and contemplated joining up in the Confederate army (though I am not clear if any actually did so).[15] Since Pleasant Hill was situated on a major military road running north and south, which was thus made use of by both armies, the community became subject to periodic depredations and incursions from one or other side. No wonder we find one of its elders crying out in desperation: 'O God! Protect this heritage from the ravages of cruel war.'[16] In October 1862 the 'house' journal of the community included the following dramatic comments on the current situation:

> Strange events! Who ever would have thought that this secluded and sacred spot of truly Pleasant Hill would ever have been surrounded by embattled legions . . . and the warring hosts traversing our streets and premises to and fro, day and night, with their weapons of death, guns, swords, and bayonets – gleaming in the sun, with the rebel banner flying, the cannon trundling over the pavements, and even through our yards, going to meet the enemy, and while yet in sounding distance, belching forth slaughter and carnage in their ranks! . . And yet that we should have escaped, with comparatively little damage, clearly implies, that whatever of evil may be among us, . . . there is still a spark of light, a remnant of faith, a seed of truth, and a righteous few in the heritage of God.[17]

After Kentucky was permanently occupied by the Union forces, Secretary Stanton ordered that Shakers there should be covered by the administration's general exemption of the sect's objectors.

The decline of Shakerism that was becoming obvious even before the Civil War continued even more visibly in the postbellum era. Now physical extinction loomed ahead: the sect was rapidly becoming a society of the elderly – increasingly wealthy but with ever smaller numbers. Shaker leaders, like Evans or Eldress Anna White, remained indefatigable in the cause of peace. Evans, for instance, corresponded with Tolstoy on communitarianism and nonviolence. The American was something of a populist, and he had chided the Russian for his scepticism concerning the beneficial influence of American democracy with its principle of *vos populi, vox dei.* Both Evans and White participated actively in the work of the reborn American peace movement, and they attended some of the conferences organised by the radically pacifist Universal Peace Union. But their practical influence was restricted to the dwindling circle of 'believers' confined within the barriers of Shakerism's communal way of life. By the early 20th century Shakerism, though a few communities continued to exist until recently, was to all intents and purposes dead.

We have seen that the Shaker peace witness, besides being rooted historically in Quakerism, paralleled in some respects Friends' peace testimony. In particular both Shakers and Quakers agreed (though only from 1815 on) on making an unconditionalist response to the state's demand for military service. In this they differed from the reaction of those peace churches which derived from 16th-century Anabaptism. Shakers, like Quakers, also insisted on their constitutional rights: as free-born Americans they claimed the untrammelled enjoyment of religious conscience in respect of military service as in other spheres of human activity. Moreover, both groups displayed considerable – some would say excessive – scrupulosity concerning the niceties of pacifist behaviour. Shakers, for instance, insisted that those of their members, who had been veterans before joining the sect, refuse henceforward to draw the army pensions they were entitled to for service in the forces.[18] Such money, they said, was in fact 'blood money,' which the consistent Christian must reject.[19] But there was one point on which Shakers and Quakers differed regarding their peace testimony. For the Shakers felt, like the Hutterites had done, that, in addition to a far reaching nonconformity to the world including abstention from politics, the practice of communitarianism too was an essential ingredient in a fully Christian witness against war. Here, in the Shakers' opinion, the Quakers fell short of a fully acceptable testimony. As they put it in their *Declaration* of 1815:

> Until the Friends . . . can prove that they have solemnly and conscientiously dedicated both themselves and all their property to God for religious and pious uses, and that they take no part in the government and affairs of the world, not even so much as to cast in a single vote for rulers, or to accept of any part of honour or profit, they can never be justly said to stand in the same peculiar situation as us . . . but while they possess each one his own private property and are laying

up riches to bequeath to their natural posterity, and hold offices of honour, profit and distinction, and are connected with the rest of mankind by voting for rulers and taking part in their political division, they fully demonstrate that they were never yet broken off from that order, and differ as widely from us as any other people in the world.[20]

So we see that, despite the Shakers' willingness to meet the nonsectarian peace movement halfway and collaborate with it in the fight for peace, an attitude that distinguished them from most Mennonites and Brethren as well as from the other small communitarian sects of America that professed pacifism,[21] the Shakers' antiwar testimony remained essentially a narrow, sectarian affair. Only those who had abandoned private property and were prepared to adopt a communitarian lifestyle could, in their view, claim an incontestible right to be considered the followers of the peaceable Saviour of mankind.

CHAPTER XVII

Canadian Quakers, the Militia, and Rebellion

THE FIRST CANADIAN QUAKERS WERE AMERICANS – British North Americans; that is, they were United Empire Loyalists, who had left the new United States to start life afresh in the Canadian North. Their small settlements in the Maritime Provinces rapidly died out; soon early Quakerism came to be concentrated exclusively in Upper Canada (later to become the province of Ontario).[1] Here Quakers had begun to settle from 1784 on – a migration northwards that lasted into the 1820s. Whereas the political motive dominated at first, economic considerations came gradually to the fore in the decision to move from the new republic, and the Quaker migration became part of the great 'westward' movement of Americans that included Quakers as well as hundreds of thousands of others who began to open up for cultivation the vast free spaces of the continent. At first, and for long afterwards, Canadian Quakers were, with few exceptions, farmers or rural craftsmen.

In 1792 the new Lieutenant-Governor of Upper Canada, John Graves Simcoe, though a military man, was anxious to get Quakers – and other peace sectaries, too – as settlers in his underpopulated province; and he therefore wrote to the British consul in Philadelphia to try to encourage members of the Society of Friends to emigrate to Canada. He promised they would be exempt from serving in the militia.[2] And in fact the parliament of Upper Canada in its militia acts of 1793 and 1794 freed Quakers, along with Mennonites and 'Tunkers,' from bearing arms. In peace time they would be required to pay an annual fee of 20 shillings while in time of war the sum required was to be raised to £5. Refusal to pay brought with it a penalty of 'distress and sale of the offender's goods and chattels' up to the amount of the original commutation fee. Thus, while Simcoe's assurance was in a literal sense carried out in this legislation, its spirit remained unsatisfied – in so far at least as Friends understood its meaning. And they were subsequently to suffer at any rate inconvenience for their unwillingness to obey the law to the letter.

As elsewhere, in Canada too Quakers paying their militia fines or hiring a substitute (an alternative open to anyone who did not wish to attend musters) were dealt with and finally disowned if they proved unamenable to the discipline. 'To answer to one's name on the militia role,' writes Arthur Dorland in his history of Canadian Quakerism, 'was likewise forbidden' (as was of course to actually drill, whether this was done in peace time or in war). In 1810 Yonge Street Monthly Meeting, situated just north of Toronto (then called York), had reported (in Dorland's words) 'that £243 11s 6½d. had been taken from members of their Meeting alone by distraint of goods in lieu of military service, and that eight of their members had been imprisoned for one month because of their refusal to pay fines.' Thus, answering to one's name at the militia muster was obviously an easy way out of what became a financially burdensome situation but it was one that the Society naturally frowned on so that, without fail, it disciplined its weaker brethren who resorted to this practice presumably seeing in it a mere formality.

During the War of 1812-1814, when fighting took place on Canadian soil, Friends for the most part strictly adhered to their peace testimony. But the problems connected with it that they had already met in peace time[3] naturally increased, and some new ones were added. For instance, when the British military forces requisitioned supplies or horses and waggons for their use Friends were expected neither to accept money for such services, if this were offered them, nor to act as teamsters. Dealings and disownments followed for all who infringed their Society's discipline in such matters. Moreover, unseemly resistance to such demands was as blameworthy in a Quaker as was his compliance. Lewis Powell, a member of Pickering Meeting, for instance, was dealt with because, as the Meeting records put it, 'he had given way to passion so far as to threaten a man with violence who imprest [sic] his team, and also [for] using deception to the officers of the Government to prevent the teams going.'[4]

Before moving on to consider the response of Canadian Quakers to the rebellion of 1837 we must look briefly at a splinter group, the so called Children of Peace, who had broken away from the Society in 1812 under the leadership of David Willson.[5] Willson, who was himself not a birthright Quaker, had moved from New York State at the beginning of the century: he joined Friends only after his arrival in Canada. A man with little education, Willson, however, read widely in the classics of early Quakerism, including the writings of Fox, Penn, and Barclay, and he came to the conclusion that the Quakerism of his day exercised an excessive discipline over its members that was incompatible with what he believed was Fox's concept of the Inner Light. It was this, and not any disagreement over the peace testimony, that led Willson and a small band of followers to separate in 1812 from Yonge Street Monthly Meeting and establish themselves in the wilderness some miles north.[6] They called their settlement Sharon, built a wooden church there, which purportedly was modelled on Solomon's Temple, and eventually, in contrast to the silent worship of the parent Society, developed a richly musical liturgical pattern. The Children of Peace, after a not unpromising start, eventually began to decline and disappeared altogether in the 1880s.

Despite the name the sect adopted, promotion of peace however does not figure among its concerns. Willson in his writings alludes occasionally to the subject but he ceased to espouse pacifism soon after abandoning mainstream Quakerism. It seems even that his Children of Peace were prepared to attend weekly militia drill, at least 'during the summer season,' and Willson himself defended the idea of national defence to the shocked surprise of a visiting peace advocate, who talked with him on the subject in the mid-1820s.[7]

Nevertheless some remnants of Quaker pacifism lingered on in the thought of David Willson. In one instance, for instance, he says of his 'Children' – 'this little and lonesome body of people' – 'they . . . are peaceable and unoffending citizens of . . . their country, resisting not offences, and are living in peace with all men, unknown to the rest of the world.'[8] Since 'universal love' was the hallmark of a Christian, it was wrong for those who followed Christ to impose punishment on criminals: if they did so, they would be repudiating the 'meek and patient' Saviour.[9] Evidently Willson shared, at least at first, the sentiments of the Mennonites rather than the Quakers concerning government, for he wrote to the latter four years after his separation from them:

Ye can vote for a part in the governments of the kingdoms of the earth; for what reason? Because *your kingdom is of this world;* therefore ye have part *in elections,* and contend for it. Such fruits may be expected of the unredeemed and unransomed of the LORD. But how came ye to profess to be actuated by his spirit and followers of the LORD, while ye are in division about the kingdoms of the earth, and the wars and commotions that take place therein? CHRIST said unto his disciples, in these things meddle not, or be ye not troubled.[10]

Willson's strongly democratic and egalitarian leanings seem to have led him later, though, to modify, if not entirely abandon, the rigidly 'no-government' views he had expressed in 1816. At any rate in an article entitled 'The Pillars of Good Government' which he composed in December 1834, we find him pointing to 'equal principles' as the chief of these pillars. 'Equality,' he says, 'is the principle of the greatest glory in the world . . . I am content with a monarchical government, but not with unequal interests and power.'[11] This of course does not mean he was ready to vote himself or advise his 'Davidites,' as the Children of Peace were often called, to participate directly in politics. But he vigorously – and publicly – attacked Upper Canada's Tory rulers, members of the so called 'Family Compact,' and certainly did not hide his sympathy for reformers like Robert Baldwin or the even more radical William Lyon Mackenzie. We need not wonder, therefore, if the Children of Peace appear to have contributed more recruits to Mackenzie's brief and unsuccessful uprising in December 1837 than any other religious denomination in the area. 'Bombarded by strongly worded sermons and writings [by Willson] and given no clear direction as to what to do, the young men of [his] congregation turned out in the rebellion while most of the older men stayed neutral.'[12] Since Willson had abandoned the practice of disownment for his sect after himself experiencing disownment in 1812,[13] none of his erring 'Children,' it would seem, were disciplined for taking up arms against the lawful government; indeed Willson seems to have been half in sympathy himself with those who had done so.

The situation was different with the mainstream Friends, by this time divided into Orthodox and Hicksite Societies. We should turn now to examine their conduct during these turbulent events that in late 1837 troubled the usually placid tenor of life in Upper Canada.[14] North of Toronto in the area covered by Yonge Street Quarterly Meeting, which also provided the base for Mackenzie's movement of revolt, some young Quakers were indeed carried away. The aims of the reformers to some extent coincided with those of Friends, whose sympathies lay with the party which opposed the class rule represented by the Family Compact.[15] Among the young Friends who joined the insurgents was Joseph Gould of Uxbridge Monthly Meeting, son of one of the first Quaker settlers in that area. (Later Gould was to become prominent in liberal politics in the province.) According to his own account, written some time afterwards, he first opposed the resort to arms but was carried along willy nilly by his fellow reformers, arrested after the rebels' disastrous skirmish with the loyal forces, then tried and sentenced to transportation but finally amnestied. Unlike Gould, however, most Friends in this neighbourhood, especially those of the older generation, kept entirely clear of insurgent activities and thereby maintained their peace principles intact.

The story is roughly the same with respect to Friends of western Upper Canada, who lived in the district south of London and Brantford. There the radical reformers rallied around a local democratic leader, Dr. Charles Duncombe, who raised the standard of revolt in this part of the country around the time William Lyon Mackenzie and his followers took to arms. Duncombe, however, was as unsuccessful as Mackenzie in his effort to topple the Tory rulers of the province. The Quaker farmers in Yarmouth and Norwich townships were suspected by local Tories, probably correctly, of being disaffected to the existing régime and nurturing the seeds of political change in their midst.[16] Here active adherence on the part of young Quakers to the rebel forces appears to have been considerably larger than in the Yonge Street area, though some of these fighting Quakers may have been attenders rather than full members, or members whose membership was largely nominal. It also seems as if the Hicksites were more affected by militancy than the Orthodox Meetings, which represented the more conservative division of the Society. One of the leaders of the Western Ontario rebellion, who was executed in London after its suppression, was a young Quaker Joshua Doan, whose father had pioneered Friends' settlement at Yarmouth. Though Friends gave permission for Joshua's body to be interred in the Quaker cemetery at Sparta, the land for which had been donated for this purpose by his father, they impartially disowned surviving Quaker rebels, who refused to 'make satisfaction' for taking up arms, as well as any of their number who had actively supported the government in other ways, for example by complying with a requisition for military purposes.[17]

According to the recent researches of Colin Read, among the religious denominations in the area of the Duncombe revolt Quakers contributed most men to the rebel cause – or at any rate the authorities suspected this was so. Why so many young Friends – or near Friends – were involved is not entirely clear, for their upbringing and their elders would surely have inclined them differently. Read suggests that 'the general humanitarian impulse of Quakerism,' combined with acutely felt economic and political grievances against the existing Tory regime, served to propel these young and inexperienced men into the rebel ranks. They may also have been influenced by the fact that several prominent Friends of the older generation called for support of the revolt. 'Such Quakers, acting as individuals rather than as representatives of their religion, helped to persuade . . . other Friends to join the cause. Thus, ties of community and kinship' reinforced economic and political motives.[18]

We should remember that only a part of the Canadian Quaker community lived in areas affected by rebellion. No Quaker bore arms from the Meetings outside these districts. And it is clear the Society as a whole reprehended the conduct of all who bore arms during the crisis and took steps to discipline them afterwards. The prominent English Friend Joseph John Gurney (brother of Elizabeth Fry), who visited Canadian Friends' Half-Yearly Meeting held in the Yonge Street Meeting House in August 1839, reported in his diary as follows concerning the state of mind of its members after their experiences 18 months before:

The sincere and simple hearted people of whom it was composed, excited my regard and sympathy. They had been exposed to many troubles during the late political excitement. An earnest desire appeared to prevail that the members of our society, throughout the province, should keep clear of all the jarring and tumults of political parties; that they might 'study' to be quiet and mind their own business.' This indeed was already their general habit; yet every one felt that it was a day of temptation and difficulty.

Gurney goes on to record the imprisonment in Hamilton at the time of his visit of two young Quakers 'in consequence of their being unable, on conscientious grounds, to serve in the militia.'[19]

Militia troubles, no longer so frequent as in former years, ceased altogether long before the establishment of the new Dominion of Canada in 1867. After Confederation Quakers, in the absence of a compulsory militia, concentrated their attention on other aspects of the peace testimony. True, their witness against war was a somewhat pallid one, as it became throughout the Society of Friends on both sides of the Atlantic until the outbreak of war in Europe in 1914 put new vigour into their pacifism. Yet at the same time its scope broadened to include issues that had previously been considered too secular for Quakers to concern themselves with. There was, we may say, a decided 'politicisation' of Friends' peace message, though they did not neglect to emphasise the religious basis of their objection to war. For the first time Canadian Friends were prepared to associate with non-Quaker peace advocates in the pursuit of a common goal, the elimination of war and the peaceable resolution of international conflict. Two years after Confederation we find Friends stating in *An Appeal to the Christian Public* that 'wars are not only anti-Christian and inexpedient, but wholly impolitic and unnecessary' and calling upon the great powers of Europe and the United States 'to establish an international court, clothed with ample power to take cognisance of all national disputes' and resolve them by means other than war.[20]

During the near half-century that elapsed between Confederation and World War I Canadian Friends, like their coreligionists in Britain and the United States, joined with the growing nonsectarian peace movement, which was recruited largely from adherents of the Social Gospel at that time spreading its influence among North American Protestants, and called for the arbitration of international disputes as well as for the reduction of armaments as a first step toward universal disarmament. They agitated, not altogether effectually, against the rising tide of militarism that was flooding the school system and the press. In 1869, for instance, Canada Yearly Meeting began a campaign to rid text books in use in Ontario public schools of aggressive nationalism. It is not clear, however, what success they obtained in this endeavour. During the early years of this century, along with other peace groups Friends vigorously opposed cadet training in schools: they proposed instead the development of physical education as an alternative to military drill. Their ties with the liberal internationalists deepened over the years: both Friends and internationalists strongly opposed the Boer War of 1899-1901 and the imperialist way of thinking that underpinned Britain's war effort at that time. A Quaker, Ada Mary Courtrice *née* Brown, together with her Methodist minister husband and some of the Hicksite Quakers, helped in 1905 to found the nondenominational Canadian Peace and Arbitration Society: Mrs. Courtrice was active, too, in promoting the peace cause within women's groups, and in particular the Women's Christian Temperance Union. Canadian Friends also worked closely with peace organisations sponsored by Quakers in the United States, like the Peace Association of Friends in America and the Lake Mohonk Conferences on International Arbitration.

As the spectre of war loomed larger, Friends in Canada as elsewhere grew increasingly alarmed at the prospects for continuing peace in the world. In July 1913 a young Friend Arthur Dorland, a descendant of one of the Quaker pioneers and himself to become a leader in the life of his Society, published an article on 'Militarism in Canada' in the *Canadian Friend* (Newmarket, vol. IX, no. 1). In it he deplored the trend toward increased expenditure on armaments and countered the arguments used in the campaign to introduce military conscription in some form or other. 'To pretend that the purpose of all this military training in the schools and colleges is the physical development of the students, will not do,' he wrote. And he went on to warn his coreligionists against complacency, against the feeling entertained by some Quakers in Canada that the progress the peace movement had made in recent years meant that the majority of their fellow citizens were as good as won over to the Quaker position on war. Dorland emphasised the need to enlist the country's youth in the struggle for peace. 'Uniforms and guns,' he wrote, 'have a definite significance. They minister to the war passion. They signify war.' Next year Canadian Friends launched the idea of creating a 'National Peace Commission, or Department of Peace': this they felt would be a positive step in the direction of a warless world. But before anything concrete could be done to implement this proposal, world peace was shattered by the guns of August 1914.[21]

The outbreak of war, however, revealed that in Canada, as elsewhere, a deep gap existed in fact, though it had been concealed in practice, between the Quakers' faith in pacifism and the quest for peace of the liberal internationalists. 'They were,' writes Thomas Socknat of the latter, 'largely "fair-weather" pacifists, and when war became a reality they, like the majority of Canadians, eagerly or sorrowfully supported the new cause.'[22]

And the same could be said of most of the social gospellers who had become involved in the prewar peace movement.[23] In World War I, as in the Second World War, absolute pacifism found support in Canada chiefly among the Quakers and other peace sects like the Mennonites or Dukhobors.

CHAPTER XVIII

Irish Quakers in 1798: An Experiment in Nonviolence

THE PLANTATION OF QUAKERISM IN IRELAND dates back to the 1650s. Many of the first Quakers there had been soldiers in Cromwell's army. Some of these settled in that country after leaving the Commonwealth forces, and in the course of time other settlers from Great Britain joined the Irish Society of Friends. They did not belong to the Protestant establishment but they did not belong, either, to the native Irish. On the whole they kept to themselves, attempting to follow the Quaker way of life to the best of their ability.

They had experienced a time of troubles in the years 1688-90 when once again Ireland was plunged into turmoil after the replacement on the throne of the Catholic James II by the Protestant William III. A state of civil war existed in that country that persisted for some time even after James's defeat at the Battle of the Boyne in July 1690. Though very few Quaker lives seem to have been lost during this period of civil war, Friends' property was pillaged: they suffered alongside their fellow Protestants at the hands of Irish freebooters, and they also underwent looting by the English forces. 'In 1692 it was computed that the total loss of [Irish] Friends . . . was a hundred thousand pounds.'[1] Despite the temptations offered in the unsettled state of the country, we have record of only four Quakers having taken up arms at this time: three of these were afterwards disowned while one publicly acknowledged he had done wrong. Some Friends, however, were willing to accept armed protection against thieves and robbers when it was offered by James's administration: they evidently felt that this constituted police action, and most Quakers at that date, we know, did not oppose such use of 'the magistrate's sword.'[2]

The 18th century proved a fairly serene period for Irish Friends. Quakers were to be found in three of the four provinces into which Ireland was then divided: Ulster, Leinster, and Munster. They remained a small group but they prospered materially, chiefly as farmers or shopkeepers. Some of them indeed became persons of considerable culture interested in the intellectual developments of their age. The occasional militia objector appeared but on the whole the peace testimony does not seem to have occupied them greatly – until they were confronted with the issue in 1798.

It so happened that around that time Irish Friends became involved in controversy among themselves – *inter alia* over the question of Old Testament warfare. One section among them, led by a cultured school-master Abraham Shackleton and influenced by the rationalist religion of the age, urged the impossibility of a benevolent deity ever giving his approval to such sanguinary and irrational conflicts. How, they asked, could Quaker pacifists throw the mantle of religion over bloodshed of this kind and assent to it even, as it were, at one remove (for virtually all Friends agreed of course that war of any sort was forbidden after the promulgation of the Christian dispensation)? God, they believed, would not – indeed could not – commend deeds as moral that at another time he would condemn as wickedness. The other side, vehemently denouncing their opponents as deists and accusing them of denying the infallibility of Scripture, argued that indeed divine justice was on the side of 'the Hebrew wars.' God was not accountable to men for his actions: they must accept them on trust. Such views reflected, in particular, the rising Evangelical trend that would soon come to predominate among Friends on both sides of the Atlantic. The controversy eventually spilled over into the Society at large, and the 'rationalists' were officially condemned as 'disturbers' and disowned when they would not recant. This fate met Shackleton – but only in 1801.[3] Meanwhile, within Irish Quakerdom both parties continued to exist somewhat uneasily alongside each other. And in 1798 Quakers closed ranks – for the time being – while they faced the menace of civil war in their homeland.

Irish discontent toward the end of the century embraced both Protestants and Catholics. The disaffected of both faiths had then combined to form a secret organisation known as the United Irishmen, whose leaders looked to Revolutionary France to aid them militarily in their struggle against England. Whereas the authorities succeeded in nipping rebellion in the bud in Ulster, the centre of Protestant disaffection, a rebellion broke out in Leinster in the south-east where most of the insurgents were Roman Catholic peasants, led by their priests. 'It was chiefly a political struggle in the North, and religious more than political in the South.'[4] And this fact gave to the fighting in the South a peculiarly terrifying aspect. There national and religious hatred erupted with elemental force; there atrocity matched atrocity as the authorities sought to prevent the uprising from spreading. Among Friends it was the Quaker communities in the counties of Kildare, Carlow, and especially Wexford, that bore the brunt, and it is with these that we shall be chiefly concerned in the account of events that follows.

As the threat of civil strife and alarms of French invasion increased around the middle of the 1790s, Irish Friends decided to take measures to ensure that their Society would stand clear of any involvement in fighting if this were to break out. One of those then active in Quaker affairs has described what happened in his area:

> In the year 1795 the Quarterly Meeting of Leinster Province, and afterwards the Yearly Meeting of Ireland, were engaged in a concern that all Friends who had guns in their houses, or any other weapons, for domestic purposes, might have them destroyed, in order to prevent their being made use of to the destruction or injury of our fellow-creatures. It was at that time a frequent practice for parties of men to assail houses in search of arms.
>
> In conjunction therefore with this concern our Monthly Meeting for the County of Wexford appointed a number of its members as a Committee to go from family to family amongst Friends, to endeavour to prevail on them to comply with the concern of the Society. I was along with this Committee, feeling my mind nearly interested, but saw the necessity of first cleansing my own hands. I took a fowling piece which I had in my possession and broke it in the street opposite my own house, which was a matter of wonder amongst my neighbours.
>
> . . . In many families this Committee had little more to do than to communicate their business, for the concern of the superior Meetings had made its way into most of the families; and being convinced of its propriety, [they] had previously destroyed all such instruments, and others gave expectation of having it speedily done. There were a few who would not be prevailed upon to make this sacrifice, but the conduct of most of them in other respects was such as to occasion disownment.
>
> A short time after this when the Government ordered all arms to be given up to the magistrates, it was a comfortable reflection and circumstance that in a general way Friends were found clear of having any such things in their possession.[5]

The destruction of Quaker weapons proceeded during 1795-96 in all the Monthly Meetings much the way it had happened in Wexford.[6] The results of this measure proved beneficial to Friends. For one thing, the government saw the Society took its pacifism seriously and did not intend to allow its members to involve themselves in any way with insurrection, should this occur. On the other hand, the United Irishmen could also observe the inflexibly peaceable stance maintained by Quakers, even if they regretted they would no longer be able to get hold of firearms when they raided Quaker homes, as they had begun to do.[7] Lastly, the weaker brethren in the Society would be saved from possible bloodshed for, as its National Meeting frankly declared, these, 'if they had had guns in their houses, might have used them in an unguarded moment of surprise or attack.'[8]

Insurrection flared up in Leinster in the spring of 1798. The government succeeded in 'pacifying' that province by the end of June but not before the insurgents had captured Wexford and Enniscorthy and spread terror among Protestants and Royalists, many of whom were forced to flee from the smouldering ruins of their homes. An attempt by the French to give assistance to the rebels failed but fear of French invasion remained. And bands of insurgents continued for a number of months to ravage the countryside. Many civilians were killed in the guerrilla warfare that characterised the fighting both while the rebellion was on and during its aftermath. Atrocities were committed on both sides; both sides took hostages and executed them on occasion, and vied with each other in plundering the local inhabitants.

The Leinster Quakers, and especially those who resided in the county of Wexford, were placed in the middle of these sanguinary happenings. How did they react to them and how did the opposing armies and their local supporters – United Irishmen and Royalists – treat the Quakers in their midst? Throughout the Quaker accounts of these times there runs a thread of horrified surprise that human beings could act in the way they did, often in their presence. Mary Leadbeater, perhaps the most sensitive and certainly the most gifted writer among these Quaker eye-witnesses, has transmitted to us something of what her people then experienced. 'My mind,' she tells us, 'felt wearied with what appeared to me oppressive in the melancholy state of the times – rule and misrule fighting with each other, and the country torn to pieces with the strife.' About the murder nearby of a young man, who had been taken prisoner by the insurgents, she writes: 'For many days after I thought my food tasted of blood, and at night I was frequently awakened by my feelings of horror, and stretched forth my hand to feel if my husband was safe at my side.'[9]

Among the green-clad United Irishmen, in that area Catholics almost to a man, we learn of a certain amount of sympathy displayed toward the Quakers. At any rate 'the United men' obviously distinguished on most occasions between Quakers and other Protestants. They possessed, it would appear, at least a vague feeling that Friends did not share, at any rate fully, the colonialist mentality common (though by no means universal) among Protestants in Ireland. Servants in Quaker families were almost invariably Catholics: they had good opportunity to observe Quaker behaviour at close range.[10] Mary Leadbeater, it is clear, was on excellent terms with, and respected by, the Catholic villagers of Ballitore, whom she did her utmost to protect against the depredations of such bodies as 'the Tyrone militia, mostly composed of professed Orangemen, wearing the ribbon of their party,' though her efforts were not always successful.[11] True, Irish Quakers shared many of the contemporary prejudices of British Protestants against the Roman Catholic religion, and they did not swerve for an instant from their allegiance to the British Crown. Yet they strove for the most part to uphold the ideal of peace among men, and they adopted a position of neutrality between the two armed contestants. Something of all this was perceptible to their Catholic neighbours as well as to the insurgent forces, even when engaged in a plundering expedition. As Mary Leadbeater remarks, 'Quakers in general escaped; but woe to the oppressor of the poor, the hard landlord, the severe master, or him who was looked upon as an enemy!'[12]

Over 100 United Irishmen or their dependents found refuge, for instance, in the house of Mary's brother, the Ballitore schoolmaster Abraham Shackleton. 'Everyone,' she related, 'seemed to think that safety and security were to be found in my brother's house. Thither the insurgents brought their prisoners, and thither, also, their own wounded and suffering comrades.'[13] And the same kind of trust in Quaker integrity and impartiality was displayed in many other cases when Quaker homes opened their doors to the rebels – on the tacit understanding that a similar welcome would be offered persons of the other side if they were in similar need.[14]

Both Abraham Shackleton and his opponent in the Quaker controversy over Old Testament wars, the elder Samuel Woodcock, found themselves – though separately – taken hostage by the rebels. But they and other Quakers in a like situation were soon freed – 'nothing being alleged against them.' Friends of course saw all this as evidence of 'Divine protection,' since 'many other persons were put to death against whom no charge of enmity was brought.'[15] Efforts made to force Quakers, and especially Quaker hostages, to conform at gun-point to Roman Catholicism seem to have been half hearted; they were soon given up when resistance to conversion was displayed, as it invariably was.[16] There were even Friends, like Joseph Haughton, who dared to expostulate with the rebels at such cruelties inflicted on the Protestants as the massacre at Scullabogue of some 200 men, women, and children, who were herded into a barn that was then set on fire. Haughton wrote of the insurgents' response to his protests:

> I found that the more I attended to what was right in my own mind, the more I seemed to be respected by them. Even when I have expostulated with them concerning the cruelties committed by them at their camps, particularly at Vinegar Hill and at Wexford, also their burning men and

women in the barn of Scullabogue, they have quietly listened to my remonstrance and frequently acknowledged the wrong.[17]

'Cannon in Ballitore!' Mary Leadbeater had exclaimed in shocked tones as she watched British soldiers enter her village in pursuit of the rebels. Quakers also suffered, though not nearly so much as the 'native' Irish did, from the ravages of the government troops and – even more – of the Protestant militia when quartered in their area. The Royalist soldiers plundered and burnt as extensively as did the insurgents, and they did not always distinguish between the loyal and the disaffected. Indeed they were frequently trigger-happy and could shoot an innocent person on the slightest suspicion of favouring the enemy (one of them took aim at and nearly killed Joseph Haughton as he stood at his door to watch the King's troops march past). Friends on principle refused to ask for armed protection from the army authorities, who were willing to extend this to the loyal part of the population. By such refusal, says Mary Leadbeater, they risked the imputation of being disloyal.[18]

Throughout the rebellion Quakers had held their Meetings for worship and business regularly; the rebels, when they met them on their way to Meeting, sometimes threatening either to kill them or burn their homes while they were absent unless they would agree to attend a Catholic place of worship instead. There were threats, too, of burning down the Quaker Meeting House if Friends persisted in using it or of converting it into a Catholic chapel. The Protestant authorities, on the other hand, did not of course put obstacles consciously in the way of Quakers meeting for worship. But, after the United Irishmen had been defeated at Vinegar Hill, they were responsible – unwittingly – for almost deterring Friends from attending the Quarterly Meeting for the province of Leinster then being held at Enniscorthy. As Hancock relates of out-of-town Quakers on this occasion:

Friends had to pass through heaps of slain on the road, and in some instances were obliged to remove the dead bodies of the Rebels out of the way, that they might not trample on them, to the wonder of the spectators; some of whom exclaimed – 'The Quakers must be mad.'[19]

Though Quakers suffered considerable losses in property inflicted by one or other side,[20] we know of only one Friend killed during the uprising – a young man who had joined the British forces and died in a skirmish with the rebels.[21] But the defeat of the insurgents in battle did not put an end at once to the unrest: lives continued in jeopardy and dwellings to go up in flames as guerrilla bands roamed the countryside for many months afterwards, robbing and arousing terror among Protestants and government supporters. 'Where Friends lived in country places,' writes Haughton laconically, 'they were exceedingly teased with such.' However, he goes on, 'where Friends had lived simply and plainly . . . treatment [by the outlawed guerrillas] was in general respectful': these he found had trust in Quaker truthfulness and honesty. While some country Friends, following the example of their neighbours, now abandoned their homes as some of them had done earlier while the rebellion was on, again most just stayed put – and faced what was to come with as much tranquillity as they could summon up.[22]

After the troubles were over, Friends were faced with a moral dilemma of another kind (one they would be called upon to face from time to time). Might they as consistent pacifists accept compensation offered by the government for damage done to their property in the course of hostilities? We know on this occasion of at least one Irish Quaker, Jacob Goff of Horetown in County Wexford (and father of the annalist Dinah), who refused. His daughter tells us, 'as a member of the Society of Friends, and not taking up arms in defence of government, he felt he could not accept it.'[23]

Irish Quakers in 1798 succeeded in maintaining their peace testimony intact, despite many opportunities to evade or soften its implications. They remained nonviolent in the face of violence offered first by one side and then by the other. Their peaceable stance was indeed known already to both contestants, and had obtained their grudging respect. On one occasion three Kildare Friends (one of them Abraham Shackleton) were even asked to mediate between the forces of the Crown and the insurgents.[24] Though the truce they arranged soon collapsed, the incident proves that Quakers were widely regarded as being 'above the battle.' Recognition of this, and the courageous attitude of many Friends when threatened with loss of life and property, helped them to weather the storm. Nonviolence in this instance proved efficacious. But too much perhaps should not be made of this (too much certainly was made of it by its first chronicler, Dr. Thomas Hancock). Small in numbers and withdrawn from the mainstream of society, the Quaker communities of Leinster, where the troubles were centred, posed a threat neither to the English authorities or the Protestant establishment nor to the United Irishmen or their Roman Catholic base. Quakers, it was known, minded their own business and asked only to be left to themselves. When confronted by the violence of others they attempted to respond peaceably and lovingly. In the circumstances of 1798 that was no mean achievement. We should, I think, leave it at that.[25]

CHAPTER XIX

French Quakers and Military Service

QUAKERS IN 18th-CENTURY FRANCE LED a double existence – in 'literary legend'[1] and in real life. French writers from the 1660s on had shown considerable interest in the Quakers, though often their accounts of the English sect were uncomplimentary and sometimes hostile. But it was really Voltaire who, in his *Lettres Philosophiques* of 1734, started the Quaker 'legend'; it soon spread among the *philosophes* of Enlightenment France.

Alongside their simple lifestyle and high moral standards, their tolerance, love of freedom, and humanitarianism, Voltaire praised Friends especially for their pacifism. He regarded Quaker Pennsylvania as a model form of government, an exemplification of their peaceable principles, and an ideal political commonwealth in which, unlike other states, virtue and civic liberty prevailed. Though he regarded their religious ideas as irrational and overly 'enthusiastic,' he held up Friends' social and political practice for the world's admiration and contrasted these, in particular, with conditions in countries under the influence of the Roman Catholic Church. And, in the words of a Voltaire scholar, 'the unique quality of the Quakers . . . was . . . that, in his eyes, they were the perfect pacifists.'[2] For Voltaire it was their peace testimony, then, that singled Quakers out from almost all other human groups as the pioneers of a warless world.[3] Yet, we should note that Voltaire, despite his attacks on war for its senselessness and destructive qualities and for the misery it inflicted on innocent humanity, did not in fact share Friends' total rejection of war or their motivation for doing so. As W. H. Barber writes:

> The disparity between them is in fact profound, for Voltaire is clearly not a pacifist in the Quaker sense at all; there is nothing to suggest that he would ever have disapproved of the use of violence in the genuine and necessary defence of individual life or of civilised society, and his hostility to war rested primarily upon humane and rational considerations of a practical and mundane kind, not upon any spiritual view of the sacredness of the human personality and the value of self-abnegation

– nor, least of all, on any desire to observe to the letter the gospel exhortation to turn the other cheek![4]

The legend of the good Quaker, once started by Voltaire, increased in intensity. It was taken up by the Encyclopedists and then by Girondins like J. P. Brissot de Warville, who had met Quakers during his travels in the United States before the outbreak of the French Revolution. Many admirers of the Quakers, however, demurred at their pacifism; and their failure to support the American Revolution was generally regarded as a blemish on the sect's otherwise praiseworthy record. And none of these philosophical friends of the Friends in France contemplated joining the Society or starting up on their own a religious group with similar principles. 'For the most part,' as Edith Philips says, 'the Quaker was regarded as a type to be admired and even idealised, but not imitated.'[5]

So much for the literary legend. Now let us turn to the reality, and examine the way a small group of indigenous French Quakers eventually emerged and how they grappled with the problem of military service when in 1792 the Revolutionary authorities imposed universal conscription on the country just as the Allies were invading with intent to restore the monarchy to France.

The first French Quakers had originated among a group of *inspirés* who, beginning around the mid-1730s, gathered in small numbers for worship at Congénies in the La Vaunage district of Languedoc. Some of their ideas paralleled those of Friends, and this made it easier for them to accept Quakerism when they finally came in contact with it. We may note that the parents of the well known 18th-century American Quaker philanthropist and peace activist, Anthony Benezet, had been connected with the *inspirés* before they emigrated to Philadelphia. Members of the Bénézet family who remained in France eventually became Quakers but the person who effectively linked the Congénies group with Friends was a young Protestant gentleman, Jean de Marcillac, who joined it in 1784.[6] Marcillac had resigned from the army seven years earlier after a reading of Barclay's *Apology*, as well as an article on Quakers in the *Encyclopédie*,[7] convinced him of the incompatibility of war with the Christian religion and left him with the wish for closer contact with Friends. Meanwhile he had decided to train as a doctor: he completed his medical studies at the University of Montpellier in 1789.

Marcillac and the Congénies group were led to establish a direct and effective link with English Quakers through an interesting sequence of events. Early in 1785 an English Quaker, Edward Long Fox, had gone over to Paris, at the request of his father, Dr. Joseph Fox, of Fowey in Cornwall, in order to insert an advertisement in a number of Paris newspapers. The notice informed readers of the latter's wish to compensate any persons who had received damages during the recent war between Britain and France, the ally of the Americans in revolt, due to the activities of two vessels of which Dr. Fox had been part owner. During the war these ships had been converted into privateers – against the Quaker doctor's wishes. In his advertisement he stated plainly the Quakers' objection to all war and to any profits that might, even inadvertently, accrue to them from warmaking. Though the matter was not finally settled until after 1815, one of its immediate results was to establish direct contact between the group at Congénies and the Society of Friends in England.

On 1 April Fox junior received a letter addressed to 'the virtuous Fox' and written in the name of 'the Quakers of Congénies' and its environs. The writers, while welcoming the English Quaker's initiative, at the same time took the opportunity of recording their own principled opposition to all forms of warfare. They had, they said, been for long opposed to participation in war, especially in those conflicts fought for religious issues, and had thereby incurred the hatred of both Catholics and Protestants. The group now numbered over 200 persons, chiefly farmers and tradespeople. Later, during the same year, Marcillac visited London as their spokesman. In a letter introducing him to Friends there, the group spoke of 'the detestable business of war (*métier abominable de la guerre*).' It was not long before the informal Quakers of Congénies became formally part of the Society of Friends.[8]

Prior to their linking up definitively with Quakers the pacifism of the Congénies group, though obviously deeply felt, seems to have possessed a somewhat amorphous character. They certainly abjured violence in matters of religion, having themselves experienced the dire effects of religious persecution. They were repelled by the idea of war but the nuances of their objection to it remained unclarified until after Marcillac's arrival and the subsequent establishment of relations with London Yearly Meeting. Before the outbreak of the French Revolution, however, there is no record of any trouble over military service. Under the *ancien régime*, as we know, the draft was sporadic and irregular and there were plenty of ways of opting out. Perhaps it never even touched this tiny rural community of devotees.

Things changed however after 1789. Even before service in the National Guard became compulsory for all ablebodied young males in 1792, French Quakers made representations to the central authorities aimed at obtaining exemption for its members who might become liable for the draft. For this they might expect would now be more strictly enforced than it had been in earlier and more peaceable times.

It appears to have been Marcillac who was the moving spirit behind the presentation in February 1791 of their petition to the National Assembly asking *inter alia* for the exemption of Quakers from bearing arms. In his task he was joined by William Rotch, an American Friend from Nantucket who, with other members of his family and some associates, had settled at Dunkirk in 1785 to carry on for the next few years their whaling enterprise: this had collapsed at home as a result of British attacks during the War of Independence.[9] The French government guaranteed Rotch's group on settling the free exercise of their religion, and 'an entire exemption from military requisitions of every kind' on the grounds of their being 'a peaceable people [who] meddle not with the quarrels of princes, neither internal nor external.'[10] But of course there was now a new form of government in France, so that the immigrant Friends of Dunkirk also needed an assurance of military exemption from it as much as did the indigenous Quakers from Languedoc, who had previously been without this protection.

'The way was prepared with much care,' writes Philips. Marcillac had already established good relations with the Girondin party which then occupied an important position in the National Assembly. Among the Girondin leaders not only Brissot de Warville but Condorcet, the Abbé Gregoire, and others were believers in the legend of the good Quaker and therefore likely to give the Quaker petition a friendly reception. They already knew that Marcillac was a man of progressive views, an active member of the antislavery Société des Amis des Noirs, and a protagonist of enlightened religion. Therefore, the prospects for the Quakers' obtaining from the Assembly what they wished for seemed good.

The petition, after recording Quakers' satisfaction at the religious toleration now existing in France, had stated their settled belief in the incompatibility of war with the Christian religion. This it was that led them to refuse 'to bear arms and kill men,' and it was this conviction, too, that had inspired their experiment in nonviolent government in Pennsylvania. Their only request on this score was to remain 'here, as elsewhere, brothers to all men without ever having to take up arms against their fellow beings.' They stressed that in whatever land they lived they were dutiful subjects who led simple, industrious, and moral lives, loved their country, and eschewed all thought of conspiracy. Surely, the petitioners concluded, France, now become the bulwark of Liberty, would grant them the same rights of conscience as had been given to them in Great Britain and the United States.[11]

Mirabeau, who acted as the Assembly's president, replied at some length to the petition. At the outset he expressed his respect for the Quakers: 'as a philanthropic system your principles command our admiration,' he told his listeners. But he soon made clear that he disagreed with their pacifism.

You say . . . that an article of your religion forbids you to take arms, and to kill, on whatever pretext. This is doubtless a beautiful philosophic principle, which makes a sort of cult of humanity; but take care, for the defence of one's fellow men may also be a religious duty! You would then have succumbed to tyrants? Since we have gained our liberty, for you as well as for ourselves, why should you refuse to keep it? . . . The Assembly will discuss your petition, but if ever I meet a Quaker, I shall say to him: 'Brother, if thou hast the right to be free, thou hast also the right to prevent others from making thee a slave. If thou love thy fellow man, do not let him be crushed by tyranny; that would be to kill him thyself. Thou wouldst have peace? Then weakness only causes war; general resistance would be universal peace.[12]

Within two months of the presentation of the petition Mirabeau was dead. Events then began to move forward swiftly. When war broke out next year, it ushered in a period of over two decades of almost uninterrupted hostilities. How did the small Quaker community in France fare during such an inauspicious time for a pacifist group? Information about the fate of its conscientious objectors unfortunately remains fragmentary. Despite Marcillac's efforts, Quakers failed to persuade the successive revolutionary administrations to grant them any overall exemption from military service such as the Mennonites in France succeeded in obtaining in 1793 from the Jacobin *régime*. But the Mennonites were willing to perform the alternative service offered them in this decree, an alternative then unacceptable, at least in principle, to the Quaker conscience. With the introduction of the *levée-en-masse* in 1792 the situation became acute. It seems, however, that for the time being at any rate a practical solution was found, with compromise being acceded to by both sides; for we learn the rural Quaker conscripts in Languedoc were now permitted to join district patrols armed merely with a truncheon in lieu of regular military service.[13]

However, a scheme of Marcillac's to set up, with British Friends' support, an industrial school at Chambord in order to train poor children in a useful trade or craft came to grief, in part because of insistence on the Quaker side that any of its pupils who were Friends of at least a year's standing should be freed from military service (as well as from taking oaths). While the Directory of neighbouring Blois supported governmental acceptance, feeling it 'wise to attract to the Republic these men so celebrated for the purity of their principles and the austerity of their morals' (despite their pacifism), the municipal council on the other hand strongly objected to the idea of military exemption. This indeed aroused so much local opposition that in the end Quakers decided not to proceed at all with the scheme.[14]

Marcillac at this time also encountered trouble for refusing to wear the *cocarde tricolore* that the Revolution had adopted as the national symbol. For the Quaker, to do so seemed to conflict with Friends' principles while for the authorities, not to do so seemed to merit arrest. Meanwhile, the Quakers at Dunkirk, as many of their coreligionists had done before, were incurring popular hostility from their unwillingness to illuminate their house windows, the inhabitants being at various times required to do this to manifest their support of the Revolutionary cause. When illumination to honour a French victory took place throughout the cities of France and only the Dunkirk Quakers refrained, the Mayor on being appealed to by William Rotch showed, however, unusual understanding. He told him, 'We are now about establishing a government on the same principles that William Penn the Quaker established in Pennsylvania – and I find there are a few Quakers in this town, whose religious principles do not admit of any public rejoicings, and I desire they may not be molested.'[15]

After first the Quakers' admirers, the Girondins, and then the Jacobins had been swept away, and the Directory which followed them had gone too, the Napoleonic *régime* brought increased hardship for the Quakers of the Midi; the draft for the *grande armée* indeed weighed ever more heavily on the whole French people. Some young Friends, faced with the alternatives of serving a long prison term or of accepting call-up, chose the latter – albeit with an uneasy conscience and with the utmost reluctance at being forced to leave home for a war in which they did not believe. A few may have been able to hire substitutes, which the Napoleonic draft still permitted though it cost a lot of money. When in 1815, after the renewal of contacts between England and France, British Friends heard of all this[16] and wrote to express their disapproval of the fact that some of their young men had borne arms in the recent struggle, French Quakers defended their brethren showing a certain asperity in doing so. Such people, they thought, were victims rather than offenders and, therefore, should be regarded with compassion rather than disapprobation. 'Not one of our members has to blush for having done violence to any. We think ourselves happy . . . in having never been engaged in any action where blood was spilt.'[17] By this I think they meant their sons who were inducted into the army, though outwardly combatants, had in fact somehow refrained from using their firearms to kill the enemy. Presumably they had by some means or other successfully avoided becoming involved in action.[18]

Immediately after the Bourbon King Louis XVIII was restored to the throne of his ancestors, Friends petitioned the monarch for exemption both from taking oaths and from military service.[19] Instead of appealing to the Rights of Man as they had done at the time of the Revolution, they now referred to the recently issued Constitutional Charter as guarantor of religious freedom, in which, at least by implication, they included the right of conscientious objection. The government responded politely but negatively; it was put off in particular by the fact that Quakers, unlike Mennonites, would not accept alternative duties such as working as teamsters for the army.

After the Restoration French Quakers, always very small in numbers, began to dwindle still further. Their young men often chose to emigrate rather than face repeated imprisonment for refusing military service (finding a substitute was both distasteful to the Quaker conscience and extremely expensive). 'The list of membership in 1822 showed two hundred names, of whom ninety belonged to the Congénies Meeting and the remainder to Nîmes, Fontanes, and St. Gilles.' By the time of the Franco-Prussian War of 1870 numbers had declined still further. Though no Friend actually served during the war, one member Jean Bénézet underwent, according to Margaret Hirst, 'severe trials for his refusal to train as a National Guard.' In 1914 only a couple of elderly women were left of the once flourishing, though always tiny, Society of Friends in France.[20] Conscription had certainly constituted one of the chief factors in hindering the growth of Quakerism in that country.

CHAPTER XX

Quaker Conscientious Objectors in 19th-Century Prussia

IN THE 17th-CENTURY SMALL Quaker Meetings for Worship had emerged in northern Germany as well as in Danzig, then an autonomous German speaking city State within the Polish Commonwealth, and in Holland. But they were comparatively short-lived. A rebirth of Quakerism in Protestant Germany took place on a modest scale in the 1790s after a pastoral visit to that country of some American and British Friends at the beginning of the decade. As a result, several already existing small religious groups declared their acceptance of Quaker doctrines and practice and were accepted as members of the Society of Friends. This happened both at Pyrmont, a spa town in the principality of Waldeck-Pyrmont, and at Minden in the part of Westphalia ruled by the King of Prussia. Later a short-lived Quaker Meeting was set up at Barmen, which became Prussian territory in 1815. The military question does not seem to have arisen with respect to the Pyrmont Friends but it cropped up periodically for Quakers who lived on Prussian soil. And, as a recent writer on this question has remarked, 'Precisely because Prussia became a military State, the problem of resistance to military service [there] is one of special interest.'[1]

Conscientious objection, it is true, was not a new problem for the government of Prussia, since Mennonites had lived within its borders from early in the 18th century. Thus, coexistence of pacifist sect and militarist State had not proved *ipso facto* impossible. By the end of the 18th century the Prussian State had in fact accepted this situation in the case of the Mennonites and was not basically hostile to extension of similiar privileges in respect of military service to another nonresistant group. Frederick (II) the Great, in particular, had shown a degree of tolerance surprising perhaps in such a militaristic monarch, though we should not forget he was a man of the Enlightenment and the friend of Voltaire.[2] But it was easier for the Prussian authorities to reach agreement on the matter with the more accommodating Mennonites, even with those of them who clung tenaciously to that sect's traditional nonresistance, than it was to do so with the Quakers. For Mennonites accepted in principle the idea of comutation for military service, while we know the Quakers did not. However, the fact that Quakers in Prussia numbered, even at the peak period of their development, less than 100 members prevented the issue from becoming a very serious one for the State.

Frederick William III (1797-1840), grand nephew of Frederick the Great, was also a man of tolerant views in matters of religion. But he and his officials looked with some alarm at the new religious body that had taken root in the western part of his dominion. How could the Quaker brand of pacifism, with its rejection of any alternative offered by the State in exchange for exemption from military service, be squared with the requirements of even the most tolerant government? Suppression was considered. In answer to a Quaker delegation from the two German Meetings (Minden in Prussia and Pyrmont outside) that visited him on 2 June 1799, the King told them frankly:

> His royal majesty the King of Prussia holds sacred the liberty of conscience in matters of faith of all his subjects. But civil institutions, and especially the fulfilment of those civil duties without which were the dispensation general, the State could not exist, have nothing in common with this. No religious sect like that of the Quakers, whose confession of faith excludes its followers from the most important civil duties in an independent State, can therefore lay claim to the right of the public exercise of their religion. Even to tolerate them is a favour which must not be extended too far, lest the State should suffer by it.[3]

In the end the central authorities relented to some degree, and on 23 February 1800 the monarch issued an edict granting limited toleration to the Quakers. But the grant applied only to the six Minden families who had joined Friends together with their descendants who remained Quakers. Admission of new members would lead immediately to withdrawal of toleration. With regard to military duties, the penalty for refusal to serve was to be a fine followed by distraint of property if the fine were not paid.

During the 15 years that preceded the signing of the peace treaty in 1815, when from 1807 to 1813 Minden was included in the Napoleonic Kingdom of Westphalia, young Quakers called up for military service were duly fined and their property distrained, and thereby they were freed from the clutches of the military – except of course for the few who agreed to serve. The total amount of fines then imposed amounted 'to three per cent of the Friends' income.'[4] When in December 1813, during the War of Liberation from the Napoleonic yoke, a Royal Cabinet Order was issued exempting Mennonites from conscription on payment of a contribution to the army, the Quakers were included. In 1814, after returning to Prussian rule, 'the Friends,' writes Hirst, 'paid the contribution not (so they ingeniously explained afterwards) as a contribution towards the war, but as a token of gratitude for the toleration they had of late enjoyed.'[5] The evasiveness of their statement indeed proves that Minden Friends shared, at least in theory, the viewpoint of their coreligionists and condemned, if here only by default, the payment of commutation for acting as they believed was right.

From 1818 on, however, confrontation did occur between Minden Friends and the Prussian State over the conscientious objection of at least some of their young conscripts and the conscription of some young men who, while not Quakers themselves, stood close to the Society and shared its testimony against war. The courts, to their credit, refused on account of accession of new members to deprive Friends of the toleration that had been granted them (though a narrow interpretation of the decree of 1800 might have done this). But they hesitated to extend such privileges of membership as exemption from military service to those who had joined Friends after 1800. Here indeed was room for conflict.

The Barmen Quakers, for instance, who, having previously belonged to the Duchy of Berg, became Prussian subjects in 1815, were not included in the Minden Quakers' military exemption. It is not known, however, if any of them suffered on this account: their little Meeting may have become extinct as early as the mid-1830s.[6] But some young Minden Friends – and friends of the Friends – suffered over the next half century – often severely – for their pacifist convictions. Since the records of the Meeting are no longer extant, we may not know of all such instances, though because of the small numbers involved the total cannot have been very numerous.

The first case to come to attention was that of Christian Peitsmeier. Christian was the second of three brothers who had joined the Meeting at Minden around 1816-17. Their family farmed at nearby Eidinghausen: neither parent, however, had belonged to the Society of Friends. The eldest brother fought in the war against Napoleon, was severely wounded in 1815, and later received a veteran's pension, which he at once renounced on joining Friends, explaining to the authorities that the activity in connection with which he was awarded this money – namely soldiering – conflicted with the beliefs of the religious body of which he had become a member. Presumably he was no longer liable for the draft. But his younger brothers were. Christian was first called to the colours in 1818 when he refused induction because, as he stated, of his 'conscientious scruple against all war.' Of course, as a new recruit to Quakerism he was not eligible for the exemption of 1800, and the government refused to recognise that the Royal

Cabinet Order of 1813 applied to peacetime as well as to wartime conditions. The officers tried to intimidate the young man who, we learn, was first 'stripped, and beaten with swords and sticks,' and 'then kicked, and when he could not stand any longer, he was tied to a stake, and again cruelly treated.' Though he would not submit, it seems he was soon released and not again called up for military service.

In 1822 came the turn of the youngest Peitsmeier brother, Ernst. His case this time dragged on for several years and led to the intervention of British Friends on his behalf. What happened at first comes out in the account they have left of the affair. When summoned before a military tribunal, Ernst had

> informed the court he could not without violence to his conscience take the military oath and bear arms, [and] was committed to prison for six weeks. At length a process of confiscation of property was instituted against him, but he was freed from this by the first court of magistrates, and not considered as contumacious; because the law applied only to those who left their country on refusing to bear arms, and not to one who refused on Christian principle. But the fiscal officer of the regiment appealed against the decision, and the second court reversed it, and condemned him to the loss of all his little property, as well as his right of inheritance, and has disqualified him from conducting any business; the court considering him of the same class with those who leave the country.

Ernst Peitsmeier, we may note, had been offered and had refused alternative duties in the army either as a drummer or as a craftsman. He had turned such offers down 'since passive as well as active participation in military service, and in all affairs which were even distantly connected with it, stood in direct conflict with his religious principles.' Such a stand, however correct from the Quaker standpoint, cannot have endeared him to the army authorities and may have been the reason for his regiment appealing his acquittal.

At one stage in the proceedings Ernst, being asked to explain his objection to fighting, had replied that a Christian could employ only spiritual weapons against wrong. 'This is my belief and my principle, based not on stubbornness but on the living conviction of the spirit of Christ.' That was the kind of declaration that evidently appealed to the religiosity of the king who, on being appealed to by two English Quakers on Ernst's behalf, declared his continued belief in the sacredness of conscience – and added, 'the young man shall not suffer.' In the end the Minden Friend was released from threat of further imprisonment. Since, however, Prussian officialdom regarded with extreme disfavour any unwillingness to perform what they considered to be the foremost duty of a subject, that of defending his country by arms, Ernst was deprived of most of his citizen rights.[7]

Several other Quakers of military age were refusing military service around this time, including a young man from the same village as the Peitsmiers came from named Heinrich Schmidt. Schmidt was duly arrested and forcibly clothed in military uniform, then a rifle was strapped onto his back and he was marched off to the regimental parade ground. For refusing orders he was put into prison and, before being finally released from custody, underwent both a bread-and-water diet and 'the punishment of the laths' (as did two other Quaker objectors from the Minden area). An English Friend described what happened to those given this punishment as 'a horrid torture indeed': 'Their clothes are taken off and a very thin covering given them instead. They are then shut up in a kind of closet, where they have nothing to stand or rest upon in any way, but the edges of laths shod with iron, about the thickness of the back of a knife and placed about two inches asunder.'[8] Since Schmidt and the others were only 'adherents,' i.e., attenders at Quaker Meeting, and not actually members of the Society, they did not of course qualify for exemption according to the strict letter of the law; and their eventual pardoning, therefore, came as a matter of grace.

London Yearly Meeting soon became very concerned at this treatment of their German coreligionists, and on 15 January 1826 it drew up a 'Memorial, respectfully addressed to the King of Prussia, concerning the cases of some individuals professing their religious principles, and living in the neighbourhood of Minden.' After describing 'these young men' as 'industrious and peaceable subjects [who] are endeavouring to live a Christian life among their neighbours,' London Friends appealed directly to Frederick William II's 'clemency' in the following words:

We venture earnestly to solicit that he will be pleased to make such regulations as in his wisdom may seem expedient, in order that relief may be extended to those of his faithful subjects, who sincerely believing all war to be inconsistent with the peaceable principles of the Gospel of Christ, cannot from tender conscience towards God, obey military requisitions. In conclusion we take the liberty to express our conviction that a sincere Christian cannot but be a good subject, for the same authority which commands him to fear his God enjoins him also to honour his King; and permits us to add the sentiment, that in proportion as real liberty of conscience is suffered, on Christian principles, to prevail in a country, so will its government be strong – strong, not only in the wisdom of its policy, but strong also in the affections of its people, and it is our sincere and respectful desire that the blessing of Almighty God may rest upon the King and his government.

English Friends proceeded to mobilise powerful support for their Memorial before handing it to the Prussian ambassador for transmission to Berlin. On 8 March the latter reported to his Minister of Foreign Affairs: 'Several prestigious members of the local Quaker community, with the strong recommendation of the banking house of N. M. Rothschild, asked me to deliver to his royal Majesty the enclosed petition, in the English original and in German translation.' In reply the King expressed his dissatisfaction with 'the proceedings of the military authorities,' which he stigmatised as being 'against the law and contrary to my intentions.' In due course some of Ernst Peitsmeier's civil rights were restored to him, and in 1830 a royal decree granted Quaker conscientious objectors exemption from military service, provided they paid an additional three per cent on their taxes. This eased the situation for them, at least for the time being.[9]

Nevertheless, despite the efforts of the army authorities to avoid a confrontation situation,[10] members of the Minden Quaker community, especially if they did not yet enjoy full membership, continued to experience difficulty over the military question. Many young men emigrated, as in Norway or France: sometimes whole families did this in order to escape the burden of conscription on future generations. In 1839 the Minden Meeting had even contemplated emigrating *en masse* but were dissuaded from doing so by English Friends, who saw in such a step an admission of defeat. Minden Quakers, therefore, persevered. They consistently disowned any member who, when drafted, agreed to bear arms, and they supported the stand of any member or 'adherent' who felt called upon to resist conscription. Cases of this kind indeed occurred fairly regularly, though with decreasing frequency as numbers at Minden dwindled.[11]

In 1855, for instance, Franz Anton Finke, a former Catholic theological student, refused to serve when drafted: his refusal had resulted from his contacts with the Minden Friends, whose Meeting he eventually joined. The chaplain of the military citadel in which Finke was incarcerated described him as 'friendly, modest, but unyielding.' He had refused while still in camp all offers of work, 'even . . . in the kitchen of the punishment section,' because labour of this kind possessed he said 'a military purpose.' On the intervention of London Friends the Prussian King, now Frederick William IV, agreed to reduce Finke's sentence of three and a half year's hard labour to two years in a civil prison.[12] In fact he was released from jail after having served only one year; then, on completing studies in chemistry abroad, he returned to Prussia and took charge of the little school which Minden Quakers had established for their children.[13]

Thereafter, conflict between Minden Quakers and Prussian military authorities seems to have ceased altogether. Quakerism in Germany was disappearing, and would not again revive until after World War I. In Prussia, despite the strength of the army tradition there and the rising tide of militarism throughout Germany, Quakers had been allowed to be conscientious objectors, just as Mennonites had been, even though Quaker absolutism led to occasional confrontation (which did not happen in the case of the Mennonites); and the problem of defining exactly who qualified for exemption as a Quaker caused trouble for some of their young men. The penalties we have seen inflicted for resisting the draft, often harsh and sometimes brutal, were such as were inflicted on the rank-and-file soldiery of those days (though this perhaps is no excuse for them) and not something reserved solely for the conscientious objector. We have seen Friends met with respect and understanding from at least some sections of the Prussian bureaucracy, and successive monarchs, when approached, showed themselves not unsympathetic. But, as Lawrence Baack remarks, since 'it was clear that the Quakers could not perform the full duties of citizens of Prussia . . . in general [they] remained . . . second-class members of the political and social community.'[14] Expansion of the sect was thus hindered, and before long its young men sought a more hospitable environment abroad, either in Britain or more frequently in the United States.

CHAPTER XXI

Norwegian Quakers, Conscription, and Emigration

I

EMIGRATION TO THE UNITED STATES also depleted the ranks of the Society of Friends in Norway, though there Quakers never disappeared altogether. Norwegian Quakerism had begun in a small way on the completion of the Napoleonic Wars in 1814, and Quakers, never to become a large community, remained for several decades a tiny group indeed. Yet, despite their continued lack of numerical strength, Norwegian Quakers succeeded eventually in making a valuable, if modest, contribution to their country's history: first, in stimulating the expansion of religious freedom and then in helping to promote Norway's burgeoning peace movement. They also played an important role in the development of another reform cause, the temperance movement in Norway, through the activities of the most prominent figure they produced during this period, Asbjørn Kloster (1823-1876).

The birthplace of Norwegian Quakerism was the English naval port at Chatham. There Norwegian and Danish sailors, captured at sea after Denmark (to which Norway was then attached) had in 1807 become a belligerent on the side of Napoleon, were kept prisoner for a number of years aboard the *Fyen*. These prisoners of war included a number of men whose spiritual awakening occurred during their long and weary years of captivity. During this period Quakers from the neighbouring town of Rochester had made contact with them, visiting them on the prison ship and distributing Quaker literature in Danish translation, including that basic exposition of Quaker faith and practice, Barclay's *Apology*.[1] Since literary Norwegian differed little at that date from Danish, the Norwegian members of the small group of religious enthusiasts, who numbered around 20 to only about 10 from Denmark, had no difficulty in reading such works. A Quaker

Meeting for Worship began to be held regularly on board ship and those attending Meeting, encouraged by their English Quaker visitors, began to consider themselves Friends. When peace came in 1814, they all, of course, returned home to their families. They left England, though, with the intention of bringing the Quaker message to their countrymen – and with the support of English Friends in this undertaking.[2]

The Society's peace testimony was naturally one of the most important Quaker doctrines they took home with them. Local Friends had supplied each returning prisoner with a certificate, dated 12 February 1814 and addressed 'To all whom this may concern,' confirming each man's adhesion to Quakerism. Quakers, stated the document, were

> a people . . ., who amongst other noble testimonies, hold the inconsistency of war with the gospel dispensation, and therefore cannot, for conscience sake, engage therein. And we believe that he, with others of his countrymen, are made partakers with us of the same precious peaceable testimony; and we are desirous of recommending him to the kind attention of those with whom his lot may be cast, that he may be permitted to have their religious scruple . . .[3]

In Denmark the Quaker converts failed to set up any permanent organisation. Though some persisted in isolation in maintaining their Quaker faith, all trace of them disappears after several decades.[4] But things turned out differently in Norway, which as a result of the peace settlement was now detached from Denmark to become an independent kingdom with its own parliament (*Storting*) and autonomous administration under the Swedish Crown. In Norway the returning Quakers succeeded in setting up a Meeting at Stavanger, a seaport on the west coast, and also one in the capital Christiania (now Oslo) under the leadership of Enoch Jacobsen, who had been chiefly responsible for establishing the original Quaker group on the *Fyen*. It was, however, in Stavanger and not Christiania that Quakerism took root, for it was from that area that most of the returning sailors came. They formed a cohesive group there with a firm base from which, once the opportunity opened out, Quakers could expand to other areas of the country.

But expansion came only later. At first, the little group of Quakers had a hard time in keeping together and, more than once, it seemed as if they were on the verge of extinction. The Lutheran state church at that time occupied a dominating position within the ecclesiastical life of the country: the established church could call upon the state to suppress spiritual dissenters and enforce religious uniformity throughout the country. This ascendancy, however, had not gone unchallenged. From 1796 on, a lay preacher named Hans Nilsen Hauge (1771-1824) had led an evangelical revival, a religious awakening pioneered by laymen that pursued its way independent of the state church and often fiercely denounced by it. Hauge indeed spent many years in prison for his religious protest. 'Haugeanism' was in many respects akin to the Methodist movement in England. Like John Wesley, Hauge too never broke decisively with the established church from which he had emerged, though his followers formed in practice a separate religious community.

With Quakerism the Haugean movement also shared some tenets: refusal to take oaths, for instance, as well as opposition to a 'hireling ministry' and belief in the priesthood of all believers, embracing women as well as men.[5] On the question of war Hauge also inclined toward the Quaker position. In 1813 he had written from his prison in Christiania: 'Christ has taught us to do good to, and to love, our enemies. If we do this, we shall experience, that we shall be happy when we return good for evil.' On the question of military service, however, he adopted a somewhat ambiguous stance, recommending his followers to obey the summons to arms if called upon to serve by the authorities.[6] Whether any Haugeans refused to fight on conscientious grounds is unclear; I rather think that none did.[7]

Nevertheless, a certain interplay existed between Haugeanism and Quakerism. It had been one of Hauge's followers among the sailors interned on the prison ship who had started Enoch Jacobsen on the spiritual quest that soon led him and his companions to become Quakers. In the early years of Norwegian Quakerism after 1814 Friends perhaps had even hoped to win Hauge himself for their new faith; such expectations, though, soon proved unwarranted. Hauge, by now worn down by years of persecution, had become more accommodating toward the established church: he frankly advised his disciples in the Stavanger area to have nothing to do with Quakers, in part because of their unwillingness to support national defence and their declared readiness to disobey the law rather than take up arms.[8] Occasionally a group of Haugeans joined Friends, as happened for instance at Skjold much later.[9] But on the whole the two movements went their separate ways.

Despite able leadership, and the support derived from the occasional visits of British Friends, the Stavanger Quaker Meeting remained for some time a very small one.[10] For over two decades its membership did not rise above a dozen, though a number of attenders also participated in its worship without formally joining the Society. The official church was bitterly opposed to the new religious group fearing it would help swell the rising tide of resentment against ecclesiastical oppression. Friends were repeatedly punished – by the state – for refusing to pay tithes to the local clergyman or the church-school tax, or for marrying or burying their members in their own fashion. Some Quaker families already began to look to emigration overseas as the only solution for what appeared to be an impossible situation at home. Thus Quakers predominated among the 52 persons who, under the leadership of a Quaker Lars Larsen Geilane (one of the sailors on the prison ship *Fyen* who had become Friends), set sail for the United States in 1825 in the small sloop *Restaurationen*, in this manner preparing the way 'for a mass immigration' of Norwegians across the Atlantic that continued on into the 20th century.[11]

It was not until after the passing of the Dissenter Law in 1845 relieving Friends and other religious nonconformists of the most glaring disabilities under which they had previously suffered, that we hear of cases of conscientious objection to military service and of young Quakers being imprisoned for refusal to do their turn of conscript service in the armed forces. Since the union with Sweden in 1814 military service had constituted one of the obligations of Norwegian citizenship. Despite the understanding of the Quaker position shown by the first Bernadotte king, Charles John, who had told a delegation of Friends that he knew they were 'a peaceable people, opposed to wars and the shedding of blood,' whose scruples on this account deserved royal protection,[12] Quakers remained liable to be called up for military service.[13] But for three decades this does not appear to have happened. For one thing, the Society of Friends in Norway was, we know, a tiny body; few of its members can, even in theory, have been subject to conscription. Again, as dissenters deprived of many civil rights they were not expected to perform all the obligations, including serving in the militia, that were incumbent on full-fledged citizens. Besides, most Quakers in the Stavanger area were poor people – farming folk and fishermen or village craftsmen[14] – who would not have enjoyed full citizenship rights even if they had not been dissenters. But the situation altered radically with the passing of the Dissenter Law of 1845. For the *Storting* could not then be persuaded to exempt Friends on grounds of conscience from bearing arms when the state required them to do so (nor did it free members of the Society from paying either tithes or the church-school tax to which they also objected strongly).

From 1845 onward the military question, therefore, becomes an acute one for Norwegian Quakers. Since from around the same date their Society underwent a decided – even if modest – expansion in numbers, we need not be surprised to learn of a steady stream of conscientious objectors emerging from its ranks to undergo periodically short spells of imprisonment: liability to annual bouts of military training lasted five years in Norway. The situation for Friends did not change basically until, in 1902, the imprisonment of religious objectors virtually ceased (see below). By this time the missionary zeal of mid-century, generated in part by the pastoral visits of a series of earnest and energetic evangelical Quaker ministers from

England, Ireland, and the United States, had finally spent itself. At its peak around 1865 the Norwegian Society had numbered 584 registered members,[15] with many more persons associated closely with the Society without the formal ties of membership. Over a dozen Meetings had sprung up during the previous two decades, some of them formed from bands of religious seekers who had already split off from the state church and had adopted on their own, before they had come into contact with Friends, beliefs and practices usually considered peculiarly Quaker. This happened, for instance, in the early 1850s in the remote mountain valley of Røldal under the leadership of a sturdy young peasant named Knud Knudsen. Though the area around Stavanger remained the centre of Norwegian Quakerism, small groups of Friends were now to be found scattered along the coastline and up the fjords, a chain that eventually stretched from Kristiansand in the south to the province of Finnmark in the far north.

During the last quarter of the 19th century and on into the 20th, numbers slowly declined. Though doctrinal squabbles imported chiefly from the American Society were eventually overcome, and despite continued able leadership from men like Endre Dahl (who died in 1885), the state of the Society did not augur well for the future development of Quakerism in Norway. By 1890 membership had dropped to 231. In 1900 there were only 175 registered Quakers, in 1910 143, and in 1920 a mere 73.[16] The small rural Meeting-Houses mostly closed; only in the town of Stavanger itself was there throughout this period a fairly flourishing Quaker community.

Among the reasons for Norwegian Quakerism's decline the emigration, often of whole Quaker families, to the United States occupies a foremost place. And among the chief motives for Quaker emigration, along with the greater economic opportunity that the New World offered, was the wish to live in a land free of the burden of military conscription that lay oppressively on every Quaker household in the homeland.[17]

How, then, did the Quakers fare once their young men became liable regularly to undergo annual military training for the statutory five years? We know the names of 21 Friends of military age who were imprisoned before 1902 for refusing to train.[18] The number would undoubtedly have been larger if it were not for the well authenticated fact of young male Quakers emigrating in considerable numbers to the United States. This almost certainly accounts for the gap in the record between 1874 and 1896 when there appear to have been no cases of conscientious objection in the Quaker community. A well informed Norwegian Friend wrote a little later of this '20-year pause': the Society's young men 'saw no point in lying in prison in a land where the government was completely deaf with regard to conscience and the claim of Truth.'[19] However, when in the 1890s a serious attempt on the part of the emergent Norwegian peace movement was set going to improve the legal position of religious objectors, non-Quakers as well as Quakers, we find Quaker conscripts once again preferring prison to emigration. The outlook no longer seemed entirely hopeless: public opinion as well as the authorities, we shall see, were beginning to consider it might be wrong, or at any rate inadvisable, to punish otherwise good citizens for following their consciences, however mistaken they might be in doing this.

Treatment of Quaker C.O.s varied from case to case. The first recorded instance occurred in 1845: then the delinquent, Andreas Bryne, was simply fined. Later, fines were rarely imposed. When they did occur, Friends, as we know from their practice everywhere else, simply refused to pay them preferring to undergo distraint of property, however heavy, than purchase in this way exemption from what they considered to be – for them – a wrongdoing.

Imprisonment, sometimes with the additional punishment of a bread-and-water diet or solitary confinement (or both combined), became the usual fate of objectors, with terms ranging from five days to six months and the fortress at Bergen as the usual place of incarceration. Elias S. Stakland in the 1850s[20] and Gudmund I. Erland in the 1860s served out five annual terms of imprisonment at the end of which, like other conscripts, they ceased to be liable – in peace-time – for service, while in the 1890s Elias's son, Søren Stakland was imprisoned thrice between 1896 and 1898. The overwhelming majority of Quaker objectors, however, seem to have suffered only one prison term. I am not clear why they were not jailed repeatedly as the Staklands and Erland were. Perhaps the military authorities relented, feeling that they had made their point and that it would not be right to continue to harass a man for doing what his religion told him was right. At any rate this must sometimes have been the way the situation developed. John F. Hanson, who knew Norwegian Quakerism at first hand, wrote in his memoirs published in 1903:

> In justice to the officers it should be said that there have been found those who felt sympathy for the conscientious youths; as in the case of Karl Tollagsen [1864] when an officer treated him well and made the sentence as light as possible. Also the testimony of Peter Fugelie might be mentioned; military officers stopped at his house and conversed freely, admitting that the entire military system was wrong, and that they were heartily sick of the whole business.[21]

Nineteenth-century Norway might be fervently nationalistic but its nationalism was qualified, as was that of the early American Republic, by a strong democratic impulse and – at least in some quarters – a genuine desire to respect the rights of conscience.

Sometimes, however, failure to incur further penalties for refusal to attend drill beyond the first spell of imprisonment must have been due to the delinquent's departure from the country. In such cases the immigrant ship, and not the army officer's kindness, was the reason why the young Quaker's name disappears from the Society's list of military 'sufferings'.[22]

Did some young Quakers consent to bear arms and what happened to them if they did so? If they did this willingly and defended their action they would, I think, have been disowned by the Society (though I have not come across any cases where this actually happened). We know that, toward the end of the century, young Friends in increasing numbers left the family farm and lost touch with the Society in their new, usually urban, environment. As an elderly Norwegian Friend lamented to two foreign Quaker visitors in 1894: 'We manage to retain very few of our young people among us; either they leave and go into the world with no interest in religion, or they go away to America, often to avoid military service.'[23] But where the young Friend, still a mere boy, yielded to pressure and agreed to muster, the Society surely, if we may judge by what usually happened in similar circumstances in other branches of Quakerism, was likely to have taken a more sympathetic view and have received the young conscript back into its rank if it were convinced that he had acted against his better self and was sorry he had not stood firm – or emigrated!

The dilemma faced by young Norwegian Quakers of this time emerges from the account given by the British Friend Sarah Ann Doeg of the pastoral visit she made in 1856 – in the company of her husband Robert – to the isolated Friends of the Røldal valley. She records the following incident that occurred during the return journey:

> Off again next morning very early. As we stood waiting for the boat, my mind was drawn in sympathy and love to a youth who had come with us, in obedience to the powers that be, summoned to prepare for service as a soldier. One of our company asked him if he would be a man's soldier or a soldier of Jesus Christ? He turned away and wept. I endeavoured to encourage him to be faithful to his God, and not to fear man.[24]

Then, 'as our boat lay at rest on the still waters of the fjord,' they knelt and prayed. As a result of Sarah Doeg's endeavours, this Quaker peasant lad decided to follow the practice of his people and refuse to serve, and for his refusal, the English visitor concludes, he afterwards 'cheerfully' endured imprisonment in the fortress at Bergen.[25]

The best documented case of conscientious objection among Norwegian Quakers was undoubtedly that of Søren Olsen in 1848. For Olsen has left us a 'handwritten report of more than 50 small pages about his experience'[26] that we may compare to the account composed a little later by the American

Quaker Cyrus Pringle of his experiences as a Civl War C.O. While Pringle was better educated and of a more introspective and contemplative nature than Olsen was, both men displayed the same punctiliousness concerning moral behaviour and the same striving after the Truth that has marked the Quaker conscience at its best. Whereas Pringle's narrative has been reprinted several times, Olsen's, though now in print, remains accessible only in Norwegian. It may be of some value, therefore, to look at how this young Norwegian peasant, possessing, it was said, 'scarcely any school learning' except what he had taught himself after he had grown up,[27] succeeded nevertheless in maintaining his Quaker peace witness intact despite constant pressure from the authorities to conform.

Actually, Olsen was not yet formally a member of the Society of Friends when he made his stand against conscription. There had, moreover, been very few conscientious objectors in Norway before him: the phenomenon, therefore, was one that was virtually new for both the civil and the military authorities as well as for the community at large. During the spring and early summer of 1848 a tense situation had arisen in Norway on account of the growing crisis in relations between Prussia and the neighbouring kingdom of Denmark over Schleswig-Holstein that was next year to erupt into open war. Hostilities were then soon over but throughout this period Norwegian naval and land forces were on the alert in case trouble should spill over onto Norwegian territory.

It was in this atmosphere of war preparation that, on 2 June 1848, the 21-year-old Olsen received his call-up notice. A farm-hand from the island of Rennesøy not far from Stavanger, hc seems to have been drawn toward Quakerism by the influence of his paternal uncle, who was a member of the Society. But Olsen did not imbibe Quaker pacifism straightaway, for we hear of him when he was 16 volunteering for the Royal Norwegian navy. Though he was not accepted at the time, he did take the oath – certainly an unquakerly proceeding – to serve king and country in case of need. By the time he was drafted, however, his Quakerism had matured and, while not yet accepted into membership of the Society (he still remained formally a member of the state church), he was no longer willing to serve his fatherland by arms. But his previous oath to do so seems to have counted against him in his dealings with the authorities after being called up for service. His assignment to the navy – an unusual proceeding with draftees – must also have been connected with his youthful attempt to enter that branch of the armed forces.

At Stavanger, where Olsen was brought under military escort on 7 June, the military officer in charge of the recruiting centre (*Krigskommissær*) was indeed puzzled to know what to do with this strange recruit he now unfortunately had on his hands. What sect do you belong to? he first asked

Olsen, for the officer at least knew of the existence of Quaker and other dissenters in that area. 'I share Quaker principles,' Olsen answered; he could not – indeed certainly he did not wish to – say that he was himself a Friend. And he had adopted such principles, he added, 'because I have found them to be the most true.' Then why, asked the officer, have you not resigned your membership in the state church? 'I told him,' Olsen goes on, 'that I would have done so but I believed it would not be good to be hasty in such matters, and I explained that the most important thing was that I should be a real Christian.' The reply, however, did nothing to appease the officer's rising anger against the refractory conscript sailor.[28]

A few days later Olsen arrived at the naval station at Horten, to which he had been taken by sea. And here, when the able seaman (*matros*) was again ordered to work, he once more refused to do so believing that might compromise the stand he had taken. He now told the naval lieutenant set in charge of him that this refusal had stemmed from the fact of his religion commanding him to do good to enemies and not to harm them.[29] The next stage in Olsen's odyssey came with his transference on 18 June to Fredriksvern where the admiralty court sat. At his hearing there Olsen was called upon once again to account for his conduct and explain why he felt he could not fight when practically everyone else in the country, including its venerable churchmen, thought differently from this youthful and semi-literate tar. Olsen's reply followed the same pattern as his previous statements to the authorities at Stavanger. He said:

> It has been for conscience sake that I have refused to serve. For if I have not felt at liberty to attack my fellow men, and were I then to do so against my true belief, I believe I would experience on this score a continuing uneasiness in my conscience . . . True, one must obey king and magistracy so long as they act in accordance with God's law but, when they do not do so, I believe that it is right to obey God and not men.

He told the court, too, that it was all the same to him whether it was peacetime or wartime: his religion forbade him to participate in any action associated with fighting. When passages from the Mosaic Code were cited against him, Olsen answered with the Sermon on the Mount and with the assertion, we have seen so often made from the pacifist side, of the superiority for the followers of Jesus of the New over the Old Testament. A minister of the established church, Pastor Sverdrup, paid Olsen a visit while he was in detention. Though they conversed for a whole hour, the pastor failed to convince the Quaker seaman of his error. As Olsen relates, 'he maintained that it must be right to defend our fatherland, and so on. I told him that we are commanded to "love" our "enemies", etc.' In the end they parted on good terms, each however maintaining the correctness of his own position.[30]

The court's sentence, when it came, proved a heavy one: Olsen was to be flogged – nine lashes with the cat-o'-nine-tails for three consecutive days, a total of 27 strokes. A penalty of this kind, though by no means unusual in the navies of that day, could have left the victim, especially one unused to the hardships of sea life, maimed for life. There was therefore no time to lose if Olsen's friends, including the Friends of Stavanger Meeting whom the authorities had permitted him to contact, meant to save the young man from undergoing this savage sentence. The Meeting forthwith issued a certificate confirming that Olsen was a convinced pacifist. For at least a year, it said, he had demonstrated his belief in the Quaker – and gospel – doctrine of love toward enemies and had been closely associated with Friends as an 'attender (*tilhenger*)' at their Meetings. The certificate testified also to his being 'a trustworthy, kindly and upright man,' who sought to act according to his religious beliefs.[31] At the same time a petition was sent to Stockholm by Friends in London addressed to the liberal minded Oscar I, ruler of the joint kingdoms. And in fact, soon afterwards, the King commuted Olsen's sentence to a period of brief imprisonment, including however the penal condition of a bread-and-water diet.

The Norwegian press, meanwhile, had given the case a considerable amount of publicity, much of it favourable to the C.O., who was regarded, at least among liberals, as a protagonist of religious liberty. On 21 October Olsen was freed from the military prison in Fredriksvern after having been in confinement for 20 weeks. Immediately after he returned home he commenced work on his memoir to which he gave the title 'A Little Witness against War and Fighting'; he had completed it before the end of the year. In the event his treatment while in detention proved to have been fairly mild: in his memoir Olsen has recorded his gratitude for kindnesses received from both ordinary soldiers and noncommissioned officers during the period he was incarcerated at Fredriksvern.[32] Whereas the senior officers for the most part felt alarm, as the outcome of their puzzlement, at Olsen's – to them – extraordinary behaviour and feared his 'insubordination (*subordinationsstridigt forhold*)' might spread, lower ranks felt more sympathy with the simple and obviously sincere young fellow with whom they were in daily contact.[33]

We do not hear of Olsen being called up for duty during the years that followed. At this date drafting does not yet seem to have been placed on a regular basis: some of those eligible were called each year while others escaped for the time being. But the threat remained. With this hanging over his head Søren Olsen too, like so many other Quaker young men, eventually chose to emigrate rather than risk further confrontation with the military.

He left Norway for good in 1854, aged 27. Eventually, with his wife Anna Ravnaas, an ardent abolitionist and also of Norwegian origin, whom he had married in 1858, he became one of the mainstays of the new Friend's community at Stavanger in Marshall County, Iowa, which formed North America's only Norwegian language Quaker Meeting – until it too adopted English.[34] Søren Olsen died in 1879.

II

Olsen, although he resigned from the state church a couple of years before he left Norway, did not become a Friend until after he had settled in America; the reasons for this delay are not clear. There were, we know, in this period other C.O.s in Norway who did not belong to the Society (e.g., the 'priestless' Peder Andreas Tou[35]), but they were all closely associated with it and are usually reckoned as Quakers in the statistics. We do not know exactly when other dissenting churches started to produce members who objected to military service. By the 1890s we already begin to hear of such people; but the phenomenon must certainly date back several decades, even if there is no longer any trace of it in the records of the earlier period. Even afterwards indeed we tend to learn only by chance of religious conscientious objectors unconnected with Quakerism.

Among these men were members of long established nonpacifist denominations like the Baptists or the Methodists, which had begun to find an increasing number of adherents throughout the Scandanavian lands. There were also objectors from entirely new groups, including several Pentecostal churches as well as the Seventh-day Adventists who were imported from the United States and the Salvation Army that had originated in England. But several indigenous groups, all of them fairly small, had by now sprung up in Norway itself, most of whose young men refused to bear arms as a result of their religious beliefs.[36] There was the Assembly of Christ (*Kristi Menighed*) in Christiania, for instance, which frowned on its members serving as soldiers, and the Pedersen group at Trøndelag (not all of whose conscripts however refused to bear arms) – and perhaps most interesting of all, the so called Free Friends (*Frie Venner*) in the far north. One or two objectors stated they belonged to the Lutheran state Church, while a revival movement that broke away from it under the leadership of one of its pastors, Gustav Adolph Lammers (1802-1878), and became known as the Free Church, also produced a few conscientious objectors, though pacifism did not constitute one of its tenets. But, as Nils Agøy points out, in Norway pacifism at this date was essentially a product of religious dissent (*et dissenterfenomén*) – with Quakers of course the leading component in it, even if the Society of Friends supplied only a small percentage of the total number of those now refusing on conscientious grounds to perform military duty.[37]

The Free Friends, who lived in isolated farming and fishing communities on the Lofoten and Viktna islands in northern Norway, had around 1890 abandoned the state church and adopted Quaker forms of worship and some Quaker beliefs – without seemingly ever having heard of the Society of Friends. There were about 300 of these people when the American Quaker minister, John F. Hanson, visited them in 1900. He had learnt of their existence only after reading by chance in a Norwegian newspaper of several young men from their communities being put in jail for refusing to drill when required to do their spell of conscript service. He immediately set out to visit them, and thus began a long connection between Friends and Free Friends. The latter, however, while they appreciated such contacts, retained their separate identity and never merged with the mainstream Quaker Society. They seem in fact to have found even Norwegian Friends rather too liberal in their attitude to scripture, and the two religious communities in the end agreed to differ.[38]

The pacifism of the Free Friends as well as other special practices they adopted appear to have originated spontaneously from their reading of the New Testament; though their interpretation may also have been shaped in part by a feeling of profound dissatisfaction with official religion shared at that time by many thousands of others throughout Norway. It was this spiritual dissatisfaction, a feeling of restlessness that sought satisfaction outside the state church, which had led to the expansion of the Society of Friends during the third quarter of the 19th century. Among the areas of conduct where many of these religious seekers found fault with the state church was its blanket approval of war, provided it was undertaken by a properly constituted authority. Lutheran theologians and Lutheran pastors condemned the C.O.'s stand unreservedly as one they thought could not find confirmation in the scriptures;[39] apart from a handful of mavericks, pacifist Lutherans, we may note, were to emerge only after 1914.

Even though the Quakers of Norway toward the end of the century had begun to decline in vigour as well as in numbers, the Quaker stand on war symbolised for most Norwegians the idea of Christian pacifism. The Friends at Stavanger though a tiny group, especially when compared to the congregations of the state church, exercised nevertheless an influence quite out of proportion to their numbers – and perhaps also to their actual spiritual strength. It is interesting to note in this connection that at least a third of the religious objectors whose cases Agøy examined for the period 1885-1901 came from the Stavanger area, even though most of them were not Quakers or closely connected with the Society of Friends.[40] Norwegian

Friends, like those elsewhere, were unwilling to claim rights of conscience for themselves if they were denied to the conscientious who were not Quakers. Since the 1850s they had in fact been pressing for the exemption of all genuine objectors to military service. But their pleas evoked no response in governing circles.[41] The successive military laws passed by the *Storting* in 1854, 1866, 1876, and 1885, contained no provision for conscientious objection, and we have seen how religious pacifists, whether Quaker or not, fared at the hands of the military when their turn came to train for national defence.

In 1898 the Clerk of Norway Yearly Meeting, Thorstein Bryne, took a bold step when in a letter of protest he sent to the Sheriff of Rogaland on behalf of his Quaker Society, he intimated their intention of no longer supplying the government with the names of members who had become eligible for the draft. Though previously Friends sometimes failed to comply with this requirement, they had made no official protest in the matter hitherto. Well disposed local authorities were ready, in case of need, to forward the relevant names to the military, so no trouble had arisen because of any omission on this point on the Quakers' part. Now, after Bryne had been twice fined for not reporting the names of Quaker conscripts, the Society decided to relinquish its status as a legally recognised religious body: a status which had brought with it the obligation Quakers were now categorically rejecting. 'This duty,' they stated, 'Friends considered contrary to their testimony against the military system.' They did not again receive government recognition until the 1930s.[42]

Four years later however, in 1902, all religious objectors became free in practice, if not in law, from the annual obligation to drill for the statutory five years, which rested on other able bodied male citizens. This exemption had come as a result of an army circular issued on 18 February 1902 (*Kommanderende Generals Cirkulære nr. 1*),[43] and it remained in force until in 1922 the *Storting* finally passed a law allowing genuine conscientious objectors, whether they refused military duties on religious or nonreligious grounds, to perform alternative civilian service instead of being required to bear arms.

The 1902 circular had a long history behind it. In 1896, and again in 1898 and in 1900, a group of liberals under the leadership of Nikolai Julius Sørensen (1850-1923), a Christian pacifist and ardent antimilitarist, of whom I shall have more to say below, and warmly supported both by the Norwegian Quakers and the small but expanding peace movement, had attempted to persuade the *Storting* to pass a law allowing conscientious objection to bearing arms as an option for the country's conscripts. There was indeed a widespread feeling by now that it was wrong for Norway to jail men for acts they considered to be inconsistent with their religion. Sørensen and others pointed out that, among those punished by imprisonment under the existing law, were members of the widely respected Quaker community. Rather than face repeated incarceration and all that this brought subsequently in the way of social and civil disabilities, many young Friends and others who shared their testimony against war had been driven to leave their native land, which could ill afford to lose such people. On the other hand, there were politicians and publicists, particularly on the political right, who remained unwilling to make an exception in their case, believing it would create widespread resentment and ultimately might even undermine the national defence system. So the successive attempts to change the law in such a way as to allow conscientious objection proved abortive, despite the fact that in the two latter bills Sørensen proposed the institution of civilian work to be performed by C.O.s as an alternative to military training.[44]

In 1900 the Department of Defence, in a circular dated 6 August (no. 29), had recommended to the army that it employ those conscripts expressing an objection to handling weapons solely on noncombatant duties – in the kitchens and transport section or as medical orderlies or in the workshops. A concession of this kind, however, could not satisfy either the Quakers or the overwhelming majority of non-Quaker objectors.[45] London Friends expressed as follows the standpoint of their Norwegian co-religionists in a letter dated 18 December 1900, which they sent to the Swedish-Norwegian consulate in London:

> Circular No. 29 will not give any relief to their members, for they see little difference between a man being employed to transport army stores, including ammunition, or otherwise serving the soldiers with food, horses, etc., and the actual use of the horses or ammunition against an enemy. They also point out that men employed in the services named as non-combatant will be in military clothing, under military command, and be regarded as soldiers, and thus will form an integral part of the system of warfare, in which they feel themselves forbidden to take any part by the spirit and teaching of the New Testament.[46]

It had indeed soon become clear that the Department of Defence's solution allowing noncombatant army service for conscientious objectors would in fact resolve nothing. With the stalemate in the *Storting*, the army command's decision two years later simply to release religious C.O.'s from all military obligation – and leave it at that – appeared at the time to provide a way out, at least for the immediate future, and until something better had been thought up, from a situation that was gaining undesirable publicity and could ultimately harm the armed forces and the interests of national defence. The 1902 circular did not satisfy Sørensen, however, and next year he once again, and once again unsuccessfully, brought forward a parliamentary bill allowing nonreligious as well as religious objectors to perform alternative service under genuinely civilian control in lieu of service in the army.

Sørensen was particularly concerned with the plight of nonreligious objectors. From 1905 (the year of the dissolution of Norway's union with Sweden), they began to come forward in significant numbers and on them the full burden of resistance to military conscription now rested. Sørensen was himself a Christian pacifist, but he believed at the same time that refusal to train for war or participate in any preparation for it was a common concern of peace people, whatever their religious beliefs or lack of belief.[47]

To the fate of these nonreligious objectors over the next decade or so we should, I think, devote several paragraphs,[48] even if the subject bears only indirectly upon Quaker antimilitarism in Norway.

Nils Agøy, in his account of Norwegian anticonscriptionism from 1885 to 1922, has described correctly the army command's circular of 18 February 1902 as marking 'an important landmark in the history of conscientious objection' in his country.[49] Henceforward there were no more prosecutions of religious objectors; provided these could prove the validity of their claims to be treated as such they escaped scot free – to the chagrin of many supporters of military preparedness in the Norwegian community. Very occasionally a miscarriage of justice did indeed occur, and a genuine religious objector might find himself under constraint. But the injustice was soon righted and the man set at liberty. It all meant a lot of work of course for the army authorities, who seem to have taken their task of investigation seriously. They were mainly concerned at obtaining proof of the objector's affiliation, either by membership or close association, with a pacifist sect or confirmation of his sincerely holding pacifist views from his pastor if he belonged to a nonpacifist denomination. They also sought evidence of behaviour consistent with the moral stand being taken by the objector. Quakers, as one might expect, got off lightly, for the Society of Friends was universally respected and their testimony against fighting well known, if not always properly understood. If of course a religious objector could be persuaded to undertake noncombatant duties within the army, well and good. Otherwise, apart from exceptional circumstances,[50] and with the unspoken proviso that the country remained at peace, the religious objector was allowed to stay at home.

But for nonreligious antimilitarist objectors, a virtually new phenomenon as we have just seen, 1902 came to mean a change not for the better but decidedly for the worse. While such men remained liable to serve in the armed forces for the statutory period, the usual penalty each time for refusing to shoulder a rifle (for most nonreligious objectors rejected noncombatant army service as vehemently as did the religious ones) became more severe. Agøy has shown that terms of imprisonment now increased in length:[51] it was easier to understand a man who based his objections to fighting on the Bible than one who did not plead religion for his peculiar behaviour, and the new sentencing situation reflected this. The non-religious objectors were nearly all drawn from the political left; among them left socialists and anarchosyndicalists predominated. Whereas the social democratic Labour Party, founded in 1887, like most of its counterparts on the European continent, upheld, at least in theory, the idea of national defence, many of its members were hostile to the existing system of conscription and sympathised to a greater or less extent with those who went to prison because of their unwillingness to kill on behalf of a capitalist state. Beginning in 1906 opposition to compulsory military service became the official policy of the Labour Party. But it was particularly in the left wing socialist youth movement that the idea of refusing military service received widespread support. From this time forward we find a steady trickle of young socialist objectors. They took the 'broken rifle' as the symbol of their war resistance.[52] Few of them, however, were pacifists on principle; they mostly supported armed defence of a future worker's state. But, during the early years of this century at any rate, there were some, often influenced by reading Tolstoy's antimilitarist writings, who objected on ethical grounds to war of every sort;[53] in their case humanist ethics rather than religion *sensu stricto* motivated a pacifism that was in some ways akin to that of the sectarians.

Interest in the question of conscientious objection, once the concern only of the tiny body of Quakers and a few other obscure peace sectaries, had greatly increased in the course of the 1890s as a result of the activities of the newly born Norwegian peace movement. That movement was not specifically Quaker. But Quakers played, both in its inception and in its early development, a role quite out of proportion to the numerical strength they possessed within it. For the Society of Friends in Norway, peace activity of this kind provided a welcome means for expressing the positive aspect of their testimony against war which the negative act of their young men in refusing to bear arms, however essential a part of their peace witness they all considered this to be, could not provide.

A short lived peace society had come into existence in Christiania in 1885, its founder a liberal politician and pillar of the *Venstre* (Left) Party, Willert Konow. But long before that date Asbjørn Kloster, the Quaker schoolmaster and temperance advocate – he was himself a total abstainer – had been hard at work spreading ideas of international law and arbitration of disputes between states. He was clearly influenced in his antiwar activity by the example of British Friends, whom he knew at first hand,[54] and of their support of the Peace Society in their country; he was also well acquainted with the work of Henry Richard, the Welsh born peace advocate and long time secretary of the London Peace Society, whom he greatly admired. But Kloster died prematurely – in 1876 – before his labours, often almost singlehanded, could bring into being in Norway a peace society on the English model. In the journal he established in 1861 to promote the causes he had chiefly at heart like temperance and peace – it was called *The Philanthropist (Menneskevennen)*[55] – Kloster published, in almost every issue, articles condemning war, both from the point of view of the Christian religion and because of the material damage war inevitably inflicted on humanity, and urging at the same time practical measures for eliminating it from civilised societies.

Actually, because of the multiple nature of his reform interests, it was only during the last five or six years of his life that Kloster could at last find time to devote himself extensively to the cause of peace. He had come to see such activity as of increasing urgency for the future of humankind. Kloster's friend and disciple, Sven Aarrestad, wrote of him many years later: 'The cause of peace was, I can almost say, part of his religion . . . He did not differentiate between wars of defence and wars of aggression; he condemned them both because . . . under all circumstances . . . war remained a crime . . . He was in no doubt as to what must be done.' And, Aarrestad relates, Kloster's eyes would start to glow as, with increasing excitement, he began to outline the various means by which he believed the earth might be freed from the scourge of war: the establishment of peace societies as widely as possible and the resolution of international conflicts through arbitration and the development of a code of international law.[56]

A Norwegian Peace Society *(Den norske Fredsforening)* did not in fact emerge on a permanent basis until 1895, 19 years after Kloster's death; its central office was in Christiania. But its foundation had been preceded by the setting up toward the end of the previous year of a local peace society at Stavanger, largely under Quaker auspices. In 1897 this was, with 545 members, the new Society's second largest affiliate. The majority of its members could not have been Friends but it was the latter who played the leading role and shaped the policies which the Stavanger Society promoted. Quaker women were particularly active in peace work here; they served on the executive committee alongside the menfolk. The pacifist component was reinforced by periodic visits from Quakers from overseas like the peace activist and protagonist of Quaker renewal from Baltimore, Richard H. Thomas, and the Norwegian born Friend, John F. Hanson, from the American West. These experienced speakers and organisers helped the Quaker peace people in Norway to hold public meetings, circulate propaganda, get up petitions in favour of international arbitration and disarmament and, finally, to agitate in favour of recognition of the right of conscientious objection.[57]

Among Stavanger Quakers the lead in peace work came from Tønnes Sandstøl (1845-1924).[58] Liberal in his religious views as well as in his political sympathies, Sandstøl, though he never actually became a member of the Society of Friends, regularly attended their Meetings for Worship and was in fact a Quaker in all but name. For a number of years he acted as headmaster of the Quaker school at Stavanger. Along with the Thomases, Anna B. and Richard H., who were then visiting from America, Sandstøl had been responsible for seeing that from the outset the Stavanger Peace Society, though open to all who sincerely desired to work against the institution of war, should be firmly based on pacifist principle. Its constitution, adopted at its foundation in November 1894, included a clause condemning war as incompatible 'with the teaching of Jesus Christ.'[59] In the early years of the new century Sandstøl was active in the central organisation of the Norwegian Peace Society, acting for a time as its chairman and later as its secretary and treasurer and editing its journal *The Standard of Peace (Fredsbanneret)* from 1907 until 1917. Himself a searcher for the Truth who never felt completely at home spiritually even among the Quakers, Sandstøl experienced a sense of kinship with Tolstoy, and in particular with the Russian's radical antimilitarism. Like Tolstoy, the Norwegian too considered pacifism a matter that transcended denominational boundaries and even the Christian religion itself. As he wrote: 'To be sure, I share the Friends' view that war is incompatible with Christianity. But it does not follow from that I therefore agree with them in everything, and in my opinion we have to guard against giving the cause of peace a definitely religious character.'[60]

Sandstøl possessed a close ally within the Peace Society's leadership in the talented journalist and energetic parliamentarian, N. J. Sørensen,[61] who was the leading personality in the Christiania branch of the Peace Society – small in numbers but important as the centre of peace activities in the capital. Like Sandstøl, Sørensen also was a liberal Christian and a member of the leftwing of the Liberal Party.[62] The two men were both convinced religious pacifists, who believed a Christian antimilitarism based on the Sermon on the Mount implied the obligation to refuse to bear arms when called upon to do so. Military service, Sørensen argued, constituted a form of war making and world peace would never arrive until conscription had been everywhere abolished. We have seen above that Sørensen had acted as the *spiritus movens* behind a number of bills introduced into the *Storting* to legalise conscientious objection, whether the motives for this were religious or nonreligious. Sørensen was never as close to Quakers as Sandstøl was; still, it was the Quakers on whom he chiefly relied to give him regular support in his struggle for peace and the rights of conscientious objectors.[63] Sørensen's journal *Peace (Fred: Tidsskrivt for folkeret og voldgift)*, which he started up in 1898, became the leading organ of the peace movement in Norway until its demise in 1907; the editor frequently had to write most of an issue himself. In its pages, as well as in a number of books and pamphlets he published between 1896 and 1901,[64] Sørensen pleaded the case not only for absolute pacifism as the proper foundation of all peace endeavours but also for the arbitration of all interstate disputes and an international court of justice as practical measures to end war, on which both pacifists and nonpacifists could unite.

It soon became clear that peace advocates in Norway, though a small company if compared with those who shared the traditional outlook toward war, were nevertheless divided in their attitude toward national defence. The Norwegian Peace Society contained both pacifist absolutists and nonpacifist relativists who strove to eliminate war from civilised society but continued to believe it right to wage a defensive war if their country were invaded. The peace relativists were naturally reluctant to support the stand of the conscientious objector; for the Peace Society to do so, they felt would be to court increased unpopularity among the populace at large. The question was discussed vehemently at meetings of the central Peace Society as well as among the local branches and in the movement's publications. Officially, the Society never wavered in its policy of accepting both absolutists and relativists into membership. But sometimes the one faction and sometimes the other predominated at the annual meetings and an absolutist majority alternated with a relativist one in the Peace Society's executive committee.[65]

During the decade or so before World War I, however, the issue subsided. Even Sørensen's concern for promoting the interests of conscientious objectors waned, though he did not abandon the pacifist cause. The Peace Society, we should note, drew its main support from the liberal minded bourgeoisie. Since in this period only left socialists had to suffer for refusing to bear arms, discussion of conscientious objection then appeared to most members of rather minor importance. Even the Quakers, with their fellowship now much reduced in numbers, were no longer busy in the matter, though they continued to maintain their peace testimony intact. Their sons, of course, were now automatically exempted by the military: it was hard for most Friends, by this time somewhat higher up in the social scale than any of them had been during Quakerism's début in Norway, to become excited over the misfortunes of working-class youths who, though they were taking a stand against war, held agnostic or atheist views, which shocked most of the Christ-centred Norwegian Quakers, and in many cases also expressed a readiness to overthrow the existing social order by violence.[66]

If Sørensen and Sandstøl were the foremost representatives of the absolutists in the Norwegian peace movement,[67] the relativists possessed an eloquent spokesman in a young historian, Halvdan Koht (1873-1965), later to become one of modern Norway's most prominent scholars, a leader of its Labour Party, and for a time the country's foreign minister.[68] Early in 1901 Koht published an article in the Peace Society's journal *Fredstidende* (Peace News), in which he strongly criticised the Quaker controlled branch of the Society at Stavanger for its pacifist absolutism and its promotion of conscientious objection. He deeply regretted, he wrote, their total opposition to the idea of defence: this 'defence nihilism (*forsvarsnihilisme*)' he felt indeed as a serious hindrance to spreading pacificist ideas among the general public and something that he thought could only do harm to the cause of peace. Sandstøl reacted at once against what he considered an unfair attack on Koht's part: pacifism, he pointed out, differed for one thing from nihilism in its steady adhesion to nonviolence. From the correspondence that developed over the next few years between them,[69] it is clear that their disagreement stemmed from a basic difference of outlook on life. Sandstøl's absolutism was part of his religion whereas Koht was a religious sceptic. Moreover, whereas the former, intellectually a product of the 19th century, held fast to political liberalism and moved among the liberal and radical bourgeoisie of Stavanger and Christiania, young Koht, although not yet a member of the Labour Party, was an enthusiastic socialist who regarded the working class as the champion of world peace.[70]

Yet, for all their differences, relativists and absolutists succeeded on the whole in peacefully coexisting within the Norwegian Peace Society. More than once schism threatened but in the end the movement's two factions perceived they had more in common with each other than either of them had with the world outside that continued to accept war as a natural phenomenon. They must therefore agree to differ and respect each other's point of view. For the peace forces were tiny indeed in comparison with those upholding the war system, and they surely could not afford to be permanently divided.

Due to men like the near-Quaker Tønnes Sandstøl, 'Norwegian Quakers made an important impact on the Norwegian peace movement'[71] during the two decades preceding the outbreak of World War I. The Quaker presence within that movement distinguished it from all the other peace movements that had arisen in conscriptionist countries on the European continent in the course of the 19th and early 20th centuries. For only Norway's Peace Society resembled the Anglo-American peace movement in its inclusion of an absolute pacifist contingent alongside those peace advocates whose view of peace allowed for the possibility of defensive wars and, therefore, denied in the existing circumstances the utility of urging unilateral disarmament. Norway's pacifists – *de absolutte fredsvennene* – embraced of course not only Quakers and Quaker sympathisers but also pacifists like N. J. Sørensen or that ardent and active antimilitarist Ivar Elias Larsen,[72] all of them persons who worked with Friends but who at the same time belonged to another religious fellowship. But without the Quaker input it is doubtful if pacifism would have found an effective voice – or at any rate its voice would soon have been drowned out – amid the relativism that prevailed everywhere else in the peace movements on that continent.

Thus Quakerism in Norway, whose peace witness had been otherwise confined to the negative act of refusal of military service and constantly diminished too by the emigration of its young people to escape the burden of conscription, found a positive role to play in asserting the right of pacifism to a place in the discussions of the emergent Norwegian peace movement over issues of peace and war. In its public peace activities the Society of Friends in Norway, with steadily declining numbers, always found welcome support and strength at this time in the Quakers who visited them from Britain and America – all of them active peace people. It is to the development of the Quaker peace testimony in England and the United States that we must, once again, now turn our attention in order to trace how renewal there eventually transformed a somewhat moribund pacifist witness into a vital force with sufficient energy to face the problems of a world at war.

CHAPTER XXII

Jonathan Dymond and the Advocacy of Peace

QUAKERS HAD LACKED A SYSTEMATIC exposition of their Christian pacifism until Jonathan Dymond (1796-1828) provided this in writings which appealed not only to Quakers of his time but to a wider public that had become interested in promoting the cause of peace. Though he died prematurely in 1828 at the age of 31, his influence as a peace advocate continued into the present century. Some of his arguments have dated but his work remains imposing through the strength of his convictions and the cogency of his reasoning. True, as Michael Howard remarks, 'Dymond said nothing that had not been said before . . . but he said it with great power.'[1]

Dymond[2] was the son of a Quaker linen-draper in Exeter in the southwest English county of Devon. Both his parents were 'recorded ministers' of the Society of Friends. Although his formal education was slight he acquired an extensive fund of knowledge, particularly of classical literature. Working as a youth in his father's shop he used to spend his leisure hours in composing verse and writing essays on religious and moral problems. At the same time he remained a devoted member of the religious denomination into which he had been born. Dymond was a sensitive spirit and he shared the moral earnestness of many of the best minds of his age. He had early in his career determined to devote his energies to peace: indeed 'the honour of advocating peace' he held to be the chief mission of his life.[3] And he believed the time had arrived for a concerted effort by all persons of good will to eliminate war as a method of settling international disputes, for war, as he wrote, constituted 'an evil before which, in my estimation, slavery sinks into insignificance.' Slavery anyhow was on the point of disappearing while war remained to menace civilised society.[4] In 1825, after attending the annual meeting of the Peace Society in London,[5] Dymond was instrumental in setting up a branch of this Society in Exeter. Ill health, however, soon led to his having to withdraw from active involvement in the work of the Exeter auxiliary Peace Society, and three years later he was dead.

Dymond's view of the role the Quaker peace testimony should play in contemporary society differed from that of many American Friends. He was anxious to collaborate with other pacifists and near pacifists in an interdenominational peace movement and opposed any talk of confining the Quaker peace effort within their own ranks. His spirit was in no way sectarian: he welcomed all who wished to work sincerely for peace and it was as much for non-Quakers as for Quakers that he composed his works on the subject.

In 1823, aged only 27, he brought out his most substantial discussion of the moral and religious implications of pacifism. He entitled the work *An Inquiry into the Accordancy of War with the Principles of Christianity, and an Examination of the Philosophical Reasoning by which it is defended: with Observations on Some of the Causes of War and on Some of Its Effects.*[6] Two years later, in 1825, the London Peace Society published a brief version of his pacifist exposition as its Tract No. VII: *Observations on the Applicability of the Pacific Principles of the New Testament on the Conduct of States, and on the Limitations which Those Principles impose on the Rights of Self-defence.* Finally, his most important book was published posthumously in 1829 in two volumes: *Essays on the Principles of Morality, and on the Private and Political Rights and Obligations of Mankind.* 'The leading theme of the *Essays* was that deviations from rectitude were impolitic as well as wrong.'[7] And one of these essays Dymond devoted to the subject of war. In it he rearranged and slightly revised the views he had expounded in his earlier *Inquiry* while at the same time giving them added cogency and additional strength of argument. This essay was soon reprinted separately and the many subsequent editions down to 1915 testify to its continued popularity in peace circles. Indeed 'Dymond on War' became a standard reference, and we find it quoted copiously in the literature of the 19th-century peace movement on both sides of the Atlantic.[8]

What was Dymond's moral philosophy of peace? It was of course essentially a Christian philosophy. Roughly half the text of his *Essay on War* is devoted to proving the incompatibility of war with the Christian religion. But he is also concerned to show its incompatibility with human reason and common morality as well as to prove the practicality of pacifism as national policy. In his pragmatism he contrasts with most previous Quaker expositors of their Society's peace testimony. In fact Dymond believes Quaker pacifism is not only good Christianity but good sense as well. That is the reason why in his *Essay on War* he discusses its cause and consequences before he moves on to disprove its 'lawfulness' from the Christian point of view. He nowhere presents his arguments against war and in favour of pacifism as specifically Quaker: they are ones he hopes may appeal to all Christians, and some of them he couches in rational rather than religious terms.

In his discussion of the bases of Christian pacifism he reminds one of Erasmus (whom Dymond admired) rather than some of its earlier exponents in the Anabaptist-Mennonite tradition. Dymond does deal with certain New Testament texts and incidents but his appeal is above all to the spirit of Christ's teachings, to the gospel of love. He is not bothered by the fact that the Christian Scriptures contain 'no specific prohibition of war,'[9] for the whole tenor of the gospels, he believes, confirms Jesus' rejection of all forms of violence, and of war in particular. He writes:

> In examining the arguments by which War is defended, two important considerations should be borne in mind. First, that those who urge them are not simply defending War, they are also defending *themselves*. If War is wrong, their conduct is wrong; and the desire of self-justification prompts them to give importance to whatever arguments they can advance in its favour. Their decisions may therefore with reason be regarded as in some degree the decisions of a party in the cause. The other consideration is, that the defenders of war come to the discussion prepossessed in its favour. They are attached to it by their earliest habits. They do not examine the question as a philosopher would examine it to whom the subject is new . . . They are discussing a question which they had already determined; and every man who is acquainted with the effects of evidence on the mind, knows that under these circumstances a very slender argument in favour of the previous opinions possesses more influence than great ones against it. Now all this cannot be predicated of the advocates of Peace; they are *opposing* the influence of habit; they are contending *against* the general prejudice; they are perhaps dismissing their own previous opinions; and I would submit it to the candour of the reader, that these circumstances ought to attach in his mind *suspicion* as to the validity of the arguments against us.[10]

Christians, Dymond argued, should not base their conduct on that of the Jews as depicted in the Old Testament. Even some Quakers, like Dymond's contemporary the evangelical Friend Joseph John Gurney, took a positive view of the wars waged under the Old Dispensation. Dymond was shocked by the attitude displayed by certain contemporary Friends, who claimed to be pacifists. 'It is sorrowful,' he wrote to his brother-in-law, 'to think that believers in the gospel of peace should allow themselves to be, in any degree, shaken from their intention of disseminating that peace by a passage from Genesis.' 'There are,' he went on, 'an abundance of matters in the Old Testament which were sanctioned by the will of God, and which we all *agree in rejecting* . . . A precept of the Old Testament does not bind Christians if an observance of it would violate the Christian law.' Dymond was frankly puzzled by the seeming unpredictability of God in sanctioning wars waged by the Jews in Old Testament times while forbidding them to Christians under the New Dispensation. However, 'such is, indeed the fact: we cannot account for it; and we have nothing to do with it.'[11] Instead, Christians should take as their model the primitive church, which had he believed rejected war unequivocally. Its members 'lived nearest to the time of our Saviour' and, therefore, were in the best position to know what he intended for his followers.[12]

Dymond did not evade the problem of the magistrate's sword. Was force permissible within the confines of the state in order to maintain order and to protect the innocent and repress the wrongdoer? He conceded 'the lawfulness of coercion on the part of the civil magistrate' while opposing capital punishment as barbarous and unchristian.[13] And even if, for the sake of argument one sanctioned the death penalty (as some peace advocates actually did), Dymond denied that such a use of force by the state could be employed as a justification for war. 'I contend,' he wrote of capital punishment, 'that it has little or nothing to do with the question of war. For . . . the indispensable requisite of the lawfulness of taking . . . lives . . . is, that *each individual should be proved to be a murderer.*'[14]

Nor would Dymond admit the possibility of any war being a truly defensive war. 'We say that if Christianity allows defensive war, she allows all war' since, if one delves deeply into the question, it is in fact virtually impossible to discover who the aggressor really is. 'Does any man believe that a war was ever waged in Europe, for a thousand years past, which could be' properly defined as a defensive one? Guilt and innocence, right and wrong become inextricably mixed once war has broken out.

> When nations are mutually exasperated, and armies are levied, and battles are fought, does not every one know that with whatever motives of defence one party may have begun the contest, both in turn become aggressors? In the fury of slaughter soldiers do not attend, they cannot attend, to questions of aggression. Their business is destruction, and their business they will perform. If the army of defence obtains success, it soon becomes an army of aggression. Having repelled the invader, it begins to punish him. If a war has once begun, it is vain to talk of distinctions of aggression and defence. Moralists may *talk* of distinctions, but soldiers will *make* none; and none can be made: it is outside the limits of possibility.[15]

In view of all this, Dymond believed that Christians must not only refrain from acts of violence in their individual lives but that what he called 'the universality of Christian obligation' required them also to apply 'the pacific injunctions of the Christian Scriptures . . . under every circumstance of life,' including relations between states.[16] This should be done regardless of the consequences: the Christian must trust in God's providence to protect him from harm. 'Christianity . . . wants men who are willing to *suffer* for her principles.'[17]

In both his major works Dymond includes an analysis of the causes of war. Here he shows his talent as a political scientist, although the moral element lies scarcely concealed below the surface of his argument. However lofty the ideals nations claim to be fighting for, the Quaker detects largely material and selfish motives lying at the root of such conflicts: it is these motives that have propelled armies into the field and that are ultimately responsible for the slaughter and devastation of war. Moreover, since men have tended to accept war as one of the facts of life, they have failed to investigate adequately either the reasons for its occurrence or the possible alternatives. A general complacency has prevailed. 'They who are shocked at a single murder on the highway, hear with indifference of the slaughter of a thousand on the field.'[18]

National prestige – which Dymond calls 'national irritability' – is another potent cause of war, for 'if on every offence we fly to arms, we shall of necessity provoke exasperation' and evoke counter measures from the other side. 'In the present state of men's principles, it is not probable that one nation will observe another levying men, and building ships, and founding cannon, without providing men, and ships, and cannon themselves.' Thus an arms race ensues with war as the inevitable outcome, for the 'balance of power' (which Dymond defines as a belief that states are prevented from destroying each other only by 'an equality of the means of destruction') has proved a mirage deluding Europe's statesmen into thinking it can safeguard peace. Self-interest on the part of those hoping to profit from armaments and international conflict helps to foment war, too. For, if war were abolished, not only would military and naval officers lose their profession but many industrialists and business men would lose their profits as well. These sections of society stand to gain by the continuance of the war system. And thus,

> By depending upon war for a subsistence, a powerful inducement is given to desire it; and when the question of war is to be decided, it is to be feared that the whispers of interest will prevail, and that humanity, and religion, and conscience, will be sacrificed to promote it.

The ambitions of princes and statesmen also act often in favour of war. Cabinets by their secret schemes to promote the aggrandisement of their countries tend to speculate 'in the lives of men' and use war as an instrument of policies they dare not openly avow. Most dangerous of all, in Dymond's opinion, are the ideas of military glory which are so deeply rooted in the populace that people are conditioned beforehand to accept any armed conflict that their rulers choose to indulge in. Poets and historians, and even clergymen, have frequently been guilty of creating a martial spirit, of whipping up patriotic emotions, and of influencing public opinion decisively to reject the ways of peace in exchange for the pursuit of a glory that is both 'factitious and impure.'[19]

In his discussion of the consequences of war Dymond is treading on familiar ground. As he remarks himself, 'To expatiate upon the miseries which war brings upon mankind, appears a trite and a needless employment. We all know that its evils are great and dreadful.'[20] Yet he felt it necessary to say something about war's social and moral effects, since familiarity with these had tended to blunt men's consciences and accustom them to consider warfare an inevitable accompaniment of human history. War, he points out, cannot be fought without extensive loss of life, a grave financial burden on the inhabitants of states engaging in it, and widespread moral depravity. The profession of soldiering he finds degrading for the human personality since 'military power is essentially arbitrary' and this arbitrariness forms an unavoidable concomitant of war. A fervent antimilitarist, Dymond saw armies as enemies of liberty and physical and moral subjection as a necessary condition of army life.

> The soldier is compelled to obey, whatever be his inclination or his will. Being in the service, he has but one alternative – submission to arbitrary power, or punishment – the punishment of death perhaps, – for refusing to submit. Let the reader imagine to himself any other cause or purpose for which freemen shall be subjected to such a condition, and he will then see that condition in its proper light. The influence of habit and the gloss of public opinion make situations that would otherwise be loathsome and revolting, not only tolerable but pleasurable. Take away this influence and this gloss from the situation of a soldier, and what should we call it? We should call it a state of degradation and bondage.[21]

Like many 19th-century peace advocates in Britain and America, Dymond tended to think in terms of a voluntary army. He does not consider, either, the relevance of pacifism in a war of national liberation. Concerning Poland which had lost its independence in 1795 and again in 1815, he wrote: 'The inhabitants might be supposed to have learnt the value of pacific morality by their experience of the effects of its contrary; if we did not know how often experience preaches in vain.'[22] It was not the *levée-en-masse* such as revolutionary and nationalist France had brought into existence in 1792 but the old fashioned British army of his day that Dymond had in mind when he denounced the antilibertarian tendencies of military life.

Dymond did not deny war had certain compensating features; it brought out courage in men, for instance, and a willingness to sacrifice.[23]

But its evils far outweighed any good qualities it might possess. In fact Dymond regarded war as the greatest evil then afflicting humankind. For him peace had always proved preferable to war; to avoid war now should be the chief aim of the non-Christian as much as for the follower of Jesus. As he wrote:

> Even waiving the obligations of Christianity, we have to choose between evils that are certain and evils that are doubtful; between the actual endurance of a great calamity, and the possibility of a less. It certainly cannot be proved that Peace would not be the best policy; and since we know that the present system is bad, it were reasonable and wise to try whether the other is not better. In reality I can scarcely conceive the possibility of a greater evil than that which mankind now endures; an evil, moral and physical, of far wider extent, and far greater intensity, than our familiarity with it allows us to suppose. If a system of Peace be not productive of less evil than the system of war, its consequences must indeed be enormously bad; and that it would produce such consequences we have no warrant for believing, either from reason or from practice, – either from the principles of the moral government of God, or from the experience of mankind. Whenever a people shall pursue, steadily and uniformly, the pacific morality of the Gospel, and shall do this from the pure motive of obedience, there is no reason to fear for the consequences: . . . the surest and the only rule of wisdom, of safety, and expediency, is to maintain [Christianity's] spirit in every circumstance of life.[24]

In other words, pacifism if pursued consistently would lead not to martyrdom (which Anabaptists and Mennonites and some early Quakers had asserted as a possibility) but to practical success. As proof of this Dymond pointed to the experience of Quakers in Pennsylvania and in Ireland in 1798. He fervently believed it was part of God's plan that war would disappear from human society and that Christianity, understood as pacifism, would be His instrument in bringing about permanent peace in the world. Therefore, Providence might be relied on to protect those who refused on grounds of conscience to participate in war.[25] While we thus see Dymond urged the adoption of pacifism on pragmatic and prudential grounds, we should not forget, however, that his objection to war was basically religious and ethical.

Dymond never denied the existence in humankind of bellicose instincts. Yet 'the question' he wrote, 'is not with what instincts are we naturally endowed? – but in what degree does the Creator require us to restrain them?'[26] He did not think the restraint needed to eliminate war as a method of solving national disputes could be found only in a spiritual élite such as the Society of Friends constituted:[27] he believed human beings in general, or at any rate all Christians, were capable of it. His work, therefore, made an appeal to a much wider audience than any exposition of pacifism addressed primarily to persons who accepted the doctrines of the Society of Friends. That many of 'Dymond's conclusions appear simplistic to a 20th-century student of peace and war' (N. C. Miller) does not detract from the forcefulness of many of his arguments or the persuasiveness – and good prose – of his presentation of the case against war.

Unlike his fellow Quakers, Penn and Bellers, or contemporary pacifists like the American William Ladd, Dymond failed to provide institutional alternatives to the war method. As Geoffrey Carnall points out, 'For him the question of means was secondary, . . . his great contribution to the nineteenth-century peace movement lay in his cogent exposition of the basic convictions of the Christian peacemaker.' For him the Sermon on the Mount and the other peaceful injunctions of the New Testament applied as much to public life and interstate relations as most of his contemporaries believed they did in respect of the conduct of individuals. He strove to show that war, both with regard to its causes and its effects, ran counter to Christian principles of action and that those who, like his own Society of Friends, tried to live according to the precepts of the gospels had something to teach the statesmen and politicians concerning the way the affairs of the world should be run for the general good of humanity. Thus, for all their shortcomings Dymond's writings on war proved a seminal influence on the peace movement. They showed that pacifism was not merely a sectarian belief; it could generate a nondenominational campaign aimed at ending war and inaugurating the reign of peace on earth. There was a lot of naivety in Dymond and his disciples. But the very simpleness of their vision enabled them to overcome the obstacles and difficulties they encountered as pioneers in the struggle for peace.

CHAPTER XXIII

English Quakers in the Crimean War

BETWEEN THE END OF THE ARMED struggle against Napoleon I in 1815 and the outbreak of World War I in 1914 Great Britain became involved in only one European conflict: the war against Russia fought out in the Crimea from March 1854 to April 1856 in alliance with Napoleon III and Turkey. The Crimean War saw the first example of Quaker 'diplomacy' exercised in an attempt to avert threatened hostilities and also the display of a more 'public response' than English Friends had hitherto shown when their country went to war.[1]

Their new stance reflected the active role many Quakers had been taking in the British peace movement which emerged after 1815: an attitude that contrasted, we have seen, with the aloofness, amounting sometimes even to hostility, of American Friends to peace organisations in their country during this period. Jonathan Dymond was only one among many English Quakers who helped to form the thought and practice of the early peace movement. Indeed the early history of the movement is intelligible only if the part played in it by Quakers is fully realised. At the London Peace Congress in 1851, for instance, 207 out of 969 delegates were Friends. 'In other words, Quakers in 1851 accounted for only one-tenth of one per cent of the total population of Great Britain, but they sent twenty-two per cent of the delegates to the Peace Congress.'[2] And not only did Quakers form a leaven inside the British peace movement; their activity within this area of public life helped to reinvigorate their own hitherto somewhat inward looking and enclosed peace witness and give it an outreach lacking until then. They continued to conduct their antiwar activities soberly and quietly but now they obviously aimed at a public outside the confines of their own membership. They saw peace as a common concern of all Christians and strove to convince as many of their fellow citizens as possible of the incompatibility of war with the religion their country officially upheld. Few British Friends became militant pacifists of the Garrisonian variety but many of them now strove to make their peace testimony a public witness, especially in periods of national crisis. By mid-century militia conscription had ceased to be operative in Britain,[3] and support of Quaker conscientious objectors was no longer a concern of the Society. It concentrated its peace efforts henceforward on ways to lessen the threat of war and reduce international tension and the rising scale of armaments.

By mid-1853 the possibility of war against Tsarist Russia began to loom large – with France, England's traditional foe, as a likely ally. As that staunch Quaker pacifist, Joseph Sturge, informed the abolitionist and peace advocate, Lewis Tappan, in New York:

> We are here in much uneasiness as to whether this Russo-Turkish affair may not lead to a European war. What strangely inconsistent beings professing Christians are! A few months ago Louis Napoleon was held up as a monster in human shape and we were put to great expense to prepare against the pretended danger, that he and his people would turn pirates and suddenly come over to murder and rob us. Now we are uniting our fleet with that of this very monster to fight with the Turks against a professedly Christian country.[4]

By the end of the year the situation had deteriorated still further, and pressure for war was mounting in the country with a bellicose press urging the government to take strong measures against Russia. The idea of sending a Quaker deputation to St. Petersburg to plead with the Tsar and his ministers on behalf of peace seems to have originated with Sturge.[5] He raised it at the Meeting for Sufferings early in January 1854. That body then approved the project on 17 January, its minute on the subject beginning with typical Quaker restraint: 'This Meeting has been introduced into much religious concern in contemplating the apparent probability of war between some of the nations of Europe.' An Address was drawn up for presentation to the Tsar and three delegates appointed to hand it over, if possible in a personal interview with that monarch. As Frick remarks: 'The deputation . . . would be decidedly a last ditch effort.' Its sponsors knew this and were prepared to take the risk of failure rather than omit any effort that might possibly avert the tragedy of war. Besides, the deputation offered an opportunity to bring the Quaker point of view to the attention of the Russian government as well as of public opinion at home. Not all peace advocates were sympathetic, however. For instance, the Peace Society's secretary, Henry Richard, and his *Herald of Peace*, remained cool for a time while Richard Cobden had tried to dissuade Sturge from undertaking the mission. The latter told Sturge on 3 January:

> I rather think you overrate the effect of deputating to crowned heads. 'Friends' have been charged with being too fond of the 'great,' and . . . biographies [of certain Quakers] give some colourable sanction to the

suspicion that you have *tuft-hunters* among your body. If a party of Friends were now to set off on a visit to Nicholas, it might I think expose them to the charge of seeking their own glorification. Nothing short of a miracle could enable such a deputation to accomplish the end in view; and miracles are not wrought in our times.

Moreover, since in Cobden's view it was Britain which was responsible for the blood about to be shed, he felt (as he put it in a letter written a week later) 'that we have too much to do at home to allow such diversions.' But Sturge remained undiscouraged by this and other adverse criticisms of the venture he was about to embark on.[6]

The Meeting for Sufferings appointed two other delegates besides Sturge himself: Robert Charleton, a Bristol pin manufacturer who had devoted a large part of his considerable fortune to various philanthropic endeavours, and Henry Pease, the railway magnate who was active in the Peace Society as well as in Liberal politics. All three, therefore, were men of substance since Sturge, for all his radicalism, had made a big success of his business as a Birmingham corn merchant. At the same time the three men had proved their loyalty to Quaker peace principles and to the Society as a whole by a lifetime of service on its behalf. Charleton, moreover, spoke fluent French which proved an asset in St. Petersburg. Thus the delegates were well chosen for the mission they now set out to accomplish.

The journey from London to St. Petersburg took 13 days, the three Quakers arriving in the Russian capital on 2 February. The latter part of their travels had been by sleigh through the Russian countryside then covered with deep snow. After arrival they set immediately to work, contacting members of the British community in St. Petersburg as well as Russian bureaucrats who might prove helpful. They were thankful to find war had not yet broken out between their two countries: since they did not enjoy diplomatic status, they ran the risk of being interned if this happened. None of them expected to achieve any miracles. As Pease wrote toward the end of their journey: 'I do not think so far as human reason goes [we have] any right to see fruit . . . [Yet] I do not doubt it is right that a Christian community as Friends should maintain this testimony against war.'[7] At any rate, whatever the outcome of their mission, they would have brought the Quaker concern for peace before the Russian ruler. They believed Tsar Nicholas, though an autocrat and portrayed in dark colours in the British press, was not as sinister a figure as he had been depicted. As Sturge wrote: 'The Emperor has qualities of private character which we in England do not give him credit for: that he is not only kind but affectionate in the private and domestic relations of life, and it is said on pretty good authority that he devotes nearly an hour to his private devotions.'[8] Moreover, Quakers had earlier enjoyed friendly relations with his brother and predecessor

Alexander I: hopefully memories of this relationship persisted among members of the Imperial family.

On 10 February the hoped-for interview with the Tsar took place. It was Sturge who read the Society's Address to the Russian ruler. This document stressed the religious basis of Friends's rejection of war. It was, it said, 'under a deep conviction of religious duty, and in the constraining love of Christ our Saviour,' and 'apart from all political consideration,' that they now came to plead for peace. Quakers had already made their position clear to England's rulers: 'in language of bold but respectful remonstrance, we have urged upon them the maintenance of peace, as the true policy as well as the manifest duty of a Christian Government.' It was not their intention now to argue the rights and wrongs of the respective parties in the present quarrel. They wished only to point out that both sides claimed to be followers of one who commanded love of enemies and blessed the peacemakers. Surely then, 'the more fully the Christian is persuaded of the justice of his own cause, the greater his magnanimity in the exercise of forbearance.'[9]

Nicholas listened carefully as the Address was read out. Sturge in conclusion explained that neither the Quakers, 'nor a large proportion of the rightly thinking part of the English public,' supported the pro-war press in Britain, and he added that they had thereby 'incurred unpopularity with those who wished to depend on physical force, by advocating the settlement of international disputes by arbitration.' The Tsar's reply emphasised both the justice of Russia's case and his own desire for peace and his abhorrence of war ('I abhor it as sincerely as you do'). He respected and admired England's Queen. Yet, while unwilling to take the first step in launching a war, he felt it his Christian duty to defend his country's honour and interests by arms against attack from whatever quarter it might come. The interview was conducted in a friendly atmosphere. At the end, as Charleton wrote his wife, 'he shook hands with us all very cordially, and with eyes moistened with emotion, turned hastily away, as we believe to conceal his feelings.' The Quakers were then introduced to the Tsarina and her daughter, Grand Duchess Olga. A small gift proffered by the Tsar was refused since the delegates feared this might be represented by the hostile British press as a bribe.[10]

At home the press, with a few notable exceptions, proved indeed hostile to the Quakers' peace initiative. The *Times* called it a 'piece of enthusiastic folly.' Sincere but misguided and naive, this constituted the essence of most comments on the deputation. *John Bull* went so far as to accuse Friends of 'sectarian vanity' and a desire 'to parade themselves before the world as more righteous than the rest of mankind.' *Punch* published an article entitled 'Save Us from Our Friends.' Ridicule as well as invective were directed against the three delegates. But surely, as one of them (Pease) remarked, 'There was . . . nothing unreasonable . . . in a body of men who had been in existence for 200 years, who had always believed that the disputes of nations could never be settled by appealing to the sword, sending three of their number to endeavour to bring about a pacific settlement of the dispute, without appealing to such an awful thing as war.'[11]

The delegates, despite their disclaimers of 'anything political in connexion with our present mission,' had evidently hoped for a moment that the Tsar, 'in the present suspended state of diplomatic relations,' might use them as a means to transmit some message to the British cabinet that could even then have averted war.[12] This did not happen, however. And on 28 March, not long after their return home, war was declared. The mission had proved fruitless, at least as to immediate results. In the prospective of Quaker development, however, it proved the first of a long series of attempts by the Society at 'private diplomacy' aimed at fostering and maintaining peace: attempts that have continued down to the present.

Christian pacifism had formed the chief motive impelling these three middle-aged Quaker gentlemen to brave the rigours of winter travel in Russia. But it cannot be denied that at least one of them (and he certainly did not stand alone among Friends) was concerned, too, with the material losses war with Russia would bring for English trade and commerce. Shortly before leaving St. Petersburg Henry Pease had told his relatives at home:

> We came here to represent [the Christian] precept as opposed to war but the commercial one is no trifle. In this respect Russia is comparatively a young country and a very large portion of the capital so employed in this city is English, in connection with flax, corn, tallow, etc. which are obtained from the interior . . . Russia [is] of vast extent, and unmeasurable resources if opened out on free trade principles . . . the life blood of the government revenues is to a large extent caused by British capital and the trade with England is nine-tenths of the exports at Cronstadt.[13]

After hostilities had broken out the Society of Friends continued to voice its opposition, even though virtually every other religious group in the country now gave its approval to the war.[14] In contrast to earlier conflicts the Society decided to bring this opposition to public notice as widely as possible. Meeting for Sufferings, therefore, appointed a Committee to draw up a statement outlining Friends' position on the war. After receiving the Meeting's approval on 8 December the statement, entitled *A Christian Appeal from the Society of Friends to Their Fellow-Countrymen on the Present War*, was printed as a leaflet early in 1855. It was to be circulated 'in as extensive a manner as . . . expedient.' In fact at least 220,000 copies of the *Appeal* were circulated throughout Great Britain, mainly through the agency of the Society's Monthly Meetings, and it was translated into German and French. In many places Friends succeeded in getting their local newspapers to print the text of the *Appeal*, which was thus brought to the attention of many people who would not otherwise have come across the leaflet.[15]

The *Appeal's* argument centred on the Christian pacifist objection to war, which it explained Friends had always considered to be 'unlawful under the gospel dispensation': use of armed force was wrong for nations as well as for individuals. 'That which is morally or religiously wrong cannot be politically right' – or even expedient, it added, for war threatened the country's financial position in addition to exacting its toll in human lives. Therefore, Friends called upon their government to restore peace to Europe, despite the difficulties they realised would have to be overcome – an inflamed public opinion at home and a formidable enemy abroad.[16]

It is difficult to assess the amount of support the *Appeal* gained in Britain. Antiwar sentiments were naturally unpopular at this time.[17] The widely acclaimed Hungarian nationalist leader, Lajos Kossuth, for instance, attacked Friends in a letter he sent to the *Sunday Times* on 15 January. He accused them of seeking 'peace at any price' and propagating the 'false doctrine' that war was always unchristian and that it would be wrong to try and overcome tyranny by the sword. Kossuth believed that sometimes force must be used to overthrow despots. For him the present conflict was indeed a 'necessary' war.[18] Arguments of this kind failed of course to convince Quakers just as their pleadings for peace left the advocates of armed victory unmoved.

Friends realised conduct counted as much as, perhaps more than, argument in persuading their countrymen of the validity of their views – or at any rate of the sincerity of their convictions. They repeatedly stressed the importance of members of the Society acting in their everyday lives consistently with the principles of peace they professed as a religious body. We find, for example, the Meeting for Sufferings in a minute of 13 December 1854 warning members that they should

> be careful not to seek or accept profit by any concern in the preparations so extensively making for war; for how reproachfully inconsistent would it be to refuse an active compliance with warlike measures, and, at the same time, not to hesitate to enrich ourselves by the commerce and other circumstances dependent on war.[19]

A case immediately presented itself that proved it was not always easy to draw the line between warlike activity and humanitarian concern. In 1851

Yearly Meeting had ruled that for Friends to supply clothing for use in the army 'was clearly a violation of our testimony.' Therefore, when it became known that, during the winter of 1854-5, C & J Clark, the highly respected Quaker leather merchants of Street in Somerset, had accepted a contract to supply the British forces in the Crimea with sheepskin coats, voices were at once raised in criticism. Many Friends felt the Clarks had directly contravened the recent decision of Yearly Meeting and deserved a stern reproof for unquakerly conduct. The Clarks, however, explained they had reluctantly acceded to the War Office's request only after discovering their firm alone possessed the skins needed to provide such garments as would protect the troops from death in the icy Crimean winter. They had refused to accept the profits from this transaction, donating the money instead to construct a new building for the village school in Street. Most Friends seem to have accepted the Clarks' explanation and exonerated them from the charge of war profiteering.[20]

Quakers proved ready to succour the victims of war on an individual basis. But for the most part they refrained from contributing to such efforts as the Patriotic Fund set up to aid the widows and orphans of those killed either in battle or by the diseases which were decimating the troops in the Crimea.[21] The losses suffered there served to strengthen their resolution to oppose the war on principle. But, after issuing their *Christian Appeal* at the beginning of 1855, they did not again attempt any public initiative. It was left to two prominent members of the Society to present the Quaker point of view in politics and the press. We should, therefore, turn now to survey briefly the antiwar witness of Joseph Sturge and John Bright. Neither were acting as representatives of the Society: each spoke only for himself, yet each (Sturge perhaps even more than Bright) reflected in his public utterances and endeavours something of the Quaker spirit in its struggle against war.

Sturge had been a committed pacifist since his early years: in 1813, when aged 20, he had refused to serve in the militia.[22] Moving off the family farm he soon succeeded in making a fortune in the grain trade. A man whose personal integrity even his opponents fully recognised, he had then thrown himself successively into a number of reform causes which included antislavery, universal suffrage, and the Anti-Corn Law movement. 'Peace, however, was his primary concern,'[23] although it was not until mid-century that he was able to devote all his energies to its promotion. He became, alongside its secretary Henry Richard, the mainstay of the Peace Society (being elected its president not long before his death in 1859). Sturge opposed war with Russia as a Quaker but he also condemned it on political grounds, though for him – as for many other Friends – Christianity and 'true policy' coincided. Both required the British government to adopt 'the full principle of non-intervention' in its relations with foreign powers. 'Christianity,' Sturge claimed, 'destroyed all nationalities'; the Christian, that is, should regard the interests of other nations as much as those of his own.

Sturge's radical antimilitarism comes out in a placard which he wrote for distribution in his home town of Birmingham. Dated 2 December 1854 it was entitled *The Russian War. To My Fellow Townsmen of the Working Classes*. The war, he told them, had – among other evils – been responsible for the high price of bread, the staple diet of Britain's labouring classes, for Russian grain was no longer available. England moreover he condemned for its self-righteous attitude *vis-à-vis* Russia. Its imperial record he felt was no better, perhaps not even as good, as the latter's had been.

> When we reflect on the atrocities committed in wars of aggression by this country within the last twenty years, in India, in China, in Afghanistan, and lastly in Africa and Burmah, it will be seen that, however, unjust towards Turkey the invasion of the principalities by Russia might be, it sinks by comparison into insignificance.[24]

After returning from the mission to St. Petersburg Sturge's next big antiwar enterprise was the creation of what has been described as 'the world's first daily newspaper dedicated to the cause of peace.'[25] The idea, says Frick, originated with Richard Cobden, and he and Bright gave Sturge strong support throughout in promoting it. In a letter to the latter dated 14 December 1853, Cobden had remarked: 'By the way, what an advantage it would be if . . . we could have a daily paper . . . advocating peace and constantly keeping before the public the evils of past wars, and the terrible consequences of future hostilities . . . It is only by a *daily* paper that we can really influence public opinion.'[26] Despite further promptings Sturge only acted on Cobden's suggestion around mid-1855, when the war had reached an *impasse* and the chances of such a paper becoming a success appeared to be more promising. Henry Richard gave his support also. The paper would advocate international arbitration and the regular holding of peace congresses; it would urge 'non-intervention in the affairs of foreign states'; and would in general represent radical liberalism, the kind of views held by the 'Manchester party.' Control was to lie with Cobden, Bright, and George Wilson who had been chairman of the Anti-Corn Law League, Sturge himself preferring to remain in the background. On practical issues, indeed, his standpoint almost invariably coincided with theirs.

Sturge now threw all his energies into raising money to launch the paper, and he succeeded in tapping the resources of a number of well-to-do Quakers as well as other wealthy middle-class sympathisers. Both Cobden and Bright felt it would be unwise to make the paper merely 'a daily *Herald of Peace*': its editor, they thought, should preferably be one who did not subscribe to 'the abstract peace principle.' They presumably feared if he were committed to absolute pacifism this would diminish the influence the paper could exert on public opinion. Sturge seems to have gone along with them on this point as on the rest of the paper's programme. It finally made its appearance on 17 March 1856 as *The Morning Star* (with a later edition entitled *The Evening Star*).[27] Shortly afterwards, Cobden told Sturge: 'You ought to be proud of your work. It is the most successful effort in the cause of peace and intelligent progress which even you have ever made.'[28]

The war was over next month, and although the *Morning Star* continued to appear for another 13 years it scarcely fulfilled the high hopes of its sponsors. Cobden at the beginning had believed it could sell as many as '30 or 40,000' copies daily: in fact it never reached the figure of 15,000. Without Sturge's efforts his colleagues all agreed the paper would never have come into existence. If indeed it failed to give birth to a new form of peace journalism, it did constitute the most practical peace initiative so far launched by a Quaker in time of war. Sturge, as Frick remarks, had succeeded in resisting not simply 'the temptation to support the war, but the more subtle one of not supporting, yet saying nothing against the conflict.'[29]

Much more than Sturge it was Bright who personified Quakerism in the public mind, even though Bright, however close he felt himself to the Society of which he remained a respected member, never committed himself openly to Quaker pacifism. In fact more than once he proclaimed his disbelief in the validity of 'that abstract principle,' at any rate in so far as the state was concerned.[30] Although most wars, he believed, could have been avoided – indeed should never have been fought in the first place – he considered certain armed conflicts to have been inevitable and consistent with public morality as at present constituted. For instance, the rebellions against arbitrary colonial rule, which took place in Upper and Lower Canada in 1837-38, he regarded as 'wholesome'[31]: later he supported the Unionist side in the American Civil War. But the Crimean War he strongly condemned; to him it seemed a 'miserable and wicked war,' due to 'the immorality of government and people' in Britain[32] and he spoke out against it in parliament. But, as a recent biographer writes, 'his opposition was based on grounds which were generally accepted in the House.'[33]

Unlike Sturge, Bright was unwilling to confront the public with the Quaker interpretation of the Sermon on the Mount, and in his denunciations of the war he confined himself solely to arguments he thought would be acceptable to the overwhelmingly nonpacifist population. Blue-books formed, as it were, his Bible, though he continued to frame his condemnation of war in terms of morality. He appealed to Englishmen – as Christians – to put a stop to the unjustifiable slaughter. He injected into reasoning founded seemingly on expediency and national self-interest a tone of indignation that accorded with the stand taken by those, like Sturge, who avowedly opposed war on principle. No wonder Friends regarded Bright, for all his caution concerning 'the abstract principle,' as in a special way the spokesman for their peace testimony, as one who knew – better than they did – how to present its essence in a form that made political sense. And Bright himself seems to have been aware of the close connection between his antiwar activity and his Quaker upbringing. He wrote later of his stand during the Crimean War:

> I do not know why I differed from other people so much, but sometimes I thought it happened from the education I had received in the religious sect with which I am connected . . . Now, my having been brought up as I was would lead me naturally to think that . . . the war with Russia in the Crimea was a matter that required very distinct evidence to show that it was lawful, or that it was in any way politic or reasonable.[34]

For its opponents the war seemed in retrospect, as it had already appeared to them likely to become while it was still in progress, a 'resultless' war.[35] At any rate it failed to bring freedom to the Poles or the Circassians or to stem Russia's advance in the Balkans for long. English Quakers, we have seen, had displayed a more political witness during the war than they had ever done before, even if they had refrained from giving official support to the antiwar activities of Friends like Bright and Sturge who took an overtly political stance. The Society's testimony for peace still remained firmly embedded in its religious faith. But now the division between religion and politics had become less inflexible.

The Crimean War was fought by professionals and volunteers, and this meant young male Quakers – and their relatives and friends – no longer faced the issue of personal war resistance. There were no longer any conscientious objectors since there was no longer any conscription. Thus Friends personally suffered little, if at all, from the incidence of war. As one of them put it (rather smugly perhaps), they had to endure 'none of that suffering, death and dying so prevalent in the Crimea, none of the bemoaning of parents over their wounded sons, no sorrow or wailing of our widows, no crying of our orphans.'[36] Yet as a whole, the Society was becoming more, rather than less, sensitised to the obligation resting on Quakers from their refusal to take part in fighting, of helping relieve the misery and devastation war invariably brought with it.

They demonstrated this, for instance, in Finland (then part of the Russian Empire) soon after the Crimean struggle was over. Since the British navy had in 1854 inflicted severe damage on the property of the innocent inhabitants along the northern coastline of the Gulf of Bothnia, often wholly destroying their means of livelihood, Quakers now raised almost £9,000 for relief, most of the money being contributed by Friends. The Committee managing these funds explained to the people in the devastated area that the Quakers' main object, apart from relief of actual suffering, was 'to endeavour by some reparation to allay the angry feelings which may have been aroused' by the damage inflicted by their fellow countrymen.[37] The association of war relief with war resistance, along with the increased 'politicisation' of their peace testimony, was to make the Crimean War a landmark in the development of the English Society's response to international conflict.

CHAPTER XXIV

Quakers and Antimilitarism in
Australia and New Zealand

I

QUAKERS FIRST CAME TO AUSTRALIA in the early 1830s[1] and to New Zealand at the beginning of the 1840s. They had left Great Britain for much the same reasons as other emigrant families had done – primarily to seek a more prosperous livelihood in these fertile lands that were then being opened up for settlement. In Australia Hobart, the capital of Tasmania, became a Quaker centre, and in 1877 Friends opened a school there which still continues to flourish under Quaker auspices.[2] But the capital cities of most other Australian colonies also got their Friends' Meeting House, while in New Zealand Quakers were to be found in very small numbers on both islands. Australian Friends began publicly to proclaim their message of peace from at least the 1860s[3] – through the press and in leaflets which they tried to circulate as widely as possible, and by petitions presented to the State legislatures, calling in particular for the settlement of international disputes through arbitration. They occasionally held public meetings, too, to bring the subject of peace to the attention of their fellow citizens.[4] But, as the historians of Australia's peace movement remark, since the Quakers there 'were isolated and few in number, their conciliatory brand of pacifism went almost completely unnoticed.'[5]

When the Boer War broke out Friends took a strong stand against it, as did a small number of antimilitarists and a sprinkling of nonsectarian religious pacifists. But again this made little impact on the Australian public, who tended to dismiss such protests saying 'Oh, the Quakers, of course – that's their religion!' – or words to that effect.[6]

Compulsory militia service lingered on in these British colonies after it had been abolished in the mother country. Whereas in Tasmania, presumably because of a substantial Quaker presence there, religious objectors were exempt from mustering, in the rest of Australia the only legal way out for such persons was to hire a substitute (which we know no good Quaker would dream of doing) or pay a fine – with distraint of goods if the fine were unpaid. It seems the latter procedure occurred in the infrequent cases of Quaker conscientious objection.[7]

In New Zealand the authorities at first do not seem to have envisaged the possibility of conscientious objection. At any rate no provision was made for it in the militia regulations. Thus, when the two sons of Thomas Mason, the first Quaker to settle in that country (he emigrated in 1841), reached the age for service in 1864, the family was faced with a difficult situation. The local militia captain, though himself sympathetic, felt obliged to refer the matter to higher authority for decision; he was then told he must 'swear in [sic!] and drill the Quakers, and in case of actual hostilities to employ them as clerks.' On the boys' father explaining the Quaker position to the commanding officer in Auckland, the latter agreed to give them indefinite 'leave of absence,' stating at the same time 'he would not allow anyone but a Quaker to shelter himself under the same plea.' The colonial government finally confirmed this decision, and henceforward the Mason boys – and by implication other Quaker conscripts – were freed from the obligation to muster with the militia. Mason senior, from whose account I have quoted, commented on the affair with prophetic insight: 'Few seem able to understand the great law of Christianity – love to all. Would it were more greatly recognised. How different then would the intercourse of the settlers and natives be!'[8]

With the slow growth of Quakerism in these colonies the Society there eventually acquired a structure of its own. In 1902 the first General Meeting for all Australian Friends was set up, while in 1909 New Zealand held its first Annual Conference which continued thereafter on a regular basis. But in both countries numbers remained very small. On the eve of World War I Australian Friends amounted to only 664 members, and in New Zealand there were as few as 143 members.[9] Even if the presence of regular 'attenders' at Quaker Meetings must have slightly increased the actual strength of the Society, Quakerism in this part of the world had obviously failed to expand to any considerable extent. Nevertheless, when the conscription crisis of the years immediately preceding 1914 arose in Australasia, the tiny Society of Friends played a role in the anticonscription movement in each country that was quite out of proportion to the Society's actual numbers.

In Australia the Defence Act of 1910 made military training compulsory for all ablebodied males between the ages of 12 and 26. Such persons would be obliged to drill for 16 days a year – or its equivalent if the conscript was not able to put in a whole day's service at one time. Exemption from handling weapons was granted to members of a recognised peace church: claimants to this had to prove they were 'forbidden by the doctrines of their religion to bear arms.' If the applicant were successful he would be assigned – 'so far as is possible' – to noncombatant duties such as ambulance training or clerking or work in the commissariat. Probably the government had Quakers chiefly in mind when making this exception to the universality of the service required.

The major impulse leading to the passing of the Act derived from the fear widespread among Australians that their still sparsely settled country could one day be threatened with invasion from Asia. As Senator George Pearce put it: 'Australians must be prepared to fight for a White Australia. The time might come and men must be trained for it. No white man worthy of the name could refrain from defending his country and his women-folk against the Asiatic.'[10] The Act came into force at the beginning of 1911.

Opposition to 'boy conscription' had appeared already while the Act was being debated in parliament. The Australian peace movement in this period was still rather weak, and what were in effect the country's first peace organisations had been set up only a few years earlier at the time of the Boer War. Neither the short lived Peace and Humanity Society founded in June 1900, nor the Anti-War League set up six months later which enjoyed an equally brief life span, had made pacifism a prerequisite for membership. The same may be said of the Peace Society established in 1905 on the model of the London based body of that name; even though its founder, the Liberal Christian clergyman Dr. Charles Strong, had already come out warmly in defence of Christian pacifism during the recent conflict,[11] and its active membership included a number of Quakers. The peace propaganda carried on by the Australian Peace Society was rather sedate, matching in this way the respectable middle class people who formed the bulk of the membership in its various branches. Like the London Peace Society, it made international arbitration the centre of its programme, while it also attacked the rise in armaments and secret diplomacy. The expansion of militarism in Australia and that country's almost paranoiac concern with national security prevented the Peace Society, however, from making much headway: its protests tended to be 'brushed aside as unrealistic and even dangerous.'[12] And, when the conscription crisis came, the Peace Society was scarcely the body to undertake a militant campaign against the drafting of the country's youth 'for defence.'

The main impetus behind the anticonscription movement derived in fact from three separate sections of the community: first, leftwing socialists and trade unionists, including members of the anarchosyndicalist and strongly antimilitarist I.W.W. (Industrial Workers of the World); secondly, pacifists and other antiwar elements in the Protestant churches; and lastly the Society of Friends.[13] As I am mainly concerned in this chapter with the latter, I shall give them a prominence that at any rate their numerical strength scarcely justifies. The reader should, therefore, bear in mind the fact that the bulk of the anticonscriptionists were either secular leftwingers or non-Quaker Protestants. There was also strong opposition to boy conscription from women's organisations, like the Woman's Christian Temperance Union, on the grounds of the harm it might do to the boys' morals as well as of 'the morality of war' itself.[14] Finally, we may mention the aversion many parents felt to the whole business, even if their objections were based more on sentiment and emotion – on their not unreasonable fears of their sons being released, even if briefly, from the guidance of their parents and exposed to bad influences in the course of their training – than on a well thought out opposition to militarism and war. There was indeed a widespread feeling that compulsion in this matter, especially as it applied to mere children, contradicted the British tradition of liberty which Australians shared with the mother country.

In April 1912 the anticonscriptionists joined together in resistance to boy conscription to form the Australian Freedom League (AFL).[15] The League agitated vigorously for the repeal of the compulsion clauses in the Defence Act and warmly supported the boys who were refusing to drill for one or another motive. Over the next two years it published a series of pamphlets and leaflets which expounded its viewpoint, and it also lobbied members of parliament and other persons of influence in an effort to get their support for repeal. It succeeded in getting cases of ill treatment of conscientious objection discussed in both the federal parliament and in the press. The League's target, however, was not war as such but the military conscription of youth. In its propaganda the libertarian argument figured prominently, though it attacked boy conscription on a number of other grounds too.[16]

The AFL had come into existence as the result of the efforts of three Quakers: John Francis Hills and Thomas Hubbard of Adelaide and John Percy Fletcher, who had been sent out to Australia by English Friends to help the Society there to fight conscription.[17] A man of great vigour and considerable enterprise and eloquence, Fletcher was to play a key role in the anticonscriptionist movement in both Australia and New Zealand. Returning to England just prior to World War I, he became shortly thereafter a prime mover in setting up the No-Conscription Fellowship in Britain and was himself imprisoned for an extended period as an absolutist objector rejecting any alternative to unconditional exemption. Hubbard, too, was a strong individualist who, quite apart from his Quaker pacifism, felt it was wrong to force boys to learn to kill without allowing them to decide for themselves whether this were right or not. Hills, the third

Quaker responsible for founding the AFL, felt much the same way as Hubbard did. The headmaster of a boarding school for boys, he also emphasised the value of outdoor life for producing healthy bodies and balanced minds. He was, he said, 'a strong believer in the physical training of boys . . . and would much like to see the rifle taught, not as a distinctly military weapon, but for its usefulness in training the eye and nerve.' Like Gandhi, he admired the Boers; in Hills's case it was 'because their boys were hardy, tough and vigorous, and could shoot straight.'[18] For all this, he became indignant when he saw the way the government had imposed military training on voteless youths, and he threw himself with his accustomed energy into the work of organising opposition to the 'Black Statute', as the AFL called the Defence Act. We should mention a fourth Quaker, John Barry who, as Commonwealth organiser for the AFL until his departure for England at the end of 1913, was largely responsible, along with Fletcher, for composing the propaganda brochures and leaflets circulated by the League. Thus, despite the fact that the bulk of the membership was non-Quaker – indeed nonpacifist[19] – the Quaker presence made itself felt in all the AFL's activities, down to the appointment of its leading officers. John Barrett describes the League as being 'dominated by the Quakers':[20] this indeed is scarcely an exaggeration. They certainly provided the main drive behind its programme of action and imparted to it much of its moral fervour.[21]

In August 1914, the AFL claimed, according to Barrett, 55,000 members: many more than all the leftwing socialist parties put together then possessed. Yet undoubtedly many of its members were 'deadheads,' who did little or nothing to promote the work of the League. Barrett is probably not far off the mark when he writes:

> In the final count, not much had been achieved by the Australian Freedom League when it suspended its activities in August 1914. It maintained a position, gave help to some victims of conscience, and helped keep the cause of conscience and anti-compulsion before the public, claiming a membership of 1.2 per cent of the total population. Yet for all the League's protests and energy, boy-conscription did not break down, but kept on working.[22]

However one assesses the successes and failures of the AFL 'in the final count,' this organisation undoubtedly provided Australian Quakers with the means to extend their influence for peace and to bring pressure on government and politicians in an effort to rescind a measure they found ran contrary to their pacifist convictions. As a Quaker told the Minister of Defence in a letter he wrote in August 1912: We are 'conscious that though ourselves a small people, we are now the spokesmen of a large and growing number outside our body.'[23] Reinforced by Fletcher and several other

Friends from England who had come out specially to help in the anticompulsion struggle, and supported wholeheartedly by London Yearly Meeting which condemned conscription in Australasia in no uncertain terms,[24] Australian Quakers pressed their government to do away with the draft (a measure, they pointed out, which, though passed when the Liberals were in power, was subsequently carried into effect by a Labour cabinet). While a few Friends advocated alternative civilian service for conscientious objectors,[25] the Society as a whole rejected alternative service, whether under civilian or military control. Of course the noncombatant duties the Act offered to members of peace sects like the Quakers were quite unacceptable to virtually all members of the Society. For they sought to get rid of conscription *in toto* and fought for the rights of all conscripts regardless of religious affiliation. Moreover, they demanded specifically the same treatment of nonreligious objectors as for members of their own denomination.[26] As Quakers in Adelaide – a major centre of opposition to the Act – declared, 'as followers of Christ,' they intended to give 'uncompromising resistance to the Commonwealth Defence Act in its violation of conscience.'

During its sessions in 1910 the Society's General Meeting had passed a strong resolution deploring the impending conscription of the country's youth and rejecting categorically the noncombatant option offered its draftees. 'Therefore, [though we] desire to remain law-abiding citizens of the Commonwealth, we are reluctantly compelled to declare that if these proposals are passed into law we shall be bound by our Christian conscience to refuse to yield them obedience.'[27] The Clerk of the General Meeting, William Cooper, along with other prominent Friends, presented the Quaker view to the government which, however, remained adamant and refused to make any concessions in response to the Friends' pleas. We also find individual Friends pressing the case against conscription in the labour movement, in the Liberal Party, in women's organisations, and in the Council of Churches as well as in the various branches of the Peace Society. 'Whenever peace and anticompulsion were mentioned in those years,' writes Barrett, 'up sprang a Quaker, fighting and trying to force the government's hand.'[28]

Once the draft came into force, Friends, along with other anticompulsionists, launched out boldly into a civil disobedience campaign. Quakers did this, as their spokesman Cooper stated, in obedience to 'the higher law written in [man's] heart,' which told them it was wrong to fight. And since 'an army exists as a unit, and every part administers to the whole, morally . . . so-called noncombatants stand in the same position as combatants.'[29] Collaboration with the machinery of conscription ended for Friends when the Quaker parents had filled out their sons' registration forms, with a statement appended in most cases explaining why Friends objected to serving in the army in any capacity. A few parents failed to register their sons so that the first clash with the law would be theirs, and not their boys'. Fines, with brief imprisonment if the fines were not paid, soon resulted from such infractions of the law. The authorities, however, still proceeded with the induction of the draftees. Thus, as Barrett remarks,[30] 'sons sometimes suffered with their fathers.[31] . . . Most often, of course, sons rather than fathers suffered.'

By the outbreak of world war in August 1914 some 30,000 prosecutions had occurred in connection with the Defence Act, and about 6,000 cadets had received short – but sometimes repeated – sentences of detention for refusing to drill.[32] The vast majority of these refractory boys, however, were not *conscientious* objectors to military service. With some their delinquency was simply the result of a desire to shirk responsibility and dodge discomfort: others were genuine hardship cases, which the authorities should have been able to deal with by other means than prosecution and imprisonment. A few were libertarians like the Size brothers, John and William, farm lads who, no longer under compulsion, were later to be among the first to volunteer for service overseas after war had broken out. There is no way of telling exactly how many of the boys who were put in jail or military fortress belonged to the C.O. category. Probably most of the genuine C.O.'s – 'the victims of conscience,' as Barrett calls them[33] – came from families with leftwing socialist views. A centre of this kind of working-class antimilitarism lay in the mining area around Broken Hill in the so called Barrier district in eastern New South Wales. Here war resistance drew considerable support from the mining population. But there were socialist objectors from all the big urban areas, too. The boys from socialist homes formed the backbone of the Passive Resisters' Union, which was run by the youths themselves – with some guidance from adults, like the broad minded Quaker John Fletcher, whose support and aid were given freely to all objectors on grounds of conscience, whatever their views on religion might be.[34]

Pacifist parents from major Protestant denominations like the Methodists or the Baptists also inspired sons to resist conscription when drafted. Barrett in his account of the war resisters cites several cases of this kind as well as cases where the motive for a boy's refusal stemmed from a secular, humanitarian objection to war in his background. There were also Seventh-day Adventists in Australia who refused to drill on Saturday, their Sabbath, and objected in addition to the actual killing of their fellow men. But Adventists amounted to a mere 0.14 per cent of the population. Though the Quakers were numerically an even smaller group (Barrett reckons they formed only 0.015 per cent, with only nine of their boys liable for cadet training in 1911), their stand against the draft attracted from authorities and general public alike as much attention as – indeed possibly more attention than – that of any of the other groups in the anticonscriptionist movement.

Let us now look a little more closely at the fate of the Quaker 'boy objectors' once they had become involved with the military. What happened to them was of course, broadly speaking, the same as what happened to the other conscientious objectors, whether socialist or religious. At the beginning refusal to drill usually brought brief imprisonment in a civilian jail, and later, incarceration in a military fortress for periods from a few weeks to a few months. Sentences of detention could be repeated for subsequent refusals – a kind of cat-and-mouse treatment that became familiar to C.O.s in Britain during World War I. Conditions in prison or fortress seem to have been fairly harsh and not infrequently included punishments like solitary confinement and bread-and-water diet. The silence rule was sometimes enforced, as in British prisons of that period.

Threats of corporal punishment and actual rough handling occurred from time to time in an effort to force acceptance of drilling or (especially in the case of Quakers) of at least noncombatant duties. But treatment could also be lenient. This happened, for instance, with a Quaker boy detained in Fort Queenscliff for several weeks after he had had second thoughts about training, which he had at first agreed to do. In the fortress, despite his refusal to drill there either, he was left alone to do what he liked and, after release, was not called back again for service.[35] Barrett thinks, probably correctly, that most young fortress detainees, whether conscientious or not, did not really have very much to complain of, though he willingly concedes that there were instances of ill treatment of conscientious objectors.[36]

Among Quakers perhaps the boy objectors whose cases became best known to the public were Herbert Ingle and Thomas Roberts. Ingle's father, a gardener who had emigrated only recently from England, had brought his son up in the spirit of the Society's peace testimony and its belief in human freedom. Both these aspects of Quakerism come out clearly in the letter young Herbert wrote (possibly with some help from his father) to Captain Hutchinson, the local cadet officer:

> In answer to your letter requesting me to drill, you never enclosed forms. Seeing you have registered me against father's and my wish, I thought you would have been manly enough to have fought against a man instead of a boy, for that is only what I am – 15 years old, August 4 – only three years older than Christ was when He chose to do our heavenly Father's will, and I am just as prepared as He was not to stand in my own strength, but to stand with God against this Military Act. I wish you to

let it be a fight to a finish, and test whether the military power or the power of God within is the strongest. Only one request, and that is that I am treated with the same respect and food equal to a man sentenced to murder. For what I read of the treatment of boys in New Zealand, I think they are being treated worse than many a murderer. So I shall be pleased if you will take proceedings at once, as I refuse to acknowledge the Act in any way whatever.[37]

Barrett's comment on this is (as often) well taken. 'There,' he writes, 'was Quaker principle and pluck – not *quite* Quaker peaceableness – under the acid test.'

In the event, Herbert's father, William Ingle, received from an Adelaide court a sentence of 14 days in prison for failing to register his son, while Herbert himself, after being involuntarily enrolled in the cadet corps, was imprisoned for 15 days in Fort Largs for refusing to train. He spent part of this time 'on No. 1 [punishment] diet, which consists of one slice of dry bread and a mug of tea, without sugar or milk, three times a day.'[38] After the boy's release his father decided to move back with the family to Britain – where ironically, with the onset of world war, an even more onerous form of conscription would be imposed on the young men of that country.[39]

Tom Roberts was 16 years old when in June 1914 he was sentenced to detention in a military prison for failure to attend compulsory drilling. During the 21 days of his incarceration in Queenscliff Fortress he spent seven days in solitary confinement on reduced diet in a small and unlighted cell as a result of his refusal to co-operate in any way with military orders. This punishment was inflicted on the boy despite the fact he was only just recovering from typhoid fever. Roberts was a working class lad. Both his father, a plumber and active trade unionist, and his mother were staunch antimilitarists and upholders of the peace testimony of the Society of Friends to which they belonged. They had brought their son up in the Quaker tradition of peace. So we find Tom writing to his parents from the Fortress:'I am not going to do anything as I know that you would sooner me not, but you wouldn't tell me so.' The boy's sentence structure may be a little shaky but his sense is clear. The Roberts case became momentarily a *cause célèbre* – due to the efforts of Tom's parents and the anticonscriptionist movement in gettng the matter raised in the press and in parliament.[40] In fact, 'the case aroused so much public indignation that the government had to announce that no more solitary confinement would be inflicted.'[41]

II

We have read above how the 15-year-old Australian Quaker conscript, Herbert Ingle, had been confirmed in his will to resist conscription by what he had read of the harsh treatment boys were receiving in neighbouring New Zealand if they refused to train to kill. The New Zealand Defence Act of December 1909 had imposed compulsory military service on all boys between the ages of 14 and 20.[42] But it took over a year before the Act went into operation, so that it was not until late in 1910 that the anticonscriptionist forces began to organise. As in Australia, the resistance movement here too drew its support from a coalition of socialist antimilitarists, libertarians, and religious pacifists. Middle-class liberals and liberal Christians united with labour militants in a cause that embraced 'anticonscription, free speech, and the cause of the conscientious objector.' The antimilitarists however remained a minority in a population that often showed an intolerance that contrasted with the democratic spirit the community claimed to uphold.

Christchurch on the South Island became the centre of opposition to the Defence Act. An Anti-Militarist League had come into existence there in June 1910: its founder, Louis P. Christie, editor of the *Christian Herald*, had got the idea from Henry Corder, a visiting English Quaker sent out to assist in the anticompulsionist movement. After drafting got under way, some of the boys themselves in February 1912 started up, with some adult help, a Passive Resisters Union, which seems to have been more vigorous than its Australian counterpart. Like the latter body it had a distinctly leftwing flavour. Members referred to themselves as the 'We won'ts,' and took a pledge 'to resist coercion, conscription, and compulsory military training under all circumstances, and in defiance of all pains and penalties which may be imposed.'[43] A young Auckland (North Island) Quaker, Egerton Gill, a few months later launched the New Zealand Freedom League, which worked for the repeal of 'boy conscription' and agitated against compulsory military training in general right up to the outbreak of war when, like the Australian Freedom League, it suspended operations.

Among a number of other organisations that opposed the compulsory clauses of the Defence Act I shall concentrate here on the Society of Friends. New Zealand Quakers had of course opposed conscription from the outset. In May 1909, while the Defence Bill was under discussion in parliament, their first annual conference had told the government that in their view 'the combative tendency of our New Zealand lads needs to be restrained rather than encouraged.' Next year, with the measure now become law, the Society through its Clerk, Thomas Wright, made it clear to the authorities that Friends felt unable to collaborate officially with them in working out a scheme of alternative service. The noncombatant service in the army, which the Act offered conscientious objectors of the Quaker variety, was clearly unacceptable to almost all Friends. Though, as Wright stated, 'it is difficult for any body of men to anticipate the objections of the individual conscience,' he thought the least the government was in duty bound to offer conscientious objectors was an 'equivalent in civil service outside the field of warfare or preparation for war.' This question of alternative service continued to bother New Zealand Friends. They debated it again at their annual conference in 1911. In 1912, when already a number of (non-Quaker) boys had been put in jail for either failing to register or for refusing to train after registration, the Quakers' annual conference decided, after some discussion, it would be wrong for them to perform 'any duty that will bring them under military control or the operation of the Defence Act.' 'Nor,' they went on, 'can they define any alternative duties that, whilst meeting the consciences of some, may violate those of others.'

In their uncompromising stand New Zealand Friends found staunch support from the three members of the deputation sent out from London Yearly Meeting – William H. F. and Harriette Alexander and Alfred Brown – as well as the ubiquitous John Fletcher, who included New Zealand in his anticonscriptionist bailiwick. In 1913 the New Zealand Society of Friends, in conjunction with the National Peace Society of New Zealand, established in 1911, published and circulated widely W. H. F. Alexander's militantly antimilitarist pamphlet entitled *The Peril to Civil and Religious Liberty from Modern Imperialism*. There Alexander argued that the powers the Defence Act gave to the military were subversive of British freedom and would lead eventually to the establishment of an autocracy. Of the New Zealand Defence Act he wrote, 'this law . . . violates the right of the parent who believes that his boys were given him to train up in accord with the words of Christ, that they should love their enemies.' Instead, by this new law 'his son is fined when in obedience to his father he declines to train to shoot his fellow-men. . . . The Defence Act aggressively demands that their immature conscience shall be moulded into the military groove.'[44] Alexander and his companions now toured the country, speaking at anticonscription rallies and encouraging resistance to the Act. In 1914, at their last Annual Meeting before the outbreak of war, New Zealand Friends stated categorically their unwillingness to 'recognise the Defence Act in any way' or 'to perform alternative service under it.' As Fletcher said, the main thing was to get rid of conscription: 'We cannot do anything that will help to make conscription popular.' If Friends were to collaborate in any scheme for alternative service for religious objectors, which the government were indeed now anxious to set up, this, he believed, would leave the nonreligious war resisters in the lurch, for then they would face an even more difficult situation than hitherto. And Alexander underlined Fletcher's point by praising 'the . . . lads [imprisoned] . . . on Ripa Island,' all of them socialist antimilitarists, who by their staunch resistance there were bringing the abolition of conscription closer.[45]

The Quaker attitude, while it disappointed the authorities, brought praise from sections of the community sympathetic to the anticompulsion movement. For instance, the *Christian World* wrote of Friends, 'Though few in number, they are attracting attention to a degree far beyond their numerical strength by their vigorous resistance to the . . . Defence Act.'[46] Indeed it is true their stance – and that of their English visitors – far transcended a merely pacifist protest, and – by no means for the first time in the history of the Society of Friends – opposition to war was combined with the defence, as Quakers saw it, of civil liberty and religious freedom.

By the end of 1912 around 120 teenage boys had been thrown into jail, with a much larger number incurring fines for nonregistration (by no means all of whom of course were conscientious objectors). In December of that year, however, the Defence Act was amended, and thereafter such offenders were placed in military detention instead of in civil prisons. James Allen, the Minister of Defence in the new Reform government which had recently replaced the Liberals in power, considered – perhaps correctly – that this was a more appropriate form of punishment in the circumstances. 'With respect to detention,' writes Weitzel, 'Allen argued that it would provide a more suitable alternative to prison and would be used primarily as a means of persuading a man to do his duty.' And Allen claimed that, unlike prison, 'military detention was not essentially penal.' He also sought to meet the needs of religious objectors while remaining unwilling to provide relief for other conscientious objectors.[47] But, as we have seen, the Quakers rejected his overture, and there were few others entitled to apply for the exemption from bearing arms which the amended Act now granted.[48]

In fact neither before nor after the Defence Amendment Act of December 1912 does the theoretical exemption for religious objectors seem to have functioned in practice. Weitzel explains the earlier situation as follows:

> The Defence Act [of 1909] was not without provisions for objections to military service, but they were poorly elaborated. An Army Department Memorandum of April 1911 stated that religious objectors, but not [other] conscientious objectors, would be trained in the non-combatant branches as far as possible. The burden of proof of religious convictions lay on the objector who could argue his claim through the non-commissioned officer of the Army Permanent Staff in charge of the area where he resided. However, the law suggested that the potential objector must first register, be enrolled, take the oath of allegiance, be ordered to parade, and only then be in a position to state his religious objections to bearing arms . . . For the individual who objected to military service, it was necessary to belong to the military before he could object.[49]

The Amendment Act certainly improved the situation, since it allowed a magistrate to grant exemption if he was satisfied that the applicant fulfilled the conditions for exemption laid down in the Act. But again all this was more a matter of theory than reality, since up to the outbreak of war no programme of alternative service had as yet been devised by the government. The Quakers refused to co-operate while, though from a different standpoint, local authorities, when canvassed by Allen, the Minister of Defence, at the end of 1913, reacted in similar fashion. 'The civic bodies,' writes Weitzel, 'indicated that they were unwilling to help in any way . . . to provide public work projects for religious objectors.' Even as regards the question of who counted as a *religious* objector, the situation remained confused. Allen, more tolerant on this point than some of his Reform colleagues, was anxious, as he told the Solicitor-General, 'so to widen the clause as to make the religious objection of the individual, as apart from the denomination, . . . ground for exemption from military training.' But the Solicitor-General felt unable to assure him that the Act could in fact be interpreted in accordance with this view. Therefore, the meaning of the Act remained ambiguous. Did exemption apply only to boys brought up in a pacifist denomination or did it cover all those whose personal 'religion' – or the religion of whose parents – included pacifism, even if the church to which they belonged did not collectively support this 'doctrine'?[50]

Quakers could certainly claim to be conscientious objectors within the meaning of the Act. But we know few, if any, of their boys were likely to apply for exemption as such, whether under the initial Act or the amended one, since Friends aimed at the abolition of military conscription and disapproved, therefore, of any accommodation that might help prolong its existence.[51] In fact, we do not hear of any young Friends being conscripted. A few, we presume, must have been called up, though the very small size of the Society in New Zealand precluded there being more than a handful of Quakers of registration age. Nevertheless, at one point New Zealand Friends had considered the possibility of large scale emigration, until assurances from the government of consideration for their scruples – as well as a feeling of responsibility for bearing their share in the general fight against compulsion – led them to decide against such a desperate course of action.[52] (It was one, though, that European Mennonites as well as Scandanavian Quakers had resorted to in earlier times.) Like Australian Friends, those in New Zealand remained, and continued their war resistance into the post-1914 era.

Historians differ in their assessment of the pre-1914 war resistance movement in the two countries. In neither land was this movement successful in lifting the load of conscription before the onset of war brought the anticonscriptionist struggle temporarily to a standstill. It is probably true, too, that even 'boy conscription' won greater support in both communities – whether among parents or among sons – than contemporary anticompulsionists were prepared to admit. The Australian Barrett writes in support of this view : 'For some lads there were fortresses and cells by the sea, but for more trainees there were drill halls and training grounds that were almost clubs. So say many old men, as they stir and stretch their memories.'[53] Even among detainees, while undoubtedly there were a few 'who . . . suffered severely' along with their families, Barrett thinks the overwhelming majority did not fare too badly : indeed there were many, he says, who even 'found detention enjoyable,' for it brought them healthy bodily exercise and an out-of-door life.[54] This may well be true. And one might even go further and argue that, compared with – let us say – contemporary conscientious objectors in Tsarist Russia, whether Dukhobors or Tolstoyans or Baptists, even the genuine Australasian objectors to military service suffered little. Their time in jail or fortress was brief and their experiences there mild if measured by what the Russian C.O.s went through. And yet in Russia (so far as I know) they did not throw boys in their mid-teens into prison – even for a few weeks or months – because their own consciences, or their family tradition, told them it was wrong to bear arms or to kill their comrades in other lands.[55] Quakers of Australia and New Zealand, in their struggle to uphold the rights of conscience not merely for themselves but for all their fellow citizens, may, like other anticompulsionists, have sometimes exaggerated the hardships imposed by boy conscription. But, as many outside antimilitarist circles also sensed, there was something peculiarly distasteful in this enterprise when it led to the kind of things we have described above. To the credit of Australasian Friends – and their supporters in British Quakerism – we must put the fact that, despite their small numbers, they pioneered the kind of antimilitarist and libertarian protest that emerged in the mother country during World War I in such organisations as the – largely non-Quaker – No-Conscription Fellowship.[56] Once again we find the Quaker peace testimony stretching out beyond the confines of the sectarian conscience and into the wider world where wars arise and where alone the spirit from which wars proceed can finally be overcome.

CHAPTER XXV

The Peace Testimony and Anglo-American Quaker Renewal

DURING THE HALF CENTURY OR SO before the outbreak of war in Europe in 1914 neither British nor American Quakers displayed a consistently vigorous peace witness. The witness was loyally adhered to certainly – with some exceptions – but extensive and energetic exposition of Quaker pacifism only emerged in the last decades of this period as a result of a general resurgence of the Society's spirituality. This renewal was spearheaded by a number of concerned – and mostly young – Friends and is more visible at first in Britain than in the United States. But it made its appearance there too, though not in all branches of the American Society. Due to the lack of scholarly work on the subject hitherto, the impact of Quaker renewal on the Society's peace witness is not always easy to trace on either side of the Atlantic. What follows in this section is only a sketch; the details must await further research in depth.

As Margaret Hirst has noted in her account of English Friends' peace testimony, there were few new departures during the last three decades of the 19th century.[1] We should mention, though, the campaign initiated, and run almost single-handed by Priscilla Peckover,[2] for enrolling British women in the work of promoting peace. Peckover belonged to a wealthy Quaker family (her brother was made a peer of the realm); she became active in peace work only when freed from domestic and family duties around the age of 45. It was while attending a Quaker Meeting in 1878 that she had been inspired to action by the query read out at regular intervals during worship: 'Are you faithful in bearing your Christian testimony against all war?' She responded by founding next year the first Women's Local Peace Association in her native town of Wisbech in Cambridgeshire.

Over the next decades more than 30 branches of the WLPA were set up in Britain with some 15,000 members, and with affiliated societies abroad. With payment of a small subscription membership was open to all women who were ready to sign a statement declaring: 'I believe all war to be contrary to the mind of Christ . . . and am desirous to do what I can to further the cause of Peace.' In 1882 Peckover established, and edited from her home in Wisbech, a quarterly magazine entitled *Peace and Goodwill*. In addition, she used her knowledge of foreign languages for translating peace literature that had appeared in English and organising its distribution from her home 'depot' throughout the European continent. A woman of private means, she financed most of her work from her own resources, subscriptions and membership fees proving insufficient to cover costs. Her peace programme coincided more or less with that of the Peace Society: international arbitration; reduced armaments as a prelude to their total abolition; the fight against the militarisation of youth. Though no peace radical, she strove to establish close links between Quaker work for peace and the wider peace movement, including those whose motivation was secular rather than religious. 'She strongly supported the collaborative pacifism that became a central feature of the twentieth-century British peace movement.' Among Quaker women she found some staunch co-workers: one of these was Ellen Robinson, a Quaker minister from Liverpool who, until her death in 1912, was indefatigable in writing and public speaking on behalf of peace.[3]

Most English Quakers at that date were Liberals. Even though a few became Liberal Unionists (and thus eventually Conservatives) or Liberal Imperialists (who tended the same way), Quaker politics adhered generally to the anti-Imperialist wing of the Liberal Party.[4] The Society as a body condemned colonial wars against Afghans, Chinese, and Zulus as well as similar ventures in Egypt and Sudan. While its protest was restrained, it was transparently sincere. But the renewed vigour with which the Society opposed the major Imperialist contest in which Britain became involved – the Boer War – was undoubtedly due mainly to the activities of a group of young reformers, men like William C. Braithwaite, John W. Graham, Edward Grubb, and John Wilhelm Rowntree. Liberal in theology and at the same time well grounded in the history of Quakerism (Braithwaite, for instance, became one of its most accomplished historians), they succeeded in transforming the thinking of the Society and remoulding its outlook to accord with the modern world, thereby *inter alia* stemming the disastrous decline in the Society's numbers that had set in earlier in the century.

'The leaders of this reform movement . . . wanted a sounder basis for their beliefs than the inward-looking theology which had turned their once dynamic Society into a virtual carbon copy of any number of dissenting religious sects.'[5] They rejected evangelicalism in favour of a return to what they regarded as the roots of the Quaker faith, and among the basic tenets of this faith they stressed pacifism. They saw the peace testimony primarily as a reflection of the Quaker doctrine of the Inner Light rather than as a biblically based injunction, and they urged Friends to join with non-Christians in the fight against war. When Grubb took charge of the *British Friend* in 1897 (he continued as proprietor-editor until 1913) the reformers came into possession of an effective organ with which to influence opinion within the Society. There, as well as in books and pamphlets, they campaigned against militarism in all its aspects as well as against imperialism and jingoism as fomenters of war.[6] Over-optimism coloured their outlook as well as a tendency to over-simplify: but this perhaps was needed at that juncture. They had to effect a re-evaluation of the Society's stance toward the underlying factors, political, economic, and social, that led to the repetition of international conflict; for a peace witness based solely on the Sermon on the Mount they saw as inadequate in the age of imperialism.

In the Boer – or South African – War of 1899 to 1902 powerful Britain was pitted against two small farmer republics, the Transvaal and the Orange Free State, where the Afrikaners, colonists of Dutch origin, ruled over a Black majority. This majority was then sunk from view, and it was the white Afrikaner minority that held the world's interest throughout the prolonged struggle that ended with a British victory and the incorporation of the two republics into the Empire. Friends as a whole ranged themselves with the unpopular 'Pro-Boer' minority that saw the war as an unjustified attack on a small people for the sake of imperial aggrandisement, and many Quakers suffered social ostracism as well as sporadic mob violence for standing out against a nation at war. They were attacked in the press and on the platform, though they were only rarely threatened with physical attack or damage to their property.

Basically the Quaker attitude remained the same as in previous wars: 'all war was sinful.'[7] And this was still about as far as the Society was prepared to go in its official pronouncements. But Friends of standing spoke out more plainly and more forcibly. John Wilhelm Rowntree, for instance, felt it was 'no time for soft speech.' In 'this miserable war' Friends must replace the 'passive resistance' and the 'patient consistency,' which some members recommended, by a more militant attitude. Writing in the *Friend* of 26 January 1900, he argued: 'Our testimony against war, if it is to be vital, must not be mere testimony against the use of armed force – it must cut at the roots of war, at the pride of Empire; the narrow popular patriotism rendered ignoble by its petty hatreds and the insatiable hunger for wealth visibly threatens our ruin.' Utterances such as this aroused an echo even among sober and 'weighty' Friends, who gave Rowntree support in his efforts to broaden the meaning of Quaker opposition to war.[8] Quakers like Joshua Rowntree or Robert Spence Watson (then President of the National

Liberal Federation) played an active part in such 'Pro-Boer' organisations as the South African Conciliation Committee and spoke at public meetings to protest against the war.[9] And almost all the Quaker members of parliament (a group numbering about 10) voted with the antiwar Liberals, among whom most prominent – at least in the public eye – was Lloyd George. Friends also supported the efforts of the Anglican Emily Hobhouse to expose the ill treatment, and alleviate the miseries, of Afrikaner women and children in the detention camps set up by the British authorities. Hobhouse and her Quaker allies also denounced the burning of Boer farms, a form of reprisal that offended many Britishers when it was brought to their attention.[10]

But there were nevertheless members of the Society, who did not merely wish to soften the Quaker peace witness in time of war but felt the struggle against the Boers was a righteous one. The most vocal of these was John Bellows, the lexicographer, who, while claiming to be still a pacifist on the personal level, argued for support of the war on the political level. Others, like young Robin Hodgkin, the future historian of the Anglo-Saxons and then an undergraduate at Oxford, considered pacifism an 'extreme . . . position.' Speaking he thought for a number of younger Friends, he urged that the question of whether or not Quakers ought to participate in war 'should be left entirely to the individual conscience.'[11] Since in the Boer War, as in the Crimean War, there was no conscription, this issue remained for the time being a largely theoretical one but it was to emerge again with the outbreak of World War I to demand an answer from Friends.

The support given by most Quakers to the Society's stand against the war helped to consolidate the position of the reformers during the postwar years and spread concern for the peace testimony among an increasing number of members. Many were ready now to respond to such an appeal as was made by Joshua Rowntree in a widely circulated pamphlet dealing with the issue of war and peace: 'It is time,' he wrote, 'for Christians to face this question more fearlessly . . . It is for our generation to do its part. The earnest application of the life and teachings and spirit of Christ to the grave and perplexing problems that confront us, cannot but clear the vision, improve the relationship, and sweeten the very existence of men . . . No hope is ever forlorn which is led by the Prince of Peace.'[12] Vehicles of the Quaker 'Renaissance' like the Summer School Movement and Woodbrooke Settlement ('for religious and social study') served also as instruments for promoting interest in, and for deepening appreciation of, the peace testimony. Kennedy has pointed out the connection between the Young Friends movement of the early 20th century and 'Quaker resistance against the Great War.' As an example, he cites the fact that 'at least eight of the eleven young men appointed to the Young Friends' Sub-Committee at [the first Conference of Young Friends held at Swanwick in 1911] would suffer imprisonment or detention as conscientious objectors.'[13]

Pressure to reintroduce conscription in some form had been mounting during the early years of the new century. When in 1909 J. St. Loe Strachey, the editor of the influential weekly journal *The Spectator*, published a plea for compulsory military service entitled *A New Way of Life* he took care to include expressions of respect for the Quakers. In an answering pamphlet which appeared the same year Edward Grubb voiced the opinion of young pacifist Friends when he wrote: 'Even if exemption were offered to the Quakers, it is doubtful whether they would accept the privilege, unless it were extended also to other conscientious objectors.'[14] This statement reflected the growing desire to link Quaker opposition to war with peace advocacy by other Christians as well as by non-Christians. It represented a wish to achieve a wider outreach for the peace testimony which we have seen was typical of the Quaker renewal of this time.

Above all, Friends now saw pacifism as central to their Quakerism – or at any rate those Friends who were more and more giving tone to the Society's utterances did so. The Yearly Meeting of 1912 had accepted an address drawn up by its Peace Committee entitled 'Our Testimony for Peace,' which stated this viewpoint clearly. It was pacifism, it said, the belief 'that war, with the whole military system, is contrary to the Spirit of God whose name is love,' which distinguished Quakerism from virtually all other Christian denominations. The testimony for peace formed 'an organic outgrowth of our faith as Christians and as Friends, which cannot be abandoned without mutilating our whole message for the world.'[15]

A renewed peace testimony would mean stronger resistance and greater personal suffering. It also implied an increased emphasis on positive action: helping the victims of war, the restoration of war damage, the reconstruction of what war had swept away. All this constituted indeed part of the practice of Quaker relief to all who needed help which, 'to the general public,' eventually became 'the best-known activity of the Religious Society of Friends.'[16] We have seen how Quaker war relief as an expression of the Society's testimony for peace traced its origins in a small way back to the 18th century. In the 19th century it is mainly British Friends who are occupied in such activity: they were nearer the areas where such help was called for. The equivalent for American Quakers lay in their work, after the Civil War was over among the freedmen in the South as well as among the Indians of the frontier: that, though, is a chapter of Quaker history that really lies outside the scope of this book.[17]

In Greece in the 1820s, during the Irish Famine of 1846, as well as later in the Near East, Quakers were active in relieving suffering. But the best known and most extensive example of such work had occurred in France after the Franco-Prussian War of 1870. Some 40 Quaker workers were then sent by London Meeting for Sufferings to the war devastated districts with such supplies as were needed to rehabilitate the area. It was at this time that Friends chose as their distinguishing mark the red-and-black star; the star became in our century a symbol of the Quaker relief that seeks to help the victims of war regardless of the side to which they belong.[18] Such activity Quakers now regard as an essential element of their peace testimony.

American Friends were to participate alongside British Quakers in the relief activity conducted during and after the two world wars of the 20th century. On both sides of the Atlantic the Quaker philosophy of relief has flowed from the same premises and emerged from a similar religious faith. We must now turn to the American Society and review the evolution of its peace testimony from the conclusion of the Civil War down to 1914. Here, too, we find decline and then renewal but the course of development differed to some extent from that of the mother Society.

The official pronouncements of the American Society continued to restate in familiar phrases the Quaker position on peace but the post-Civil War period saw a decline of interest in this aspect of Friends' witness, which was reflected particularly in the Quaker press. Despite general Quaker opposition to the imperialist trend that culminated in the Spanish-American War of 1898, little was being done institutionally for the promotion of peace until after the turn of the century.[19] Of the three branches into which the Society had separated the evangelical Orthodox branch showed perhaps most vitality in this area. Orthodox Friends had been responsible for setting up the Peace Association of Friends in America in 1867:[20] this organisation eventually became the Peace Board of the Five Years Meeting which was established in 1902 to coordinate the activities of the various Orthodox Yearly Meetings. From 1870 on, the Peace Association published a monthly paper entitled *The Messenger of Peace* that provided a forum for discussing peace issues – and especially the subject of international arbitration – as well as a means of propagating Quaker views on war and rebutting the arguments of the militarists whose influence was steadily growing in the country. The Association also circulated peace literature in the form of books, pamphlets, and leaflets, often distributing these free among ministers of religion and educational institutions. But it proved an uphill struggle. The *Messenger of Peace,* for instance, had a hard time to survive. At best no more than 4,000 copies of an issue were sold, usually less, and between 1894 and 1900 it had to cease publication as a separate paper altogether. Revived again in 1900 it struggled along until, in 1912, it was forced to assume a reduced format; it henceforward circulated merely as a bulletin for consumption mainly within Friends' Meetings. While the Association and its journal, largely carried along by a small group of enthusiasts, helped to keep the pacifist flame alight in one important section of the Society of Friends, its impact outside Quaker circles must have been rather limited. Though it achieved something, it certainly did not fulfill the hopes of its founders who had seen it as the instrument of a potential Quaker pacifist revival.

This did not in fact come until near the end of the century and resulted from another quarter. The founders of the Peace Association had been strongly evangelical: the makers of the renewal, which embraced all aspects of Quaker faith and action and not only peace, were religious liberals even when their birthright was in the Orthodox branch, and they were influenced by – and interacted closely with – the liberal renewal movement among English Friends discussed above. I am referring here to young men like Elbert Russell, Richard H. Thomas, Alexander C. Wood, and above all Rufus M. Jones. In 1893 Jones became a teacher of philosophy at Haverford College and editor of the Orthodox journal shortly to be known as *The American Friend*. 'Ably supported by a group of liberal Friends [he] proposed to make the new paper the organ not of a party or sect but of a liberal Quakerism. His emphasis was upon the religion of inward experience; upon the realities of the Christian faith rather than any theological formulation of them, and especially upon the first-hand experience of God. The paper was committed to the search for truth without theological limits or sectarian reservations.'[21] And for Jones and his associates search for truth naturally included investigation of new ways to achieve peace as well as exploration of the historical roots of Quaker pacifism and its meaning for the modern world. They saw pacifism not simply as a function of personal sanctification but as a quest undertaken, along with persons of other creeds and other faiths, to eliminate war from the planet. Thus, they sought contacts with the wider peace movement that was expanding during this period and strove so to shape Quaker peace endeavours that they would make a relevant contribution to the contemporary struggle against war and militarism.

American Quakerism had its counterpart to Priscilla Peckover in Hannah J. Bailey, who for a dozen years edited and distributed from her home in Winthrop Center, Maine, a periodical devoted largely to peace for adult readers, *The Pacific Banner* (1889-1895) and a similar publication intended for children, *The Acorn* (1889-1901). For Hannah Bailey peace advocacy formed just one link in what she liked to call 'the grand work of moral reform.' She insisted on the essential role American women might play, whether as mothers or as teachers, in instilling peace principles and a spirit of internationalism in the young. 'It is early training,' she wrote in 1895, 'that exerts the [greatest] influence. Mothers should not allow their children to have military toys, to practice warlike games, or anything that makes them familiar with taking life, as a pastime. They should be early taught the divine law as to the sacredness of human life, and also the golden rule.'[22] In her papers she did not stress her absolute pacifism, though at the same time she did not conceal it. The same might be said of the scholarly mid-West Friend, Benjamin F. Trueblood, who was secretary of the American Peace Society from 1892 to 1915.[23] His views on peace were neither innovative nor exciting. He excelled, instead, rather as an organiser and as an interpreter of what others had written on the subject. Above all, he strove to unite the whole peace movement behind such practical objectives as a world federation and permanent international arbitration. Similar aims motivated another Quaker, Albert K. Smiley, when in 1895 he organised the first of 22 annual Conferences on International Organisation at Lake Mohonk in the Catskills. 'Smiley . . . sought out statesmen, educators, religious leaders, lawyers, and even generals and admirals to attend the Mohonk conferences.' But his outlook was even more conservative than Trueblood's.

> Desiring to maintain harmony at the conferences Smiley played down the division between advocates of extreme nonresistance and individuals who maintained the right of defensive war. In fact, he discouraged discussion of such matters and even tried to limit debate on the usefulness of armament reductions. For the same reason, Smiley refused to approve or disapprove America's role in the Spanish-American war and its imperialistic aftermath.[24]

The efforts of Friends like Bailey, Trueblood, and Smiley, for all their shortcomings, witnessed to a growing desire in many sections of the Society to break out of the Quaker enclosure and mingle with those fellow citizens who were also engaged on the quest for peace.

But alongside all this we must note within American Quakerism a trend not found on the English scene. I refer to the drift away from pacifism among fundamentalist Quakers of the mid and far West. Though evangelical Quakerism in many places had already replaced the silent meeting with a pastoral system and a programmed form of worship, and had finally rejected the concept of the Inner Light as unscriptural, it still clung to the peace testimony as part of its Bible-centred faith. But wherever the revivalism engendered by the extremist Wesleyan holiness movement got a firm foothold in a Quaker community, there pacifism began to wither and finally disappeared almost totally (though this retreat from pacifism happened on a wide scale really only after the period with which this book deals[25]). In Yearly Meetings like Ohio and Kansas,[26] where Quakers of this kind finally broke away to become separate religious bodies – though still bearing the Quaker name – antipacifism formed part of the antiliberal thrust of the new theology they had imported from outside. Here little remained to distinguish Quaker churches from other denominations that had undergone the same revival experiences.

The renewal of Quaker pacifism in Britain and the United States found its *dénouement* during and after World War I. Those Friends who most effectively shaped the Society's response to that conflict had received their peace training in, or their pacifist inspiration from, the decades that preceded 1914. Indeed, without a knowledge of the Quaker renaissance prior to 1914 we cannot fully comprehend the character of the post-1918 peace initiatives either of the English Friends or of an organisation like the AFSC[27] that have since made pacifism and Quakerism almost synonymous terms with so many outside the Society (which of course they are not). Quaker pacifism in 1914 stood, then, on the threshold of a new era just when humankind itself was entering on a new – and infinitely dangerous – stage in its development.

Notes

Chapter I
(pages 1-8)

Pre-Quaker Pacifism in England

[1] H. S. Cronin, ed., 'The Twelve Conclusions of the Lollards,' *The English Historical Review* (London), vol. XXII, no. 2 (April 1907), pp. 302, 303. I have modernised the spelling of my citations from the English version of the Conclusions which Cronin prints alongside a Latin – and probably later – text.

[2] Quoted in Philippe Contamine, *War in the Middle Ages*, transl. from the French by Michael Jones, Oxford, 1984, pp. 294, 295.

[3] *English Historical Documents*, vol. IV *(1327-1495)*, ed. A. R. Myers, London, 1969, p. 865. For further examples of Lollards in the course of examination condemning all forms of homicide, whether in battle or by legal process, see Norman P. Tanner, ed., *Heresy Trials in the Diocese of Norwich, 1428-31* (Camden Fourth Series, vol. XX), London, 1977, pp. 42, 71, 86, 96, 142, 148, 153, 166. These men and women, who spoke out against war and the death penalty (even for murder or treason) on the grounds of their being forbidden by Christ, were all simple people unversed in theology. Vengeance, they repeat, must be left to God.

[4] C. E. Whiting, *Studies in English Puritanism from the Restoration to the Revolution, 1660-1688*, London, 1931, p. 286. See also William Nigel Kerr, 'Henry Nicholas and the Familists: A Study of the Influence of Continental Mysticism on England to 1660,' unpublished Ph.D. diss., University of Edinburgh, 1955, pp. 349, 350. The carrying of staves instead of swords was almost certainly a borrowing from the practice of the Anabaptist *Stäbler* on the continent.

[5] Albert Peel, ed., 'A Conscientious Objector of 1576,' *Transactions of the Baptist Historical Society* (London), vol. VII, no. 1/2 (1920), pp. 80, 86, 93, 108, 109, 123. The Schleitheim Confession of Faith was drawn up at a meeting of the Anabaptist Swiss Brethren in February 1527. It included the first official statement of their nonresistance.

[6] Quoted in Peter Pauls, '"A Pestiferous Sect": The Anabaptists in England from 1530-1660,' *Journal of Mennonite Studies* (Winnipeg), vol. III (1985), p. 66.

[7] Champlin Burrage, *The Early English Dissenters in the Light of Recent Research (1550-1641)*, 2 vols., Cambridge, 1912, vol. I, pp. 224-6. The pamphlet referred to was written in English by one John Payne, and published in Haarlem.

[8] Timothy George, 'Between Pacifism and Coercion: The English Baptist Doctrine of Religious Toleration,' *The Mennonite Quarterly Review* (Goshen, Indiana), vol. LVIII, no. 1 (January 1984), p. 38.

[9] *Ibid.*, pp. 34-36. The full Latin text of the section of the document devoted to the office of the sword is given in *The Works of John Smyth Fellow of Christ's College, 1594-8*, ed. W. T. Whitley, Cambridge, 1915, vol. II, pp. 696, 697.

[10] Burrage, *op. cit.*, vol. II, pp. 197, 198. See also Smyth, *Works*, vol. II, p. 748; J. G. de Hoop Scheffer, *History of the Free Churchmen called the Brownists, Pilgrim Fathers and Baptists in the Dutch Republic 1581-1701*, Ithaca (New York), 1922, p. 250; R. E. E. Harkins, 'Early Relations of Baptists and Quakers,' *Church History* (Chicago), vol. II, no. 4 (December 1933), p. 233.

[11] Burrage, *op. cit.*, vol. I, p. 271; vol. II, p. 232.

[12] Louise Fargo Brown, *The Political Activities of the Baptists and Fifth Monarchy Men in England during the Interregnum*, Washington, D.C., 1912, p. 9.

[13] Quoted in George, *op. cit.*, p. 30.

[14] Christopher Hill in Hill *et al.*, *The World of the Muggletonians*, London, 1983, pp. 76, 77.

[15] See in general Whiting, *op. cit.*, ch. VI. Tryon felt Quakers, because they were not vegetarians, had fallen short of the nonviolent ideal. Another, we may note, who was later to feel Friends were not living up to their pacifist principles on this issue (though perhaps he was not being wholly serious), was Sir Walter Scott. See his novel *Redgauntlet* (1844), Letter 7, with respect to the young Scottish Quakeress Rachel Geddes (a fictional character of course).

[16] Hill, *The World turned upside down: Radical Ideas during the English Revolution*, Harmondsworth (Middlesex), 1975 edn., pp. 210-12. As Hill points out, Coppe's 'pacifism was different from that which Quakers were later to profess.' Fox met Coppe, together with 'a great company of Ranters' in 1655: however, they found little common ground. See *The Journal of George Fox*, ed. John L. Nickalls, Cambridge, 1952, p. 195. In his monograph *Blasphemy, Immorality, and Anarchy: The Ranters and the English Revolution*, Athens (Ohio) and London, 1987, Jerome Friedman places his chapter on Coppe (5) in the section devoted to 'Sexual Libertines'.

[17] Rufus M. Jones, *Spiritual Reformers in the 16th & 17th Centuries*, London, 1914, p. 337. See also pp. 348, 349.

[18] *Ibid.*, pp. 199, 220-27, 343. Boehme denounced war and exalted peace but, unlike evangelical Anabaptists or Mennonites, he believed in the possibility of just wars and refrained from advocating conscientious objection to military service. Though his major works became available in English between 1647 and 1661, and Jones believed Fox as well as other Seekers who eventually became Quakers were indebted to him for some of their ideas, I doubt if pacifism was one of them.

[19] *Ibid.*, pp. 143, 144, 146.

[20] Cf. Jones, *The Later Periods of Quakerism*, London, 1921, vol. I, p. 157: 'The spiritual reformers of the sixteenth and seventeenth centuries had arrived at an apostolic type of Christianity which allowed no place at all for war, and George Fox had risen by a leap of experience to the full height of this apostolic ideal.' With respect to the peace testimony, I think it likely that pacifist

inclined Baptists constituted a more visible influence on the early Quakers than spiritual reformers. How many Baptists joined the Quaker movement in its beginning stages remains unknown but 'many of the known converts' assumed positions of leadership in it; see Craig W. Horle, 'Quakers and Baptists, 1647-1660,' *The Baptist Quarterly* (London), vol. XXVI, no. 8 (October 1976), p. 347. Of course, for the most part these early leaders of Baptist origin did not adhere to pacifism right away. Yet surely if they knew of former coreligionists who were pacifists this would have made it easier for them to accept the Quaker peace testimony when it came to be officially adopted.

Chapter II   (*pages 9-23*)
Quaker Attitudes to War before the Peace Testimony

[1] Frederick B. Tolles, Introduction to William C. Braithwaite, *The Second Period of Quakerism*, Cambridge, 1961 edn., p. XXVII.

[2] Christopher Hill, *The World turned upside down: Radical Ideas during the English Revolution*, Harmondsworth (Middlesex), 1975 edn., p. 14.

[3] Geoffrey F. Nuttall, *The Holy Spirit in Puritan Faith and Experience*, 2nd edn., Oxford, 1947, p. 183.

[4] Barry Reay, *The Quakers and the English Revolution*, London, 1985, p. 3. Cf. Alan Cole, 'The Quakers and the English Revolution,' reprinted from *Past and Present*, no. 10 (1956), in Trevor Aston, ed., *Crisis in Europe 1560-1660*, London, 1965, p. 348: 'In the first phase of its history, Quakerism was essentially a movement of protest against the suppression of the "good old cause".' But, we may ask, was political radicalism really the 'essence' of early Quakerism? I do not think Cole's equation holds.

[5] Reay, *op. cit.*, p. XIII, quotes the following passage from a work by a young Quaker James Parnell, *A Shield of the Truth* (1655): 'And now is the separation, the sheep from the goats, the wheat from the tares, and Christ is come to set at variance father against son, and son against father, and wife against the man, and the man against the wife, and to turn the world upside down; and this is the cause why the world rages.'

[6] Cole, *op. cit.*, p. 343. On p. 346 he writes: 'Pacifism was not a characteristic of the early Quakers: it was forced upon them by the hostility of the outside world.'

[7] Reay, 'Quakerism and Society,' in J. F. McGregor and B. Reay, eds., *Radical Religion in the English Revolution*, Oxford, 1984, p. 153, and his *Quakers and the English Revolution*, p. 41.

[8] Hill, *The Experience of Defeat: Milton and Some Contemporaries*, London, 1984, pp. 18, 130, 160, 161. See also his Introduction to Reay's book cited above, p. VII. In his 'Quakerism and Society' (p. 152) Reay, though he denies Quakers were 'consistent pacifists' in the 1650s, adds: 'True, some do seem to have reached the pacifist position before 1660,' and in a footnote gives three citations in support of this. One of them refers to the former Leveller leader, John Lilburne, who became a Quaker two years before his death in 1657.

[9] Reay, *The Quakers and the English Revolution*, pp. 18, 19.

[10] Hill, *The Experience of Defeat*, p. 129. For a long list of soldiers and sailors who became Quakers before 1660 – certainly not a complete one – see Hirst, pp. 527-29.

[11] See especially Kenneth L. Carroll, 'Quakerism and the Cromwellian Army in Ireland,' *JFHS*, vol. LIV, no. 3 (1978), pp. 135-54; also Reay, *The Quakers and the English Revolution*, pp. 50, 51, and his 'Quakerism and Society,' pp. 153-55.

[12] Quoted in Reay, 'Quakerism and Society,' p. 155.

[13] *To the Generals, and Captains, Officers, and Souldiers of This Present Army; the Just and Equal Appeal, and the State of the Innocent Cause of Us, who have been turned out of Your Army for the Exercise of Our Consciences, who are now persecuted amongst Our Brethren, under the Name of Quakers*, n.n.p., [1657], pp. 1, 7. Hirst, pp. 530, 531, prints a manuscript entitled 'A Testimony of Some of the Soldiers that were turned out of the Army who owned themselves to be Quakers 1657.' While this document makes no mention of any objections to fighting, the printed pamphlet we quote from here does contain phrases that might be given a pacifist interpretation, e.g., 'our kingdom, and victory, and weapons are not from below, but from heaven, and out of wars and strife' (p. 7). However, I doubt if such an interpretation would be correct. The explanation of such passages lies, in my view, much rather in the Quaker ex-soldiers' desire to distance themselves from those leaders whom they considered to have betrayed the Good Old Cause.

[14] Cole, 'The Quakers and Politics, 1652-1660,' unpublished Ph.D. dissertation, University of Cambridge, 1955, p. 25. Actually Cole is referring here to early Quakers generally and not merely to those who had been serving in the army.

[15] E.g., in his *Experience of Defeat*, pp. 130-34.

[16] *Ibid.*, p. 133.

[17] *Ibid.*, p. 149.

[18] Cole, 'The Quakers and Politics,' p. 283, referring to a work by Francis Howgill and Edward Burrough, *The Visitation of the Rebellious Nation of Ireland*, dated 23 May 1656.

[19] Edward Burrough, *The Memorable Works of a Son of Thunder and Consolation*, London, 1672, pp. 93, 94; from his pamphlet entitled 'An Invitation to All the Poor Desolate Soldiers to repent, and make Their Peace with the Lord, and Their Duty shewed them what the Lord requires of them' (1655).

[20] John Audland, quoted in Hill, *The Experience of Defeat*, p. 149.

[21] *Ibid.*, p. 149.

[22] In a letter to Oliver Cromwell in 1657 Burrough protested vehemently against the expulsion from the army of its Quaker converts, 'though they have not denied to serve thee and the Commonwealth.' See his *Works*, p. 558; from his pamphlet 'Good Counsel and Advice rejected by Disobedient Men' (1659). When the Saints had gone, Burrough's chiliastic hopes for the army began naturally to wane, too.

[23] Hill, *The Experience of Defeat*, p. 138. Nayler, so far as I know, did not touch directly on the issue of war in any of his extant writings. However, his well known soliloquy spoken on his deathbed in 1660 on the 'spirit . . . that

delights to do no evil' accurately expresses the message of nonviolence that lies at the core of Quaker pacifism. Nayler, a former Cromwellian soldier, though he had brought discredit on Quakers by his extravagant behaviour in 1656, seems, if we may judge by these final utterances of his, to have come fully to accept the emergent Quaker peace testimony before his death.

[24] *The Journal of George Fox*, ed. John L. Nickalls, Cambridge, 1952, p. 389.

[25] A concise statement of this viewpoint is given in Hill, *The World turned upside down*, p. 252: 'It seems to have been the approach of the restoration that decided Fox in favour of pacifism and non-participation in politics. His turn witnesses to acceptance of the fact that the Kingdom of God is not coming in the near future. So long as that appeared to be on the agenda, political attitudes had necessarily to remain fluid.'

[26] Fox, *Journal*, pp. 64, 65, 67. See also H. J. Cadbury, '"The Occasion of Wars" and Its Occasion,' pp. 152, 153, in his *Friendly Heritage: Letters from the Quaker Past*, Norwalk (Connecticut), 1972.

[27] Hill, *The Experience of Defeat*, p. 160. Cf. his *World turned upside down*, p. 242, where the same view is expressed in slightly less categorical terms: 'In the *Journal* [Fox] tells us that he refused [the captaincy] on pacifist grounds . . . It is at least possible that his refusal in 1651 sprang from political objections to the government of the commonwealth rather than pacifist principle.' But we may ask, did Fox at that time indeed have 'political' objections to the Commonwealth government?

[28] George Fox, *A Collection of Many Select and Christian Epistles, Letters and Testimonies . . .*, London, 1698, no. 131. For similar statements from the 1650s, see T. Canby Jones, *George Fox's Attitude toward War: A Documentary Study*, Annapolis (Maryland), 1972, pp. 70-73.

[29] Canby Jones, *op. cit.*, p. 99. See also pp. 102, 111.

[30] Fox, *Epistles*, no. 171. We can see what he meant by this – to us today – rather startling phrasing in another epistle (no. 172), also dated 1659. Referring to his sect he says there: 'We are of the royal seed, elect and precious, before the world began.' Nuttall in his 1970 Frederick Denison Maurice Lectures says of Fox that from the 1650s on he repeatedly 'summons Friends to exercise patience' and that throughout his career patient suffering, like that of Christ on the cross, was at the centre of his attitude to violence. *Christianity and Violence*, Royston (Herts), 1972, p. 15.

[31] Mabel Richmond Brailsford, *A Quaker from Cromwell's Army: James Nayler*, London, 1927, p. 17, in her introductory chapter entitled 'Cromwell's Quaker Soldiers,' originally published in 1915 in briefer form as an article. Other writers have drawn attention to Fox's ambiguity in this matter.

[32] Reay, *The Quakers and the English Revolution*, p. 41.

[33] Hill, *The Experience of Defeat*, p. 157, quoting from *To All Officers and Soldiers of the Armies in England, Scotland and Ireland*. Fox's words echo those of John the Baptist to the Roman soldiers who visited him in the desert.

[34] Quoted in Hugh Barbour, *The Quakers in Puritan England*, New Haven and London, 1964, p. 196.

[35] See, for example, Hill, *The Experience of Defeat*, pp. 157, 158.

[36] Some writers have doubted Fox's authorship. See, for example, Hirst, pp. 120-22, who writes, 'It seems impossible either to prove or disprove the authorship of Fox.' Rufus M. Jones in his article 'Were the Quaker Founders consistent Peace-Makers?,' *The Friend* (Philadelphia), vol. CXVI (29 April 1943), p. 346, was even more emphatic: 'George Fox's connection with that Tract seems to me an impossibility.' Coming from a Quaker author, it was 'undoubtedly a compromising document,' which Jones could not conceive was a product of the founder of Quakerism's pen. But it now appears to be virtually certain that it was by Fox. See Cadbury, 'A Disputed Paper of George Fox,' *BFHA*, vol. XIII, no. 2 (Autumn 1924), pp. 78-82; and also his 'Did George Fox write it?', published in the Philadelphia *Friend*, 10 June 1943, where Cadbury presents additional evidence in favour of Fox's authorship. 'The style of the pamphlet,' he writes, 'is much of it unmistakably of the style of Fox' (p. 396). The most recent discussion of the problem (agreeing with Cadbury's conclusions) is in Canby Jones, *op. cit.*, appendix B.

[37] Cf. Canby Jones's perceptive comments on pp. 124, 125, of his book.

[38] Quoted in Canby Jones, *op. cit.*, p. 82. (My italics.)

[39] Fox, *Epistles*, no. 188 (1659). See also no. 177 (1659), where too Quakers are described as weaponless and nonviolent. 'As for the rulers, that are to keep the peace, for peace's sake and the advantage of truth, give them their tribute. But to bear and carry carnal weapons to fight with, the men of peace (which live in that, which takes away the occasion of wars) they cannot act in such things, under the several powers.'

[40] Braithwaite, *The Beginnings of Quakerism*, Cambridge, 1961 edn., pp. 310-14.

[41] *Ibid.*, p. 312.

[42] An even more exact parallel can be found in the Civil War stance of the famous American evangelist, Dwight L. Moody. Moody, though a strong abolitionist, refused on grounds of conscience to join the Unionist army. 'In this respect I am a Quaker,' he said. But his pacifism did not prevent him from evangelising among the troops, and he was welcomed by the military authorities in army camps and hospitals and among prisoners of war. (We even find him taking part in patriotic rallies.) At the same time he never seems to have expressed his pacifism in his ministry among soldiers, still less undermined their military zeal. See my book *Pacifism in the United States*, p. 822, n.l. For Garrison's attitude to the American Civil War, see pp. 697-701.

[43] Carroll, *op. cit.*, p. 154.

[44] Norman Penny, ed., 'The First Publishers of Truth' . . ., London, 1907, p. 106.

[45] Reay, *The Quakers and the English Revolution*, p. 42.

[46] Braithwaite, *Beginnings*, pp. 229, 230.

[47] See *The Fighting Sailor turn'd Peaceable Christian: Manifested in the Convincement and Conversion of Thomas Lurting* . . ., London, 1710.

[48] Joseph Besse, *A Collection of the Sufferings of the People called Quakers*, . . . *Taken from the Original Records and Other Authentick Accounts*, London, 1753, vol. II, pp. 378-80. There is admittedly some vagueness in dating here. Besse writes (on p. 378) that in Maryland 'the earliest sufferings we meet with are without any particular dates' but they 'appear to have been transacted in or

before the year 1658.' The official order quoted from Carroll in my next note seems to indicate that Besse's dating is nevertheless accurate – at any rate as regards the majority of cases of militia refusal cited by him.

[49] Carroll, 'Persecution of Quakers in Early Maryland (1658-1661),' *QH*, vol. LIII, no. 2 (Autumn 1964), p. 75.

[50] Hirst, p. 55.

[51] Barbour, *op. cit.*, pp. 194, 202; Braithwaite, *Beginnings*, pp. 461-63. See also James F. Maclear, 'Quakerism and the End of the Interregnum: A Chapter in the Domestication of Radical Puritanism,' *Church History*, vol. XIX, no. 4 (December 1950), pp. 240-70; Douglas Gwyn, *Apocalypse of the Word: The Life and Message of George Fox (1624-1691)*, Richmond (Indiana), 1986, pp. 38-41.

[52] Cole's statement on p. 351 of his article cited above – 'In the weeks which followed [the restoration of the Rump, Quakers] seem to have acted for a [short] time as a united political force' – perhaps overstates the degree of unity, though something like a consensus certainly existed in some sections of the movement.

[53] *Ibid.*, p. 352.

[54] Quoted in Hill, *The Experience of Defeat*, p. 157.

[55] Cole, 'The Quakers and the English Revolution,' p. 345, quoting from Penington's pamphlet *To the Parliament, the Army, and All the Well-affected in the Nation*.

[56] Reay, 'The Quakers and 1659: Two Newly Discovered Broadsides by Edward Burrough,' *JFHS*, vol. LIV, no. 2 (1977), pp. 101-11. Reay prints the texts of the broadsides, seemingly unpublished hitherto, and discusses their dating in his introduction. On p. 105 he comments: 'if after the work of Professor Cole, anyone still believes in Quaker pacifism prior to 1660 [apart from individuals like William Dewsbury], Burrough's declaration should put an end to it.' See also his article, 'The Quakers, 1659, and the Restoration of the Monarchy,' *History* (London), vol. LXIII, no. 208 (June 1978), esp. pp. 193-95, 200-03.

[57] Braithwaite, *Beginnings*, p. 463.

[58] Reay, *The Quakers and the English Revolution*, pp. 41, 42.

[59] That this path now seemed uncertain to many Quakers can perhaps be taken as evidence of a growing, if still amorphous, sentiment among them that use of the sword was incompatible with the basic principles of their movement. Of course the issue was wider than that of pacifism alone but embraced the whole problem of participation in political life.

[60] Barbour, *op. cit.*, p. 202; Hill, *The Experience of Defeat*, p. 160.

[61] Cf. the rather similar mental crisis – *mutatis mutandis* – which occurred in Gandhi's career in 1918 when he, the apostle of nonviolence and practitioner of *satyagraha* before 1914, now engaged on a recruiting campaign for the British army among Indian peasants. See my book *The Mahatma and Mother India*, pp. 65, 66.

[62] Quoted in Reay, *The Quakers and the English Revolution*, p. 100. Cf. the perceptive passage by Tolles (*Quakers and the Atlantic Culture*, New York, 1960, p. 41) explaining the motives which led some Quakers in 1659 'to take

up the magistrate's sword, in the interests of establishing the Rule of the Saints.' 'Given the apocalyptic atmosphere of the time,' writes Tolles, it must have seemed to them as if 'the regime of the righteous' was at hand. Once this was established, then 'all swords would, no doubt, be turned into plowshares and all spears into pruning hooks.' But, of course 'the revolution of the Saints did not come off.'

[63] Fox, *Journal*, p. 357. See also Canby Jones, *op. cit.*, pp. 27-29, 116-18.

Chapter III *(pages 24-31)*
The Crystallisation of the Quaker Peace Testimony

[1] Christopher Hill, *The Experience of Defeat: Milton and Some Contemporaries*, London, 1984, p. 130.

[2] Philip S. Belasco, *Authority in Church and State*, London, 1928, p. 64.

[3] George Fox, *A Collection of Many Select and Christian Epistles, Letters and Testimonies* . . . , London, 1698, no. 239 (1664).

[4] Quoted in Barry Reay, *The Quakers and the English Revolution*, London, 1985, p. 64.

[5] Norman Penney, ed., *'The First Publishers of Truth'* . . ., London, 1907, p. 324.

[6] Hill, *op. cit.*, pp. 161, 162. See also the rather similar statement Fox made around this time on his own behalf, which was also addressed to the King; quoted in T. Canby Jones, *George Fox's Attitude toward War: A Documentary Study*, Annapolis (Maryland), 1972, pp. 31, 32.

[7] *The Journal of George Fox*, ed. John L. Nickalls, Cambridge, 1952, pp. 398-404. The Declaration was dated 21 January 1661.

[8] William C. Braithwaite, *The Second Period of Quakerism*, Cambridge, 1961 edn., p. 615.

[9] 'What started as a solution of a particular practical problem became, in the process, the statement of a principle of far-reaching effect.' D. Elton Trueblood, *The People called Quakers*, New York, 1966, p. 195.

[10] However, as Henry J. Cadbury remarks: 'It sounds a little like the boy who said when being punished, "I didn't do it and I'll never do it again."' *Friendly Heritage: Letters from the Quaker Past*, Norwalk (Connecticut), 1972, p. 253. We can indeed detect in the Declaration some of that unconscious 'projecting pacifism backwards' into the previous decade that Alan Cole finds a characteristic of past-Restoration Quakerism.

[11] 'It can be too easily construed as mere personal abstention,' writes Cadbury (*ibid.*, p. 254) not unjustly.

[12] Stephen C. Morland, ed., *The Somersetshire Quarterly Meeting of the Society of Friends 1668-1699*, Somersetshire Record Society, vol. LXXV, n.p.p., 1978, p. 63. See also pp. 36-39, 62-65, 171. That disagreement with pacifism never disappeared from the Quaker family, though indeed it became a submerged element within it, will come out later in this book. Suffice it now to point to just one more case: that of James Logan, William Penn's nonpacifist secretary, who was accepted as a respected member of Pennsylvania Yearly Meeting.

[13] Hill, *op. cit.*, p.162.

[14] Reay, *op. cit.*, pp. 108, 109. See also Richard L. Greaves, *Deliver Us from Evil: The Radical Underground in Britain, 1660-1663*, New York and Oxford, 1986, pp. 11, 29, 34, 55, 65, 68, 80, 91, 93, 99, 102, 116, 137, 177-82, 190, 200, 201.

[15] Reay comments on the cases he lists (*ibid.*): 'It is . . . becoming clear that the famous Quaker peace testimony was slower in developing and less universally accepted after 1660 than most historians have assumed . . . I emphasise this lack of commitment to pacifism not because it was widespread – as far as we know it was not – but because it is seldom mentioned in histories of Restoration Quakerism.' For further examples of the survival of Quaker militancy during the 1660s (isolated cases, though, based mostly on extremely shaky evidence), see William Wayne Spurrier, 'The Persecution of the Quakers in England: 1650-1714,' unpublished Ph.D. dissertation, University of North Carolina at Chapel Hill, 1976, pp. 35-37, 42-44, 46-52.

[16] Reay, *op. cit.*, p. 109.

[17] Hill, *The World turned upside down: Radical Ideas during the English Revolution*, Harmondsworth (Middlesex), 1975 edn., p. 351. See also his *Experience of Defeat*, pp. 151, 153, where Hill comments, 'He died too soon for us to know whether he accepted pacifism as a temporary expedient or as a long-term principle.' See also T. Vail Palmer, Jr., 'Quaker Peace Witness: The Biblical and Historical Roots', *Quaker Religious Thought* (Greensboro, North Carolina), vol. XXIII, nos. 2/3 (June 1988) pp. 40-48.

[18] Hill, *The Experience of Defeat*, p. 126.

[19] Isaac Penington, *Somewhat spoken to a Weighty Question, concerning the Magistrate's Protection of the Innocent* (1661), quoted in Trueblood, *op. cit.*, p. 200.

[20] Jonathan M. Chu, *Neighbors, Friends, or Madmen: The Puritan Adjustment to Quakerism in Seventeenth-Century Massachusetts Bay*, Westport (Connecticut), 1985, pp. 53, 107, 108. Chu gives the names of these men: Nicholas Shapleigh, James Hurd, and Miles Thompson.

[21] Canby Jones, *op. cit.*, pp. 84-86.

[22] This time I have used the edition issued by the Friend's Book Store in Philadelphia in 1906.

[23] Barclay's *Apology* (1906 edn.), pp. 526, 527, 531.

[24] *Ibid.*, p. 528.

[25] 'It is as easy to obscure the sun at mid-day, as to deny that the primitive Christians renounced all revenge and war.' *Ibid.*, p. 533.

[26] *Ibid.*, pp. 531, 532.

[27] Geoffrey F. Nuttall, *Christian Pacifism in History*, Oxford, 1958, pp. 57, 60, 61.

[28] Barclay's *Apology* (1906 edn.), p. 538. His *Epistle of Love and Friendly Advice, to the Ambassadors of the Several Princes of Europe, met at Nimeguen to consult the Peace of Christendom*, . . . (1678-9) contains similar humanitarian denunciations of war.

[29] Trueblood, *Robert Barclay*, New York, 1968, pp. 243-45.

[30] Quoted in *ibid.*, p. 246, from *The Apology Vindicated* (1679).

[31] Barclay's *Apology* (1906 edn,), pp. 529, 536, 537.

[32] William Penn, *The Rise and Progress of the People called Quakers*. This originally appeared as a preface to the first edition of Fox's *Journal* published in 1694. I have used the Philadelphia (1855) edition of Penn's work where the passages cited appear on pp. 26, 27. See also p. 25.

[33] Friends in Britain, because of the political situation prevailing in that country well into the 19th century, were rarely to find it difficult to square their pacifism with their rights and obligations as citizens under a sword-bearing magistracy. In his novel *Redgauntlet* (1824) Sir Walter Scott makes one of his characters, the Scottish Quaker Joshua Geddes, answer a threat to damage his property with the following words: 'Friend . . . we [Quakers] are under the protection of this country's laws; nor do we the less trust to obtain their protection, that our principles permit us not, by any act of violent resistance, to protect ourselves.' Geddes goes on to justify Quaker pacifism by saying, 'there is . . . more cowardice . . . in the armed oppressor, who doth injury, than in the defenceless and patient sufferer, who endureth it with constancy.' (See Letter 6.) Obviously Friend Geddes, despite the Quaker experiment in governing Pennsylvania, still did not envisage Quakers ever participating in framing or enforcing his own 'country's laws.' Though fiction and set not in the novelist's own day but in the third quarter of the previous century, Scott's narrative nevertheless reflects accurately, I think, an attitude long common among Quakers in Great Britain.

[34] See Howard H. Brinton, *Quaker Journals: Varieties of Religious Experience among Friends*, Wallingford (Pennsylvania), 1972, pp. 61-63, for an example of a Quaker practising nonviolence when shipwrecked among fierce Indian tribesmen on the coast of Florida (Jonathan Dickenson), and for a Quaker woman preacher's discussion of the implications of Quaker nonviolence in respect of self-defence (Catherine Phillips).

Chapter IV *(pages 32-46)*
The Pattern of Quaker Conscientious Objection in England

[1] Michael Walzer, *Obligations: Essays on Disobedience, War, and Citizenship*, Cambridge (Massachusetts), 1970, p. 124.

[2] Jurgen Schreiber, 'Kriegsdienstverweigerung, eine historische und rechtsvergleichende Untersuchung,' unpublished doctoral dissertation, Faculty of Law, University of Bonn, 1952, p. 37.

[3] Quoted in Hirst, pp. 211, 212.

[4] Her chapters on Britain, however, are much stronger than those dealing with North America, since she was unable to do research in American archives and libraries.

[5] Hirst, p. 75. In the early days 'the total volume of [militia] suffering was very considerable' but not so 'spectacularly oppressive' as in the case of other Quaker testimonies, e.g., against paying tithes; Alfred W. Braithwaite, 'Early Friends' Testimony against Carnal Weapons,' *JFHS*, vol. LII, no. 2 (1969), p. 104.

[6] Henry J. Cadbury, ed., 'Questions to a Conscientious Objector and Answers, 1679,' *Fellowship* (Nyack, New York), vol. XXVI, no. 9 (1 May 1960), pp. 29-31. Ford's later career alas was not very glorious: as Penn's financial agent he was to be involved in a series of transactions whereby he shamelessly exploited his master's lack of acumen in business affairs and inflicted considerable material losses on him.

[7] Hirst, 185, 188-91.

[8] Beryl Williams, *Quakers in Reigate 1655-1955*, n.p.p., 1980, p. 51.

[9] *Ibid.*, p. 67. The Library of the Society of Friends in London contains some fascinating manuscript material on the imprisonment of propertyless objectors during this same year 1809. The increase in the number of cases of imprisonment was due to a reorganisation of the militia carried out by the Secretary of War two years earlier in an effort to make that body a more efficient instrument for backing up the army in case of French invasion. We may note the future radical Joseph Sturge (along with John Bright the best known Quaker politician of the 19th century) narrowly escaped imprisonment when, aged 20, he was drawn for the militia in 1813. Later Sturge commented dryly, 'but for the fact of having a small farm with a flock of sheep upon it, he should have gone to prison, as a testimony against any appeal to arms.' Quoted in Henry Richard, *Memoirs of Joseph Sturge*, London, 1864, p. 24.

[10] Hirst, p. 244. The penalty of imprisonment was specifically abolished in the case of Friends in 1852. See *ibid.*, p. 246.

[11] *Ibid.*, p. 74.

[12] A dramatic depiction of an impressment is to be found in Elizabeth Gaskell's novel, *Sylvia's Lovers* (1863), with its scene set on the Yorkshire coast in an area even in her day still with a considerable Quaker component.

[13] Our Friend, Thomas Lurting, when pressed onto a man-of-war in 1662, had so provoked the anger of its captain by his exposition of pacifism that he cried, 'Turn him away, he is a Quaker.'

[14] Joseph Besse, *A Collection of the Sufferings of the People called Quakers, . . .*, London, 1753, vol. II, pp. 112-20.

[15] Hirst, p. 78.

[16] *Epistles from the Yearly Meetings of Friends, held in London*, London, 1858, vol. I, p. 72.

[17] Henry Cadbury notes, in connection with this whole problem, that even Friends of unimpeachable pacifist credentials were sometimes obliged to travel on a man-of-war when there was no other means of transport to their destination. See his *Friendly Heritage: Letters from the Quaker Past*, Norwalk (Connecticut), 1972, p. 19.

[18] W. Pearson Thistlethwaite, *Yorkshire Quarterly Meeting (of the Society of Friends) 1665-1966*, Harrogate, 1979, p. 375.

[19] *Ibid.*, p. 373.

[20] Hirst, p. 230. The date is 1781, and the Clerk's name Samuel Clemesha. He was soon afterwards relieved of his office.

[21] How difficult it was to eradicate such practices from the life of the Society emerges from the case of John Hunt, a London merchant and also a highly

respected member of the Meeting for Sufferings. When in 1748 a Philadelphia Friend had charged him with purchasing a prize ship and then installing armaments on it, 'Hunt answered that he did not know when he had purchased the vessel, that it was indeed a prize, and that the few cannon on board were not for defense.' See J. William Frost, *The Quaker Family in Colonial America: A Portrait of the Society of Friends*, New York, 1973, p. 202. Hunt's explanation appears to be extremely weak, at any rate as coming from a Quaker minister. Should he not have got rid of the ship once he knew it was a prize? And what were the cannon doing on board if not for use in some emergency?

[22] One is reminded of the fictional English Quaker William Walters in Daniel Defoe's novel *The Life, Adventures and Piracies of the Famous Captain Singleton* (1720). Walters, after being captured by pirates, tells their captain: 'But thou knowest it is not my business to meddle when thou art to fight. No, no, says the captain, but you may meddle a little when we share the money' (chap. 10).

[23] Cadbury, *op. cit.*, p. 20.

[24] Marjorie Sykes, *Quakers in India: A Forgotten Century*, London, 1980, p. 19.

[25] *Adventures by Sea of Edward Coxere*, ed. E. H. W. Meyerstein, Oxford, 1945.

[26] *Ibid.*, pp. 86-92.

[27] A medley of such 'troubles' appears, for instance, in the report of Yorkshire Quarterly Meeting for March 1812: 'Two cases under care, of watchmen provided with firearms for the protection of property, and an instance of a young man serving on board an armed vessel and one inadvertently taking down names on account of the militia.' Quoted in Thistlethwaite, *op. cit.*, p. 374.

[28] Barclay speaks in his *Apology* (Philadelphia, 1906 edn., p. 533) of what Friends had suffered: 'Because we could not hold our doors, windows, and shops close, for conscience' sake, upon such days as fasts and prayers were appointed, to desire a blessing upon, and success for, the arms of the Kingdom or commonwealth under which we live; neither give thanks for the victories acquired by the effusion of much blood.'

[29] Hirst, pp. 182, 183. There is some doubt if Cumming was formally a member of the Society, though he undoubtedly stood close to it.

[30] *Ibid.*, p. 214.

[31] *Ibid.*, pp. 233-40. The younger Galton, however, 'disregarded the disownment and, with his wife, continued to attend the worship of Friends. Of course he could take no part in business meetings.' *Ibid.*, p. 240.

[32] I should mention, albeit in a footnote, the clandestine involvement around the mid-18th century of certain prominent English Quakers like the wealthy London merchant and bulwark of Yearly Meeting, John Hanbury, in British military activities on the American frontier. Such men probably numbered only a handful, still there were more of them than earlier Quaker historians realised. We owe our knowledge of this rather shady chapter in Quaker history to the researches of such historians as Guy F. Hershberger. Hershberger's findings have alas only been published in part.

[33] *Epistles*, vol. I, p. 72.

[34] Of course Quakers refused as far back as around 1660 to pay a fine (which might sometimes be referred to as a tax) in lieu of bearing arms in the militia. The argument here, though, was on a rather different plane. It was wrong, Friends said, to pay a penalty for doing something that was right. It was not only wrong to pay but of course also wrong for the state to require such payment. If it did so, its request must be rejected, and any further penalties in the way of distraints or imprisonment suffered quietly – though not necessarily unprotestingly.

[35] Hirst, p. 198.

[36] *Ibid.*, p. 214.

[37] *Ibid.*, p. 213. The Society took care not to support volunteer campaigns to help finance war. For instance, in 1798 the merchants of the City of London attempted to gain support of this kind from Friends with an argument they hoped would carry weight with Quakers, namely that 'it is not to make war, but to prevent the continuance of war, that we call upon you to join us in giving public aid at this awful moment.' The Clerk of the Meeting for Sufferings answered by rejecting the appeal on the grounds that a contribution from Friends 'would be a violation of our religious testimony against all war.' See Cadbury, *op. cit.*, pp. 159-61.

Chapter V   (pages 47-61)
Quaker Conscientious Objectors in Colonial America

[1] By 1775 Quakers numbered around 50,000 out of a total North American population of around 2,500,000. The Quaker community of course, like the population at large, was much smaller in earlier periods. In the 18th century a few Quakers were to be found in South Carolina and Georgia but very little is known about them.

[2] Quoted in Howard Beeth, 'Outside Agitators in Southern History : The Society of Friends, 1656-1800,' unpublished Ph.D. dissertation, University of Houston (1984), p. 338.

[3] David W. Jordan, ' "God's Candle" within Government : Quakers and Politics in Early Maryland,' *WMQ*, series 3, vol. XXXIX, no. 4 (October 1982), p. 650.

[4] R. R. Russell, 'Development of Conscientious Objector Recognition in the United States,' *The George Washington Law Review* (Washington, D.C.), vol. XX, no. 4 (March 1952), pp. 412, 413.

[5] In Britain, and so far as I know in colonial America too, a militia objector was usually imprisoned only if he did not own property on which distraint might be made. But Arthur J. Worrall refers to two Quakers in Barnstable (Massachusetts), who in May 1757 had refused to serve in the militia and then been 'imprisoned and fined.' This is rather confusing. But what I think must have happened here was that the two men first received a fine which, their being for some reason then unable to pay, led on to their subsequent incarceration. Under the new militia act passed on 31 December of that year they appear to have been subjected to distraint alone. It is still not clear to me

why distraint was not carried out also in the first instance, unless later distraint was in fact a result of their delinquency the previous May. See Worrall, *Quakers in the Colonial Northeast,* Hanover (New Hampshire) and London, 1980, p. 138. However, ambiguous cases like this one do not alter the general rule.

[6] *Records of the Colony of Rhode Island and Providence Plantations, in New England,* ed. John Russell Bartlett, Providence, vol. I (1856), p. 379. See also pp. 374-8, 380.

[7] A reference to the existence within the colony of 'diverse persons of several societies, who are one in that point of conscience, of not training and fighting to kill,' shows there were others in Rhode Island besides Quakers, who held pacifist views. The legislators, although they do not name them, were probably thinking of the small local sect of Rogerenes; they may also have been thinking of certain individual Baptists who believed in pacifism. For further discussion of the working out of the Quaker peace testimony in colonial Rhode Island, see ch. XI below.

[8] *Ibid.,* vol. II (1857), pp. 495-99.

[9] Just as the conscience clause in the act of 1673 had undoubtedly been due in large measure to the powerful Quaker presence in both the provincial assembly and the provincial administration, so its withdrawal three years later certainly stemmed from the – temporary – anti-Quaker reaction in that year. According to Worrall (*op. cit.,* p. 131), the act was 'briefly repealed and reinstituted in 1676, and then finally repealed in 1677 under Governor Benedict Arnold.'

[10] Worrall, *ibid.*

[11] Russell, *op. cit.,* p. 413. Russell sees in the 1730 act 'a forerunner of the "noncombatant" and "work of national importance" provision of modern Selective Service Acts.' But of course the same might be said of the earlier act of 1673, which was, I think, the first piece of American legislation granting the right of conscientious objection to war.

[12] Worrall, *op. cit.,* pp. 131, 132, writes of Rhode Island Quakers from 1700 to 1750: 'Despite their release from military service, Friends still had to contemplate alternative service much as they had in the seventeenth century . . . Alternative service remained a requirement, and Rhode Island Friends apparently observed it during the colonial period to the extent that they served when required. They did not raise the question whether specific alternative service, by contributing to the war effort, compromised their pacifism. It was sufficient to avoid carrying weapons.' But the only example he cites of such alternative service is that of watching performed in 1704 during the War of Spanish Succession. I am not convinced, however, that the watching under discussion here was done as an alternative to militia service. (I deal briefly with this incident below.) Of course it is possible that Rhode Island Quakers, some of whose members, we shall see in ch. XI below, were active in the military aspects of provincial government, were more flexible, too, in allowing members to perform civilian service as an alternative to bearing arms in the militia. But, if they were, they were acting clean contrary to the practice of other branches of the Society in North America as well as to that of the mother Society in England (which however was not completely consistent in

this respect, either). At any rate, it would be interesting to see some further evidence on this point, if indeed such evidence exists.

[13] Worrall, *op. cit.*, p. 136.

[14] Originally a separate unit West Jersey, 'founded and settled by people with scruples against war,' possessed at first 'no provisions for defence.' East Jersey, on the other hand, although its early proprietors included Quakers of such eminence as William Penn and Robert Barclay, did provide for military defence and militia conscription. But the balance of Quaker and non-Quaker interests resulted in 1683 in a compromise being worked out whereby 'those who objected to bearing arms would not have to do so and would provide substitutes, but those who supported defence could do so in a legal manner.' The management of military affairs was to be consigned exclusively to non-Friends, but Quakers sitting on the Great Council, with which body lay the ultimate decisions, would, it was hoped, succeed in speaking there on defence matters 'after the manner of men, and abstractly from a man's persuasion in matters of religion,' i.e., would be able to put aside their Quaker scruples when invasion or war threatened. In addition, the costs of defence would be covered by non-Quakers, with Friends bearing 'so much in other charges, as may make up that portion in the general charges of the province.' As J. William Frost remarks: 'The law was a fascinating attempt, however unworkable in practice, to guarantee the civil and religious liberties of two groups.' See his article 'Religious Liberty in Early Pennsylvania,' *PMHB*, vol. CV, no. 4 (October 1981), pp. 430, 431, on which I have based the above account. We may note that, while the kind of payment envisaged in place of a direct contribution toward military expenses might then have been acceptable to Friends, providing a substitute to perform military service in one's stead definitely was not. I am not clear why the Quaker proprietors allowed this provision to go through.

[15] Edwin P. Tanner, *The Province of New Jersey 1664-1738*, New York, 1908, pp. 556, 567.

[16] *Ibid.*, p. 571.

[17] Sometimes Friends were urged to send their servants, if these were non-Quakers, to perform militia service in their stead. Sending a servant to the militia in his master's place – or sometimes it was in place of his master's son – was a not an uncommon practice in those days, but of course one that could not be countenanced by the Society, at least officially.

[18] *A Narrative of Some Sufferings for His Christian Peaceable Testimony, by John Smith, late of Chester County, Deceased*, Philadelphia, 1800, pp. 6-10. Smith's autobiographical 'narrative' was published long after his death. See also Thomas Story's *Journal*, Newcastle upon Tyne, 1747, pp. 264-70, 309-12, 339.

[19] *The Colonial Records of North Carolina*, ed. William L. Saunders, Raleigh, vol. I (1886), p. 810. See also pp. 808, 809. These pages reprint extracts from the 'Journal of Virginia Council.'

[20] *Ibid.*, p. 811.

[21] *Ibid.*, p. 812.

22 Certainly Spotswood was badly informed about the attitude of contemporary Quakers in neighbouring North Carolina. In 1711 the antiproprietary party there had resorted to insurrection, the so called Cary Rebellion, and the rebels gained the support of a few prominent Friends. Even though North Carolina Yearly Meeting took disciplinary action against any members who participated in the rebellion, Spotswood in his letter to the Board of Trade states categorically that 'in [North] Carolina . . . they were the most active in taking arms to put down that Government (tho they now fly again to the pretence of conscience to be excused from assisting against the Indians).' It seems hardly likely he would have been better informed about the attitude of Quakers in distant Britain than he was about those living in the province next door. But here lay an equally handy argument for use against the then very unpopular sect.

23 Colonial Quakers were sometimes required to contribute financially to the construction of fortifications. An instance of this occurred in New York City in 1672. The Friends there firmly refused to do so writing at the same time to the governor of the province in explanation of their stand. It seems that the authorities accepted this and freed Quakers from further demands of this kind. See John Cox, Jr., *Quakerism in the City of New York 1657-1930*, New York, 1930, p. 70-72. But see Sydney V. James, *A People among Peoples: Quaker Benevolence in Eighteenth-Century America*, Cambridge (Massachusetts), 1963, p. 81, for behaviour of the opposite kind. In 1757 the Preparative Meeting at Providence on the Virginia frontier was dissolved because, according to a report from the Monthly Meeting within whose jurisdiction it lay, 'all of them [had] been concerned in building a fortification and dwelling therein for defence against the Indian enemy,' with whom it seems local Quakers were involved in a land dispute that the latter had as yet not succeeded in settling satisfactorily.

24 For background, see Steven Jay White, 'The Peace Witness of North Carolina Quakers during the Colonial Wars,' *The Southern Friend* (Greensboro, North Carolina), vol. V, no. 1 (Spring 1983), pp. 13-22.

25 Quoted in Beeth, *op. cit.*, p. 338.

26 For the encounter that took place in 1756 between seven Quaker conscientious objectors to service in the Virginia militia and the future President of the United States, George Washington (then a colonel in the same militia), see my article, 'Colonel Washington and the Quaker Conscientious Objectors,' *QH*, vol. LIII, no. 1 (Spring 1964), pp. 12-26. The article prints the text of a Quaker manuscript entitled 'A Narrative of the Conduct and Sufferings of Some Friends in Virginia . . .'

27 Letter from John Woolman to Abraham Farrington, dated 1 October 1757, printed in *PMHB*, vol. XVII (1893), no. 3, p. 371.

28 Smith, *op. cit.*, pp. 10-18.

29 The only auxiliary service then performed by Friends – or rather, some of them acting in a private capacity – lay in supplying the British army with woollen waistcoats 'to keep them warm.'

30 *Rules of Discipline and Christian Advices of the Yearly Meeting of Friends for Pennsylvania and New Jersey*, Philadelphia, 1797, p. 131.

[31] Frost, *The Quaker Family in Colonial America: A Portrait of the Society of Friends*, New York, 1973, p. 202.

[32] Worrall, *op. cit.*, p. 132.

[33] *An Account of the Life of That Ancient Servant of Jesus Christ, John Richardson*, London, 1757, pp. 128, 129.

[34] Worrall, *op. cit.*, pp. 137-39.

[35] We learn of some 10 or more New Hampshire Quakers enrolling at this time in the armed forces: they were presumably disciplined for such un-Quakerly behaviour. Worrall (*ibid.*, p. 220, n. 24) mentions the existence of a group of ex-Quakers living at Brentwood (N.H.) in the early 1760s, who had served recently in the army yet still called themselves Quakers, despite having been formally disowned by Dover Monthly Meeting.

[36] *The Book of Discipline, agreed on by the Yearly-Meeting of Friends for New-England*, Providence (Rhode Island), 1785, p. 148.

Chapter VI   (pages 62-74)
Quaker Conscientious Objectors in the West Indies

[1] The last foothold retained by Quakerism in the Caribbean area was ironically not on British but on Danish territory. On the small island of St. Croix (now one of the Virgin Islands belonging to the United States) a small Meeting functioned between 1760 and 1785, presumably an outgrowth of the neighbouring Quaker communities of Antigua and Nevis. One of the leading Quaker converts on St. Croix was, we learn, an Englishman Thomas Lillie. Of him it was said, 'Although he was a captain of the burghers in Christianstadt [on St. Croix] . . . and also a member of the burgher community, yet he forsook all for Christ,' abandoned his weapons, and joined Quakers. See Harriet Frorer Durham, *Caribbean Quakers*, Hollywood (Florida), 1972, pp. 68, 69, 72.

[2] See Henry J. Cadbury's Foreword to Durham, *op. cit.*, p. V.

[3] Joseph Besse, *A Collection of the Sufferings of the People called Quakers for the Testimony of a Good Conscience*, London, 2 vols. 1753. The West Indies are dealt with in volume II: Barbados (to 1695), pp. 278-351; Nevis (to 1677), pp. 352-66; Bermuda (to 1672), pp. 366-70; Antigua (to 1695), pp. 370-78; and Jamaica (to 1689), pp. 388-91. It will be seen that only Barbados receives lengthy treatment, a treatment which is in fact out of proportion to that assigned the other islands. Besse, for instance, allots only a few pages to Jamaica, despite its size and importance. Obviously for some reason Besse had at his disposal a disproportionate amount of documentation relating to Barbados and correspondingly little concerning Jamaica and the other islands. However, despite these shortcomings Besse's work, because it reproduces a wide variety of documents no longer extant, remains an invaluable source of information on the peace testimony of Caribbean Quakers as well as on such matters as their opposition to taking oaths or paying tithes. But it stops before the end of the 17th century; thereafter,

except with regard to Tortola (and Antigua in 1708-9), we are almost completely without documentation.

4 Besse, *op. cit.*, vol. II, p. 331 (Barbados, 1685), records that John Gittings was fined 'for not sending men to work at the fortifications,' 'for refusing to take the oath of a juryman,' and 'for church and priest's dues.'

5 *Ibid.*, p. 278.

6 Nevis, 1677, in *ibid.*, p. 362.

7 *Ibid.*, p. 280.

8 Quoted in Hirst, p. 313.

9 *Ibid.*, pp. 314, 315.

10 See *ibid.*, ch. XII, *passim*, for details of militia legislation passed in some of the other islands. The pattern follows more or less that of Jamaica, though with a multitude of minor variations.

11 Musterings were often held every month. We learn that in Barbados during the 1670s 'in the exercising week some of them [i.e., Quakers] had been charged with the penalty for absence of a foot-man for each day.' Besse, *op. cit.*, vol. II, p. 318.

12 Barbados, 1693, quoted in Besse, *op. cit.*, vol. II, p. 341. Friends complain there of 'a new and great addition [to their trials on account of military demands] by an Act made for persons to ride armed with swords and pistols, by reason of which, divers of us have been haled off our horses by soldiers, our horses taken away and kept for some time from us ; our saddles sold by public outcry for our pretended forfeitures, with many other abuses, . . .'

13 Besse, *op. cit.*, vol. II, pp. 295, 296.

14 For example, in Jamaica in 1685 a Quaker named William Davis was fined first for failing to buy arms for himself and then for refusing to send 'his servant to exercise military discipline.' Next year he was again fined 'for not appearing personally in arms' as well as 'for not accounting and sending his servant to the muster.' A distress was levied each time on his goods as a result of his refusal to pay the fines. *Ibid.*, p. 389.

15 According to Hirst, p. 310, Barbados in 1660 laid down in its first legislation directed against militia objectors that all who refused to serve should be fined 'five hundred pounds of sugar for the first offence, one thousand pounds of sugar for the second offence, and a thousand pounds for every default after the second, and to be committed (to gaol) until the same be paid.' For Quakers who were not planters, sugar had to be converted for the purpose of fining into some other commodity which the delinquent possessed. We learn, for instance, that in 1669 Richard Marshal, a Barbados Quaker, 'for not sending people in arms to the fort' had taken from him 'one young Negro man, about the age of 19 or 20 years, worth 3000 lb. of sugar.'

16 Besse, *op. cit.*, vol. II, p. 391.

17 Besse records in his second volume a number of 'sufferings' on account of military demands of various kinds experienced by George Gray between 1665 and 1693. See pp. 283, 288, 314, 332, 338, 342. Gray was a barber by trade.

18 From *A Short Account of the Manifest Hand of God that hath fallen upon Several Marshals and Their Deputies, who have made Great Spoil and Havock of the Goods of the People of God called Quakers, in the Island of Barbados, for Their*

Testimony against Going or Sending to the Militia . . ., London, 1696, p. 14. (See also p. 3, for a description of another Barbados marshal, Samuel Buckley, who battened on the spoils accruing from Quaker 'overpluses.') This 23-page pamphlet (reprinted in large part in Besse, *op. cit.*, vol. II, pp. 344-51) illustrates a curious – and not altogether pleasing – aspect of the Quaker mind of those days in the story told there of how some 40 'persecutors,' who had harried Friends on account of their objection to bearing arms, were struck down by God prematurely through unexpected illness or accident. We also meet with the same kind of postponed – or, perhaps we should say, vicarious – revenge, with a similar feeling of satisfaction at the destruction of the oppressor by means of divine intervention, in the case of some 16th-century evangelical Anabaptists.

[19] Besse, *op. cit.*, vol. II, p. 281. Gittings's name, like that of many others from the islands, appears repeatedly on Besse's pages: fines, distresses, and imprisonment appear to have been frequent occurrences for such men.

[20] *Ibid.*, p. 377.

[21] *Ibid.*, p. 352.

[22] For Dashwood, see *ibid.*, p. 390; for Mallet's excesses, see *ibid.*, pp. 372, 373. It is interesting to note that Besse at the conclusion of his section on Antigua (on p. 378) notes that Major Mallet eventually was struck down unexpectedly by 'a deadly fit,' which finished him off in the course of 10 days. This Besse takes as 'a token of the divine vengeance upon him, who had been a busy persecutor, and seemed to delight in oppressing his innocent neighbours.'

[23] Barbados's militia act of 1675 laid down in section 18: 'That if any servant or hired man . . . shall omit making his appearance at the place appointed to him for exercise . . . such servant or freeman so defaulting and neglecting his and their due appearance in arms as aforesaid, shall for every such offence be by the commander in chief there present, censured to lie his neck and heels at the head of the company whereto he belongs, so long as the commander shall think fit, not exceeding the space of one hour.' Printed in Besse, *op. cit.*, vol. II, p. 300. (I do not think the limit of one hour was always strictly observed.)

[24] *Ibid.*, p. 366.

[25] *A Short Account*, p. 22.

[26] Besse, *op. cit.*, vol. II, p. 322 (1673).

[27] J. H. Lefroy, ed., *Memorials of the Discovery and Early Settlement of the Bermudas or Somers Islands 1511-1687*, 2nd edn., London, 1932, vol. II, p. 137; Besse, *op. cit.*, vol. II, p. 366.

[28] Besse, *op. cit.*, vol. II, p. 367; Durham, *op. cit.*, p. 48.

[29] Besse, *op. cit.*, vol. II, pp. 291, 313.

[30] George Fox, *A Collection of Many Select and Christian Epistles, Letters and Testimonies* . . . , London, 1698, pp. 363-68, no. 319; summarised in Hirst, pp. 316, 317.

[31] Quoted in Hirst, pp. 317, 318.

[32] The dissidents signing the second letter were John Brennan, John Butler, John Darlow, Jr., John Fallowfield, William Hague, and Henry Hodge. I think these names deserve mention here.

[33] *Ibid.*, pp. 322-26. Hirst's account is based on manuscript correspondence preserved in the Library of the Society of Friends in London.

[34] Charles F. Jenkins, *Tortola: A Quaker Experiment of Long Ago in the Tropics*, London, 1923, p. 89.

[35] Pickering wrote of his unregenerate days: 'For my part, I owned the [Quaker] way, but never lived any way answerable to it, but had always a great love and tenderness for them [*sic*] people above all others.' Quoted in *ibid.*, p. 7.

[36] *Ibid.*, pp. 8, 19.

Chapter VII *(pages 75-86)*
Early Quaker Plans for World Peace

[1] I have used the facsimile reprint of the first edition of Penn's *Essay* (published in London) that has been brought out by Olms-Weidmann (Hildesheim-Zürich-New York, 1983). The volume contains a long and informative introduction by Peter van den Dungen (cited below as Dungen). The title-page of the original edition contains two mottoes: *Beati Pacifici* and *Cedant Arma Togae*.

[2] I have used the original 1710 edition published in London. An abbreviated reprint appears on pp. 89-103 of A. Ruth Fry's study on *John Bellers 1654-1725: Quaker, Economist and Social Reformer*, London, 1935. The most convenient edition is probably the reprint in George Clarke, ed., *John Bellers: His Life, Times and Writings*, London and New York, 1987, pp. 134-53.

[3] The two peace plans are summarised (among other places) in Hirst—Penn on pp. 158-65 and Bellers on pp. 166-9. Dungen, pp. xxxv, xxxvi, has noted the curious fact that monographs on Penn as a peace planner 'have appeared only in French, and with impressive regularity' – usually as doctoral theses. He lists six titles, dating from 1926 to 1973, and adds the comment: 'They are, on the whole, neither original nor thorough in their analysis, and very derivative.' I have only consulted one of them (Terasaki, see below).

[4] Dungen, pp. vii, viii; Kurt von Raumer, *Ewiger Friede: Friedensrufe und Friedenspläne seit der Renaissance*, Freiburg and Munich, 1953, p. 107.

[5] Quoted in Hirst, pp. 156, 158.

[6] The *Essay* did not appear with official Quaker approval, and Penn probably had the early editions printed by a non-Quaker printer (though there is a little uncertainty on this point); Dungen, p. xiii.

[7] Dungen, p. viii; von Raumer, *op. cit.*, p. 98 (also p. 113).

[8] Von Raumer, *op. cit.*, p. 99, argues cogently for an Erasmian influence on Penn's *Essay*, either directly or indirectly. He writes: 'Erasmus of Rotterdam is clearly among the ancestors of Penn's peace idea, although it is difficult to decide whether Penn had actually read him or whether he had merely absorbed him somehow through his own extended Dutch connections and through the inner relationship between various humanistic and moral-religious components of his world view.'

[9] *Essay*, pp. i, iii ('To the Reader'), 1 (Sec. 1).

[10] *Ibid.*, pp. 64, 65 ('The Conclusion').

[11] *Ibid.*, pp. 4, 5 (Sect. 1).

[12] *Ibid.*, p. 10 (Sect. 2).

[13] *Ibid.*, pp. 11, 13-15 (Sect. 3).

[14] Penn saw 'a long and undoubted succession' and 'purchase' as the best titles a prince could possess to his territories. But he did not altogether exclude 'conquest.' For conquest, though its claim to recognition was, 'morally speaking, only questionable,' had nevertheless 'obtained a place among the rolls of titles, but it was engrost and recorded by the point of the sword, and in bloody characters. What cannot be controlled or resisted, must be submitted to . . . there is a little allowed to conquest too, when it has had the sanction of articles of peace to confirm it . . . when conquest has been confirmed by a treaty and conclusion of peace. I must confess it is an adopted title; and if not so genuine and natural, yet being engrafted, it is fed by that which is the security of better titles, consent.' *Ibid.*, pp. 23, 24 (Sect. 6).

[15] Taro Terasaki, *William Penn et la paix*, Paris, 1926, p. 133.

[16] Elsewhere (*Essay*, pp. 20, 21 [Sect. 5]) Penn lists three causes of war: 'To keep, to recover, to add.' While the prince's motive in the first instance is 'purely defensive,' in the second it is 'offensive,' i.e., a desire to recover what he believes has been unjustly taken from his ancestors by force. A third motive operates where a prince seeks to extend his dominion for purely expansionist reasons. 'This last will find no room in the Imperial states: They are an unpassable limit to that ambition. But the other two may come as soon as they please, and find the justice of that sovereign court.'

[17] *Ibid.*, pp. 7-9 (Sect. 3). See also pp. 22-25 (Sect. 6).

[18] Sect. 4. See also von Raumer, *op. cit.*, pp. 108, 109; Thomas Raeburn White, 'Influence of William Penn on International Relations,' *PMHB*, vol. LXVIII, no. 4 (October 1944), p. 390.

[19] 'Penn uses no less than twelve different names to describe . . . the European parliament which is in the centre of his plan'; Dungen, p. xxv.

[20] *Essay*, p. 18 (Sect. 4).

[21] Cf. von Raumer, *op. cit.*, p. 109: 'The world to which he himself belongs is that of the nobility, and the world at which he is looking [in the *Essay*] is everywhere still princely.'

[22] *Essay*, p. 63 ('The Conclusion'). 'Penn sought stability through a registration of dynastic titles'; Benjamin Sacks, *Peace Plans of the Seventeenth and Eighteenth Centuries*, Sandoval (New Mexico), 1962, p. 15.

[23] Sylvester John Hemleben, *Plans for World Peace through Six Centuries* (1943), ed. Walter F. Bense, New York and London, 1972, p. 53.

[24] As a precaution against disputes arising between the representatives over 'precedence,' Penn proposed that 'the [assembly] room may be round and have divers doors to come in and out at, to prevent exceptions.' Voting, moreover, was to be by secret ballot: Penn feared the ill effects of corruption and bribery among the delegates if voting were open. A quorum – 'three quarters of the whole, at least seven above the balance' – would be necessary for any measure to pass, with the further prerequisite that throughout each session 'every sovereignty should be present under great penalties.' Latin or French were to be the official languages of debates. *Essay*, pp. 30-35 (Sect. 8).

[25] F. H. Hinsley in his *Power and the Pursuit of Peace: Theory and Practice in the History of Relations between States*, Cambridge, 1963, p. 34, speaks of Penn's 'hesitation about including Russia' and adds, 'it does not seem that he thought Turkey's inclusion worth serious attention.' But Penn's own words (on p. 29) do not support this conclusion, for he specifically states it as his view that it would be 'but fit and just' to grant representation in the Diet to both these powers.

[26] Hemleben, *op. cit.*, p. 52; White, *op. cit.*, pp. 390, 391.

[27] *Essay*, pp. 36-43 (Sect. 9).

[28] *Ibid.*, pp. 43-60 (Sect. 10).

[29] *Ibid.*, pp. 45-48 (Sect. 10). Penn's observation that his plan 'will end blood, if not strife' is striking. Understood literally at any rate, it cannot mean simply that he realises the plan does not entirely do away with armies and any further possibility of war, for in that case he would not have said it would 'end blood.' Is it too far fetched for us to see in this phrase a dim realisation on Penn's part of the concept of nonviolent conflict resolution developed in our time by Mahatma Gandhi and certain Western thinkers? Is he in fact saying that, while his plan would put a stop to war, 'strife,' that is, conflict, would continue between states and need some nonmilitary means of resolution?

[30] *Essay*, p. 53 (Sect. 10).

[31] See, for example, Hinsley, *op. cit.*, pp. 38-41; also White, *op. cit.*, pp. 394, 395, where Penn's standpoint is presented as follows, 'Hating war, recognising its essential wrongness, and desiring above all things its abolition, he yet fully recognised that the preservation of order in the world and the prevention of war required the use of force.'

[32] On the other hand, Henry J. Cadbury, in his *Friendly Heritage: Letters from the Quaker Past*, Norwalk (Connecticut), 1972, p. 79, seems to me to underestimate the role military force plays in Penn's scheme. He is right, though, in stressing that Penn's emphasis was 'upon consultation, organisation, judicial procedure,' and reduced armaments.

[33] In 1696, three years after drafting his peace plan, Penn composed a somewhat similar project designed to show how a union of England's American colonies might be effected. The scheme, which Penn drew up for presentation to the Board of Trade, included *inter alia* provisions for recruiting troops in time of war and other measures for defence. White, *op. cit.*, p. 397, comments as follows: 'This . . . proposal . . . is . . . interesting as showing beyond any question that at that time Penn realised the necessity for the use of force for self-defence and in the preservation of peace.' I do not think this interpretation is correct; at any rate, it is wrong if my argument concerning Penn's *Essay* is correct, for that, I think, applies equally to his plan for colonial union.

[34] Dungen, p. xxvii.

[35] Bellers, *Some Reasons*, pp. iii, 8. In contrast to the misery of war, 'peace, with industry and virtue, brings all the happiness that this world can give to a country.' See also his remarks in the Conclusion (p. 20): 'Nothing makes nations, and people more barbarous than war . . . War is destruction, and puts men (they think) under a necessity of doing those things, which in a time

of peace, they would account cruel, and horrid.' Peace, on the other hand, 'must be the first step, to fit mankind for religion.'

[36] *Ibid.*, pp. iv-vi, 9. On pp. 17-19 Bellers prints 'an abstract' of the *grand dessein* for European peace devised by Henry IV's minister Sully.

[37] *Ibid.*, p. 20.

[38] Cf. Philip S. Belasco's comment: '[Bellers] saw more clearly than Penn the importance of armaments. When Penn had only given the Diet the right to question the amassing of armaments of a separate power, Bellers definitely suggests their limitation as a condition of peace.' From his article on Bellers in *The Friend* (London), vol. LXV, no. 52 (25 December 1925), p. 1161.

[39] *Ibid.*, pp. 4-7 ('The Proposal').

[40] *Ibid.*, pp. 14-16. 'All the powers on earth cannot make one man sincere by force; tho' they make millions conformable' (p. 14). Like Penn, Bellers included a special appeal to the European clergy of every denomination for support of his plan; *ibid.*, pp. 10-14. War, he told them, remains 'your greatest enemy.'

[41] Karl Seipp, *John Bellers: Ein Vertreter des frühen Quäkertums*, Nürnberg, 1933, pp. 63, 64: 'He grants the masses nothing, he accepts only the prerogatives of the hitherto privileged classes.'

[42] T. A. Pavlova, *Dzhon Bellers i angliiskaya sotsial'no-ekonomicheskaya mysl' vtoroi poloviny XVIIv.*, Moscow, 1979, p. 165.

[43] *Ibid.*, p. 161, n. 21. See Bellers, *Some Reasons*, pp. 1-3.

[44] Bellers, *Some Reasons*, p. 3.

[45] Seipp, *op. cit.*, p. 60.

Chapter VIII *(pages 87-101)*
The Pacifist Ethic and Quaker Pennsylvania:
The First Phase

[1] I may cite as a – perhaps extreme – example of this view the work by E. Dingwall and E. A. Heard, *Pennsylvania 1681-1756: The State without an Army*, London, 1937. A typical pre-scholarly treatment of Quaker rule is found in Samuel M. Janney, *Peace Principles exemplified in the Early History of Pennsylvania*, Philadelphia, 1876. These works present Quaker Pennsylvania as a pacifist model: an interpretation that is frequently found in the literature of the 19th- as well as the 20th-century peace movement in America and Britain.

[2] Melvin Endy, Jr., *William Penn and Early Quakerism*, Princeton (New Jersey), 1973, pp. 348, 349.

[3] Richard S. and Mary Maples Dunn, eds., *The Papers of William Penn*, Philadelphia, vol. II (1982), p. 108.

[4] 'It would be impossible to discredit the tradition that William Penn and his friends were primarily interested in planning a utopian community, based on the beliefs of the Society of Friends.' Edwin B. Bronner, *William Penn's 'Holy Experiment': The Founding of Pennsylvania 1681-1701*, New York, 1962, p. 14.

[5] E.g., Penn, *Papers*, vol. I (1981), p. 439: 'For we believe, magistracy to be both lawful and useful for the terrifying of all evil doers; and the praise and encouragement of those that do well' (from his letter to King Jan III of Poland, August 1677). Penn refers from time to time to a specifically Christian magistracy.

[6] *Ibid.*, vol. II, p. 212.

[7] 'Because of royal restrictions, liberty of conscience was limited to Protestants. Roman Catholics could not legally become naturalised and hold property, but they [like other theists – P.B.] could worship openly. Discriminations remained at the level of English policy, but in practice in Pennsylvania even Catholic priests owned property.' J. William Frost, 'Religious Liberty in Early Pennsylvania,' *PMHB*, vol. CV, no. 4 (October 1981), p. 450. True, atheists were precluded from expressing their views freely, but there must have been very few atheists at that date.

[8] When in January 1705 the Board of Trade asked Penn to define what he understood by 'liberty of conscience' he replied: 'I mean not only that relating to worship, but education, or schools, a coercive ministerial maintenance, *the militia*.' (My italics.) Elsewhere he lists among the rights he strove to safeguard for the Quakers (and presumably other nonresistants) of his province: 'To be exempted from militia services and charges thereof so as well watch and war in times of troubles.' See Frost, 'Religious Liberty,' p. 427.

[9] Frost, 'Religious Liberty,' pp. 431, 449.

[10] Frederick B. Tolles, 'Nonviolent Contact: The Quakers and the Indians,' *Proceedings of the American Philosophical Society* (Philadelphia), vol. CVII, no. 2 (April 1963), p. 95.

[11] Penn, *Papers*, vol. II, p. 261.

[12] G. W. Knowles, ed., *Quakers and Peace*, London, 1927, pp. 36-38. Geoffrey F. Nuttall comments on the Treaty as follows in his *Christian Pacifism in History*, Oxford, 1958, p. 63: 'This . . . is great humanism. It is also great Christianity; but it would hardly be possible, historically speaking, without the respect for man as man which at the Renaissance was regained from the ancient world.' We may note the impact which the conclusion of the treaty made on one present at the signing – the Welsh Quaker Thomas Wynne. It confirmed Wynne's belief in nonviolence; this comes out clearly in the exposition of Quaker pacifism which the Welshman composed – in English – for his Friends four years later. See Geraint Jenkins, ed., 'Llythyr Olaf Thomas Wynne o Gaerwys: "A Farewell of Endeared Love to Ould England and Wales, 1686",' *The Bulletin of the Board of Celtic Studies* (Cardiff), vol. XXIX, pt. 1 (November 1980), pp. 91-110.

[13] Penn's conciliatory spirit comes out, posthumously, in the renewed treaty of friendship concluded in 1728 between the Lieutenant Governor of Pennsylvania and the Indian tribes living in the province. The Governor, among other Quakerly things, expressed his hopes, 'That the doors of the Christians' houses should be open to the Indians, and the houses of the Indians open to the Christians, and that they should make each other welcome as their friends.' *Memoirs of the Historical Society of Pennsylvania* (Philadelphia), vol. III, pt. 2 (1836), pp. 200-03.

[14] George Staughton *et al.*, *Charter to William Penn, and Laws of the Province of Pennsylvania passed between the Years 1682 and 1700*, Harrisburg, 1879, p. 88.

[15] Hermann Wellenreuther, *Glaube und Politik in Pennsylvania 1681-1776: Die Wandlungen der Obrigkeitsdoktrin und des 'Peace Testimony' der Quäker*, Cologne and Vienna, 1972, pp. 61, 62; and his article, 'The Political Dilemma of the Quakers in Pennsylvania 1681-1748,' *PMHB*, vol. XCIV, no. 2 (April 1970), p. 145.

[16] 'James Logan on Defensive War, or Pennsylvania Politics in 1741,' *PMHB*, vol. VI (1882), no. 4, p. 407.

[17] Frost, 'William Penn's Experiment in the Wilderness: Promise and Legend,' *PMHB*, vol. CVII, no. 4 (October 1983), p. 586. In an anonymous pamphlet written to induce non-Quakers to settle in the newly founded province the Quaker author, William Loddington, wrote: 'If any carper should buzz protection into planters' ears saying, how shall you be secured, if W.P. [William Penn] will not fight,' let them rest assured that, despite the absence of weapons for defence, 'in these parts of America, where the Indians are not exasperated by any of our European pious cheats, our [Protestant nonconformist] planters in all probability may expect better measure than in Europe while they behave themselves justly and honestly in all their dealings with them.' From his *Plantation Work the Work of This Generation, Written in True-Love to all such as are weightily inclined to transplant Themselves and Families to any of the English Plantations in America . . .*, London, 1682, pp. 8, 9.

[18] David E. Shi, *The Simple Life: Plain Living and High Thinking in American Culture*, New York and Oxford, 1985, pp. 28, 33.

[19] Endy, *op. cit.*, pp. 363, 368. The Quaker historian Frost is quite as severe in his judgement as the non-Quaker Endy: 'Philadelphia did not become a new Jerusalem; Quakers proved to be extraordinarily contentious.' In his article 'Penn's Experiment,' p. 604, Frost contrasts this contentiousness with 'the beauty of [Penn's] religious life' and 'the depth of his spirituality,' which displayed themselves in the course of his two visits to Pennsylvania.

[20] Endy, *op. cit.*, p. 366.

[21] Quoted in Guy Franklin Hershberger, 'Pacifism and the State in Colonial Pennsylvania,' *Church History* (Chicago), vol. VIII, no. 1 (March 1939), pp. 62, 63.

[22] E. Digby Baltzell, *Puritan Boston and Quaker Philadelphia: Two Protestant Ethics and the Spirit of Class Authority and Leadership*, New York and London, 1979, p. 154. I do think, though, that Baltzell in his major thesis (see p. 20) may exaggerate the degree of influence Quaker antiauthoritarianism exercised throughout the history of Philadelphia. But this is a subject that is really outside the scope of my book.

[23] Endy, *op. cit.*, pp. 371-6.

[24] 'By opening the doors of Pennsylvania to people of every nation and every religion he [Penn] established a situation of cultural pluralism.' Frederick B. Tolles, *Quakers and the Atlantic Culture*, New York, 1960, p. 131.

[25] By this I mean the practical working out in Pennsylvania of what Hermann Wellenreuther has called the Quakers' *Obrigkeitsdoktrin* or *Obrigkeitsbegriff*.

[26] Jack D. Marietta, 'The Course of Quaker Pacifism in the Colonial Wars: Pennsylvania's Legislatures, 1693-1748' (1980), p. 18. I am grateful to the author for sending me a typescript of this hitherto unpublished conference paper.

[27] Wellenreuther, *Glaube und Politik*, p. 15.

[28] Alan Tully, *William Penn's Legacy: Politics and Social Structure in Provincial Pennsylvania, 1726-1755*, Baltimore and London, 1977, p. 154.

[29] Quoted in Wellenreuther, *Glaube und Politik*, p. 93.

[30] *Ibid.*, pp. 80, 81.

[31] Quoted in James Bowden, *The History of the Society of Friends in America*, London, vol. II (1854), p. 145.

[32] Wellenreuther, *Glaube und Politik*, pp. 123, 124.

[33] Frost, 'Religious Liberty,' pp. 444, 445.

[34] Wellenreuther, 'The Political Dilemma of the Quakers,' p. 155. I would like, though, to add that, despite disagreement with some of his conclusions, I have found Wellenreuther's work both in English and in German an invaluable source of information on the history of Quaker pacifism in Pennsylvania.

[35] *Pennsylvania Colonial Records: Minutes of the Provincial Council of Pennsylvania*, vol. I (Philadelphia, 1852), pp. 306-11.

[36] Wellenreuther, 'The Political Dilemma of the Quakers,' pp. 149, 150. See also his *Glaube und Politik*, pp. 83-87, 98.

[37] See Marietta, 'The Course of Quaker Pacifism,' pp. 306. According to Marietta, 'Fletcher . . . believed the legislators objected to the uses of their taxes for warfare and were ethically constrained from paying such taxes. But that was not the case; the Quaker obligation to pay such taxes made no exception for the bellicose use of the tax. Friends had to pay . . . And whereas Fletcher believed that his promise to the Quaker Assemblymen was permissive – it freed them to pay – the Quakers' ethic was not permissive, but obligatory. They had to pay when the Crown demanded taxes. Friends were subordinates and subjects to Caesar and were not to question whether that which was the monarch's was to be rendered upon his demand.' But this, I think, is only partially true. We know from the English minister John Richardson's statement, made less than a decade later, that in his country 'many Friends are not so easy as they could desire' in paying taxes of which even a part went for purposes of war. Why should not many Friends in Pennsylvania, too, including Quaker Assemblymen, feel hesitation of this kind in voting, and subsequently paying money, exclusively – if perhaps not quite explicitly – for military ends? And why the repeated reluctance and prevarication shown by Quaker Assemblymen with respect to voting war credits if this did not reflect at least a residual objection on pacifist grounds? It could surely not have been due only – or even mainly – to financial or other prudential considerations. We may note, too, that in 1696 Governor Markham observed that Quakers 'for conscience cannot contribute to war' directly. (Quoted in *ibid.*, p. 7.) Though Marietta finds this remark 'curious,' I cannot help feeling it was based on the Governor's correct perception of an underlying reluctance on Friends' part to collaborate in any way in war-making.

[38] Marietta, *op. cit.*, p. 5; Wellenreuther, *Glaube und Politik*, pp. 86-88.

[39] Quoted in Isaac Sharpless, *A History of Quaker Government in Pennsylvania:* Vol. I, *A Quaker Experiment in Government,* Philadelphia, 1900, p. 191.

[40] Marietta, *op. cit.,* p. 9.

[41] Quoted in Henry J. Cadbury, *Friendly Heritage: Letters from the Quaker Past,* Norwalk (Connecticut), 1972, p. 53. See Wellenreuther, *Glaube und Politik,* pp. 88, 89, for Governor Andrew Hamilton's complaint, voiced in 1702, that Quakers were not ready to respect the consciences of those who believed in fighting, though they expected others to respect their own conscientious scruples against bearing arms. The Assembly, urged the Governor, represented the province as a whole and should take into consideration the views of the non-Quaker section of the population as well as those of their own coreligionists. Otherwise, where was the freedom of conscience that Quaker legislators made so much of in their political pronouncements? The thrust of this question was directed in particular against the repeated refusal of the Quaker controlled Assembly to approve the establishment of a provincial militia, even though Friends and other pacifists would be exempt from serving in it. Such arguments of course later gained increased cogency – and were used with increasing frequency – when the Quakers became a minority in Pennsylvania.

[42] Marietta, *op. cit.,* pp. 9-11; Wellenreuther, *Glaube und Politik,* pp. 94-96.

[43] Marietta, *op. cit.,* p. 23, n. 22.

[44] Tully, *op. cit.,* p. 243, n. 62.

[45] Marietta, *op. cit.,* pp. 11-13. I shall have a little more to say about Rakeshaw later in my overview of the Quaker attitude to war taxes.

[46] Wellenreuther, *Glaube und Politik,* p. 97. Wellenreuther, pp. 93, 98-100, seems, if I have understood him correctly, to make a distinction in substance between the formula adopted by the Assembly in 1693 for its appropriation – 'for the support of government' – and that used for this in 1709 and 1711 as well as subsequently – 'for the Queen's [or King's] use.' In the first case the purpose of the allocation remained more vague, more general, than in the second where it became more specifically military. But I am not sure if such a distinction really has much meaning: in each instance there was a vagueness and in each, at the same time, a barely concealed recognition that the money was in fact destined for war.

Chapter IX   *(pages 102-111)*
The Pacifist Ethic and Quaker Pennsylvania: The Second Phase

[1] *The Ancient Testimony of the People called Quakers, reviv'd. By the Order and Approbation of the Yearly Meeting, held for the Provinces of Pennsylvania and New Jersey, 1722,* Philadelphia, 1773 edn., pp. 18, 19, 23.

[2] Hermann Wellenreuther, *Glaube und Politik in Pennsylvania 1681-1776: Die Wandlungen der Obrigkeitsdoktrin und des 'Peace Testimony' der Quäker,* Cologne and Vienna, 1972, p. 122.

[3] Wellenreuther, 'The Political Dilemma of the Quakers in Pennsylvania, 1681-1748,' *PMHB*, vol. XCIV, no. 2 (April 1970), p. 139.

[4] Wellenreuther, 'The Quest for Harmony in a Turbulent World: The Principle of 'Love and Unity' in Colonial Pennsylvania Politics,' *PMHB*, vol. CVII, no. 4 (October 1983), p. 553. See also Gary B. Nash, *Quakers and Politics: Pennsylvania, 1681-1726*, Princeton (New Jersey), 1968, pp. 236, 237; Richard Alan Ryerson, 'Portrait of a Colonial Oligarchy: The Quaker Elite in the Pennsylvania Assembly, 1729-1776,' in Bruce C. Daniels, ed., *Power and Status: Officeholding in Colonial America*, Middletown (Connecticut), 1986, pp. 107-9, 127; Alan Tully, 'Quaker Party and Proprietary Policies: The Dynamics of Politics in Pre-Revolutionary Pennsylvania, 1730-1775,' in Daniels, pp. 75-78, 81-84, 104; and Wellenreuther, *Glaube und Politik*, pp. 170, 171, 197, 198.

[5] The description is Tully's (in Daniels, p. 76).

[6] Tully, 'Ethnicity, Religion, and Politics in Early America,' *PMHB*, vol. CVII, no. 4 (October 1983), p. 497.

[7] Wellenreuther, *Glaube und Politik*, pp. 122, 171, 195, and his article 'The Political Dilemmas of the Quakers,' p. 164.

[8] Tully, in Daniels, p. 81.

[9] See Jack D. Marietta, 'The Growth of Quaker Self-Consciousness in Pennsylvania,' in J. William Frost and John M. Moore, eds., *Seeking the Light: Essays in Quaker History in Honor of Edwin B. Bronner*, Wallingford and Haverford (Pennsylvania), 1986, pp. 86-99.

[10] In 1742 a leading English Quaker, Dr. John Fothergill wrote to Israel Pemberton, Jr.: 'If I may be permitted to give my opinion of the management of your controversy with the governor, I can scarcely upon the whole forbear to take his side. Your cause is undoubtedly good, but I am afraid you discover a little more warmth than is quite consistent with the moderation we profess . . . The arguments made use of by the Assembly are strong and cogent, but he justly accuses you with too much acrimony.' Quoted in Guy Franklin Hershberger, 'Pacifism and the State in Colonial Pennsylvania,' *Church History* (Chicago), vol. VIII, no. 1 (March 1939), p. 66.

[11] Wellenreuther, *Glaube und Politik*, p. 128.

[12] *Ibid.*, pp. 145, 152. Whereas Logan remained a Friend till his death in 1751, both Strettell and Chew were eventually disowned for actions contravening the Quaker peace testimony.

[13] See especially Tully, 'King George's War and the Quakers: The Defense Crisis of 1739-1742 in Pennsylvania Politics,' *Journal of the Lancaster County Historical Society* (Lancaster, Pennsylvania), vol. LXXXII, no. 4 (Michaelmas 1978), pp. 176-85, 188-92.

[14] Tully, 'King George's War,' p. 191.

[15] Marietta, 'The Course of Quaker Pacifism in the Colonial Wars: Pennsylvania's Legislatures, 1693-1748' (unpublished conference paper, 1980), p. 14.

[16] Quoted in Wellenreuther, 'The Political Dilemma of the Quakers,' p. 161. See also his *Glaube und Politik*, p. 148. Marietta, *op. cit.*, p. 25, n. 34, thinks Benjamin Franklin incorrect in his assertion that the phrase 'other grain,' inserted at the end of the list of foodstuffs which the Assembly authorised to

be bought for the troops' needs, meant gunpowder. (See the *Autobiography of Benjamin Franklin*, ed. Leonard W. Labaree, New Haven, 1964, pp. 188-90.) Certainly no positive proof in favour of Franklin's statement has so far been discovered. In addition (and this now is on the debit side of the Assembly's activities), Marietta (p. 15) believes its delegation of the task of buying these foodstuffs to two Quaker merchants, John Mifflin and John Pole, created a dangerous precedent: 'For the first time the Assembly entered into the forbidden degree of complicity with war of directly purchasing and supplying the sinews of war.'

[17] Quoted in Wellenreuther, *Glaube und Politik*, p. 149.

[18] *Ibid.*

[19] *Ibid.*, pp. 156, 157, 190. Curiously, one of those who led in the moves to bring about the disownment of these delinquent Friends was John Reynell, who in 1745 had sent a parcel of pistols (for what purpose is not clear) on a 40-gun ship. See J. William Frost, *The Quaker Family in Colonial America: A Portrait of the Society of Friends*, New York, 1973, p. 215. Of course Reynell's was a venal offence compared to the ones he helped to 'deal with' a few years later.

[20] *Pennsylvania Colonial Records: Minutes of the Provincial Council of Pennsylvania*, vol. V (Harrisburg, 1852), p. 236.

[21] Wellenreuther, *Glaube und Politik*, pp. 150-152, 157. The Assembly's declaration was made on 10 June. It is interesting to note that a Friend in good standing like William Logan – James's son and much closer to the mind of the Society than his father had been – sat at this time on the Provincial Council, which was directly concerned with the organisation of the province's military defence.

[22] Quoted in *ibid.*, pp. 162, 163. Smith seems to have presumed that the money subscribed would have been repaid by the Assembly at its next sitting.

[23] Tully, *William Penn's Legacy: Politics and Social Structure in Provincial Pennsylvania, 1726-1755*, Baltimore and London, 1977, p. 158.

[24] *An Account of the Gospel Labours, and Christian Experiences of a Faithful Minister of Christ, John Churchman, late of Nottingham in Pennsylvania, deceased*, Philadelphia, 1779, pp. 69-73. Another prominent Quaker minister, Thomas Chalkley, had presented the Pennsylvania Quaker community with somewhat similar views during the defence crisis of 1740.

[25] Quoted in Wellenreuther, 'The Political Dilemma of the Quakers,' p. 169.

[26] This religious revival among Quakers was a phenomenon common to all parts of the Transatlantic Quaker community, and its roots went back at least to the 1730s. In Pennsylvania its climax of course came in 1756 but the crisis of that year was the outcome of a long process of growth. See Kenneth L. Carroll, 'A Look at the "Quaker Revival of 1756,"' *QH*, vol. LXV, no. 2 (Autumn 1976), pp. 64, 74, 79, and *passim*.

[27] David E. Shi, *The Simple Life: Plain Living and High Thinking in American Culture*, New York and Oxford, 1985, p. 38.

[28] Norman C. Freund, 'Pacifism and the Holy Experiment: The Reasons for Its Failure,' *Gandhi Marg* (New Delhi), N.S., vol. VII, no. 12 (84) (March 1986), esp. pp. 829-31.

[29] The phrase is Tully's, *William Penn's Legacy*, p. 160.

[30] Quoted in Richard Bauman, *For the Reputation of Truth: Politics, Religion, and Conflict among Pennsylvania Quakers 1750-1800*, Baltimore and London, 1971, p. 63.

[31] Nash, *op. cit.*, pp. 341, 342.

Chapter X   *(pages 112-131)*
John Woolman and the Renewal of Pacifism
among Pennsylvania Quakers

[1] Frederick B. Tolles has described Woolman's *Journal* as 'the classic expression of the Quaker spirit at its best'; 'the crystal purity, the functional simplicity of his style' reflect Woolman's deep understanding of Friends' ethos. 'In the character of John Woolman,' writes D. Elton Trueblood, 'we do not learn what every Quaker is, but we do learn something of the richness of the Quaker potential' (*The People called Quakers*, New York, 1966, p. 153). Trueblood points out that, although Woolman was an exceptional Quaker, he was at the same time a product of his Quaker culture and background, his life and activities resting 'squarely on a Quaker base' (p. 152).

[2] The phrase is Edwin H. Cady's (*John Woolman: The Mind of the Quaker Saint*, New York, 1966, p. 89).

[3] Nancy Slocum Hornick, 'Anthony Benezet: Eighteenth Century Social Critic, Educator and Abolitionist,' unpublished Ph.D. dissertation, University of Maryland, 1974, pp. 228, 235, 241.

[4] Quoted in Jack D. Marietta, 'Conscience, the Quaker Community, and the French and Indian War,' *PMHB*, vol. XCV, no. 1 (January 1971), p. 14. There, Marietta comments, 'Benezet offered a prescription in terms more acerbic than Woolman's.'

[5] Richard Bauman, *For the Reputation of Truth: Politics, Religion and Conflict among Pennsylvania Quakers 1750-1800*, Baltimore and London, 1971, p. 61.

[6] A third Pemberton brother, John, worked closely with Woolman and devoted most of his energies to the reform cause. The Pembertons, we may note, were reckoned among the wealthiest Quaker merchant families of Philadelphia.

[7] *Ibid.*, pp. 71, 72, 221.

[8] Quoted in Herman Wellenreuther, *Glaube und Politik in Pennsylvania 1681-1776: Die Wandlungen der Obrigkeitsdoktrin und des 'Peace Testimony' der Quäker*, Cologne and Vienna, 1972, p. 225.

[9] Marietta, *The Reformation of American Quakerism, 1748-1783*, Philadelphia, 1984, p. 141. There had been a precedent for such procedure in 1745 but this seems to have been overlooked at the time.

[10] Dietmar Rothermund, *The Layman's Progress: Religious and Political Experience in Colonial Pennsylvania 1740-1770*, Philadelphia, 1961, pp. 174, 175 (Documents).

[11] Alan Tully, 'Politics and Peace Testimony in Mid-Eighteenth-Century Pennsylvania,' *The Canadian Review of American Studies* (Winnipeg), vol. XIII, no. 2 (Fall 1982), p. 172. See also his book *William Penn's Legacy:*

Politics and Social Structure in Provincial Pennsylvania, 1726-1755, Baltimore and London, 1977, pp. 159, 160.

[12] The militia bill, though passed by the Assembly, was later quashed by the British government on constitutional grounds.

[13] Quoted in Wellenreuther, *Glaube und Politik*, p. 239.

[14] Letter dated 27 November 1755, quoted in Tully, 'Politics and Peace Testimony,' p. 173. On 17 November we find James Pemberton's brother Israel telling Dr. Fothergill that 'times of floods and tempest . . . seem now to come upon us or very near us.' Rothermund, *op. cit.*, pp. 175, 176 (Documents).

[15] *Pennsylvania Archives*, 1st series, ed. Samuel Hazard, vol. II (Philadelphia, 1852), pp. 487, 488.

[16] *The Journal and Major Essays of John Woolman*, ed. Phillips P. Moulton, New York, 1971, pp. 85, 86. Though the reformers' Address to the Assembly in November condemns the supplies bill for appointing commissioners to control expenditure of the money granted, the *Epistle* does not mention this, concentrating its fire on the military purposes to which most of the money would go. Marietta in his book seems to me to give undue prominence to the former point, for it was undoubtedly the latter one that ultimately bulked largest in the reformers' campaign for tax refusal.

[17] *Ibid.*, p. 84.

[18] Letter dated 14 October 1755; quoted in Wellenreuther, 'The Quest for Harmony in a Turbulent World: The Principle of "Love and Unity" in Colonial Pennsylvania Politics,' *PMHB*, vol. CVII, no. 4 (October 1983), p. 563.

[19] Marietta, 'Conscience, the Quaker Community, . . .,' p. 9.

[20] Jonah Thompson, an English Friend recently returned from a visit to Pennsylvania, told John Smith on 26 June 1756: 'That letter wrote to Friends to dissuade them from paying the tax . . . has given great disgust at court . . . and many Friends look upon it as a reflection on the conduct of our Friends here . . . as we have always cheerfully paid all taxes imposed for the support of government.' Quoted in Wellenreuther, *Glaube und Politik*, pp. 262, 263. The same sentiments appear in a letter which a prominent London Quaker, Robert Foster, wrote to John Pemberton on 9 September 1756. Meeting for Sufferings, said Foster, would be most anxious to know 'on what principle you refused the payment of the tax levied by your government . . . your refusal cast great reflection upon the conduct of all that have gone before. In this light that affair is viewed by many.' Pemberton Papers (Historical Society of Pennsylvania MSS.), vol. XI, p. 119.

[21] *Chain of Friendship: Selected Letters of Dr. John Fothergill of London, 1735-1780*, ed. Betsy C. Corner and Christopher C. Booth, Cambridge (Massachusetts), 1971, pp. 173, 180.

[22] Quoted in Marietta, *Reformation*, p. 164.

[23] Marietta, *op. cit.*, pp. 162-64, 167. Among country Quakers in the United Kingdom, there was, according to Marietta, even talk of refusing to pay the 'land tax' because part of it was used for war, though in the end nothing came of this proposal.

[24] Wellenreuther, 'The Quest for Harmony,' p. 363, note 69. It is interesting to read that 'when John Woolman's *Journal* [first published in 1774] was reprinted in England in 1775 the whole section on paying or not paying taxes was omitted.' Henry J. Cadbury, *Friendly Heritage: Letters from the Quaker Past*, Norwalk (Connecticut), 1972, p. 304.

[25] Wellenreuther, *Glaube und Politik*, p. 308. The phrase quoted was James Pemberton's.

[26] Quoted in Isaac Sharpless, *A History of Quaker Government in Pennsylvania*: vol. I, *A Quaker Experiment in Government*, Philadelphia, 1900, p. 249.

[27] *Ibid.* (letter of 11 January 1757).

[28] Woolman, *Journal*, pp. 83, 84, 86, 87.

[29] *Ibid.*, p. 90.

[30] *Ibid.*, p. 87. See also Cadbury, *op. cit.*, pp. 303, 304; Wellenreuther, *Glaube und Politik*, pp. 329-31.

[31] *An Account of the Gospel Labours, and Christian Experiences of a Faithful Minister of Christ, John Churchman, late of Nottingham in Pennsylvania, deceased*, Philadelphia, 1779, p. 175.

[32] The majority of non-Quakers in the province identified, not entirely without reason, the traditional pro-Indian policy of the Pennsylvania administration with its Quaker orientation. While strict Friends regarded a Quaker presence in the wartime Assembly as an embarrassment feeling it cast doubt on the integrity of the Society's witness for peace, an Assembly controlled even by largely nominal Quakers was considered by many non-Friends to be an ineffectual instrument for carrying on war both on account of the Society's official pacifism and its tradition of good relations with the Indians. In fact we know the majority of Quakers in the House, though undoubtedly desiring friendship with the neighbouring Indians, were not on the whole impeded by pacifist scruples from a thoroughgoing prosecution of the war. For instance, in 1760 Isaac Norris, Jr., then Speaker of the Assembly (who nevertheless retained his membership in the Society of Friends), spoke of 'this just and necessary war' (quoted in William T. Parsons, 'Isaac Norris II, the Speaker,' unpublished Ph.D. dissertation, University of Pennsylvania, 1955, p. 233). His sentiments would have been echoed by most of his Quaker colleagues who had remained in the House after the withdrawal of some in 1756.

[33] J. William Frost, *The Quaker Family in Colonial America: A Portrait of the Society of Friends*, New York, 1973, p. 202. See also Tully, 'Politics and Peace Testimony,' p. 173, and Wellenreuther, *Glaube und Politik*, p. 292.

[34] Marietta, *Reformation*, pp. 158, 320, note 26. Cf. Wellenreuther ('The Quest for Harmony,' p. 570, note 86), who considers it 'unlikely' that the resignations resulted from the influence of the revival group. However, I find Marietta's arguments in favour of this more convincing than Wellenreuther's thesis against.

[35] Marietta, 'Conscience, the Quaker Community, . . . ,' p. 18; Wellenreuther, *Glaube und Politik*, p. 306.

[36] Parsons, *op. cit.*, p. 196.

[37] Tully, 'Ethnicity, Religion, and Politics in Early America,' *PMHB*, vol. CVII, no. 4 (October 1983), pp. 504, 505; Richard Alan Ryerson, 'Portrait of a

Colonial Oligarchy: The Quaker Elite in the Pennsylvania Assembly, 1729-1776,' in Bruce C. Daniels, ed., *Power and Status: Officeholding in Colonial America*, Middletown (Connecticut), 1986, pp. 128, 135.

[38] Letter to Israel Pemberton (who was the moving spirit in this undertaking), London, 9 April 1759, quoted in Wellenreuther, *Glaube und Politik*, p. 327.

[39] See especially Theodore Thayer, 'The Friendly Association,' *PMHB*, vol. LXVII, no. 4 (October 1943), and Bauman, *op. cit.*, chap. 6: 'The Quaker Politiques and the Career of the Friendly Association' (pp. 77-101).

[40] Marietta, 'Conscience, the Quaker Community, . . . ,' p. 25. Though Marietta states there that 'the application of the article . . . proved equivocal, for . . . no Quaker officeholder was disciplined between 1758 and 1775,' he cites in his book (*Reformation*, p. 324, note 28) – on the authority of James Pemberton – at least one case where an 'official was disowned for distraining Friends' property in lieu of their paying taxes.' The general failure to apply disciplinary action, we may note, applied not only to the lower magistracy but to Friends who continued to sit in the Assembly. It is interesting to note, too, that in his book (pp. 78, 79), Marietta refers to Bradford Monthly Meeting in Chester County, where the majority upheld the actions of those members who were justices or constables in distraining the property of local Quaker tax objectors. In the end the Meeting conformed – but not without a struggle!

[41] Marietta, *Reformation*, p. 178.

[42] *Ibid.*, pp. 180-82.

[43] Quoted in Wellenreuther, *Glaube und Politik*, p. 345.

[44] David Sloan, '"A Time of Sifting and Winnowing": The Paxton Riots and Quaker Non-Violence in Pennsylvania,' *QH*, vol. LXVI, no. 1 (Spring 1977), p. 3. This article gives the best presentation of Quaker attitudes and actions during the Paxton disturbance.

[45] Bauman, *op. cit.*, p. 109, describes Israel Pemberton as 'a symbol of all that the westerners identified as hostile to their interests: the wealthy, pacifist, Quaker, Indian-loving, eastern ruling class.' See also Brooke Hindle, 'The March of the Paxton Boys,' *WMQ*, 3rd Series, vol. III, no. 4 (October 1946), p. 476; James H. Hutson, *Pennsylvania Politics 1746-1770: The Movement for Royal Government and Its Consequences*, Princeton (New Jersey), 1972, pp. 94-96; as well as James E. Crowley, 'The Paxton Disturbance and Ideas of Order in Pennsylvania Politics,' *Pennsylvania History* (University Park), vol. XXXVII, no. 4 (October 1970), pp. 324, 325.

[46] Peter A. Butzin, 'Politics, Presbyterians and the Paxton Riots, 1763-64,' *Journal of Presbyterian History* (Philadelphia), vol. LI, no. 1 (Spring 1973), p. 82.

[47] 'The frontiersman had never made the nice Quaker distinction between friendly and enemy Indians. To him all Indians were treacherous.' Hindle, *op. cit.*, p. 466.

[48] How many Quakers bore arms is not certain. Estimates run from around 140 to 200 – or even more. About 200 seems the most likely figure.

[49] Bauman, *op. cit.*, pp. 110, 112.

[50] Quoted in Butzin, *op. cit.*, p. 83.

[51] Tracts for and against the Quakers have been republished in the volume edited by John R. Dunbar, *The Paxton Papers*, The Hague, 1957.

332

[52] Sloan, *op. cit.*, pp. 13-22. See also Bauman, *op. cit.*, pp. 118, 119; Marietta, *Reformation*, pp. 194, 195.

[53] Ryerson, *op. cit.*, pp. 106, 134.

[54] Rothermund, *op. cit.*, p. 96, note 31.

[55] Wellenreuther, *Glaube und Politik*, p. 426.

[56] In 1760 Quaker Assemblymen, when a Committee of Philadelphia Meeting for Sufferings attempted – yet once more – to persuade them to resign, answered their coreligionists' appeal as follows: 'Tho' they have been concerned in granting large sums of money at several times for the King's use, which were intended and have been applied to military purposes, yet as they are not active in the immediate application of the sums granted, they do not acknowledge that they have wounded the testimony of Friends.' Quoted in *ibid.*, p. 352. But, as Wellenreuther goes on to point out (p. 353), the Assembly's increasingly frequent practice of controlling the allocation of such supplies through the appointment of commissioners responsible to the House meant that, in large part, the House itself had taken charge of the warmaking process. Cf. Marietta (*Reformation*, p. 172), who seems to me to over-emphasise the role protest against direct expenditure by the Assembly played in the tax objection movement.

[57] Quoted in Wellenreuther, *Glaube und Politik*, p. 369.

[58] *Ibid.*, pp. 384-86, 388, 389.

[59] Wellenreuther (*ibid.*, p. 358) speaks of the 'basically new positions' that the *Quäkerprediger* came up with in 1755 in connection with the peace testimony and Friends' *Obrigkeitsdoktrin*. See also pp. 217, 267. In his article 'The Quest for Harmony,' p. 562, note 68, he states that (along with William Frost) I have expressed in my book *Pacifism in the United States* . . . (1968) 'traditional opinion,' namely, 'that the revival group's concept of the peace testimony had held sway since the founding of Pennsylvania.' Rereading what I wrote in that volume Wellenreuther's view does not seem to me correct (unless it is that I failed to make myself clear). See pp. 138, 141, 944.

Chapter XI   *(pages 132-141)*
The Quaker as Magistrate in Colonial Rhode Island

[1] D. Elton Trueblood, *The People called Quakers*, New York, 1966, p. 4.

[2] David W. Jordan, '"God's Candle within Government": Quakers and Politics in Early Maryland,' *WMQ*, vol. XXXIX, no. 4 (October 1982), pp. 631ff, 637, 643, 644.

[3] Trueblood, *ibid.*

[4] Cf. Sydney V. James, *Colonial Rhode Island: A History*, New York, 1975, p. 40: 'So many Friends occupied high offices that historians, uncritically believing some accusations made at the time, have written of their "controlling" Rhode Island by 1670 or of a Quaker party capturing the government a couple of years later. There was no such party, however, although there may have been something of a religious block vote.'

[5] Rufus M. Jones *et al.*, *The Quakers in the American Colonies*, London, 1911, pp. 173, 174. Jones's chapter in this volume entitled 'New England Quakers in Politics' (pp. 171-212) is devoted exclusively to Rhode Island; it remains the most comprehensive treatment of the subject, though by now in some ways outdated.

[6] James, *op. cit.*, p. 216.

[7] Easton was the Committee's chairman. See Jones, *op. cit.*, pp. 174-6.

[8] *Ibid.*, pp. 177ff.

[9] Arthur J. Worrall, 'Persecution, Politics and War: Roger Williams, Quakers, and King Philip's War,' *QH*, vol. LXVI, no. 2 (Autumn 1977), p. 80.

[10] Jones, *op. cit.*, pp. 179-84.

[11] *Ibid.*, p. 179.

[12] *Ibid.*, p. 200. Worrall, *op. cit.*, p. 85, writes of Quaker members of the government during King Philip's War: 'Quaker governor William Coddington signed John Cranston's commission as major of the colony's forces. Deputy-governor John Easton, Walter Clarke, and John Coggeshall, all Friends, were members of a Committee appointed in April 1676 to command Newport's defensive fleet. Walter Clarke became governor in May 1676, and he too signed a commission for Captain Arthur Fenner.' Cranston and Fenner of course were not Friends. The commission Coddington signed for Cranston empowered the latter to exert his 'utmost endeavour to kill, expulse, expel, take and destroy all and every the enemies of this His Majesty's colony'; quoted in Jones, *op. cit.*, p. 188. According to Worrall in his *Quakers in the Colonial Northeast*, Hanover (New Hampshire) and London, 1980, p. 130, John Easton on various occasions not only made military appointments, but also 'approved the expenditure of funds, and commissioned privateers.' Whatever may be said about the irregularity of the first two activities on the part of a Quaker, association with privateering was surely a prohibited occupation deserving disownment if persisted in after discovery.

[13] Quoted in Jones, *op. cit.*, p. 184. Jones defines a ketch as 'a strong two-masted vessel, generally carrying guns.'

[14] *Ibid.*, p. 200.

[15] *Ibid.*, pp. 188, 189. Edmundson adds, 'but the Governor being a Friend (one Walter Clarke) could not give commissions to kill and destroy men.' But it is clear that Edmundson was wrong in thinking Clarke (or probably any other contemporary Quaker politician in the province) objected to doing so. Jones cites further evidence for this on p. 189, n.1.

[16] *An Account of the Life of That Ancient Servant of Jesus Christ, John Richardson*, London, 1757, pp. 128, 129. See above, ch. 5.

[17] Worrall, *Quakers*, p. 129.

[18] Not long before his death in 1733, William Wanton returned to his ancestral Quakerism, remarking on that occasion, 'My father's God is my God and I shall die in the faith of the Quakers.' Quoted in Jones, *op. cit.*, p. 203. He lived, however, in a spirit that seems to have had little in common with the peaceable ethos of Friends (see p. 202).

[19] *Ibid.*, p. 203.

[20] *Ibid.*, p. 204; John Russell Bartlett, *History of the Wanton Family of Newport, Rhode Island*, Providence, 1878, pp. 53-55; Worrall, *Quakers*, pp. 129, 130.

[21] Worrall, *Quakers*, p. 130. Bartlett, *op. cit.*, p. 76, remarks of Gideon Wanton, 'It is evident . . . that, although a Quaker, he was a belligerent one.' See also pp. 69-75.

[22] Jones, *op. cit.*, pp. 205-7. Partridge's military concerns throw an interesting light also on the state of mind of English Friends of his time. The latter must surely have known about these concerns of Partridge's, yet he remained a respected member of the London Meeting for Sufferings. And there indeed he must have become acquainted with another of the Meeting's members, John Hanbury, whose military entrepreneurship (largely clandestine) I have referred to in an earlier chapter.

[23] Worrall, *ibid.*

[24] Jones, *op. cit.*, pp. 207-12. In 1776, Hopkins, no longer of course a Friend, was one of the signatories to the Declaration of Independence. We may note that Hopkins maintained a lifelong friendship with Moses Brown, like him a convert to Quakerism and a friend of the 'patriot' cause, but unlike Hopkins a staunch upholder of the peace testimony.

[25] Worrall, *Quakers*, pp. 130, 131. One of the five was Gideon Wanton, Jr.. Worrall notes that, for lack of evidence, 'we cannot say whether Quaker Assemblymen from Quaker centers like Portsmouth voted for war taxes without scruple.' My guess would be that, at any rate before 1757, some did and some did not. After that date I imagine most, if not all, Quaker Assemblymen voting in this way at least would have felt such 'scruples.' But of course that is merely a supposition.

[26] James, *op. cit.*, p. 224.

Chapter XII (*pages 142-154*)

Quaker Conscientious Objectors and the American Revolution

[1] Robert F. Oaks, 'Philadelphians in Exile: The Problem of Loyalty during the American Revolution,' *PMHB*, vol. XCVI, no. 3 (July 1972), p. 299.

[2] Walter H. Conser, Jr., Ronald M. McCarthy, and David J. Toscano, 'The American Independence Movement, 1765-1775: A Decade of Nonviolent Struggles,' p. 17, in Conser *et al.*, eds., *Resistance, Politics, and the American Struggle for Independence, 1765-1775*, Boulder (Colorado), 1986.

[3] Arthur J. Mekeel, *The Relation of the Quakers to the American Revolution*, Washington, D.C., 1979, p. 48. This monograph, which draws on a wide array of archival sources, including many Quaker records, provides the most comprehensive account of the Society of Friends' activities during the Revolution and the years preceding it. I have profited much from Mekeel's thorough research.

[4] Hermann Wellenreuther, *Glaube und Politik in Pennsylvania 1681-1776: Die Wandlungen der Obrigkeitsdoktrin und des 'Peace Testimony' der Quäker,*

Cologne and Vienna, 1972, pp. 405, 408, 409. The sentiments expressed here by Philadelphia Quakers were of course held by Quakers in general. As London Meeting for Sufferings put it in an epistle sent to New England Friends in November 1774: 'When ye shall hear of wars and rumours of wars, see that ye be not troubled . . . Mix not in the various outward consultations, dwell alone.' Quoted in Mekeel, *op. cit.*, p. 78.

5 William H. Nelson, *The American Tory*, Oxford, 1961, p. 90.

6 Mekeel, *op. cit.*, pp. 71, 92, 93.

7 Isaac Sharpless, *A History of Quaker Government in Pennsylvania:* vol. II, *The Quakers in the Revolution*, Philadelphia, 1900, pp. 125-28; Wellenreuther, *op. cit.*, pp. 414-20; Mekeel, *op. cit.*, pp. 137-40.

8 Quoted in Wellenreuther, *op. cit.*, p. 416. See also Mekeel, *op. cit.*, ch. 7, and C. C. Bonwick, 'English Radicals and American Resistance to British Authority,' pp. 404, 408, 412, in Conser *et al.*, eds., *op. cit.*

9 On 11 May 1775 he wrote to a friend: 'My religious principles, thou art, I presume, sensible, do not admit of my interfering in war, but my love for my country and sense of our just rights is not thereby abated.' Quoted in Henry J. Cadbury, 'Quaker Relief during the Siege of Boston,' *Publications of the Colonial Society of Massachusetts* (Boston), vol. XXXIV (1943): *Transactions 1937-1941*, p. 52. Cadbury's study was also published separately as a pamphlet (Wallingford, Pennsylvania, 1943). We may note Brown was a convinced, not a birthright Friend.

10 Wellenreuther, *op. cit.*, p. 418.

11 Mekeel, *op. cit.*, pp. 214, 217, notes that the Revolutionary authorities treated Quakers more severely in Pennsylvania and in Rhode Island than in the neighbouring areas, a difference that may be attributable to their previous close connection in the former with government.

12 A brief summary of the conclusions on this point of three leading historians of loyalism is given by Joseph S. Tiedemann, 'Queen's County, New York Quakers in the American Revolution: Loyalists or Neutrals?' *Historical Magazine of the Protestant Episcopal Church* (Austin, Texas), vol. LII, no. 3 (September 1983), p. 215.

13 *Rhode Island Quakers in the American Revolution 1775-1790*, [Providence], 1976, p. 30.

14 Tiedemann, *op. cit.*, pp. 224, 225.

15 Cecil B. Currey, 'Eighteenth-Century Evangelical Opposition to the American Revolution: The Case of the Quakers,' *Fides et Historia* (North Newton, Kansas), vol. IV, no. 1 (Fall 1971), p. 28, quoting from an epistle sent by the New England Meeting for Sufferings to the Monthly Meetings, 10 July 1776.

16 Jack D. Marietta in his book *The Reformation of American Quakerism, 1748-1783* (Philadelphia 1984) has argued that the Society's pacifist stand during the Revolution might have been modified if the political circumstances of the conflict had been different. He writes (p. 233): 'Enforcement of the prohibition on military service should not be taken for granted. In the Revolution, military service was more than just another article of discipline; it became a very special case historically, for which exceptions conceivably might have been made.' He goes on to cite the mild reaction of the Society to

its young members who had taken up arms during the Paxton disturbance, as proof it might have been equally, if not more, lax in its treatment of fighting Quakers in the subsequent hostilities. But 'the rigor of the discipline in the past twenty years and the belief that Friends' adversaries in this revolution were their old adversaries from 1763 kept them to the pacifist and neutral line.' Yet, however desirable this might have been, I do not think it at all likely that the Society at this date would ever have allowed fighting Quakers to remain in good standing, unless they had first expressed regret for their action.

[17] Mekeel, *op. cit.*, p. 167. See also pp. 224, 225, 264, 268.

[18] *The Life and Travels of John Pemberton, A Minister of the Gospel of Christ*, London, 1844, pp. 97, 98. See also *A Journal of the Life, Travels and Religious Labours, of William Savery*, ed. Jonathan Evans, London, 1844, p. 6.

[19] Friends were also active in preventing the conscription of freedmen, even though these presumably did not have any conscientious objection to fighting. Tiedemann, *op. cit.*, p. 225, writes of New York Quakers: 'If a freedman were taken by either army, concerned Friends searched after him to make certain he was not forced to bear arms or return to slavery.'

[20] Mekeel, *op. cit.*, pp. 218, 219.

[21] *Ibid.*, p. 251.

[22] *Friends' Miscellany* (Philadelphia), vol. VIII, no. 2 (January 1836), p. 61; *Rhode Island Quakers*, p. 32.

[23] Mekeel, *op. cit.*, pp. 194, 250, 251, 270.

[24] Oaks, *op. cit.*, p. 300.

[25] Arthur J. Worrall, *Quakers in the Colonial Northwest*, Hanover (New Hampshire) and London, 1980, p. 144. Tiedemann (*op. cit.*, p. 225) gives an interesting instance of Friends' strictness in this regard: 'When a young Friend from Queens . . . decided on becoming a merchant in New York, other Friends cautioned him against going because of the temptations that were present to purchase prize goods. When he refused to heed their advice, they anxiously checked on all his transactions.'

[26] *Rhode Island Quakers*, p. 33. Further examples of disciplinary action by Quaker Meetings against members who took service on a privateer are given in Dorothy Gilbert Thorne, 'North Carolina Friends and the Revolution,' *The North Carolina Historical Review* (Raleigh, N.C.), vol. XXXVIII, no. 3 (July 1961), pp. 325, 326.

[27] *Biographical Sketches and Anecdotes of Members of the Religious Society of Friends*, Philadelphia, 1870, pp. 326-28. See also Mekeel, *op. cit.*, pp. 195, 234, 235.

[28] *Journal of the Life, Travels and Gospel Labours of That Faithful Servant and Minister of Christ, Job Scott*, Wilmington (Delaware), 1797, p. 50.

[29] See Ezra Michener, *A Retrospect of Early Quakerism; being Extracts from the Records of Philadelphia Yearly Meeting and the Meetings composing it*, Philadelphia, 1860, p. 303-06, for the case of Thomas Watson, a prosperous Quaker farmer in Bucks County who refused to handle the Continental paper currency on grounds of conscience. 'It was made for the express purpose of carrying on a war,' he said. Watson was arrested and tried by the Revolutionary army and only escaped being hanged through the intervention

of his wife with the general in command, who then ordered his release. Refusal of the Continental currency, at any rate on political grounds, had been made a capital offence. See also Mekeel, *op. cit.*, pp. 161, 162, who cites expressions of anger from leading supporters of the Revolutionary cause like Nathaniel Greene and Samuel Adams at Quaker rejection of Continental paper currency.

[30] Quoted in Thorne, *op. cit.*, pp. 331-33. See also Michener, *op. cit.*, p. 287.

[31] Quoted in Mekeel, *op. cit.*, p. 271. See also pp. 189-91, 193, 227, 228, 272, 273. Conscientious objectors who were also punished for not taking the Test figure in A. Day Bradley, 'Quakers in the Lancaster Gaol, 1778,' *Pennsylvania Folklife* (Collegeville, PA), vol. XXXVI, no. 2 (Winter 1986-87), pp. 95, 96.

[32] Toward the end of the 1770s the County Court of Perquimans County (North Carolina), acting on the basis of a recent state law, imposed banishment and forfeiture of estates on Quakers and others refusing the Test; Mekeel, *op. cit.*, p. 272.

[33] *The Defence of Warner Mifflin against Aspersions cast on him on Account of His Endeavours to Promote Righteousness, Mercy and Peace among Mankind*, Philadelphia, 1796, p. 19.

[34] Oaks, *op. cit.*, pp. 305, 324, 325. In Oaks's view (p. 325), 'The infringement on the rights of the Quakers is an early example of a violation of civil liberties . . . Pennsylvania's Revolutionary leaders . . . compromised the ideals for which they said they were fighting.' Many documents on the affair were printed in Thomas Gilpin, ed., *Exiles in Virginia: With Observations on the Conduct of the Society of Friends during the Revolutionary War*, Philadelphia, 1848.

[35] See Mekeel, *op. cit.*, ch. 17.

[36] Quoted in Cadbury, *op. cit.*, p. 57, who however considers Brown was probably mistaken in so thinking (p. 61). Cadbury's study gives a detailed description of Quaker relief activities during and after the siege of Boston.

[37] Thorne, *op. cit.*, pp. 336-39; Seth B. Hinshaw, *The Carolina Quaker Experience 1665-1985: An Interpretation*, [Greensboro, North Carolina], 1984, pp. 50-54.

[38] Kenneth Alan Radbill, 'Socioeconomic Background of Nonpacifist Quakers during the American Revolution,' unpublished Ph.D. dissertation, University of Arizona, 1971, pp. viii, 123-25.

[39] The single Quaker Meeting in Georgia – at Wrightsborough – seems, because of its isolation from the rest of the Society, to have been peculiarly susceptible during the Revolutionary War to deviancy from the peace testimony on the part of its young men. As many as 20 of them were 'dealt with' on this account: a large number for a small Meeting. See Robert Scott Davis, Jr., ed., 'The Wrightsborough Quakers and the American Revolution,' *The Southern Friend* (Greensboro), vol. IV, no. 2 (Autumn 1982), pp. 3, 4.

[40] Mekeel's book contains, scattered among its pages, a lot of information on disownment (as well as on the wartime legislation covering militia and cognate services required by the Revolutionary administration). Among a number of items dealing with 'military' disownment, I would mention only Gilbert Cope, 'Chester County Quakers during the Revolution,' *Bulletins of the Chester County Historical Society 1902-3*, pp. 15-26, which pages are entirely devoted to that subject.

[41] See Charles Wetherill, *History of the Religious Society of Friends called by Some the Free Quakers, in the City of Philadelphia*, [Philadelphia], 1894; also Mekeel, *op. cit.*, ch. 16.

[42] Wetherill, *op. cit.*, pp. 47, 48.

[43] Webster King Wetherill, 'The Fighting Quakers,' *Proceedings of the Numismatic and Antiquarian Society of Philadelphia for the Years 1919, 1920, 1921*, vol. XXIX (1922), pp. 73, 74. The flag maker was of course 'Betsy' Ross.

[44] We hear after hostilities were over of at least one prominent Free Quaker, Owen Biddle, formerly a colonel of militia and a member of the Board of War of Pennsylvania, being received back into membership of Philadelphia Monthly Meeting – of course after making acknowledgment of error. He subsequently played an active role in the affairs of the Society. See Radbill, *op. cit.*, pp. 108, 110, 111.

[45] Richard Bauman, *For the Reputation of Truth: Politics, Religion, and Conflict among Pennsylvania Quakers 1750-1800*, Baltimore and London, 1971, pp. 186-88.

[46] Quoted in Howard H. Brinton, *Quaker Journals: Varieties of Religious Experience among Friends*, Wallingford, 1972, p. 65.

Chapter XIII   *(pages 155-165)*
Quaker Pacifism in the United States between the Revolution and the Civil War

[1] Richard Bauman, *For the Reputation of Truth: Politics, Religion, and Conflict among Pennsylvania Quakers 1750-1800*, Baltimore and London, 1971, pp. 175, 183 ff.

[2] Arthur J. Mekeel, *The Relation of the Quakers to the American Revolution*, Washington, D.C., 1979, pp. 315-27; Arthur J. Worrall, *Quakers in the Colonial Northeast*, Hanover (New Hampshire) and London, 1980, pp. 144, 145; Jack D. Marietta, *The Reformation of American Quakerism, 1748-1783*, Philadelphia, 1984, p. 267.

[3] I am indebted to Christopher Densmore for a copy of his article illustrating the Quakers' attitude on this question ('The Peace Testimony in Erie County, 1827: Talcutt Patching and the Quakers') in the newsletter of the Buffalo Friends Meeting (1986). Patching, though a Freewill Baptist by convince-ment, attended Quaker Meeting and adopted Quaker pacifism along with Quaker costume and language – yet if Densmore's identification is correct (as it seems to be) he continued to draw his army pension as a wounded veteran of the War of 1812. When in 1827 the visiting minister from England, Thomas Shillitoe, chided him with this, he said he accepted it 'not so much for his own use' as to diminish the amount of money the government could spend on military defence. His answer appeared far from satisfactory either to Shillitoe or to Erie County Friends. Later Patching broke with Quakers to found his own sect; he was indeed a somewhat troubled spirit who evidently found it difficult to submit to the Society's discipline.

[4] Richard Wilson Renner, 'Conscientious Objection and the Federal Government, 1787-1792,' *Military Affairs* (Manhattan, Kansas), vol. XXXVIII, no. 4 (December 1974), pp. 142-44. See also R. R. Russell, 'Development of Conscientious Objector Recognition in the United States,' *The George Washington Law Review* (Washington, D.C.), vol. XX, no. 4 (March 1952), pp. 414-17; Stephen M. Kohn, *Jailed for Peace: The History of American Draft Law Violators, 1658-1895*, Westport (Connecticut) and London, 1986, pp. 10, 11, 14.

[5] Sometimes militia delinquents did not have the alternative of distraint of property but were put straightaway in jail. This seems to have happened at any rate in New York state. See the account of the arrest and imprisonment in 1839 of four young New York Quakers for refusing to pay their militia fines; printed in the *Dutchess County Historical Society Year Book* (Poughkeepsie, New York), vol. LXX (1985), p. 50, from the original manuscript. 'They got along very comfortably' in confinement, according to this account, while the village constable and neighbours were friendly. Their sentence of 21 days was cut short after a week when relatives had successfully intervened at Albany.

[6] That Quakers were still subject in the late 1850s to militia fines is illustrated in the records of the Oswego Monthly Meeting (Hicksite) in New York state, as cited in Alson Van Wagner, 'Dutchess Quakers maintain Their Testimony against Military Participation,' *ibid.*, p. 56. According to the author of this article, payment of a militia fine was no longer followed by any disciplinary action on the part of the offender's Meeting. Moreover, throughout the period surveyed, '1829 through 1864,' 'it appears a young Quaker might never have been brought up to pay a fine and, if he had been, it probably was a once-in-a-lifetime event,' despite the fact of his being theoretically liable by state law to serve annually in the militia from the age of 18 to 45. 'It looks as if enforcement of the law was extremely erratic if not capricious.' See also *ibid.*, pp. 52 and *passim*.

[7] See, for example, *Autobiography of William Hobbs*, Indianapolis, 1962 edn., pp. 7, 8, and William H. Coffin, 'Settlement of the Friends in Kansas,' *Transactions of the Kansas State Historical Society, 1901-1902*, Topeka, 1902, pp. 332-35, 341-43. Also the interesting letter from the Kansas Quaker Richard Mendenhall, dated 27 July 1856 and printed in the *Bond of Brotherhood* (London), N.S., no. 76 (November 1856), p. 62. In Kansas, Mendenhall writes, 'it requires close exercise of faith for a man of peace to maintain his principles . . . If defensive warfare *could* be justified in any case, it would seem to be so in the present case . . . Some of our number have been threatened with violence . . . We are sensible that our position [as Quakers] is one liable to trial . . . Doubtless it is only by a strict adherence to Christian faith, . . . that we shall be enabled to pursue the right course.'

[8] See William Gribbin, *The Churches Militant: The War of 1812 and American Religion*, New Haven and London, 1973, pp. 120-27 for Quaker pacifism during the war.

[9] John H. Schroeder, *Mr. Polk's War: American Opposition and Dissent, 1846-1848*, Madison (Wisconsin), 1973, p. 112.

[10] John Jackson, *Reflections on Peace and War*, Philadelphia, 1846, ch. 4.

Anna Davis Hallowell, *James and Lucretia Mott: Life and Letters*, Boston, 1884, pp. 290, 291.

I have dealt in some detail with this subject in my article, 'The Peace Testimony in "a Garden Enclosed",' *QH*, vol. LIV, no. 2 (Autumn 1965), pp. 67-80. I think the subject deserves more attention than I was able to give it there.

The Friend (Philadelphia), 30 August 1834.

Ibid., 13 September 1834.

Letter to Richard Mott, 15 November 1840, in *The Letters of John Greenleaf Whittier*, ed. John B. Pickard, Cambridge (Massachusetts) and London, 1975, vol. I, p. 467.

Quoted in Otelia Cromwell, *Lucretia Mott*, Cambridge (Massachusetts), 1958, p. 111.

E.g., the saintly Quaker bookseller, Isaac T. Hopper, disowned by the Hicksite Meeting in New York in which White then held sway. The adverse effect White's rigid stand on this issue had on a young man who contemplated joining Friends comes out in the pamphlet entitled *Correspondence between Oliver Johnson and George F. White, A Minister of the Society of Friends*, New York, 1841.

Letters to Moses Austin Cartland, 15 March 1840, and Richard Mott, 15 November 1840, in Whittier, *Letters*, vol. I, pp. 393, 467. Italics in the original. Whittier of course also disagreed with the nonresistants in their eschewal of politics. His own abolitionism found expression in warm support first for the Liberty Party and then for the Republican Party.

Edmund Quincy (editor) in *The Non-Resistant* (Boston), vol. III, no. 3 (10 February 1841).

Henry C. Wright, *Six Months at Graeffenberg; with Conversations in the Saloon, on Nonresistance and Other Subjects*, London, 1845, pp. 164-66.

Odell Richardson Reuben, 'Peace against Justice: A Nineteenth-Century Dilemma of Quaker Conscience,' unpublished Ph.D. dissertation, Duke University, 1970, pp. 50-55, 100 ff. The dissertation deals largely with Whittier and his attitude to war and slavery.

Letter to W. L. Garrison, 15 January 1860, in Whittier, *Letters*, vol. II, pp. 447, 448. Cf. Reuben, *op. cit.*, pp. 120-25. In his poem on Brown Whittier had written *inter alia* the following line: 'And they who blamed the bloody hand forgave the loving heart.' For the Quaker poet Brown was a martyr, though mistaken in the means he had chosen to achieve his righteous purpose.

Dana Greene, ed., *Lucretia Mott: Her Complete Speeches and Sermons*, New York and Toronto, 1980, pp. 261, 262.

Chapter XIV *(pages 166-183)*
Quaker Conscientious Objectors in the American Civil War

Letter dated 15 September 1863, *Friends' Intelligencer* (Philadelphia), vol. XX, no. 30 (3 October 1863), p. 474.

[2] See, for example, *The Friend* (Philadelphia), 23 August 1862. This paper was the organ of the Orthodox branch of the Society. For a brief survey of the attitude of Orthodox Quakers to the war, see Thomas D. Hamm, *The Transformation of American Quakerism: Orthodox Friends, 1800-1907*, Bloomington and Indianapolis, 1988, pp. 66-69.

[3] Frederick B. Tolles, ed., 'Two Quaker Memorials for Abraham Lincoln,' *BFHA*, vol. XLVI, no. 1 (1957), p. 44.

[4] *Ibid.*, pp. 42, 44.

[5] Letter to her sister, Martha Wright, 12 September 1863, quoted in Margaret Hope Bacon, *Valiant Friend: The Life of Lucretia Mott*, New York, 1980, p. 183.

[6] Quoted in *ibid.*, p. 180.

[7] Odell Richardson Reuben, 'Peace against Justice: A Nineteenth-Century Dilemma of Quaker Conscience,' unpublished Ph.D. dissertation, Duke University, 1970, p. 144. (Reuben is dealing primarily with Whittier.)

[8] *Ibid.*, p. 170: 'One implication of Whittier's position is a double morality, or two categories of Christians. One group of Christians might engage in fighting in the Civil War, presumably with justice. The other group of Christians was justified in taking the stand of a vocational pacifist and not fighting. Whittier's position, thus, permits a double ethic for Christians.' See also pp. 151-53, 155-59, 169.

[9] *The Letters of John Greenleaf Whittier*, ed. John B. Pickard, Cambridge (Massachusetts) and London, 1975, vol. III, p. 19. Some of Whittier's wartime utterances were, however, rather ambiguous. Roland H. Woodwell in his biography *John Greenleaf Whittier*, Haverhill (Massachusetts), 1985, pp. 307, 308, cites an instance of this. 'A gunboat,' he writes, 'was being built [at a shipyard] in Newburyport with oak timber supplied by a Quaker who asked Whittier if selling timber for a gunboat was consistent with the peace doctrines of the Society of Friends. Whittier's reply was "If thee does furnish all of that oak timber thee spoke of, be sure that it is all sound".' Did Whittier intend to advise against, or for, a transaction of this kind?

[10] R. R. Russell, 'Development of Conscientious Objector Recognition in the United States,' *The George Washington Law Review* (Washington, D.C.), vol. XX, no. 4 (March 1952), pp. 418-20. The standard work by Edward Needles Wright, *Conscientious Objectors in the Civil War*, Philadelphia, 1931, contains detailed information concerning conscription laws as well as most other aspects of conscientious objection during that period.

[11] Wright's monograph contains many tributes from contemporary Friends to the leniency displayed by the civil authorities – and sometimes (though by no means always) by the army as well. To give just one example taken from a report of a Committee of New England Yearly Meeting, dated 11 June 1864, and cited in Wright, *op. cit.*, p. 194: 'In every case where the Committee have had interviews with the officers of the Government, both civil and military, they have been uniformly treated with kindness, and respect, and their representations listened to patiently and respectfully.'

[12] *The Friend*, 1 August 1863.

[13] An extraordinary degree of tolerance was displayed by Dover Monthly Meeting in North Carolina in the case of one D. W. C. Benbow, who had hired a substitute in April 1862 and seemingly violated the Quaker discipline in other ways, too. See Richard L. Zuber, 'Conscientious Objectors in the Confederacy: The Quakers of North Carolina,' *QH*, vol. LXVII, no. 1 (Spring 1978), pp. 7, 8.

[14] *Ibid.*, pp. 13, 14; Patrick Sowle, 'The Quaker Conscript in Confederate North Carolina,' *QH*, vol. LVI, no. 2 (Autumn 1967), pp. 95, 96. According to Sowle (p. 105), many of those who had purchased exemption by paying the statutory fine of $500 'later regretted that they had compromised their principles.'

[15] Jacquelyn Sue Nelson, 'The Society of Friends in Indiana during the Civil War,' unpublished Ph.D. dissertation, Ball State University, 1984. See also John William Buys, 'Quakers in Indiana in the Nineteenth Century,' unpublished Ph.D. dissertation, University of Florida, 1973, pp. 151-58, for the Civil War period. (Also Nelson's articles 'The Military Response of the Society of Friends in Indiana,' *Indiana Magazine of History* [Bloomington], vol. LXXXI, no. 2 [June 1985], pp. 101-30; 'Fighting Friends,' *Madison County Historical Gazette* [Anderson, Indiana], vol. XIX, no. 7 [July 1985], p. 2; 'Military and Civilian Support of the Civil War by the Society of Friends in Indiana,' *QH*, vol. LXXVI, no. 1 [Spring 1987], pp. 50-61.)

[16] Nelson, Ph.D. diss., pp. 163, 164.

[17] Two cases of this are given by Wright, *op. cit.*, pp. 164, 165.

[18] Nelson, *op. cit.*, pp. 78, 79. She cites here the case of Eli Patterson who entered the army voluntarily 'on the express condition that he not be required to bear arms but instead be assigned to hospital duty. When confronted by the Monthly Meeting after the war, Patterson asserted that his request was strictly adhered to by military authorities.' Among the clearly noncombatant positions occupied by Quakers who accepted conscript service in the army Nelson lists the following: surgeon, nurse, hospital orderly, ambulance driver, medical cadet, and cook. More objectionable certainly from the Quaker point of view but still essentially noncombatant were occupations such as bugler, blacksmith, carpenter, teamster, quartermaster, etc., which a few Quaker conscripts accepted for their army service. Sowle, *op. cit.*, pp. 95, 96, also gives instances of Quakers in North Carolina accepting various forms of noncombatant service offered by the Confederate authorities in lieu of bearing arms. Such service included orderly duty in military hospitals as well as employment in the state salt mine at Wilmington either in person or by substitute. The Meeting for Sufferings discouraged acceptance and, 'consequently, only a small group of Quakers engaged in non-military work.' It seems, too, that the Confederate authorities regarded employment in factories producing such items as ironware or wool (some of these owned by Quakers) as work of national importance carrying with it exemption from the draft. See also Wright, *op. cit.*, p. 146.

[19] Wright, *op. cit.*, pp. 215, 216, citing from the minutes of the Meeting for Sufferings of the Philadelphia (Orthodox) Yearly Meeting, 13 April 1865.

[20] Discussion of the issue appeared in the columns of all three Quaker papers: the *Friend*, the *Friends' Intelligencer*, and the *Friends' Review*. The latter journal has been described as 'probably the most effective instrument in promoting adherence to pacifism among Gurneyites,' i.e., evangelical Quakers, during the Civil War; Richard E. Wood, 'Evangelical Quaker Acculturation in the Upper Mississippi Valley, 1850-1875,: *QH*, vol. LXXVI, no. 2 (Fall 1987), p. 139.

[21] Wright, *op. cit.*, p. 126, says of Stanton, he 'was . . . sympathetically inclined toward those scrupulous of bearing arms, and he at all times showed an unusual degree of patience in dealing with matters of conscience.'

[22] *Ibid.*, pp. 74, 75.

[23] Sowle, *op. cit.*, pp. 94-96, 103; Zuber, *op. cit.*, pp. 17, 18.

[24] Zuber, *op. cit.*, pp. 13, 14.

[25] Cf. Sowle, *op. cit.*, pp. 99, 101, who reckons about 50 'War Quakers' were absolutists. But I am not sure if this figure is not too high.

[26] This punishment, one of the severest then in use in the army, consisted in seating a man on the ground, tying his knees and pressing his arms over them, and thus immobilising both hands and feet. He was left in this position for several hours thereafter.

[27] Wright, *op. cit.*, p. 179.

[28] Cited in *ibid.*, pp. 178, 179. (In a few places I have inserted punctuation and corrected the spelling.) The objectors mentioned in the petition were birthright Quakers who had taken the absolutist position and were willing to accept only unconditional exemption.

[29] Cited in *ibid.*, pp. 116, 117.

[30] Zuber, *op. cit.*, pp. 9-12.

[31] *Ibid.*, p. 10, where Zuber cites as an example of this the case of Joshua Davis, whose former Monthly Meeting at Black Creek, despite his no longer being a member, nevertheless backed his application for exemption as a conscientious objector. His claim was eventually turned down, and he was drafted. How Davis behaved after this is not known.

[32] Roy S. Nicholson, *Wesleyan Methodism in the South. Being the Story of Eighty-Six Years of Reform and Religious Activities in the South as conducted by the American Wesleyans*, Syracuse (New York), 1933, pp. 106-10. For pacifist pronouncements made by Wesleyan Methodists during the antebellum period, see Donald W. and Lucille S. Dayton, 'An Historical Survey of Attitudes toward War and Peace within the American Holiness Movement,' in Paul Hostetler, ed., *Perfect Love and War: A Dialogue on Christian Holiness and the Issues of War and Peace*, Nappanee (Indiana), 1974, pp. 136, 137. It is clear that in that period some Wesleyan Methodists already espoused absolute pacifism and conscientious objection, though I presume they remained a minority.

[33] Fred Albert Shannon, *The Organization and Administration of the Union Army 1861-1865*, Cleveland, 1928, vol. II, p. 249.

[34] 'The United States *versus* Pringle: The Record of a Quaker Conscience,' *The Atlantic Monthly* (Boston and New York), vol. CXI, no. 2 (February 1913), pp. 145-162. The pamphlet edition of 1962, published at Pendle Hill,

Wallingford (Pennsylvania), contains a valuable foreword by Henry J. Cadbury.

[35] But cf. Shannon, *op. cit.*, vol, II, p. 256, n. 1178, and Eugene C. Murdock, *One Million Men: The Civil War in the North*, Madison (Wisconsin), 1971, p. 213. Both authors have cast doubt on the authenticity of some of Pringle's complaints concerning his treatment while in the army, to my mind without sufficient justification. But it is true that parts of the narrative read as if they were the result of a later rewriting by Pringle rather than reproducing the actual words of the original diary.

[36] Citations from Pringle, *op. cit.*, pp. 145, 156, 157, 160.

[37] Wright, *op. cit.*, pp. 124, 194.

[38] Shannon, *op. cit.*, vol. II, p. 260.

[39] Sowle, *op. cit.*, p. 103; 'The North Carolina Friends presented the best record of adherence to [pacifist] principle of all the Yearly Meetings.' See also Zuber, *op. cit.*, p. 15.

[40] *The Friend* (New York), vol. I, no. 6 (June 1866), p. 85. The paper subsequently printed opinions *pro* and *con* disownment of Friends who had enlisted during the war; see no. 6 (June), p. 87; no. 7 (July), p. 99; no. 8 (August), p. 119; no. 10 (October), p. 147.

[41] Nelson's dissertation, *op. cit.*, pp. 44 ff., 57-65, 174-76, contains interesting statistical information on these matters with regard to Indiana Friends. Perhaps she is right in claiming as 'the major finding' of her work 'that far more Quakers from Indiana took up arms in the Civil War than was generally known' (p. i*a*), still the picture remains a little unclear despite her painstaking researches. According to her findings (p. 187), out of 1184 Indiana Friends who served in the army during the Civil War, 148 were disowned, 220 expressed to their Meetings regret for their wartime conduct, 584 were not disciplined, while 234 died in the course of hostilities. See also pp. 173-78, 188, 194. The largest number of Quaker soldiers was drawn from those aged 18 to 21 (p. 329). At least 2170 Indiana Quakers had claimed to be conscientious objectors, 'nearly 1000 more than the total who bore arms'; yet, Nelson points out, 'in at least eight Indiana counties the number of uniformed Quakers exceeded the number of "conscientious" Friends' (p. 57). I may note that the greater part of her dissertation is in fact devoted to Quaker support of the war effort – either in the army or on 'the home front.' Our knowledge of other areas of the country is even more nebulous. In contrast to Indiana, for instance, the Kansas Preparative Meeting records reveal only three members who joined the Union army, despite the strong antislavery sentiments of its roughly 200 members. See Cecil B. Currey, 'The Devolution of Quaker Pacifism: A Kansas Case Study, 1860-1955' *Kansas History* (Topeka), vol. VI, no. 2 (Summer 1983), pp. 120, 121.

[42] See Nelson, *op. cit.*, ch. 3. She remarks, on the basis of a number of manuscript letters she has examined by 'Friends in uniform,' 'that freeing the slaves prompted Quakers to enroll in the armed forces was conspicuously absent from the letters written by the soldiers themselves.' This, I find, rather surprising.

[43] Daniel Wooten to Miriam Green, 11 July 1861, in William C. Kashatus III, 'Conflicts of Conscience: The Richmond Quakers face the Civil War, 1860-1865,' *Indiana Military History Journal* (Indianapolis), vol. V, no. 3 (October 1980), p. 29.

[44] Quoted in Bacon, *op. cit.*, p. 180. Davis was eventually disowned by his Monthly Meeting, even though he belonged to the more tolerant Hicksite branch of the Society.

[45] Whittier, *Letters,* vol. III, p. 21.

[46] For Indiana Quakers, see Nelson, diss., ch. 4.

[47] See, for example, *Recollections of Lydia S. (Mitchell) Hinchman*, n.p.p. (privately printed), 1929, p. 45. Bliss Forbush, *A History of Baltimore Yearly Meeting of Friends* . . ., Sandy Spring (Maryland), 1972, p. 76, writes of the situation in 1863: 'Quaker women in most Meetings met to make bandages, cook food, and knit garments for the soldiers and refugees. Friends loaded wagons with supplies and drove to hospital or camps . . . Once [two Quaker women] called at the White House after unloading their supplies and were received with expressions of gratitude by President Lincoln for what they had done for the soldiers.'

[48] I shall deal with the most articulate of these Civil War tax objectors (Joshua Maule) in the next chapter. Maule deducted from his tax payment 8½%, which was the amount he believed the government would allocate to war purposes.

[49] Quoted in Wright, *op. cit.*, pp. 218, 219. Payment of bounties was voluntary, although of course those who refused to contribute often incurred hostility from their community. Elsewhere Wright quotes from a report from a Committee of the North Carolina Meeting for Sufferings, dated 3 August 1863, urging members not to accede to the Confederate government's 'demand for the tenth part of the produce of our lands' since, so far as it could see, this was 'designed for the direct support of the army.' Thus in the Committee's view, 'It is strictly a war measure.' It seems, however, that Friends reconsidered the matter and in the end decided this tithe should be paid. *Op. cit.*, pp. 110, 111.

[50] Nelson, *op. cit.*, p. 175. See also pp. 115-17.

[51] Arthur G. Sharp, 'Victims of Two Enemies: The Quakers in the Civil War,' *Evangelical Friend* (Newberg, Oregon), vol. XI, no. 3 (November 1978), p. 7; also his 'Men of Peace: Conscientious Objectors face Civil War,' *Civil War Times Illustrated* (Harrisburg, Pennsylvania), vol. XXI, no. 4 (June 1982), p. 37.

[52] Quoted in Zuber, *op. cit.*, p. 19, from the Minutes of North Carolina Yearly Meeting, 1865.

Chapter XV   *(pages 184-196)*
Quakers and War Taxes: An Overview

[1] Hirst, p. 73; William C. Braithwaite, *The Second Period of Quakerism* (1919), Cambridge, 1961 edn., p. 601.

[2] *A Short Account of the Life of Mr. John Pennyman* . . ., London, 1696, p. 19. Pennyman had become a Quaker in 1658.

[3] Braithwaite, *op. cit.*, p. 601, note 4, cites a minute issued by the influential Morning Meeting of London Friends in July 1695 in connection with the recently imposed duties on marriages. 'The Minute said that tribute was to be paid, without disputing or questioning the use to which the Government put it.'

[4] Henry J. Cadbury, *Friendly Heritage: Letters from the Quaker Past*, Norwalk (Connecticut), 1972, pp. 88-90. Cadbury says of Penn's letter, 'its genuineness can hardly be doubted even by those who might wish he had never written it.'

[5] *An Account of the Life of That Ancient Servant of Jesus Christ, John Richardson*, London, 1757, pp. 128, 129.

[6] Arthur J. Worrall, *Quakers in the Colonial Northeast*, Hanover (New Hampshire) and London, 1980, p. 132, comments on this: 'Like the complicity of Rhode Island Quaker leaders in wartime finance, one is struck by the inconsistency of struggling to avoid church tax on the one hand, yet paying war tax on the other. But the war tax was not continuous, as was a church tax . . . In short, political realism dictated the course Friends adopted.'

[7] Story, who was a staunch upholder of the peace testimony, had defended his position *vis-à-vis* war taxation in an interview he had had with Peter the Great during the latter's visit to England in 1697. Asked by the Tsar what possible use Quakers could be to the state if they would not fight, Story had replied: 'We can and do by His [i.e., Christ's] example readily and cheerfully pay unto every Government, in every form, where we happen to be subjects, such sums and assessments as are required of us by the respective laws under which we live . . . We, by so great an example, do freely pay our taxes to Caesar, who of right hath the direction and application of them, to the various ends of government, to peace or to war, as it pleaseth him or as need may be, according to the constitution or laws of his kingdom, and in which we as subjects have no direction or share; for it is Caesar's part to rule in justice and in truth, but ours to be subject and mind our own business and not to meddle with his.' Quoted in Braithwaite, *op. cit.*, pp. 601, 602. This classic statement of the standpoint on war taxation of early English Friends does not, of course, altogether fit the situation in Pennsylvania where Quakers were not merely 'subjects' with 'no direction or share' in drawing up the constitution and laws of the province but themselves took part in framing that constitution and the provincial laws based on it.

[8] See Jack Donald Marietta, 'William Rakestraw: Pacifist Pamphleteer and Party Servant,' *PMHB*, vol. XCVIII, no. 1 (January 1974), pp. 53-57. In 1947 Emily E. Moore uncovered the author's true identity; until then the pamphlet was thought to be the work of a Massachusetts Quaker named Thomas Maule. Thomas Story wrote a refutation of Rakestraw's views which, however, was not published.

[9] *Ibid.*, pp. 55-57.

[10] 'Pastorius' Essay on Taxes,' *PMHB*, vol. XVIII (1934), no. 3, pp. 255-59.

[11] What one does through another is accounted as done by oneself.

[12] But Peter and John said to them in reply: 'Is it right in God's eyes for us to obey you rather than God? Judge for yourselves.'

[13] Edwin Bronner, *War Tax Concerns: A Quaker History*, Washington, D.C., 1986, pp. 8, 9. A slightly different version of this pamphlet has appeared as 'War Tax Refusal in American Quaker History' in *The Friends' Quarterly* (Ashford, Kent), vol. XXIV, no. 5 (January 1987), pp. 202-13.

[14] Quoted in Bronner, *War Tax Concerns*, p. 11.

[15] Ezra Michener, *A Retrospect of Early Quakerism; being Extracts from the Records of Philadelphia Yearly Meeting and the Meetings composing it*, Philadelphia, 1860, pp. 302, 303.

[16] Marietta, *The Reformation of American Quakerism, 1748-1783*, Philadelphia, 1984, p. 266.

[17] Arthur J. Mekeel, *The Relation of the Quakers to the American Revolution*, Washington, D.C., 1979, p. 145. Brown was writing in September 1775. See also pp. 232, 233.

[18] *Ibid.*, p. 231.

[19] *Ibid.*, pp. 161, 259, 261, 265, 266, 269, 270.

[20] 'Under the present commotions' was the phrase often used by Friends to describe the Revolutionary War situation.

[21] *Ibid.*, pp. 262, 266, 268-70.

[22] Bronner, *War Tax Concerns*, p. 12. For a contemporary description of such 'sufferings,' see for example the 'essay' drawn up by Western Quarterly Meeting (part of Philadelphia Yearly Meeting) in December 1781 and printed in Michener, *op. cit.*, pp. 386-92. Complaint is made there *inter alia* of 'the insolent conduct of collectors and others under them' (p. 390). They had levied distraints on poor Quaker farmers, 'who live on poorish land, and, in prosperous times, just lived reputably above want; but are . . . reduced by the conduct of the collectors, under the sanction of law, as to have no cow left, and some but one horse, some no sheep, and greatly stripped of other utensils, clothing, etc.' (p. 392).

[23] Mekeel, *op. cit.*, p. 234. According to Mekeel, the New England Meeting for Sufferings threatened with disownment any Friends who paid taxes 'expressly or especially for the support of war, whether called for in money, provisions, clothing, or otherwise.' I cannot cite an instance of this threat ever having actually been carried out nor does such strictness appear to have been general throughout the Society at this time. Of course there was never any question, even in New England, of the discipline being applied to those who paid mixed taxes, since this was known to have been the long accepted practice of Friends.

[24] The Free Quakers of course were also in favour of unconditional payment of all taxes. This comes out in the pages of the *Serious Address* which a Free Quaker sympathiser, Isaac Grey of New Garden Monthly Meeting in Pennsylvania, published in 1778.

[25] MS. in the Haverford College Quaker Collection.

[26] *Journal of the Life, Travels and Gospel Labours of That Faithful Servant and Minister of Christ, Job Scott*, Wilmington (Delaware), 1794, p. 63. See also Mekeel, *op. cit.*, pp. 233, 234.

348

27 Hirst, pp. 212-15.

28 See John S. Stephens, 'Nathaniel Morgan of Ross,' *JFHS*, vol. XLVI (1954), no. 1.

29 Mekeel, *op. cit.*, pp. 314, 315.

30 After a brief survey based on Yearly Meeting disciplines printed during the 19th century, Bronner (*op. cit.*, p. 16) sums up as follows: 'Five of the Yearly Meeting groups included statements about war taxes in their *Disciplines* at the beginning of the century, and three did not. None of the Yearly Meetings modified these statements until after the Civil War, but the Wilburite Yearly Meeting in Ohio was the only one of the group to continue publishing its statement when the United States entered the First World War.'

31 Warner Mifflin had refused to use imported products during the Revolution – not indeed on account of any duty on them but because importation might have involved armed defence of the vessel on which they were being carried. 'In a time of national hostility,' he wrote, 'those [things] I am so fond of come . . . at a manifest risk of the lives of fellow men.' Like Joshua Evans a little later, he was forced however, while away from home, to make an exception in the case of salt. See *The Defence of Warner Mifflin against Aspersions cast on Him on Account of His Endeavours to promote Righteousness, Mercy and Peace among Mankind*, Philadelphia, 1796, pp. 19, 20.

32 Joshua Maule, *Transactions and Changes in the Society of Friends, and Incidents in the Life and Experience of Joshua Maule*, Philadelphia, 1886, esp. pp. 220-24, 233-46, 261-65, 282-85.

33 Cf. Bronner, *op. cit.*, p. 18: 'While it would be useful to make a careful study of the minutes of each Yearly Meeting, as well as articles in the Friends' papers and references to taxes in the journals and letters for the [Civil War] period, this has not been done.'

34 *Ibid.*, p. 19.

Chapter XVI (*pages 197-206*)
The Shaker Peace Testimony: A Variant of Quaker Pacifism

1 Quoted in Edward Deming Andrews, *The People called Shakers*, New York, 1953, p. 212. For Shaker pacifism during the American Revolution, see Clarke Garrett, *Spirit Possession and Popular Religion: From the Camisards to the Shakers*, Baltimore and London, 1987, pp. 167, 174-76.

2 Mary L. Richmond, ed., *Shaker Literature: A Bibliography*, Hancock (Massachusetts) and Hanover (New Hampshire), 1977, vol. I, pp. 143, 144.

3 James M. Upton, 'The Shakers as Pacifists in the Period between 1812 and the Civil War,' *The Filson Club History Quarterly* (Louisville, Kentucky), vol. XLVIII, no. 3 (July 1973), pp. 267-69. Upton makes use of manuscript sources not utilised by previous writers on the subject.

4 *A Declaration of the Society of People, (commonly called Shakers,) shewing Their Reasons for refusing to aid or abet the Cause of War and Bloodshed, by bearing Arms, paying Fines, hiring Substitutes, or rendering any Equivalent for Military*

Services, Albany, 1815. See also Doris Grumbach, 'American Peaceniks, 150 Years Ago,' *Commonweal* (New York), vol. XCIII, no. 7 (13 November 1970), pp. 164, 165; Richmond, *op. cit.*, vol. I, p. 70.

[5] *Declaration* (Albany), pp. 4-7.

[6] *Ibid.*, pp. 12-15. It is interesting to note the authors' use of phrases made familiar as a result of the French Revolution, e.g. 'the natural rights of man,' 'the friends of man,' etc.

[7] *Ibid.*, p. 19.

[8] *Ibid.*, p. 15.

[9] See Upton, *op. cit.*, pp. 271-82. Also Richmond, *op. cit.*, vol. I, pp. 148-50, 160, 164.

[10] Richmond, *op. cit.*, vol. I, p. 160.

[11] Upton, *op. cit.*, p. 282. According to Upton, 'This is the only reference found concerning military service and the Mexican War.' Shakers regarded the jointly held possessions of their communities as property consecrated to the service of God.

[12] Priscilla J. Brewer, *Shaker Communities, Shaker Lives*, Hanover and London, 1986, p. 174. Brewer's book is limited to communities in New England and eastern New York State. She has summarised the information contained in manuscript lists of Brethren of draft age in 1863 as follows: 'Sabbathday Lake, Maine, reported only four Brethren in this age group, one of whom was chronically ill. Alfred reported seven Brethren, one a cripple; Shirley eight and Harvard four, of whom two were cripples and two partly blind. Canterbury listed twenty-four men in this age group, but counted one with a hernia, two who were blind in one eye, two with maimed hands, one with bad eyes, one subject to fits, two with weak lungs, one with a weak knee, and one partly insane. Enfield, New Hampshire, similarly reported twenty-three Brethren, one third of whom were exemptible due to physical disability. Even if some allowance is made for possible exaggeration in these reports, the situation was grave indeed.'

[13] I have summarised the experiences of Horace S. Taber, a young Shaker conscript from the Shirley (Mass.) community, who was inducted into the army at this time, in my book *Pacifism in the United States* . . . (1968), pp. 828-30. The original manuscript account is in the Western Reserve Historical Society Library in Cleveland (Ohio).

[14] See Thomas D. Clark, *Pleasant Hill in the Civil War*, Pleasant Hill (Kentucky), 1972, *passim*.

[15] Cf. *ibid.*, p. 32: 'Thomas Chaplin accidentally shot himself in the foot as he prepared to join the rebels.'

[16] *Ibid.*, p. 46.

[17] *Ibid.*, p. 53.

[18] Richmond, *op. cit.*, vol. I, p. 144.

[19] Cf. Upton, *op. cit.*, p. 282, who points out that the Ohio communities disagreed with the rest of Shakerism in allowing members to collect army pensions.

[20] *Declaration* (Hartford version), p. 15.

[21] Among such sects were, in the 18th century, the Ephrata community as well as a number of similar small communities established by German immigrants to

Pennsylvania and, in the 19th, the Separatists of Zoar, the Harmonists, and the Inspirationists of Amana. All these groups were German speaking. See my *Pacifism in the United States, passim*. In addition, we may mention the Hopedale joint-stock community in Massachusetts established by the former Universalist minister, Adin Ballou, in 1841. His Hopedalers were less removed from the environing society intellectually than the Shakers were.

Chapter XVII   *(pages 207-214)*
Canadian Quakers, the Militia, and Rebellion

[1] Except for a Meeting at Farnham in Lower Canada (later the province of Quebec), which lasted from 1820 to 1902. It formed part of New York Yearly Meeting.

[2] Gerald M. Craig, *Upper Canada: The Formative Years 1784-1841*, Toronto, 1963, pp. 25, 44.

[3] An example of Quaker scrupulosity in this area can be found in their refusal to take out land which the government had set aside specifically for United Empire Loyalists, since this land was awarded ostensibly for assistance in the British Crown's war effort. To take such lands, Friends argued, constituted a breach of their peace testimony, an action 'inconsistent with our profession.' We know of members being dealt with for this offence: Dorland, for instance, cites a case from 1809.

[4] Arthur Garratt Dorland, *The Quakers in Canada, a History*, Toronto, 1968, pp. 316-19.

[5] See *ibid.*, ch. 7.

[6] Thomas M. F. Gerry, '"Amongst the Assemblies we hope no more": David Willson's Writings on His Separation from the Quakers,' *Journal of Canadian Studies* (Peterborough, Ontario), vol. XX, no. 2 (Summer 1985), pp. 102, 105, 109.

[7] This was John Casey, self-styled 'agent for promoting the establishment of peace societies' and an associate of Noah Worcester and the Massachusetts Peace Society. Casey was active during the 1820s on peace work in Upper Canada. He discusses Willson and the Children of Peace (extremely negatively) in his *Letters, addressed to Several Philanthropic Statesmen and Clergymen; vindicating Civilized and Christian Government, in contradistinction to the Uncivilized and Anti-Christian Institutions . . .*, Buffalo, 1826, pp. 50-53. It is not known for certain if Casey was a British or American subject, but he was presumably the latter. He was also the author of another pacifist work entitled *Universal Peace . . .*, Black Rock [Buffalo], 1827. I am much indebted to Christopher Densmore, Associate Archivist, State University of New York at Buffalo, for supplying me with a xerox of the pages cited above as well as with further data about John Casey's two books. Densmore also sent me a xeroxed extract from the New York *Telescope* (29 October 1826), p. 86, reporting on the readiness of the 'Davidites' to bear arms.

[8] David Willson, *The Practical Life of the Author, from the Year 1801 to 1860*, Newmarket (Ontario), p. 63.

[9] Willson, *A Present to the Teachers and Rulers of Society*, Philadelphia, 1821, p. 3, 14.

[10] Willson, *A Testimony to the People called Quakers*, n.p.p., 1816, p. 6. Italics in the original.

[11] Willson, *The Impressions of the Mind . . .*, Toronto, 1835, pp. 257, 260. In the article, alongside his political egalitarianism he also gave expression to a semi-pacifism when he wrote (on p. 259): 'Till the day cometh that the *universal love of nations and societies* – is preached from the pulpit – the *love of neighbours as ourselves*, and practiced, there will be *peace in no nation under the sun*, for these are the principles or pillars of good government.' Italics in the original.

[12] Ronald John Stagg, 'The Yonge Street Rebellion of 1837: An Examination of the Social Background and a Re-assessment of the Events,' unpublished Ph.D. thesis, University of Toronto, 1976, pp. 205, 211, 212.

[13] See Willson, *The Practical Life of the Author*, p. 61, where, writing in 1860, he confirms that the Children of Peace possessed 'no written test,' 'no written creed,' to which members were required to subscribe. 'They practice no line of distinction whereby any shall or may be excluded from participating with them in the worship of God. They continue in the first principles of union, that all that will come may come, and share alike in the favours of God. They have not varied in principle nor practice from the beginning until now.'

[14] See Dorland, *op. cit.*, pp. 319-23. See also Laura L. Peers, 'The Not So Peaceable Kingdom: Quakers took up Arms in the Rebellion of 1837,' *The Beaver: Exploring Canada's History* (Winnipeg), vol. LXVIII, no. 3 (June-July 1988), pp. 4-9, which aims at rehabilitating the 'handful of Friends' taking part in the uprisings in central and western Upper Canada. This is a legitimate endeavour, but the writer seems to me to exaggerate the significance of the fighting Quakers in the life of the Canadian Society of Friends as a whole.

[15] Arthur Carthew, an Anglican and lieutenant-colonel in the militia, wrote on 2 May 1838 to a friend as follows: 'The people in the neighbourhood of my residence [near Newmarket] are chiefly Quakers, and are, with the exception of one or two, altogether disloyal. Many of them have connections implicated in the Late Rebellion.' Colin Read and Ronald J. Stagg, eds., *The Rebellion of 1837 in Upper Canada: A Collection of Documents*, Don Mills (Ontario), 1985, p. 423.

[16] See the letter from Rev. Thomas Green, Anglican parson in London (Ontario), dated 19 February 1838, in *ibid.*, pp. 364, 365.

[17] Dorland, *op. cit.*, pp. 322, 323. According to Dorland, 'So far as our records go, Joseph Gould and Joshua Doan were the only Quakers who took any prominent part in the Rebellion.' And neither of these young men seems to have been particularly active in the affairs of the Society of which they were 'birthright' members.

[18] Colin Read, *The Rising in Upper Canada, 1837-8: The Duncombe Revolt and After*, Toronto, 1982, pp. 186-88.

[19] Joseph Bevan Braithwaite, *Memoirs of Joseph John Gurney*, 4th edn., Philadelphia, 1859, vol. II, p. 190.

[20] *An Appeal to the Christian Public, on the Inconsistency of War with the Gospel Dispensation, by the 'Society of Friends,' in Canada*, Newmarket, 1869, p. 7.

[21] Thomas P. Socknat, *Witness against War: Pacifism in Canada, 1900-1945*, Toronto, 1987, pp. 21, 30, 33, 36-38, 41, 42, 307. See also Dorland, *op. cit.*, pp. 325-29. Socknat's first chapter on 'Early Pacifist Traditions in Canada' contains much information on the nonsectarian peace movement before 1914. This, however, for the most part might be described as near-pacifist or 'pacificist' rather than as pacifist *sensu stricto*.

[22] Socknat, *op. cit.*, p. 41.

[23] James S. Woodsworth represents in this respect a link between the pre- and postwar periods. A social gospel pacifist before 1914, Woodsworth, moving now gradually from a Christian to an ethical and secular basis for his antiwar position, became an outstanding exponent of the socialist pacifism of the interwar years when the Social Gospel again became a factor in the evolution of the Canadian peace movement. See Kenneth McNaught, *A Prophet in Politics: A Biography of J. S. Woodsworth*, Toronto, 1959, pp. 67, 68; Socknat, *op. cit.*, esp. ch. 4 (II).

Chapter XVIII   *(pages 215-221)*
Irish Quakers in 1798: An Experiment in Nonviolence

[1] Hirst, p. 103. Isabel Grubb sums up the Irish Quakers' attitude at this time: 'They refused, as a whole, to take sides in the war, but submitted to whichever king was in authority.' But they suffered equally from both English and Irish armies. 'Irish Friends' Experiences of War, 1689-92,' *Friends' Quarterly Examiner* (London), April 1916, p. 186.

[2] Hirst, pp. 105, 106. It was particularly William Edmundson, the ex-Cromwellian veteran turned Quaker, who was instrumental in obtaining 'a guard of Irish soldiers' to ward off the attacks of Irish 'thieves, Raparees,' and other violators of the peace. It was not only Friends of course but also their Protestant neighbours who benefited from this protection.

[3] John Punshon, *Portrait in Grey: A Short History of the Quakers*, London, 1984, pp. 153-62. For the related Hannah Barnard case, see my *Pacifism in the United States*, pp. 371-74. In 1800 Barnard, a Friend of American origin, was accused at London Yearly Meeting of doubting 'the divine authority for the Jewish wars, as stated in the Old Testament'; William Rathbone, *A Narrative of Events, that have lately taken place in Ireland among the Society called Quakers* . . ., London, 1804, p. 108. (On p. 529 of my *Pacifism in Europe to 1914* I stated erroneously that Rathbone's book dealt with Irish Quakers in the Rebellion of 1798. This is not so.)

[4] This apt summing up of the situation comes from the work of a Quaker doctor Thomas Hancock: *The Principles of Peace exemplified in the Conduct of the Society of Friends in Ireland, during the Rebellion of the Year 1798; with Some Preliminary and Concluding Observations*, London, 1825, p. 108. Hancock's book, which was based on accounts by Friends who participated 'either as

actors or eye-witnesses, in the scenes . . . depicted,' remains – for all its inadequacies – the chief source for the situation of Irish Quakers during the Rebellion. See also Hirst, pp. 216-24.

5 Joseph Haughton, of Ferns (Wexford), printed in Alice Mary Hodgkin, ed., *Friends in Ireland*, Friends' Tract Association: London, 1910, pp. 20-22. Hancock used Haughton's narrative as one of his main sources: he describes Haughton as 'constitutionally weak in body and timid in mind' (p. 59). Weak and timid or not, Haughton was rightly valued by Hancock for his reliability and his sense for detail.

6 See Hancock, *op. cit.*, pp. 54-56. At Ballitore Mary Leadbeater (*née* Shackleton) records: 'The only person amongst us [Quakers] who was in possession of such an instrument was Molly Haughton, who resigned to destruction her husband's old fowling-piece, and joined in the laugh raised at her expense.' From *The Annals of Ballitore* (vol. I of *The Leadbeater Papers*), 2nd edn, London, 1862, p. 211. Chapters 8 and 9 of this volume give her experiences during, and in the aftermath of, the Rebellion of 1798.

7 The loyalist authorities also expressed anger and disappointment at the destruction of Quaker arms, which they would like to have used themselves against the rebels. For an example of this, see Hodgkin, *op. cit.*, p. 22 (Haughton's narrative). Quaker homes, when searched, failed to reveal any hidden weapons.

8 Hancock, *op. cit.*, pp. 58, 59. Nevertheless it seems not quite all Quakers became weaponless. According to the researches of an Irish Friend, John M. Douglas (cited in Hirst, p. 218, n. 1): 'Some thirty or forty members were disowned for refusing to destroy their weapons . . . Some retained their weapons and were not disowned. Others obeyed out of loyalty to the Society.' Douglas implies that those Friends who succeeded in retaining both their weapons and their membership in the Society had all ceased to be pacifists. That was probably true of most of these people. But could not some of them just have been cussed individuals (to be found in the Society both before and after that time), who resented being required to give up their fowling pieces, though they had no intention of using them against their fellow humans?

9 Leadbeater, *op. cit.*, vol. I, pp. 226, 231-33.

10 Hancock, *op. cit.*, p. 107, tell us, 'with few exceptions, their domestic servants, being Roman Catholics, were in secret league with the Insurgents.'

11 Leadbeater, *op. cit.*, vol. I, pp. 224-28, and *passim*. See also Hodgkin, *op. cit.*, pp. 23, 24 (Haughton's narrative).

12 Leadbeater, *op. cit.*, vol. I, p. 255.

13 *Ibid.*, p. 235.

14 See Hancock, *op. cit.*, pp. 72, 73; Hodgkin, *op. cit.*, pp. 26, 29 (Haughton's narrative). Also the narrative written in her old age by the then 14-year-old Dinah Wilson Goff, *Divine Protection through Extraordinary Dangers, during the Irish Rebellion in 1798*, Philadelphia, n.d., pp. 13, 14. It was originally published in London in 1857. An example of Quaker assistance to Protestants is provided by Haughton, who sheltered two Protestant women servants of Euseby Cleaver, Bishop of Ferns, from the rebels. After the insurrection was

over the Bishop wrote to thank the Quaker – 'My good friend' – for his 'great humanity.' The letter is printed in Hodgkin, *op. cit.*, p. 44.

[15] Leadbeater, *op. cit.*, vol. I, p. 233; Hodgkin, *op. cit.*, pp. 31, 33 (Haughton's narrative).

[16] Hodgkin, *op. cit.*, p. 33; Hancock, *op. cit.*, ch. 4: 'On the Trials to which Friends were exposed for refusing to conform to the Roman Catholic Worship.' Hancock's strong anti-Catholicism, and his deep dislike of the Roman Catholic Irish peasantry, emerge clearly on pages 96-98.

[17] Hodgkin, *op. cit.*, p. 37. Quakers of course also protested against atrocities and cruel acts perpetrated by the British army. Here, though, the risk of retaliation was less since, however vaguely, Quakers were felt to be on the Loyalist side.

[18] Leadbeater, *op. cit.*, vol. I, pp. 224, 225, 239, 241; Hodgkin, *op. cit.*, p. 35 (Haughton's narrative). Cf. the Quaker attitude now to seeking military protection with that of William Edmundson earlier; mentioned above in footnote 2.

[19] Hancock, *op. cit.*, ch. 3: 'Of the Dangers to which the Society was exposed in the Attendance of Their Meetings.' See also Goff, *op. cit.*, pp. 11, 27, 28.

[20] Hancock (*op. cit.*, pp. 121, 127, 128) related that in the town of Antrim, the only place in Ulster where Quakers found themselves in a trouble spot, the commanding officer of the British forces stationed there approved the confiscation of 'the shop-goods of a Friend living in a suspected quarter of the town' remarking, 'he was a Quaker, and would not fight; therefore the men were allowed to take his goods.'

[21] *Ibid.*, pp. 137-40. See pp. 141-49 for the tragic case of Samuel Jones who, along with his elder brother John, was shot by the insurgents on the day of the massacre at Scullabogue. Their father had been disowned by Friends for 'marrying out' but Samuel, we learn, from his childhood up had been an attender at the Quaker Meeting at Forrest near New Ross (County Wexford). He had never applied for membership yet 'was considered to make no other profession of religion,' i.e., in his own eyes and in the eyes of others he was a Quaker. 'Of a meek and tender spirit, and remarked for the benevolence of his disposition,' Samuel read deeply in devotional literature. He refused to flee from the danger of rebel arrest, though advised to do so by many of his Protestant neighbours, and when taken into custody by the United Irishmen, he refused to escape death by claiming to be one of the Quakers (whose peace testimony he obviously shared), although his captors expressed readiness to free him if he were shown to be a Friend.

[22] Hodgkin, *op. cit.*, pp. 40, 41. See also Leadbeater, *op. cit.*, vol. I, pp. 254, 260, 261. Dinah Goff (*op. cit.*, p. 29), describes the alarm caused to her family by two night visits of the outlawed rebels, who were hiding 'in caverns in the wood' nearby and who 'sallied forth by night to commit depredations on such of the peaceable inhabitants as had returned to their dilapidated dwellings.' 'On these occasions,' she writes, 'our sufferings were greater than on any during the rebellion. My father had been urged to accept the nightly services of a guard of yeomanry, but always positively refused.' See also pp. 29-36. In

the end Dinah's parents did decide to send their young daughter to stay with relatives in the town of New Ross.

[23] Goff, *op. cit.*, p. 39.

[24] Hodgkin, *op. cit.*, pp. 35, 36 (Haughton's narrative).

[25] When the Welsh pacifist Henry Richard visited Irish Quakers nearly three quarters of a century later, he found most of them lukewarm about peace and politically tending to be Conservative (because, Richard thought, the Roman Catholics there tended to be Liberal). They were on the whole wealthy by this date and unwilling to risk their possessions on behalf of their Society's pacifist principles. Though Irish Friends were 'fond of referring with some pride' to their record during the events of 1798, 'I am afraid,' Richard goes on, 'they have lost the simple faith of their fathers, and are far more inclined to trust in the arm of the flesh. And though they profess to adhere theoretically to what they call their Christian testimony about wars and fightings, they evidently don't like to have the question mooted, in any practical form, lest they be pressed to the logical deduction from their principles.' In short, Richard, who of course knew Hancock's book well, found the Irish Quakers of his own day a disappointment. See Henry Richard Journals, National Library of Wales (Aberystwyth), MS. 10207A, pp. 43-47 (entry for 20 August 1872).

Chapter XIX *(pages 222-228)*
French Quakers and Military Service

[1] In her preface (p. ix) Edith Philips, *The Good Quaker in French Legend*, Philadelphia, 1932, writes: 'a definite literary legend is involved whose development can be clearly traced . . . a traditional Quaker was evolved in the French mind who resembled but little the real Quaker of history.'

[2] Graham Gargett, *Voltaire and Protestantism (Studies on Voltaire and the Eighteenth Century*, vol. 188), Oxford, 1980, p. 415. See his ch. 8, pt. ii, for Voltaire's largely positive attitude to Quaker pacifism. See also pp. 18, 473. We may note that neither Voltaire nor any of the other French admirers of Quakerism knew of the French translation of William Penn's *Essay towards the Present and Future Peace of Europe* (1693) made around 1700, possibly by Penn himself. It was published anonymously without date or place of publication and appears to have made little, if any, impression in France. The *Essay* of course eventually became known there but through the English original. See the facsimile reprint *Essai d'un projet pour rendre la paix de l'Europe solide et durable*, York (England), 1986, intro. by Peter van den Dungen, p. viii.

[3] Gargett, *op. cit.*, p. 423: 'cette prérogative, qui les distinguait de presque tout le reste de la terre.'

[4] W. H. Barber, 'Voltaire and Quakerism: Enlightenment and the Inner Light,' *Studies on Voltaire and the Eighteenth Century* (Geneva), vol. XXIV (1963), pp. 97, 98. I feel Gargett (pp. 415 ff.) rather exaggerates the degree of affinity between Voltaire's *pacificism* and the Quaker view of war, though he does acknowledge Voltaire was not an absolute pacifist.

[5] Philips, *op. cit.*, p. 202. See also pp. 83, 92, 119, 125, 126, 131, 177.

[6] In 1769 one Paul Cadognan, a member of the Congénies group, heard about the existence of Quakers in England while he was on a visit to Holland. Crossing over to London he met with Friends there and was present at the Yearly Meeting. He returned to Congénies with some Quaker literature in French and the goodwill of London Quakers – but nothing further seems to have emerged from this contact. Or, at any rate, it took another decade and a half for contact to be renewed – and then on a more permanent basis.

[7] Philips, *op. cit.*, p. 142, comments: 'Marcillac . . . is the only Frenchman known to have been led by the philosophical writings on the subject to make a religion of Quakerism.' His early reading on Quakerism of course was not confined to the writings of the *philosophes* but included works by Quakers themselves.

[8] Henry van Etten, *Chronique de la vie quaker française 1745-1945*, 2nd edn, Paris, 1947, pp. 43, 44, 49. See also Hirst, pp. 468, 469.

[9] See *Memorandum written by William Rotch in the Eightieth Year of His Age*, Boston and New York, 1916, for Rotch's career as Quaker and whaler both on the island of Nantucket and in France.

[10] Hirst, pp. 466, 467.

[11] 'Pétition respecteuse des Amis de la Société chrétienne, appelés Quakers, prononcée a l'Assemblée Nationale le jeudi 10 février 1791,' reprinted in van Etten, pp. 72-76, from the original pamphlet. The petition was signed by Marcillac as well as by Benjamin and William Rotch.

[12] The text of Mirabeau's reply to the petition is given in van Etten, *op. cit.*, pp. 77, 78. I have quoted from the English translation by Philips, *op. cit.*, pp. 136, 137.

[13] Van Etten, *op. cit.*, p. 109.

[14] *Ibid.*, pp. 84, 85; Philips, *op. cit.*, pp. 139, 140.

[15] Quoted in J. William Frost, 'William Penn's Experiment in the Wilderness: Promise and Legend,' *PMHB*, vol. CVII, no. 4 (October 1983), p. 577. Cf. Hirst, p. 467.

[16] The 25-year-old Welsh Quaker, Evan Rees, visited French Quakers at Congénies early in 1815. In a letter dated 28 February 1815 he wrote: 'Those who profess with us here, have a testimony against war, but when compelled to march, serve in the army. Several of their young men have been taken by the conscription, few of them are returned. One of them lost both his legs in Prussia, and is supposed to have died in consequence; a second was killed in Spain; the parents of a third are still mourning, uncertain of the fate of their eldest son, swept away to the bloody plains of Moscow, where, in all possibility, he has fallen a victim to (another's) ambition. Did they possess firmness to suffer for their principles, they would enjoy a higher degree of consideration in the world.' In another letter, dated 25 March, Rees stresses the extreme difficulties which 'the little Society here,' made up of humble folk and 'subject to many trials to which we are strangers,' had had to face during the years of Napoleon's rule. *Memoirs of Evan Rees; consisting chiefly of Extracts from His Letters*, London, 1853, pp. 30, 31. After 1815 Rees became a keen member of the London Peace Society; and in 1818 he composed a pamphlet for it on the *Horrors of War*. Was he perhaps drawn toward writing

it, not only by his hereditary pacifism, but also by what he had heard firsthand of war's horrors from the Quakers of Congénies?

[17] Van Etten, *op. cit.*, p. 169; Hirst, pp. 469, 470.

[18] It is interesting to note that Stephen Grellet, a leading American Quaker who was himself of French origin, was more understanding of the wartime plight of Friends in France than English Quakers seem to have been. Hirst (p. 470) writes: 'Grellet, as an American, in spite of difficulties and dangers, was able to visit them twice, in 1807 and 1811, to their great help and comfort. He grieved for them and for his native France under the crushing burden of conscription, and tried in vain to reach and plead with Napoleon himself.' Grellet's speaking fluent French must have eased communication in his country of origin.

[19] Van Etten, *op. cit.*, where the Quakers' *Réclamation* against military service, dated Congénies, 7 August 1814, is printed on pages 305-9, with the French government's comments on pages 310 and 311.

[20] Hirst, p. 470.

Chapter XX   *(pages 229-235)*
Quaker Conscientious Objectors in 19th-Century Prussia

[1] Lawrence J. Baack, 'Frederick William III, the Quakers, and the Problem of Conscientious Objection in Prussia,' *Journal of Church and State* (Waco, Texas), vol. XX, no. 2 (Spring 1978), p. 305.

[2] Frederick, however, could not refrain from teasing Voltaire over his partiality for Quaker pacifism and the peaceable Quaker commonwealth in Pennsylvania. See Graham Gargett, *Voltaire and Protestantism (Studies on Voltaire and the Eighteenth Century*, vol. 188), Oxford, 1980, p. 422.

[3] Quoted in Hirst, pp. 471, 472.

[4] *Ibid.*, p. 473.

[5] *Ibid.*, p. 472.

[6] Heinrich Otto, *Werden und Wesen des Quäkertums und seine Entwicklung in Deutschland*, Vienna, 1972, pp. 196, 197.

[7] Hirst, *op. cit.*, p. 473; Baack, *op. cit.*, p. 308; Otto, *op. cit.*, pp. 197-99. For a detailed account of Ernst Peitsmeier's experiences as a conscientious objector, based on official documents, see Paul Helbeck, 'Deutsche Quäker als Kriegsdienstverweigerer vor hundert Jahren,' *Die Eiche* (Berlin), vol. XII, no. 2 (April 1924), pp. 172-77. See also Guido Grünewald, *Zur Geschichte der Kriegsdienstverweigerung . . . 1650 bis 1945*, Essen, 2nd edn, 1982, pp. 26-31.

[8] *JFHS*, vol. XIII, no. 3 (1920), p. 102, citing from a letter from John to Joseph Grubb, dated 18 June 1826.

[9] Baack, *op. cit.*, pp. 308-12. Baack comments as follows on the phrase employed by the king in his reply to the Quakers, 'against the law and contrary to my intentions': 'This wording symbolises the coexistence in early nineteenth-century Prussia of the *Rechtsstaat*, or State based on the rule of law . . ., and the *Obrigkeitsstaat*, or State based on royal authority and embodied in the king.'

[10] If they could get rid of a Quaker draftee on grounds of ill health, they seized on the opportunity and dismissed him. Hirst, *op. cit.*, p. 475, relates the story of a young Quaker from Obernkirchen near Minden, who 'was put . . into a lower age group, and when he came back at the appointed time the officers in dismay asked: 'Why had he come? – they would not have sent for him'."

[11] Hirst, pp. 474, 475. Curiously, after 1815 the Minden Meeting for several decades enjoyed a modest expansion, whereas the Pyrmont Meeting did not, despite the fact that Friends in the latter did not experience trouble over the draft – at any rate not until after the establishment of a united German Empire in 1870, by which time only a handful of Quakers remained at Pyrmont.

[12] Wilhelm Hubben, *Die Quäker in der deutschen Vergangenheit*, Leipzig, 1929, pp. 174-49; also Otto, *op. cit.*, pp. 199, 200.

[13] Otto, *op. cit.*, p. 200; Grünewald, op. cit., pp. 31, 32.

[14] Baack, *op. cit.*, p. 313.

Chapter XXI   *(pages 236-256)*
Norwegian Quakers, Conscription, and Emigration

[1] These translations were made a century earlier by Christopher Meidel, a Danish clergyman of Norwegian extraction. Around 1700 Meidel, having served for a time as pastor of the Danish church in London, had eventually converted to Quakerism. His efforts to spread Quakerism back at home proved however unsuccessful, and his translation of Barclay's *Apology*, one of several translations he made of Quaker writings, was in fact printed only in 1732, some years after his death. The London Yearly Meeting, which had been responsible for its publication, still retained copies in stock three quarters of a century later when members of the Society were able to put some of them to good use.

[2] Anne Emilie Jansen, *Det norske kvekersamfunns historie i förste halvdel av det 19. hundreåret*, Stavanger, 1967 (originally written in 1943), pp. 6-10; John Ormerod Greenwood, *Quaker Encounters*, vol. II: *Vines on the Mountains*, York, 1977, pp. 86, 87.

[3] Quoted in John Frederick Hanson, *Light and Shade from the Land of the Midnight Sun*, Oskaloosa (Iowa), 1903, pp. 34, 35. Hanson's book, despite its ingenuous character, constitutes an important source of information on 19th-century Norwegian Quakerism, including its peace testimony. For Hanson's Quaker ministry in the United States and in the land of his birth (he had left Norway aged 15), see Arthur O. Roberts, *John Frederick Hanson, A Biographical Study*, privately printed, Newberg (Oregon), 1988.

[4] For the replantation of Quakerism in Denmark around 1870, see Greenwood, *op. cit.*, pp. 197 ff.

[5] Greenwood, *op. cit.*, pp. 85, 86.

[6] *An Account of a Religious Society in Norway called Saints . . .*, London, 1815; Philadelphia reprint, pp. 15, 26, 27. The author of this anonymous pamphlet was the English Quaker Frederick Smith, one of those in close touch with the prisoners on the *Fyen*. See also Jansen, *op. cit.*, p. 19.

[7] Yet Smith was clearly of opinion that some did. For he writes in his pamphlet (p. 15): 'These persons, who are called Saints, though a few of them retain some of the ceremonies of the Lutheran church, such as baptism, and the Lord's supper, yet they have a testimony against war, oaths, and an hireling ministry; but, through human weakness, some of them, when commanded by the magistrates (whom they have conceived it a Christian duty to obey), have taken up arms.'

[8] Jansen, *op. cit.*, p. 19.

[9] *Ibid.*, pp. 19, 31.

[10] The figure who stands out amongst the earliest Stavanger Friends is undoubtedly Elias Tastad, a 'graduate' of the Chatham prison hulks, who guided the tiny Society through the difficult years of its infancy.

[11] T. K. Derry, *A History of Modern Norway 1814-1972*, Oxford, 1973, p. 211. The other major component among these 'sloopers', as they were later known, consisted of Haugeans. Whereas this first contingent of Norwegian immigrants to North America in modern times 'resembled the Pilgrim Fathers in being a group of religious dissidents', later immigrants leaving Norway 'had mainly secular motives.'

[12] Quoted in Jansen, *op. cit.*, p. 24.

[13] However, we hear of one of the returned P.O.W.'s – Tønnes Johnson from Kristiansand – successfully petitioning, in connection with his application to acquire full citizenship *(borgerbrev)* in February 1815, for official military exemption on account of his newly acquired Quaker scruples concerning fighting. (He also asked for exemption from taking the oath that was obligatory for gaining this status.) The official reply stated that, if called to arms, Johnson would have to fulfill some equivalent service. See Jansen, *op. cit.*, p. 51. In 1828 a Quaker named Peder Osmundsen Gilje was summoned for military duties and, when he refused, was deprived of his full citizen status. See Hans Eirik Aarek, 'Oversikt over militærnektingens historie i Norge' in his edition of Søren Olsen, *Et lidet Viidnesbyrd mod Krig og Fægtning*, a publication of the Kvakerforlaget, Ås. I am most grateful to the editor for supplying me with a corrected pre-publication page-proof copy of this book, an invaluable primary source for the history of mid-19th-century Quaker pacifism in Norway; see below.

[14] Jansen, *op. cit.*, pp. 35-37.

[15] Ernest Lapin, *Det norske kvekersamfunnet 1846-98. En undersøkelse met hovedvekt på Stavangermenigheten*, Bergen, 1983, p. 229. The figure, however, included children. At this date Quakers, though a small group, formed the fourth largest religious denomination in Norway. The state church of course was far and away the largest religious body numerically: moreover, it was for long necessary to opt out of it by a formal statement in order to be counted as a member of another denomination. Cf. *ibid.*, p. 170.

[16] Nils Ivar Agøy, *'Kampen mot vernetvangen': Militærnektersspørsmålet i Norge 1885-1922*, Oslo, 1987, p. 322. As my book goes to press, I have received a summary in English of Agøy's work: 'Regulating Conscientious Objection in Norway from the 1890s to 1922,' *Peace & Change: A Journal of Peace*

Research (Newbury Park, California), vol. XV, no. 1 (January 1990), pp. 3-25. Quakers are dealt with briefly in this article.

[17] See, for instance, *ibid.*, pp. 50, 51, 58. This last motive for Quaker emigration was commented on in the *Storting* in 1896: Norway, it was said, was thereby losing good citizens and its reputation for religious toleration was becoming tarnished.

[18] The fullest list is found in Lapin, *op. cit.*, p. 256, while the most detailed account of individual cases of Quaker conscientious objection is given by Hansen, *op. cit.*, pp. 84-87, and *passim*. See also the 'sufferings' of Quaker C.O.s ('Lidelser for vegring af at gjore krigstjeneste') printed in the shortlived Quaker paper, *Vennen* [The Friend] (Stavanger), vol. I, no. 4 (April 1901), p. 57. These however only cover the period 1848-1870.

[19] *Vennen, ibid.*

[20] The English Quaker minister Joseph Crosfield wrote home during a pastoral visit to Norway in 1868: 'Elias Stakland for five successive years underwent imprisonment for refusing to bear arms. The first year it was three weeks, then it went on to four or five weeks of solitary confinement with nothing but bread and water. Now the five years' service is over and he is not liable to anything more.' Quoted in Hanson, *op. cit.*, p. 179.

[21] *Ibid.*, p. 85.

[22] See for example Jansen, *op. cit.*, p. 52. Also Martin Nag, *Det indre lys: Strand-kvekerne—deres nærmiljø i Ryfylke og i Amerika*, Ås, 1983, pp. 183-7, 232, 233.

[23] Hanson, *op. cit.*, p. 25.

[24] *Ibid.*, pp. 159, 160, quoting from Sarah Ann Doeg's notebook.

[25] Sarah Doeg does not give the name of the young man but I think he must have been John Olsen Botn, whom the Quaker C.O. lists cited above mention as having been imprisoned in the fortress at Bergen in 1857 for 20 days (with another period of detention at Voss in 1861; this time only for five days, but 'on bread and water'). The Botns were among the Røldal Quaker families, and took their name from one of the valley's hamlets. In 1869 the Røldal Quakers emigrated as a group to North America under the leadership of Knud Knudsen of Botn – in part because of the threat of imprisonment hanging over their young men. (Another cause of harrassment was the series of heavy distraints they suffered for not paying church dues.) See Greenwood, *op. cit.*, pp. 187, 188.

[26] Aarek, 'Scandanavian Contribution to Quakerism', p. 157 in Aarek *et al.*, eds., *Quakerism: A Way of Life*, Ås, 1982. For his edition of Olsen's memoir, see note 13 above. It is cited below simply as Olsen. The memoir is printed here on pages 31-53; the editor has also included a number of documents relating to Olsen's case from official as well as from Quaker archives. See also Nag, *Det indre Lys*, pp. 69-77. For Olsen's friendship at this time with Asbjørn Kloster and for the latter's endeavours in 1848 on Olsen's behalf, see Nag, *Nytt lys over Asbjørn Kloster og hans nærmiljø i Stavanger, Ryfylke og Christiania*, Ås, 1986, pp. 39-46.

[27] George Richardson, *The Rise and Progress of the Society of Friends in Norway*, London, 1849, p. 120.

[28] Olsen, p. 32.

[29] *Ibid.*, pp. 35-39. Cf. the similar sentiments expressed in Olsen's letter to his friend Asbjørn Kloster, dated 5 September 1848 and printed in Olsen, p. 110. As he later informed Kloster in a letter dated 29 June 1848: 'I, for conscience sake, refused to work in anything appertaining to war'; quoted in Richardson, *ibid.*

[30] Olsen, pp. 42, 44, 47. Cf. the corresponding official record printed on pp. 91, 92, which confirms the general accuracy of Olsen's own account of his examination.

[31] *Ibid.*, pp. 56, 57. The certificate, dated 9 June, was signed by Elias Tastad, who was probably responsible for drawing up its text, as well as by two other Stavanger Friends, Ener Rasmussen and Iver Halvorsen Revem. The latter's relative, Halvor Halvorsen, had previously been sentenced, while serving as a sailor, to a similar flogging, as well as to six months' imprisonment, for refusing to obey certain orders – because he was a member of the Society of Friends, a 'sect [that] forbade any participation in military operations.' He suffered the 27 lashes but the prison sentence was later remitted. See Greenwood, *op. cit.*, p. 183. And Iver Revem himself – 'one of the earliest and most consistent members at Stavanger,' John F. Hanson called him – was a staunch upholder of religious freedom and a sufferer 'for the Truth'; see Hanson, *op. cit.*, pp. 59-61. For further information about Revem and Rasmussen, see Nag, *Kloster*, pp. 40, 41.

[32] Olsen, p. 51.

[33] *Ibid.*, pp. 63, 66.

[34] H. F. Swansen, 'The Norwegian Quakers of Marshall County, Iowa', *Norwegian-American Studies and Records* (Northfield, Minnesota), vol. X (1938), pp. 127, 128, 130 ff.; Wilmer L. Tjossem, *Quaker Sloopers: From the Fjords to the Prairies*, Richmond (Indiana), 1984, pp. 26, 27. We may note that Norwegian-American Quakers of military age at the time of the Civil War faced the same dilemma of conscience as young American-born Friends did. Like the latter, some of them went off to fight in a struggle they considered was being waged for the freedom of the slave; others stayed at home regarding war for however good a cause as contrary to the religious faith in which they had been raised.

[35] Nag, *Det indre lys*, pp. 183-87.

[36] Agøy, 'Kampen', pp. 24, 25, 166, 322, 323, 387.

[37] For the period between 1885 and 1901 Agøy was able to discover, from examining the military records preserved in the archives of the Department of Defence or of various branches of the armed forces, the religious affiliation of 19 out of a total of 44 objectors whose cases he dealt with. See pp. 17, 25, 53; also pp. 42-48 for four detailed case studies of non-Quaker religious objectors prior to 1902. There may of course have been a few more objectors who escaped his net. Hanson, *op. cit.*, p. 87, gives the names of 17 non-Quakers 'having more or less in agreement with Friends', who suffered imprisonment as conscientious objectors between 1890 and 1900. The list includes two intriguing entries at the end: Sergeant Rustad sentenced to 35 days in jail in 1900 and Pastor [C.V.] Ulness who in the same year received a sentence of 15

362

days. I wish I knew more about the sergeant and the pastor; the latter is also mentioned briefly in Agøy, p. 52.

[38] Greenwood, *op. cit.*, pp. 194-97; Hanson, *op. cit.*, p. 229. For the imprisonment around 1912 of a conscientious objector (almost certainly) from this sect, see the recollections of an English Quaker evangelist working among the remote and barren islands where the Free Friends were located, J. J. Armistead, *Ten Years near the Artic Circle*, London, 1913, pp. 188, 189.

[39] See Agøy, ch. 8 (pp. 302-22): 'Den norske kirkes forhold til militærnekting', which takes the story down to 1922. The state church in Norway became seriously concerned with the question of conscientious objection only in the 20th century.

[40] *Ibid.*, pp. 22, 23, 26. The other area from which many objectors came was the capital, Christiania.

[41] Lapin, *op. cit.*, pp. 183-86, 210-14.

[42] *Ibid.*, pp. 25-27, 230, 279.

[43] Agøy, *op. cit.*, pp. 80-85, 89-92, 181, 182.

[44] *Ibid.*, pp. 27-31, 48, 49, 56-80, 87 ff.

[45] *Ibid.*, pp. 71, 72. It would have sufficed, however, for a noncombatant sect like the Seventh-day Adventists, whose objection was strictly confined to carrying weapons and killing.

[46] *Extracts from the Minutes and Proceedings of the Yearly Meeting of Friends held in London . . . 1901*, p. 162. See also pp. 121, 157-61, 163, and *Extracts . . . 1900*, pp. 72-75. Cf. Agøy, *op. cit.*, p. 72.

[47] Agøy, pp. 81-83, 324-28, 383.

[48] Agøy has dealt with this subject in detail. See *ibid.*, esp. chaps 6 and 7 (pp. 210-301) for non-religious objectors from 1902 to 1922. Also pp. 165, 167-75.

[49] *Ibid.*, p. 181.

[50] See *ibid.*, pp. 200-09, for some exceptional instances of religious objectors being punished after 1902. However, in most of these cases they speedily received an official pardon.

[51] *Ibid.*, pp. 241-44, 256-58, 386.

[52] Derry, *op. cit.*, p. 203.

[53] Agøy, *op. cit.*, p. 262.

[54] Kloster's initial visit to England in 1847 as a young student-teacher may quite likely have been caused, at least in part, by his desire to escape call-up for military service. Already a convinced pacifist though not yet formally a member of the Society of Friends, Kloster on his return, however, was no longer liable for service, since school teachers under Norwegian law were exempt at that date from military obligation.

[55] The title may also be translated as *Friend of Man*. We should note, too, that Kloster was interested in social reform. He had shown interest earlier in the Utopian socialist movement of Marcus Thrane that arose in Norway around 1850. Such radical leanings on Kloster's part, however, aroused opposition from some of the more bourgeois Friends in the Stavanger Meeting. See Kloster's biography by Martin Nag, *passim;* also Lapin, *op. cit.*, pp. 87-90, and Nag, *I strid for fred: Tre kapitler av fredsbevegelsens pionértid i Norge*, Ås, 1985, pp. 10, 11, 21-37.

[56] Quoted in Nag, *Fred*, p. 36.

[57] *Ibid.*, pp. 8, 18, 38-55; Agøy, *op. cit.*, pp. 26, 75, 84, 127-29, 202.

[58] See Nag, *Det indre lys*, pp. 402-15, also his *Fred*, pp. 7, 56 ff.

[59] Nag, *Fred*, p. 38.

[60] Letter to Halvdan Koht, dated 28 August 1900, quoted in Nag, *Det indre lys*, p. 407. Sandstøl is referring here to his disagreement with Norwegian Friends over their strongly emphasised evangelicalism and Bible literalism.

[61] See the entry on Sørensen by Einar Sigmund in *Norsk biografisk leksikon* (Oslo), vol. XVI (1969), pp. 16-18; also Nag, *Fred*, pp. 14-17, 76, and Agøy, *op. cit.*, pp. 100 ff., 129-31.

[62] In 1880 Sørensen had been imprisoned for urging the establishment of a republic in the press: the crime of *lèse-majesté* made his name well known throughout Norway and, as a result, he began to enjoy considerable popularity on the left.

[63] We may note that Sørensen was also an advocate of women's rights and a keen temperance man. In both these causes he found himself working alongside Quakers.

[64] Listed in Agøy's bibliography on pp. 396, 397.

[65] See Agøy, *op. cit.*, pp. 112-22, for details of these internal struggles.

[66] But in justice to Tønnes Sandstøl I must mention his renewed concern for the C.O. question during the Great War: contrary to his previous position, he now began to urge that the Peace Society should actively encourage young men to refuse military service. See Agøy, *ibid.*, pp. 124, 125. And just before the outbreak of World War I the so called Wickman movement *(Wickmans bevegelse)* had aroused considerable interest among peace people in Scandanavia. A young Baptist minister from Lund, Albert Wickman, proposed in 1912 that Christians take an oath to refrain from all acts involving homicide, including war. But there was ambiguity as to whether such an oath would involve refusal to bear arms in peacetime. In fact the movement, overtaken by the outbreak of war in Europe, soon petered out. See *ibid.*, pp. 123, 124. Early in the war, Wickman, after refusing to bear arms when called for service and completing a prison sentence for this, finally consented to undertake noncombatant duties; Ingmar Gustafsson, *Fred och försvar i frikyrkligt perspektiv 1900-1921: Debatten inom Svenska Missionsförbundet*, Uppsala, 1987, pp. 50, 51, 120-22, 127, 128, 161, 162, 166, 194.

[67] Sympathetic, we may note, in his personal outlook to the absolutists but desiring above all to maintain the Norwegian peace movement's fragile unity was Cornelius Bernhard Hanssen (1864-1939), who represented an intermediate position between the movement's opposing wings. By profession a ship-owner, by avocation a journalist, and in his political allegiance a moderate liberal, Hanssen succeeded in making the Peace Society's branch in his home town of Flekkefjord for a time one of the most active centres of peace work in the country. The prominent parliamentarian and peace advocate, Viggo Ullmann (1848-1910), was also close to the absolutists during the 1890s, though he later became a relativist and supported national defence while remaining a *fredsvenn*. See Jens Evang, *Norges Fredsforening 1894-1937*, unpublished University of Oslo dissertation in history, 1938, pp. 18, 19. For Hanssen, see pp. 21 ff, 39, and *passim*.

[68] See, for instance, the entry on him by T. Leiren in Byron J. Nordstrom, ed., *Dictionary of Scandanavian History,* Westport (Connecticut) and London, 1986, pp. 335, 336.

[69] Extracts from this correspondence, preserved fragmentarily in the manuscript division of the University of Oslo Library, have been printed in Nag, *Fred,* pp. 57-81. Their interchange of letters continued for over a decade. A similar difference of opinion on the peace issue had cropped up in 1896 between N. J. Sørensen and the famous Norwegian writer Bjørnstjerne Bjørnson, who shared roughly Koht's viewpoint. See *ibid.,* p. 79. And for Bjørnson as a pacificist, see the entry on him by William Shank in *BDMPL,* pp. 80-82.

[70] Nag, *Frid,* p. 78. See also Evang, *op. cit.,* pp. 67-76.

[71] Agøy, *op. cit.,* p. 127.

[72] Agøy (p. 44) calls him 'the most stubborn, aggressive, and provocative C.O. whom we know of from the early period.' While acting as secretary of the Stavanger Peace Society in 1897, Larsen had received the first of a succession of prison sentences for refusal to muster. He worked with Sørensen and Hanssen to keep the question of conscientious objection before the members of the peace movement, in which he took a very active part. In 1897 he wrote to Hanssen shortly after being sent to jail for rejecting military service: 'I am doing this not simply on my own account but to arouse others to think about the matter . . . I share Tolstoy's view that only in this way can the cause of peace be advanced.' *Ibid.,* pp. 43-46, 53, 103. Ivar Larsen and his brother Matthias, also a conscientious objector, strongly opposed the idea of civilian alternative service, which moderate pacifists like Sørensen warmly supported. For the Larsen brothers work schemes of this kind appeared as devices to blunt the edge of antimilitarist activity, and they viewed such service as being essentially of a penal nature and aimed at making conscientious objection in reality an innocuous act. See *ibid.,* pp. 105, 106.

Chapter XXII   *(pages 257-264)*
Jonathan Dymond and the Advocacy of Peace

[1] Michael Howard, *War and the Liberal Conscience,* London, 1978, pp. 39, 40.

[2] See the entry on him by Geoffrey Carnall in *BDMPL,* pp. 236, 237; also Charles William Dymond, *Memoir, Letters and Poems of Jonathan Dymond,* rev. edn., n.p.p., 1911 (cited below as *Memoir*).

[3] *Memoir,* p. 115.

[4] *Ibid.,* p. 53.

[5] The Society for the Promotion of Permanent and Universal Peace was founded in London in 1816 largely as a result of the endeavours of the Quaker philanthropist, William Allen. Although the London Peace Society was nondenominational, Quakers always played an important role in its activities. For the Quaker connection during the Peace Society's first decade, see W. H. van der Linden, *The International Peace Society 1815-1874,* Amsterdam, 1987, pp. 3-26.

[6] I have used the Garland Library of War and Peace facsimile reprint, *An Inquiry into the Accordancy of War,* ed. Naomi Churgin Miller, New York and London, 1973 (cited below as *Inquiry*). This reproduces the fourth, corrected and enlarged edition published in Philadelphia in 1835.

[7] Carnall in *BDMPL*, p. 237.

[8] I have used the Garland Library facsimile reprint, *War: An Essay,* ed. N. C. Miller, New York and London, 1973 (cited below as *Essay*). This reproduces the third edition published in New York [1889] by the Friends' Book and Tract Committee, and includes John Bright's 'Introductory Words.' For a critique of Dymond on war from an evangelical standpoint, see T. Vail Palmer, Jr., *Quaker Religious Thought* (Greensboro, North Carolina), vol. XXIII, nos. 2/3 (June 1988), pp. 48-53.

[9] *Essay*, p. 34. Italics in the original.

[10] *Ibid.*, pp. 45, 46. Italics in the original.

[11] Letter to John Cadbury, 26/27 April 1827; *Memoir*, p. 109-111, 115. (Italics in the original.)

[12] *Essay*, pp. 57-62. See also *Inquiry*, pp. 70-77. Dymond was indebted to the researches on early Christian antimilitarism of the Anglican pacifist, Thomas Clarkson, which were published in 1816.

[13] *Inquiry*, pp. 101-4.

[14] *Memoir*, pp. 109, 114. Italics in the original.

[15] *Inquiry*, p. 112; *Memoir*, p. 109; *Essay*, p. 69. In his *Inquiry* (pp. 91-99) Dymond devotes considerable space to refuting the eminent theologian, Archdeacon William Paley, who in his *Principles of Moral and Political Philosophy* (1785) had argued it was 'lawful' for Christians to bear arms in a righteous cause. Paley of course was only one of many theologians to defend the just war while at the same time lauding Christianity as a religion of peace.

[16] *Inquiry*, pp. 89-91. Dymond was particularly indignant at the idea of Christians praying for victory. 'Surely,' he wrote, 'it were enough that we slaughter one another alone in our pigmy quarrels, without soliciting the Father of the universe to be concerned in them; surely it were enough that each reviles the other with the iniquity of his cause without each assuring Heaven that *he* only is in the right.' *Ibid.*, p. 154.

[17] *Essay*, p. 81. Italics in the original.

[18] *Ibid.*, p. 5.

[19] *Ibid.*, pp. 6-15. See also *Inquiry*, pp. 15-18, 32-39.

[20] *Essay*, p. 15.

[21] *Ibid.*, p. 25. His antimilitarism did not lead Dymond to reject the giving of humanitarian relief to the troops of either side: 'I should bind up the bleeding wound of a soldier,' he wrote 'although he were lying on the field of battle' (letter dated 13 January 1827; *Memoir*, p. 67).

[22] Letter to his brother, William, 8 July 1826; *Memoir*, p. 26.

[23] Inquiry, p. 154.

[24] *Essay*, pp. 82, 83.

[25] *Ibid.*, p. 82. For Dymond's *apologia* for conscientious objection, see *Inquiry*, pp. 155-58; *Essay*, p. 84. He makes clear he advocates this course not only for Quakers but for all Christians. (Though he does not consider the case of non-

Christian ethical pacifists, who indeed scarcely existed in his day, perhaps we may say that by implication he included them too.)

[26] Letter dated 13 January 1827; *Memoir*, p. 66.

[27] As a sympathetic critic of the peace movement put it in 1820: 'The principles of the "Friends" on the subject of war, are such as both governments and nations have long viewed without much apprehension of their prevalence. That respectable Society is regarded as a religious order, whose peculiar rules are not at all likely to be extensively adopted' (John Sheppard, *An Inquiry on the Duty of Christians with Respect to War . . .*, London, 1820, p. 179).

Chapter XXIII   *(pages 265-275)*
English Quakers in the Crimean War

[1] I am much indebted to the work of Stephen Frick based largely on archival sources, which he has published in the *JFHS*: 'The Quaker Deputation to Russia: January-February 1854,' vol. LII, no. 2 (1969); 'The *Christian Appeal* of 1855: Friends' Public Response to the Crimean War,' vol. LII, no. 3 (1970); 'Joseph Sturge and the Crimean War. 1. The Search for a Cause,' vol. LIII, no. 3 (1974); 'Joseph Sturge and the Crimean War. 2. The Founding of *The Morning Star*,' vol. LIII, no. 4 (1975).

[2] Frick, 'The *Christian Appeal*,' p. 205. The series of International Peace Congresses held around mid-century had originated largely from the initiative of the London Peace Society, founded in 1816 by the Quaker, William Allen, and other Christian pacifists, including non-Friends as well as Friends. Concerning the Peace Society's widely circulated series of tracts Frick comments: 'Of the eight identifiable authors . . . four were Friends': Jonathan Dymond, Joseph John Gurney, Thomas Hancock, and Evan Rees.

[3] The Militia Ballot Act officially lapsed in 1860, and Great Britain revived military conscription only in 1916.

[4] Letter dated 8 July 1853, quoted in Frick, 'Joseph Sturge. 1.', p. 243.

[5] For Sturge's role in the Quaker deputation to Russia see, in addition to Frick, the brief account given by Alex Tyrrell, *Joseph Sturge and the Moral Radical Party in Early Victorian Britain*, London, 1987, pp. 210-12. Tyrrell's monograph contains much valuable information on Sturge's work for peace, especially during his latter years.

[6] Frick, 'The Quaker Deputation', pp. 79-81; Hirst, p. 256.

[7] Quoted in Griselda Fox Mason, *Sleigh Ride to Russia . . .*, York, 1985, p. 28.

[8] *Ibid.*, p. 52.

[9] Printed in *ibid.*, pp. 63, 65; also in Hirst, Appendix D.

[10] Mason, *op. cit.*, pp. 65-70. In a letter to his nephew Pease described the Tsar as follows (p. 79): 'A fine powerful tall frame with an unmistakable countenance which one thinks quite capable of saying "Siberia" although by no means incapable of kindly relaxation.'

[11] *Ibid.*, pp. 29-32; Hirst, pp. 258-60.

[12] Letter from Robert Charleton, 13 February 1854, quoted in Mason, *op. cit.*, p. 69. Charleton concluded: 'I think it would be our duty not to shrink from

any responsibility which might thus be imposed on us; due caution being, of course, exercised not in any way to compromise either ourselves or the religious society to which we belong.'

[13] Quoted in Mason, *op. cit.*, pp. 74, 77, 78. We see the same amalgam of interest and religion in the contemporary antiwar sentiments of Henry's parent, the 87-year-old Edward Pease. See *The Diaries of Edward Pease: The Father of English Railways*, ed. Sir Alfred E. Pease, Bart., London, 1907, pp. 314, 316. For instance, the entry in his diary for 23 May reads: 'Grain has been advancing in price from the devastation of foreign exporting ports, and the wicked waste of a wicked and cruel war.'

[14] The small sect of Plymouth Brethren, which had emerged as a separate denomination around 1830, also professed a 'Quakerlike' testimony against war (though their stand resembled Mennonite nonresistance more than that of the Society of Friends). It maintained a low-key pacifism throughout the course of the war. This was very far removed, however, from the militant opposition of Quakers like Joseph Sturge. See my article 'The Peace Testimony of the Early Plymouth Brethren,' *Church History* (Chicago), vol. LIII, no. 1 (March 1984), pp. 41-44.

[15] Frick, 'The *Christian Appeal*,' pp. 207-9.

[16] *A Christian Appeal . . .*, pp. 1, 3.

[17] Frick, *op. cit.*, p. 210.

[18] 'An Answer to the *Christian Appeal* of the Society of Friends in Great Britain,' newspaper cutting in the Library of the Society of Friends (London), Box 351. Kossuth belonged to the Lutheran Church of Hungary.

[19] Quoted in Frick, *op. cit.*, p. 208.

[20] Hirst, p. 259. According to Hirst one Friend, however, accused the Clarks of being responsible for the deaths of many Russian soldiers, 'since by their supplies English soldiers were kept alive to kill the enemy, but his logic was not echoed by his fellow members.'

[21] Pease, *Diaries*, pp. 322, 323.

[22] Frick, 'Joseph Sturge. 1.', p. 237. For this offence his property had been distrained, the local constable taking from him 'two ewes and six lambs, valued at £11.6s, in order to satisfy a . . . fine of £10.'

[23] William J. Baker, in *BDMPL*, p. 917.

[24] Frick, *op. cit.*, pp. 247, 251-54.

[25] *Ibid.*, p. 255.

[26] Quoted in Frick, 'Joseph Sturge. 2.', p. 339. Italics in the original.

[27] *Ibid.*, pp. 340-5, 351-3.

[28] Letter dated 19 March 1856, quoted in *ibid.*, p. 353.

[29] *Ibid.*, p. 354. See also W. H. van der Linden, *The International Peace Movement 1815-1874*, Amsterdam, 1987, pp. 471-3.

[30] I have dealt with the question of what exactly Bright's attitude to war was in my *Pacifism in Europe to 1914*, pp. 350-55. In 1887, at a public meeting organised by the Peace Society, Bright summed up his attitude as follows: 'I do not discuss the abstract principle, I say that if you will tell me a war, I will tell you my opinion about it.' From *Mr. John Bright, M.P., and the Peace Society*, London, [1887], pp. 9, 10. And he believed that 'nearly all the wars – as far as

I know, every one of them – in which we have been engaged' hitherto had soon come to be generally acknowledged as unnecessary.

[31] Quoted in J. Travis Mills, *John Bright and the Quakers*, London, 1935, vol. II, p. 228.

[32] Quoted in Frick, 'The Quaker Deputation,' p. 96.

[33] Keith Robbins, *John Bright*, London, 1979, p. 104.

[34] Hirst, p. 276. See also pp. 275, 281-4.

[35] The term is Cobden's. He used it in a letter he wrote Sturge on 21 January 1856; Frick, 'Joseph Sturge. 2.', p. 357.

[36] Pease, *Diaries*, p. 323 (entry for 27 November 1854).

[37] *Report of the Committee for the Relief of Famine in Finland*, London, 1858, p. 10. The relief work had resulted from a fact finding mission undertaken in the autumn of 1856 by Joseph Sturge and Thomas Harvey (*Report of a Visit to Finland . . .*, Birmingham, [1856]). See also John Ormerod Greenwood, *Quaker Encounters*, vol. I: *Friends and Relief*, York, 1975, ch. 5.

Chapter XXIV *(pages 276-289)*
Quakers and Antimilitarism in Australia and New Zealand

[1] That is, excluding some 40 persons of Quaker origin who were sent there as convicts; Charles Stevenson, *With Unhurried Pace: A Brief History of Quakers in Australia*, Toorak (Victoria), 1973, p. 5.

[2] When 'boy conscription' came in 1910 the authorities, writes Hirst (p. 490), 'never enforced the provision for military drill in the case of Friend pupils, and allowed the others to perform it at a centre independent of the school.' This concession stemmed from the government's reluctance to come into open conflict with a group like the Quakers, which objected to military training on religious grounds.

[3] See Malcolm Saunders, 'Peace Dissent in the Australian Colonies: 1788-1900,' *Journal of the Royal Australian Historical Society* (Sydney), vol. LXXIV, pt. 3 (December 1988), pp. 186, 187, for details concerning the first – and Quaker sponsored – effort to establish peace societies in Australia during the early 1860s. These abortive groups were based on absolute pacifism but they included more non-Quakers than Quakers among their supporters. Saunders's article also contains information about Quaker peace activity during the second half of the 1880s (pp. 190-95), which received a boost with the visit of the British Quaker peace activist, William Jones, in 1888. However, as Saunders explains, before 1900 it is difficult to speak of a real peace movement in Australia: this really got going only after the turn of the century. I am grateful to Dr. Saunders for allowing me to read the typescript of his article before its appearance in print.

[4] William Nicolle Oats, *A Question of Survival: Quakers in Australia in the Nineteenth Century*, St. Lucia (Queensland), 1985, p. 320.

[5] M. Saunders and Ralph Summy, 'One Hundred Years of an Australian Peace Movement, 1885-1984. Part I: From the Sudan Campaign to the Outbreak of

the Second World War,' *Peace and Change* (Kent, Ohio), vol. X, no. 3/4 (Fall/Winter 1984), p. 39. For background, see also their study *The Australian Peace Movement: A Short History*, Canberra, 1986, pp. 11-17.

[6] Eleanor M. Moore, *The Quest for Peace as I have known it in Australia*, Melbourne, [1949], p. 19. See also Oats, *op. cit.*, p. 322.

[7] Oats (*op. cit.*, p. 321) comments on this situation: 'Quakers therefore had good reasons to favour the movement for Australian federation, for they hoped that this would bring with it uniform acceptance of the right of conscientious objectors to refuse military service.' However, by the time federation came – in 1901 – military conscription had, for the time being, lapsed.

[8] Margaret West and Ruth Fawell, *The Story of New Zealand Quakerism 1842-1972*, Auckland, 1973, pp. 2, 64, 65. I am grateful to Margaret West for supplying me with xeroxes of several items relating to pre-1914 antimilitarism in New Zealand.

[9] Hirst, p. 488, also Stevenson, *op. cit.*, p. 42. Because of their small numbers, Australasian Quakers remained formally part of London Yearly Meeting of Friends.

[10] Quoted in Thomas W. Tanner, *Compulsory Citizen Soldiers*, n.p.p., 1980, p. 192.

[11] In a sermon preached at his independent 'Australian Church' in Melbourne in December 1899, Strong had declared: 'I cannot reconcile war and democracy, war and the Christianity of Christ . . . Our religion knows but one law – Love, respect, serve, bless your fellow-men . . . I call on you as the Christian Democracy to discourage war.' C. R. Badger, *The Reverend Charles Strong and the Australian Church*, Melbourne, 1971, pp. 145, 278, 279. A Social Gospeller, this Scottish born minister throughout his long life supported a number of radical causes including both pacifism and socialism. See the entry on him by M. Saunders in the *BDMPL*, pp. 914-16.

[12] Saunders and Summy, in *P. and C.*, pp. 40-43; Moore, *op. cit.*, p. 22. For the Peace Society's branch in New South Wales, which came into being in 1907 with the vigorous Rose Scott as its guiding spirit – and president – until 1917, see Ann-Mari Jordens, 'Against the Tide: The Growth and Decline of a Liberal Anti-war Movement in Australia, 1905-1918,' *Historical Studies* (Melbourne), vol. XXII, no. 88 (April 1987), pp. 375 ff. Scott was not an absolute pacifist as Strong was. But the two got on well together. As Strong said, 'we have people at different stages of evolution. I think we have to be content with the general direction and strive to educate people up to what we conceive to be the ideal' (p. 376).

[13] Stevenson, *op. cit.*, pp. 29-32.

[14] John Barrett, *Falling In: Australians and 'Boy Conscription' 1911-1915*, Sydney, 1979, pp. 102, 103; Tanner, *op. cit.*, p. 212.

[15] For the League, see especially Barrett, *op. cit.*, pp. 111-27. Also Tanner, *op. cit.*, pp. 197-201, 209, 214, 217, 266, 267.

[16] 'It voiced four main objections to the scheme. Firstly, it was unnecessary. Volunteer defence forces were sufficient for Australia's needs as they were for Britain's. Secondly, the scheme threatened civil rights and religious liberties, especially since – claimed the AFL – it had been brought in without either the consideration or the consent of the people. Thirdly, it was "unspeakably

mean," because it placed most of the burden on boys who did not have the vote rather than on men who did. Finally, in a time of peace, it placed the military power above the civil authority.' Saunders and Summy, in *P. and C.*, p. 43.

[17] Leslie C. Jauncey, *The Story of Conscription in Australia*, London, 1935, pp. 67 ff. An abortive effort toward the end of 1911 at creating a general anticonscription organisation had preceded the creation of the AFL. This Anti-Compulsory Military Training League, formed to resist conscription 'on Christian and humanitarian lines' (to quote the words of its sponsors), was also largely a Quaker enterprise. See Barrett, *op. cit.*, p. 111.

[18] Quoted in Barrett, *op. cit.*, p. 112. Barrett makes the apt comment: 'Somewhere in Hills there lurked a potential warrior.' Yet we may add, like Gandhi, Hills aspired to be a nonviolent warrior. In his pamphlet entitled *Child Conscription: Our Country's Shame*, Hills had proposed an alternative civilian training programme for boys that would develop their physique as well as their mental capacity and their moral character without entailing military drilling. Barrett, *op. cit.*, pp. 120, 121.

[19] Not only was the Anglican Bishop of Tasmania a supporter of the League, but no less a personage than Colonel James W. Macarthur Onslow, Commanding Officer of the Southern and Western Districts of the First Light Horse Brigade of New South Wales, became the president of that State's AFL branch! See Tanner, *op. cit.*, pp. 198, 199.

[20] Barrett, *op. cit.*, pp. 115, 116, 119-22, 126.

[21] But we should not overlook the contribution of non-Quaker pacifists like the Rev. Charles Strong or the young Congregational minister from England, Rev. Leyton Richards. Richards had arrived in February 1913 and remained in Australia for three years as pastor of the Collins Street Independent Church in Melbourne. During this time he took an active part in the anticonscriptionist movement there. See Edith Ryley Richards, *Private View of a Public Man: The Life of Leyton Richards*, London, 1950, pp. 44-49, 58. His experiences in the movement had helped to crystalise his hitherto still inchoate antimilitarism, and he emerged at the end a full fledged pacifist. His anticompulsion utterances of this period combine economic and libertarian arguments with implicitly pacifist ones – plus a strong dose of Norman Angellism. See the following printings of sermons and addresses he gave in Melbourne: *The Futility of War*, Melbourne, [1911]; *Compulsory Military Training and the Duty of the Church: A Plea for Liberty of Conscience*, Melbourne, [1912]; and *Compulsory Military Training and Christian Character*, London, [1914]. It is interesting to note that in 1946, two years before his death, Richards became a Quaker.

[22] Barrett, *op. cit.*, pp. 116, 117, 127.

[23] Quoted in *ibid.*, p. 111.

[24] In 1912 we find the *British Friend* appealing to concerned Quakers to go out to Australasia and help organise 'an agitation' there for repeal of boy conscription, i.e., what one of those who went (W. H. F. Alexander) called 'the compulsory militarising of the boyhood of a nation.' See Thomas

Kennedy, 'Opposition to Compulsory Military Service in Britain before the Great War,' *P. and C.*, vol. VIII, no. 4 (Fall 1982), pp. 12, 13.

[25] Barrett (*ibid.*, p. 110) quotes from a letter which Norton J. Neave, a New South Wales Quaker, wrote to King George V asking that Quaker draftees be permitted to 'serve in . . . government institutions such as hospitals, gaols, etc.' And, he added, 'we would be glad to give double the time required by the Act for military service.'

[26] Indeed most anticonscriptionists of whatever hue rejected noncombatant – or any other – service as an alternative to bearing arms. Leyton Richards put their position clearly when he stated: 'An army is an engine of combat in all its branches. It is not against the mere firing of a rifle that conscience rebels; it is against the whole spirit and purpose of combat for which the military machine is called into being; and . . . compulsory military training is in effect an attempt to flout the conscience of the citizen, and where conscience cannot be coerced, to penalise the man who dared to obey its voice.' In his two pamphlets against *Compulsory Military Training* . . ., p. 4 (1912); p. 3 (1914).

[27] Quoted in Hirst, p. 488.

[28] Barrett, *op. cit.*, p. 109.

[29] Quoted in *ibid.*

[30] *Ibid.*, p. 175. Barrett, we should note, intended his comment to apply not only to Quakers but to all anticonscriptionist families in a similar predicament.

[31] In 1913 Francis Hopkins, of Rockhampton (Queensland), was fined because he refused to register his grandson. Appealing to the Supreme Court, the old man died while his case was pending. Quakers recorded 'that the worry and trial of this case greatly helped towards the closing our Friend's useful life.' Quoted in *ibid.*, p. 176. See also Hirst, p. 490.

[32] Jauncey, *op. cit.*, p. 54; Barrett, *op. cit.*, p. 206. 'It amounted,' writes Barrett, 'to a considerable penal exercise . . . about one boy in twenty was prosecuted.' However, he does not consider this a 'large-scale resistance to compulsory training.' I do not agree, though of course a judgement as to what constitutes 'large-scale' must remain a matter of opinion. In the circumstances – and considering we are speaking of children and not adults – resistance of five per cent of the group appears to me to be fairly considerable.

[33] Chapter 5 of Barrett's book ('Fines and Fortresses') provides the most detailed – and impartial – account of their confrontation with the army. He does this by giving some 17 'case studies of notable resisters' – 'the notorious cases.' There were of course other instances of victimisation by the military as well as a large number of genuine conscientious objectors who escaped more lightly than these 'victims' did. See also John Percy Fletcher and John Francis Hills, *Conscription under Camouflage: An Account of Compulsory Military Training in Australasia down to the Outbreak of the Great War*, Glenelg, 1919, esp. ch. 23, 25-28.

[34] As an example of this pacifist ecumenism I may cite the comment on the Barrier socialist objector, Alfred Francis Giles, made by Fletcher and Hills in their book: 'His stand for human brotherhood should be respected by all who follow Christ's teaching' (p. 82). Indeed the two Quaker authors give at least

as much prominence to socialist and humanitarian war resisters as they do to Quakers and other religious objectors.

[35] Barrett, *op. cit.*, p. 246. Barrett's information was based on one of the responses to his questionnaire. He does not, however, give his respondent's name, remarking only that he was then a surveyor in Victoria and 'was closely related to some prominent Quaker opponents of [pre-1914] conscription.'

[36] *Ibid.*, p. 199.

[37] Quoted in *ibid.*, p. 111.

[38] Fletcher and Hills, *op. cit.*, p. 90.

[39] Mrs. Leyton Richards, in her life of her husband, mentions another Australian Quaker family who (as we know Norwegian Quaker families had for long been doing) emigrated rather than expose their children to the trials of conscription. She writes (p. 46): 'One Quaker family, which had two boys in it, left the country rather than submit. I well remember our seeing them off at the Port of Melbourne and how sad they were to go, as it meant pulling up the roots of a lifetime.'

[40] Barrett, *op. cit.*, pp. 188-91; Fletcher and Hills, *op. cit.*, pp. 101-104.

[41] Hirst, pp. 491, 492.

[42] See R. L. Weitzel, 'Pacifists and Anti-militarists in New Zealand, 1909-1914,' *The New Zealand Journal of History* (Auckland), vol. VII, no. 2 (October 1973), pp. 128-47. I am indebted to this article for most of my information about the anticonscriptionist movement in that country. See also Fletcher and Hills, *op. cit.*, ch. 30-32; Jauncey, *op. cit.*, pp. 92-98.

[43] Quoted in Weitzel, *op. cit.*, p. 131. It was from this group that the boys imprisoned in the fortress on Ripa Island in mid-1913 were drawn. Their rough treatment there became another *cause célèbre* and brought strong criticism down upon the government.

[44] From W. H. F. Alexander's pamphlet, published in Auckland, pp. 12, 13.

[45] West and Fawell, *op. cit.*, pp. 66-69; Weitzel, *op. cit.*, pp. 143, 144, 146.

[46] Quoted in West and Fawell, *op. cit.*, p. 69.

[47] Weitzel, *op. cit.*, pp. 138, 139, 141. Fletcher and Hills (*op. cit.*, p. 110) give the total of prosecutions for the years 1911-13 as 10,245. But many of these cases must have been due to non-conscientious motives. We should note that refusal to drill – the next stage in the boys' civil disobedience after failure to register – might be accompanied by a loss of civic rights for a period up to 10 years as well as by deprivation of educational assistance from the government. See Hirst, p. 489.

[48] An objector was required to show that 'the doctrines of his religion' forbade him to bear arms. Weitzel (pp. 136, 137) comments that this provision applied in effect 'almost solely to the Society of Friends.' Weitzel does refer to one nonsectarian religious objector, who was prosecuted before the Act was amended: this was James Nuttall, a Baptist Sunday School teacher. There must have been others, including probably a few Seventh-day Adventists. But I have been unable to find references to such persons in the works I have consulted. The bulk of the objectors appear to have been socialist – or trade-unionist – antimilitarists, while the number of boys whose parents were religious or ethical pacifists was small.

[49] Weitzel, *op. cit.*, pp. 136, 137.

[50] See *ibid.*, pp. 139, 146.

[51] This comes out clearly in the slim pamphlet which the Society of Friends in New Zealand had issued in May 1912: *Peace, and the Defence Act. A Brief Statement of the Society of Friends in Regard to the Defence Acts, 1909, 1910, New Zealand.* It was signed by the Clerk of Annual Meeting, Alfred Goldsbury, and 'commended to the careful consideration of the Legislators, all Ministers of Religion, Citizens of the Dominion, and to the Press.' It stated the Society's view that noncombatant duties in the army did not differ essentially from military service on a combatant standing: 'those who perform any work in assisting combatants only set additional men free for fighting.' It also pleaded for the rights of nonreligious objectors: 'that class of people, nominally outside the Churches, who, with a keen sense of the claim of human brotherhood, look upon war as its negation.' Finally, the document condemned such legislation for violating 'our British tradition of *liberty of conscience.*' (Italics in the original.)

[52] Hirst, p. 490.

[53] Barrett, *op. cit.*, p. 207.

[54] *Ibid.*, p. 170.

[55] In New Zealand a young socialist antimilitarist Reg Williams, president of the Christchurch branch of the Passive Resisters Union, in an article entitled 'The Truth about Lyttleton Gaol', recalls asking himself, on his reception there, whether he was not dreaming. 'Was it Russia or New Zealand?' he murmured as he and four other teenagers were clothed in prison dress. *The Repeal* (Christchurch), May 1913, p. 10.

[56] Kennedy, *op. cit.*, p. 13: 'The Australasian experience gave English Quakers like John P. Fletcher practical experience in opposing compulsion which would be put to use during the war years in Britain.'

Chapter XXV   *(pages 290–298)*
The Peace Testimony and Anglo-American Quaker Renewal

[1] Hirst, p. 272.

[2] See Thomas C. Kennedy's article in *BDMPL*, pp. 736-8.

[3] See Kennedy's article in *ibid.*, pp. 811-13; also M. Muriel Shearer, *Quaker Peace Work on Merseyside*, n.p.p., 1979, pp. 15-21. 'In one year Ellen Robinson addressed 116 gatherings and in others 40 to 96 a year' (Shearer, p. 17). Like Peckover, she was also an accomplished linguist with close contacts with continental peace advocates.

[4] The number of socialists in the Society was then small, though they were growing. Moreover, Quaker socialists usually took their pacifism seriously, and as might be expected, they were concerned in particular to deepen the economic dimension of their Friends' peace witness that hitherto had been largely ignored.

[5] Kennedy, 'The Quaker Renaissance and the Origins of the Modern British Peace Movement, 1895-1920,' *Albion* (Boone, North Carolina), vol. XVI, no. 3 (Fall 1984), p. 243.

[6] *Ibid.*, pp. 243-7. See also Kennedy's articles on Graham (pp. 352, 353) and Grubb (pp. 366-9) in *BDMPL*.

[7] Mrs. George (later Dame Elizabeth) Cadbury at annual council meeting of the Women's Liberal Federation, 10 May 1901; quoted in Stephen Koss, ed., *The Anatomy of an Antiwar Movement: The Pro-Boers*, Chicago, 1973, p. 210. George Cadbury, owner of the famous cocoa manufactory in Birmingham, was himself an ardent Pro-Boer. He gave considerable financial support to the election campaign of John Burns, a leading Labour opponent of the war, and, at David Lloyd George's suggestion, he purchased the *Daily News* and established it as the organ of the Pro-Boers. See Richard A. Rempel, 'British Quakers and the South African War,' *QH*, vol. LXIV, no. 2 (Autumn 1975), p. 91.

[8] Kennedy, 'The Quaker Renaissance,' pp. 246, 247.

[9] Rempel, *op. cit.*, pp. 81, 93.

[10] *Ibid.*, pp. 90, 91.

[11] Letter to the *Friend* (London), vol. XL, no. 7 (16 February 1900), pp. 104, 105. Such views of course were not new in the Society and something akin to them was eventually to prevail within it. Young Hodgkin soon solved the problem for himself by resigning from Friends as a prelude to joining the Territorials. For the reaction to Hodgkin's letter of another young Quaker intellectual Margery Fry (who was also his cousin), see Enid Huws Jones, *Margery Fry: The Essential Amateur*, London, 1966, p. 54: 'The more I think about it, the more perplexed I become, it seems impossible to cut off the particular exercise of force which we call war from all other cases of its use, and if I should not hesitate to call in a policeman to protect us from a burglar why should I object to the use of force against an invader . . . If you feel that the utmost one can do to further the Kingdom of Heaven is to compare . . . the shades of grey and always to choose the one nearer to white, I can have no doubt whatever that war will sometimes (I do not think probably in this case) seem the lesser evil, and then, as Robin says in his letter, if you admit that it is inevitable the least thing you can do as a good citizen is to take your part in preparing for it and bearing the burden of it.' The issue raised here was not dealt with, so far as I know, by the proponents of the revived peace testimony, at least at this time.

[12] Joshua Rowntree, *Applied Christianity and War*, 3rd edn., York, n.d., p. 14; published in the Present-Day Pamphlets series for the 1905 Committee of Yorkshire Quarterly Meeting of the Society of Friends.

[13] Kennedy, 'Quaker Renaissance,' p. 249. Of Grubb Kennedy writes, 'The conflict in South Africa was . . . the first real test of [his] pacifism'; 'The Ubiquitous Friend: Edward Grubb and the Modern British Peace Movement,' *Peace Research* (Brandon, Manitoba), vol. XVII, no. 2 (May 1985), p. 2.

[14] Edward Grubb, *The True Way of Life: A Reply to Mr. J. St. Loe Strachey*, London, [1909], p. 64. Ch. 4 is devoted to the question of conscientious objection. For Friends the other side of the medal was represented by the problem of what to

do with the Quaker conscientious assentor to war. Some we have seen, like Robin Hodgkin, withdrew from fellowship. But others who joined the Territorials felt it was all right to remain members. Was the Society to allow these young men to 'go to Meeting on Sunday while they hobnob with . . . the Territorials in the week?' (Quoted from the *British Friend*, July 1911, in Kennedy, *op. cit.*, p. 251.) Young Friends were indeed cautioned against joining the Territorials but no decisive step was taken. In fact of course disownment for whatever cause had long been abandoned by the Society.

[15] Quoted in Kennedy, *ibid.*, where he writes: 'The Yearly Meeting's acceptance of 'Our Testimony for Peace' was the seminal event linking the ideals of the Quaker Renaissance to Friends' resistance to war and conscription from 1914 to 1918.' And this resistance forms one of the major themes of Kennedy's book *The Hound of Conscience: A History of the No-Conscription Fellowship, 1914-1919*, Fayetteville (Arkansas), 1981.

[16] John Ormerod Greenwood, *Quaker Encounters*, vol. I: *Friends and Relief*, York, 1975, p. v.

[17] I may mention here one dilemma Friends ran into while working with the Indians that relates directly to their peace testimony. In the course of the 1870s, as part of the arrangements made with the government for administering the reservations, their agents found themselves obliged to hand over 'contumacious,' i.e., unruly Indians to the U.S. army for punishment. This unsatisfactory situation ceased only with the withdrawal of Quakers from this work around the end of the decade. See Philip S. Benjamin, *The Philadelphia Quakers in the Industrial Age 1865-1902*, Philadelphia, 1976, pp. 111, 112.

[18] See Greenwood, *op. cit.*, esp. ch. 1-3, 5-7, 9. For the adoption of the Quaker star, see William K. Sessions, *They chose the Star*, London, 1944.

[19] In the Philadelphia area, for instance, though this represented the heartland of American Quakerism, 'both branches [Hicksites and Orthodox] entered the new century devoid of any regular standing committee to deal with challenges to the peace testimony. The Yearly Meetings did not create any until the European war confronted them with sizeable responsibilities.' Nor had the Orthodox Yearly Meeting of Philadelphia ever associated itself with the Peace Association of Friends. Benjamin, *op. cit.*, p. 195.

[20] For the Peace Association's early years, see Richard E. Wood, 'Evangelical Quaker Acculturation in the Upper Mississippi Valley, 1850-1875,' *QH*, vol. LXXVI, no. 2 (Fall 1987), pp. 142-44. Wood shows that the new organisation was centred in the mid-West, the heartland of Evangelical Quakerism, where the Gurneyite impulse was strong among Friends.

[21] Elbert Russell, *The History of Quakerism*, New York, 1942, p. 508.

[22] Quoted in David S. Patterson, *Toward a Warless World: The Travail of the American Peace Movement 1887-1914*, Bloomington (Indiana) and London, 1976, p. 25.

[23] See, for example, his essays 'The Nation's Responsibility for Peace' (1895) and 'The Golden Rule in International Affairs' (1901), reprinted in a posthumous volume entitled *The Development of the Peace Idea and Other Essays*, Boston, 1932. Here he argues that if 'the Christian law of love' is right for the individual Christian it is equally right for the nation that claims to be

Christian. In his practical activity, nevertheless, Trueblood was more of a gradualist than an absolutist.

[24] Calvin D. Davis's articles in *BDMPL*, pp. 961, 962 (Trueblood), and pp. 889, 890 (Smiley). See also C. Roland Marchand, *The American Peace Movement and Social Reform, 1898-1914*, Princeton (New Jersey), 1972, p. 19. 'Formerly a nonresister Smiley had . . . been convinced by the Pullman strike and other labor upheavals that police and government militia were necessary for internal peace and stability.' He evidently came to feel that some measure of national armaments was needed to preserve international peace, too.

[25] David B. Updegraff, a leading holiness Friend, clashed in the late 1870s on the pacifist issue with supporters of the Peace Association of Friends, including Daniel Hill, the chief spokesman for the latter. Some Quakers even went so far as to call Updegraff a 'New War Advocate.' See Thomas D. Hamm, *The Transformation of American Quakerism: Orthodox Friends, 1800-1907*, Bloomington and Indianapolis, 1988, pp. 107-99. Hamm concludes, 'the stronger the [holiness] revival impulse, the weaker the commitment to pacifism.' Some holiness Friends still 'paid lip service to the tradition and a few were fully committed to it' but by and large there was little enthusiasm for peace work among them. In fact, they were generally indifferent, if not actually hostile, to it.

[26] See Cecil B. Currey, 'The Devolution of Quaker Pacifism: A Kansas Case Study, 1860-1955,' *Kansas History* (Topeka), vol. VI, no. 2 (Summer 1983), pp. 123, 124. Pacifism, however, remained as an item embedded in the books of discipline of this branch of Quakerism, too: a curious relic of the past without meaning for those for whom the discipline was intended.

[27] American Friends Service Committee; set up in 1917.

Bibliographical Postscript

SEVERAL NEW PUBLICATIONS HAVE COME to my notice since I completed my manuscript.

Though a substantial piece of research, Craig W. Horle's book *The Quakers and the English Legal System 1660-1688*, Philadelphia, 1988, deals only very briefly with Quaker militia objectors (on pp. 11, 12, 52, 158) – and not at all with Friends who became victims of the press gang, even though such confrontations with the law would seem to fall within the book's scope. Two recent articles dealing respectively with colonial and revolutionary America are Robert Daiutolo, Jr., 'The Role of Quakers in Indian Affairs during the French and Indian War' (*Quaker History*, vol. LXXVII, no. 1 [Spring 1988], pp. 1-30), and George H. Cox, Jr., 'The Peace and Social Concerns of Wrightsborough Friends: pt. II, The Ravages of War' (*The Southern Friend*, vol. XI, no. 1 [Spring 1989], pp. 1-9). In this section of his study Cox deals with the Wrightsborough Quakers' reaction to the fighting during the Revolutionary War. He shows there were indeed Quaker enlistments on both sides, though most members remained loyal to their Society's peace testimony. Also of interest is Jacquelyn S. Nelson's article, 'Civil War Letters of Daniel Wooton: The Metamorphosis of a Quaker Soldier,' *Indiana Magazine of History* (Indianapolis), vol. LXXXV, no. 1 (March 1989), pp. 50-57. Drawing once more on her doctoral dissertation, the author presents the reactions to war of a young mid-West Friend who had joined the Union army.

The pacifism of early Canadian Quakers is touched on in two articles dealing with wider issues of Quakerism: Richard K. MacMaster (an American Mennonite historian), 'Friends in the Niagara Peninsula 1786-1802,' *Canadian Quaker History Newsletter* (Toronto), no. 45 (Summer 1989), pp. 3, 5, 14, 15, and Albert Schrauwers, 'The Politics of Schism: The Separation of the Children of Peace, 1812,' *Ontario History* (Willowdale), vol. LXXX, no. 1 (March 1988), esp. pp. 48-50. Schrauwers shows clearly that pacifism was not an issue in this schism. Separation came about largely as a result of the 'New England revivalist rhetoric' of the founder of the new sect, David Willson, and 'his . . . emphasis on the religion of experience,' things which most Upper Canada Quakers of that day found distasteful. There were fewer Friends at this period in France than in Canada. Yet, perhaps because of Voltaire's interest in Quakerism, the former have aroused more outside interest than the latter. A recent article by James C. Dybikowski on 'Edmond Philip Bridel's Translations of Quaker Writings for French Quakers' (*QH*, vol. LXXVII, no. 1 [Fall 1988]) throws light on the efforts of French Friends in 1791 to gain exemption from military conscription for their young men, in this case from the National Assembly; see pp. 114, 117.

The most important work for our topic that has appeared since I finished my book is undoubtedly the study by Hope Hay Hewison picturesquely entitled *Hedge of Wild Almonds: South Africa, the 'Pro-Boers' and the Quaker Conscience,* London, 1989. The war period is covered in chapters 6, 8, 9, and 11. The volume also includes much background material and extensive treatment of Quaker relief work and postwar reconstruction. Hewison devotes an interesting chapter (12) to the relationship between the Society of Friends and the energetic – and controversial – Anglican pacifist Emily Hobhouse, the person mainly responsible for exposing the 'concentration camps' in which the British authorities interned numerous Afrikaner women and children. British Friends indeed were divided over the war. The majority upheld their Society's peace testimony with greater or less enthusiasm, but there was a minority personified best in the redoubtable John Bellows, who warmly supported the war effort. Hewison recounts 'the Quaker debate' that ensued: as she indicates, it was the so-called 'pro-Boer', rather than the pro-war position, that expressed most accurately the feelings of those within the Society who, like John William Graham or John Wilhelm Rowntree, were at this time bringing about a much needed Quaker renaissance. Early on in her book, on pages 10 and 11, the author gives us some fascinating details about the peace activities and nonviolent stance of the carpenter and farmer Norman Gush (1789-1858), who had arrived in the Cape Colony in 1820. Hitherto a Methodist, in South Africa Gush 'became a convinced Friend, alone and solitary, worshipping in silence and endeavouring to put his [Quaker] beliefs into practice.' Despite the unsettled conditions of the country, he always refused to keep a gun and met hostile Xhosa tribesmen unarmed, managing to send them away without their doing him or his family harm. Quaker Gush, as he was known to his neighbours, 'asked the Society of Friends in London for peace tracts which he might distribute among the Cape Dutch, and he learned Dutch [presumably Afrikaans] himself.' It does not seem, however, that he made much headway with the Boer farmers in this endeavour.

I would like finally to note, in connection with the South African War, the latest product of the American historian Thomas C. Kennedy's ongoing research on the English 'Quaker Renaissance'. His article ' "They in the Lord who firmly trust": A Friend at War with the Great War'(*QH*, vol. LXXVIII, no. 2 [Fall 1989]) includes an introductory section on 'progressive' Quaker attitudes to the war in South Africa; see pages 91-93.

Thus, we see there are few signs of diminished interest on the part of historians in the development of the Quaker peace testimony since its emergence around the year 1660.

Further Reading

Alexander, Horace G. *The Growth of the Peace Testimony of the Society of Friends*, 3rd edn. London, 1982.

Barksdale, Brent E. *Pacifism and Democracy in Colonial Pennsylvania.* Stanford (California), 1961.

Brinton, Howard H. *Sources of the Quaker Peace Testimony.* Wallingford (Pennsylvania), [1941].

Brock, Peter. *Pacifism in Europe to 1914.* Princeton (New Jersey), 1972.

——. *Pacifism in the United States: From the Colonial Era to the First World War.* Princeton, 1968.

——. *Pioneers of the Peaceable Kingdom.* (Excerpted from *Pacifism in the U.S.*) Princeton, 1970.

——. *The Roots of War Resistance: Pacifism from the Early Church to Tolstoy.* Nyack (New York), 1981.

Bronner, Edwin B. *William Penn's 'Holy Experiment': The Founding of Pennsylvania 1681-1701.* New York, 1962.

Dymond, Jonathan. *An Inquiry into the Accordancy of War with the Principles of Christianity.* Ed. Naomi Churgin Miller. New York and London, 1973.

——. *War: An Essay.* Ed. N. C. Miller. New York and London, 1973.

Hirst, Margaret E. *The Quakers in Peace and War: An Account of Their Peace Principles and Practice.* Ed. E. B. Bronner. New York and London, 1972.

Jones, T. Canby. *George Fox's Attitude Toward War: A Documentary Study.* Annapolis (Maryland), 1972.

Knowles, G. W., ed. *Quakers and Peace.* London, 1927.

Marietta, Jack D. *The Reformation of American Quakerism, 1748-1783.* Philadelphia, 1984.

Mekeel, Arthur J. *The Relation of the Quakers to the American Revolution.* Washington (D.C.), 1979.

Mendl, Wolf. *Prophets and Reconcilers: Reflections on the Quaker Peace Testimony*. London, 1974.

Pringle, Cyrus. *The Civil War Diary of Cyrus Pringle*. Ed. Henry J. Cadbury. Wallingford, 1962.

Schlissel, Lillian, ed. *Conscience in America: A Documentary History of Conscientious Objection in America, 1757-1967*. New York, 1968.

Sharpless, Isaac. *A Quaker Experiment in Government*, 2 vols. in 1 edn. Philadelphia, 1902.

Wellenreuther, Hermann. *Glaube und Politik in Pennsylvania 1681-1776: Die Wandlungen der Obrigkeitsdoktrin und des 'Peace Testimony' der Quäker*. Cologne and Vienna, 1972.

Wright, Edward Needles. *Conscientious Objectors in the Civil War*. Philadelphia, 1931.

Index

384